New Ways of
Looking at Old Texts

Papers of the Renaissance
English Text Society, 1985–1991

CDEDIEVAL & RENAISSANCE
TEXTS & STUDIES

VOLUME 107

RENAISSANCE ENGLISH TEXT SOCIETY
SPECIAL PUBLICATION

New Ways of
Looking at Old Texts

Papers of the Renaissance
English Text Society, 1985–1991

edited by

W. SPEED HILL

Medieval & Renaissance Texts & Studies
in conjunction with
Renaissance English Text Society
Binghamton, New York
1993

Library of Congress Cataloging-in-Publication Data

Renaissance English Text Society.
    New ways of looking at old texts : papers of the Renaissance English Text
Society, 1985–1991 / edited by W. Speed Hill.
      p. cm.
    Includes index.
    ISBN 0-86698-153-5
    1. English literature—Early modern, 1500–1700–Criticism, Textual. 2. Manu-
scripts, Renaissance—England—Editing. 3. Manuscripts, English—Editing. 4. Renaissance—England. I. Hill, W. Speed (William Speed), 1935– . II. Title.
PR418.T48R46 1993
820.9 '003—dc20   93–936
                                                     CIP

Contents

Illustrations

Preface

In the course of preparing a survey of scholarly editing of nondramatic texts of the English Renaissance for *Scholarly Editing: A Guide to Research* (ed. D. C. Greetham, forthcoming, MLA), I discovered that there was no coherent body of scholarly literature on the editing of these texts, as there is, for example, for editors of Renaissance play-texts. Editing skills, passed on from mentor to student and exemplified in the practices of individual editions published by particular university presses (especially Oxford and Harvard), were nowhere codified in a form that a beginning editor of texts of the period might emulate or modify. To remedy that lack, my essay surveys these various practices. This in turn provided the occasion to cite a number of essays that had been prepared for panels sponsored by RETS at annual MLA conferences and distributed to members of the Renaissance English Text Society from 1985 on. They are gathered and reprinted here because, read chronologically, they supply a useful proxy for developments in the field in the last half dozen years, and many are of interest beyond their immediate conference-paper occasions. Their collection, in turn, suggested to the publisher's readers' the need for a more substantial introduction than the brief Preface originally supplied, to satisfy which I offer a modestly revised version of the originating survey, written in the summer of 1990 and scheduled for publication in 1993. Attendees at the 1991 Kalamazoo Conference will recognize it, as it was distributed at the panel organized there by Carolyn Kent.

W. SPEED HILL

Editing Nondramatic Texts of the English Renaissance: A Field Guide with Illustrations

W. SPEED HILL

NLIKE EDITORS OF SHAKESPEARE AND OTHER RENAISSANCE dramatic texts, editors of nondramatic texts in the Renaissance have not been mesmerized by that finally unanswerable question: what was the nature of the copy for the First Folio? For textual criticism and editorial practice in English—especially following World War II—have been driven by Shakespeare's being England's national poet, and editorial theorizing has accordingly been focused on the task of producing authoritative texts of Shakespeare's *plays*. No one worries about the texts of *Venus and Adonis* or *The Rape of Lucrece*, and the problems of editing *The Sonnets* are viewed as purely local, not systematic, and therefore unsusceptible of theorizing. Most theoretical work on editing texts of the period has therefore been concentrated on a subset of the whole—play-texts—and not the whole itself. Yet play-texts are anomalous in several respects. They were normally printed in quartos, even after Jonson's Folio *Workes* of 1616 attempted to elevate their literary status; many were printed from difficult copy, authorial drafts, rather than scribal transcripts; and their authors were far less likely to have overseen their printing.[1] As a result,

---

[1] F. P. Wilson, *Shakespeare and the New Bibliography*, ed. Helen Gardner (Oxford:

press work is often more careless, proofing less careful, and texts more corrupt than is the case with nondramatic texts of the same period. Yet, apart from Shakespeare's thirty-eight plays, the surviving corpus of individual play-texts (printed and manuscript, 1495–1640) numbers 900+.[2] *Everything else* written and/or published in England in the period covered by the *Short-Title Catalogue* constitutes a "remainder" that survives in a bewildering variety of textual forms. Texts continued to circulate in manuscript well into the Restoration,[3] and literacy itself was a highly variegated phenomenon.[4] This introduction cannot adequately survey the editing of a corpus of such bulk, variety, and complexity. Rather, it sketches various editorial models editors of Renaissance nondramatic texts have historically used, so as to place the essays reprinted in this volume more securely in the context of contemporary textual scholarship.

Modern editing of Renaissance nondramatic texts may be said to begin with Ronald B. McKerrow's of *The Works of Thomas Nashe* (1904–1910) and Herbert J. C. Grierson's of John Donne's *Poems* (1912), although there were obviously editors and editions before 1900. The indefatigable A. B. Grosart edited over 130 volumes between 1868 and 1896, and Edward Arber edited three series of reprints—*English Reprints* (30 vols., 1868–71), *An English Garner* (8 vols., 1877–1896), and *The English Scholar's Library* (16 vols., 1878–1884)—and transcribed as well the *Stationers' Register* (5 vols., 1875–94) and the *Term Catalogues 1668–1709* (3 vols., 1903–1906). Although Arber became a university teacher at London and Birmingham, the early editing of vernacular texts took place largely outside the universities, sponsored by such *ad hoc* organiza-

---

Clarendon Press, 1970), 70–71.

[2] Alfred Harbage, *Annals of English Drama 975–1700*, rev. S. Schoenbaum (Philadelphia: Univ. of Pennsylvania Press; London: Methuen, 1964); W. W. Greg lists 859 printed play-texts, 1516–1689; *A Bibliography of the English Printed Drama to the Restoration*, 4 vols. (London: The Bibliographical Society, 1939–1959; repr. 1970).

[3] See Peter Beal, comp., *Index of English Literary Manuscripts*, vol. 1, parts 1 and 2 (1450–1625), and vol. 2 (1625–1700), part 1 (A–K) (London and New York: Mansell, 1980–87), and D. F. McKenzie, "Speech-Manuscript-Print," *New Directions in Textual Studies, The Library Chronicle of the University of Texas at Austin*, 20.1–2 (1990): 93–94.

[4] Keith Thomas, "The Meaning of Literacy in Early Modern England," in *The Written Word: Literacy in Transition*, ed. Gerd Baumann (Oxford: Clarendon Press, 1986), 97–131.

tions as the Early English Text Society and carried on by such enthusiastic amateurs as Grosart. Only when it was tied to historical philology did it gain academic respectability.

Characteristic of these early editors is their reticence (or naïveté) about means and ends. The E.E.T.S. still issues no manual for contributors, nor does the Oxford University Press for its Oxford English Texts.[5] While every text assuredly demands its own method of editing and form of presentation,[6] this alone does not explain the absence of published guidelines. Rather, as philologically-based editing came to be concentrated in scholars attached to the colleges and libraries of Oxford, Cambridge, and London, and in the accumulated expertise of the Oxford University Press (and, to a lesser degree, Cambridge University Press) as a set of procedures handed on from teacher to student, there was less a need for a codified manual than for exemplary models or paradigms of editorial practice.[7] In order of their historical advent, these are: documentary editions, including diplomatic and photographic reprints; genealogical editions; copy-text editions; and multiple-version editions.

---

[5] In a 16 November 1988 letter to a prospective editor, Frances Whistler, the coordinating editor of English Editions of O.U.P., explains why "such a set of guidelines has never been formally drawn up": "there has been resistance in the past to the idea of regimenting what are, by their diverse nature, really very different kinds of books (if one contrasts, for example, a volume based entirely on Middle English manuscripts with a late 19th century poet where printed editions and proofs still exist)." She then sets out in some detail "the basic rules for presentation of copy" in accord with the production requirements of the Press, but she acknowledges that "I am telling you far more about the preparation of manuscript and far less about the editorial principles that may underly such editions...."

[6] As Philip Gaskell sensibly insists, *From Writer to Reader: Studies in Editorial Method* (Oxford: Clarendon Press, 1978), 10.

[7] Although Gaskell includes two Renaissance texts as sample editorial problems, Harington's translation of Ariosto's *Orlando Furioso* (11–28) and Milton's *Comus* (29–61), it is difficult to generalize from Gaskell's discussions of these two texts. As he states at the outset, "The examples were not chosen because they proved a theory or supported a preconception. As it turned out, the possible solutions to which the evidence led me were in almost every case surprising, and if this book has a message it is that the editor should not base his work on *any* predetermined rule or theory.... every case is unique and must be approached with an open mind" ([vii]). Gaskell's view typifies a certain English reluctance to theorize editorial practice; see D. C. Greetham's review of *The Theory and Practice of Text-Editing* (Cambridge Univ. Press, 1991), forthcoming, *TEXT* 7.

1. *Documentary Editions*. The rationale behind the documentary edition is to make more widely available scarce or unique texts whose inspection would otherwise necessitate a trip to a library. Before the advent of microfilm and xerography, virtually all of the texts of our period could be described as "scarce or unique." As most were originally published (if they were published at all) in the smaller formats (quarto and octavo) deemed suitable for vernacular works, they are disproportionately scarce among surviving collections of STC books. A few were so popular that entire editions have vanished. The earliest Tudor miscellany, *The Court of Venus* (ca. 1536) survives in three fragments of editions; a fourth is lost altogether.[8] Examples of such "documentary" reprints date from the eighteenth century (the *Somers Tracts*; *The Harleian Miscellany*), the nineteenth (Arber's three series), and the twentieth (Scolar Press photo-facsimiles; the Illinois Milton). These reprints range from straightforward reprints of individual texts to diplomatic type-facsimiles and photographic reproductions. Richard Proudfoot's edition of *Tom a' Lincoln* (Malone Society, 1992), derived as it is from a recently discovered manuscript play, possibly by John Heywood, is just such an edition (see his essay below). A refinement of the photo-facsimile involves selecting individual pages from a variety of exemplars and assembling them into an "ideal" volume representing the corrected state of each page, as Charlton Hinman did for *The Norton Facsimile of the First Folio*.[9]

---

[8] *The Renaissance in England: Non-dramatic Prose and Verse of the Sixteenth Century*, ed. Hyder E. Rollins and Herschel Baker (Boston: D. C. Heath, 1954), 191.

[9] Randall McLeod has demonstrated in a variety of articles and lectures how pervasive typographic distortion is in any letterpress edition. Accordingly, he consistently uses "photoquotes"—photocopied excerpts pasted in his essays—in lieu of typeset quotations, arguing "that the Camera has set us free, and that we should all work from photographic facsimiles or originals" (Gary Taylor, letter 18 August 1990). See "Spellbound," in *Play-Texts in Old Spelling: Papers from the Glendon Conference* [1978], ed. G. B. Shand and Raymond C. Shady (New York: AMS Press, 1984), 81–96; "Unemending Shakespeare's Sonnet 111," *SEL* 21 (1981): 75–96; "Tranceformations in the Text of *Orlando Furioso*," *New Directions in Textual Studies*, *The Library Chronicle of the University of Texas at Austin* 20.1–2 (1990): 61–85; and "Information on Information." *TEXT* 5 (1991): 241–281. While no editor would deny that *any* form of reproduction, however faithful, distorts an original, humanistically trained editors have always proceeded on the assumption that it was their obligation to "[take] the fruit, and lat the chaf be stille" (*Nun's Priest's Tale* 623)—that is, discriminate signal from noise—so as to supply intelligibly edited texts for students and fellow scholars of a wide range of expertise. So conceded, the "distortion" inherent in the

Documentary editions either transcribe with minimal alterations or photograph a manuscript or a single exemplar of a printed text, reserving the principal editorial work (which may be quite extensive) for an introduction that discusses the provenance of the exemplar, its language, sources, codicology (if a manuscript book), bibliographic make-up and printing history (if a printed book), and a commentary that treats questions of interpretation that extend beyond the lexical glossing set forth in a glossary. Such an edition reaches its fullest development in an edition like the Yale Edition of *The Complete Works of St. Thomas More*,[10] with its conservatively transcribed texts, full collational notes printed at the foot of the text page, lengthy introductions and running commentaries, glossary, and appendices.[11]

2. *Genealogical Editions.* In response to the need to edit classical texts that have survived in copies that post-date by many centuries the author who wrote them, Karl Lachmann (1793–1851) developed a method of organizing surviving manuscripts into genealogical trees (*stemmata*) by analyzing the patterns of unique and shared errors in order to isolate those exemplars that are closest to the lost archetype.[12] From these, a critical

---

editing process was seen as a form of translation, justified as rhetorically or pedagogically necessary. On the limits of facsimile reproductions, see G. Thomas Tanselle, "Reproductions and Scholarship," *Studies in Bibliography* 42 (1989): 25–54.

[10] The "Note on the Texts" in R. S. Sylvester's edition of More's *The History of King Richard III* occupies less than two pages of a 106-page Introduction. It specifies that "the spelling, capitalization, and punctuation of both the Latin and English texts are, unless an emendation is noted, those of the original editions. Abbreviations and contractions have been silently expanded with the exception of '&', 'y^e', 'y^t', 'y^u', and 'w^t', which are retained." Even so, as nine texts were compared, the collational notes bulk large; their function is to record the printing history of the work in the sixteenth century. Sylvester's treatment of the Arundel manuscript (MS 43) of the Latin version is even more conservative: it is ". . . an exact transcript which endeavors to reproduce all the major features of the original. The spelling, capitalization, and punctuation are given as they stand in the manuscript and emendations are rarely made. The notes record all of the cancellations, corrections, interlineations, gaps, and variant readings in the text . . ." (cv).

[11] Clarence Miller writes: "It seems to me that we are basically a copy-text edition, though sometimes not as strictly so as Bowers or Tanselle would want" (letter, 13 August 1990). Perhaps the Yale More should be thought of as a hybrid, closer to E.E.T.S. editions, from which it derives, than to Bowers's edition of *The Dramatic Works of Thomas Dekker*, which derives from a quite distinct tradition.

[12] See Paul Oskar Kristeller, "The Lachmann Method: Merits and Limitations," *TEXT* 1 (1984, for 1981): 11–20, and Paul Maas, *Textual Criticism*, trans. Barbara

text is constructed, more authoritative than any single surviving witness, that reconstructs the lost archetype. Lachmannian stemmatic analysis, then, is principally concerned with establishing the relative authority of individual manuscripts within a family of texts, few of which can be demonstrated to have been copied directly from one another, but all of which derive either from a single common ancestor or from a limited number of such ancestors (Kristeller, 14–15). Once its utility was demonstrated with classical texts, its methods were adopted by editors of vernacular texts that similarly survive in multiple manuscript forms. It is best exemplified in our period by William A. Ringler's edition of Sidney's *Poems* (see 447–457), and it is best suited to the organization of a complex tradition of manuscript transmission such as exists for Donne's poems, not collected in print until after his death but surviving in about 240 manuscripts.[13]

Its strength is its ability to reduce the multiple copies (and their variants), the inevitable products of long and complex scribal transmission, to a manageable number. Those copies that stand highest in the genealogical tree supply the readings of the constructed text; copies that are demonstrably derivative can therefore be ignored. Its weakness is its inability to cope with a transmission tradition so fragmented that its gaps preclude the construction of a viable stemma. The texts of Thomas Wyatt's poems, for example, survive in such disparate forms that the editor is bound to treat them as independent texts that can be ordered chronologically, from early to late, but not genealogically.[14] By con-

---

Flower (Oxford: Clarendon Press, 1958).

[13] The General Editor of *The Donne Variorum*, Gary A. Stringer, notes that textual data to be surveyed "include about 240 manuscript sources . . . 3 inscriptions on monuments; over 200 seventeenth-century books that collectively contain over 700 copies of individual Donne poems or excerpts . . . and over 20 historically significant editions . . . from the eighteenth century to the present" (" 'Remote low Spirits . . . finde enough to doe': How We Must Edit Donne Now," unpublished talk delivered at Society for Textual Scholarship Conference, April 11, 1991, New York City, 2). See Beal, *Index*, s.v., Donne, and Arthur Marotti, *John Donne, Coterie Poet* (Madison: Univ. of Wisconsin Press, 1986), 3–24. The editors of *The Donne Variorum*, however, are skeptical about their ability to construct viable genealogies for Donne's poems, although they are confident that they can identify the "best text" (or texts); see Ted-Larry Pebworth, "MS Transmission and the Selection of Copy-Text in Renaissance Coterie Poetry," forthcoming, *TEXT* 7.

[14] Like Donne's, Wyatt's verse circulated in MS collections, one of which (now lost) became the basis for *Tottel's Miscellany* (1557), the text by which sixteenth-century readers knew Wyatt's and Surrey's verse. British Library Egerton MS 2711 seems

trast, the ten extant manuscripts of Richard Hooker's eighth book of *The Lawes of Ecclesiasticall Politie* and the three early printed editions (1648, 1661, 1662) can be plotted onto a stemma, albeit one that must assume the prior existence of six now nonextant manuscripts, or, alternatively, that a missing manuscript that was copied and recopied six times before disappearing. These so-called inferential witnesses must be assumed because, of the ten extant manuscripts of Book VIII, only two were copied directly from an extant predecessor. Two predate the stemma, and the remaining six were demonstrably not copied from one another but were copied from now lost intermediaries.[15]

Where the editorial problems are primarily those of nonauthorial transmission, as in Sidney's *Astrophil and Stella*, genealogical analysis works brilliantly, but where textual variation is the product of authorial revision, as in his two *Arcadias*, the attempt to construct a unitary text (the Lachmannian archetype) from the three surviving disparate versions is obviously impossible. Two earlier critiques of Lachmannian analysis remain influential. In the course of editing the medieval French work, *Le Lai de L'Ombre*, Joseph Bédier came to reject the claims of stemmatic or genealogical analysis,[16] as did A. E. Housman in a classic essay, "The Application of Thought to Textual Criticism" (1921). Bédier's skepticism lead him to an editorial policy of choosing a "best text" and re-

---

to have been Wyatt's own, and so prior to the collection Tottel used. But the evidence is too scant to establish a clear genealogical connection between the two, except that the Egerton clearly predates Tottel, Wyatt having died in 1542. Other MS collections (principally Devonshire and Blage) contribute more uncertainly to the Wyatt canon. See Richard Harrier, *The Canon of Sir Thomas Wyatt's Poetry* (Cambridge: Harvard Univ. Press, 1975), 1–92, and Helen Baron, "The 'Blage' Manuscript: The Original Compiler Identified," *English Manuscript Studies 1100–1700* 1 (1989): 85–119.

[15] Richard Hooker, *Of the Lawes of Ecclesiasticall Politie*, ed. Georges Edelen, W. Speed Hill, and P. G. Stanwood, *The Folger Library Edition of the Works of Richard Hooker* (Cambridge: Harvard Univ. Press, 1978–1981), 3:lx.

[16] In 1895 Bédier first published an edition of the *Lai de L'Ombre* edited according to Lachmannian genealogical procedures. Criticized by Gaston Paris (Bédier's own teacher) for its stemmata, the edition was revised and republished in 1913, with a lengthy preface attacking Lachmannian stemmatic analysis, particularly its tendency to produce two-part (bifid) stemmata; "La tradition manuscrite du *Lai de L'Ombre*: reflexions sur l'art d'éditer les anciens textes," *Romania* 54 (1928): 161–96, 321–56; repr. as pamphlet, 1970. These articles, in which Bédier sets forth his "best text" theory, draw on his experience in the two earlier editions, especially as criticized by Paris. See Mary Speer, "Scholarly Editing in French Literature: Old French," *Scholarly Editing: A Guide to Research*, ed. D. C. Greetham, forthcoming, MLA.

printing it conservatively, with no attempt reconstruct the missing arche-type.[17] English scholars such as McKerrow were similarly skeptical, and, in effect, a "best text" editorial conservatism prevailed in the first half of the century until Greg's "Rationale of Copy-Text" (1950) offered the possibility of a logically constructed eclectic text in cases where strict stemmatic analysis was inappropriate.

As genealogical analysis is characteristically used in author-centered editions, it privileges the autonomous author and his (or her) original text, which it attempts to recover, at the expense of those forms of the text that circulated among its original audience or in subsequent, textual-ly "degraded," forms. As such, genealogical editions betray their origins in early nineteenth-century romantic ideology of the autonomous author/artist whose work derives its value from its unique authorial ori-gins, not its subsequent social distribution.[18] Margreta de Grazia's essay and Arthur Marotti's two essays in this volume acknowledge the timeli-ness of Jerome J. McGann's *Critique*.[19] However, to the extent that schedules of variants ("historical collations"), culled from later printed editions (or subsequent manuscript copies), supplement the critical text, such editions may be said to record the history of the text's later circula-tion, and a determined reader may reconstruct that record from a list of variants keyed to the critical text but physically separate from it, either at the bottom of the text page, or even less conveniently, as back-matter. But, practically speaking, such collations are so difficult to incorporate into one's experience of actually *reading* a text within such an edition that the social history encoded in those "merely scribal" variations is oc-cluded.[20]

   3. *Copy-Text Editions.* The origins of copy-text editing, the editorial

---

[17] James Thorpe, *Principles of Textual Criticism* (San Marino: The Huntington Library, 1972), 114.

[18] See Jerome J. McGann, *A Critique of Modern Textual Criticism* (Chicago: Univ. of Chicago Press, 1983; repr., Charlottesville: Univ. Press of Virginia, 1992), chap. 3, and Lee Patterson, "The Logic of Textual Criticism and the Way of Genius," in *Textual Criticism and Literary Interpretation*, ed. Jerome J. McGann (Chicago: Univ. of Chicago Press, 1985), 55–91.

[19] See also D. C. Greetham's Foreword to the recent Univ. Press of Virginia reprint, cited in the previous note.

[20] See Ted-Larry Pebworth and Ernest W. Sullivan, II, "Rational Presentation of Multiple Textual Traditions," *PBSA* 83 (1989): 43–60.

model most familiar to American literary editors,[21] lie in the attempt of
English editors of Renaissance texts, principally play-texts, to apply the
scholarly rigor of Lachmannian stemmatic analysis to a very different corpus of texts. Whereas the latter worked primarily with texts whose
authorial originals were long lost, McKerrow, Alfred Pollard, J. Dover
Wilson, and, most notably, W. W. Greg wrestled with texts that existed
in quarto prints contemporaneous with their authors but separated from
the lost authorial manuscript by what Bowers liked to call the "veil of
print."[22] Their attentions, accordingly, were turned to analyzing exactly
how early Renaissance printers transformed their texts in the course of
printing them. The "new" (i.e., analytical) bibliography was to trailblaze
"the bibliographical way" for editions of printed texts, just as codicology
and stemmatic analysis had for manuscript texts.[23]

But texts disseminated by manuscript radiate out in more or less complex families, whereas printed texts typically reprint a new edition from
its immediate predecessor; therefore, once the sequence of editions is established by bibliographical analysis of the printed *book*,[24] it is simple
enough to identify the earliest in the series, and Lachmannian analysis of
texts in derivative editions (as distinct from the physical volumes in
which they survive) is redundant. However, if a subsequent edition had
been reprinted in the author's lifetime, authorial revision was always a
possibility, and if the author was to be granted his or her last word, these
revisions belonged in any text that claimed to be *authoritative*. John
Pitcher's examples in his essay from editing Daniel demonstrate the
limitations of orthodox Gregian copy-text theory when *both* manuscript
and printed forms of the same text survive, in the production of *both* of
which the author was actively engaged.

Authorial revision, however, was a problem the Lachmannian editor
did not face: however complex and extensive the transmissional history

---

[21] See William Proctor Williams and Craig S. Abbott, *An Introduction to Bibliographical and Textual Studies*, 2nd ed. (New York: MLA, 1989).

[22] *Textual & Literary Criticism* (Cambridge: Cambridge Univ. Press, 1959), 18; also
81, 84, 172–173.

[23] *Essays in Bibliography, Text, and Editing* (The Bibliographical Society of the
Univ. of Virginia; Charlottesville: Univ. Press of Virginia, 1975), 3–108; Wilson,
Shakespeare and the New Bibliography.

[24] For classic discussions, see Ronald B. McKerrow, *An Introduction to Bibliography
for Literary Students* (Oxford: Clarendon Press, 1927; corrected ed., 1928), 175–203,
and Fredson Bowers, *Principles of Bibliographical Description* (Princeton: Princeton Univ.
Press, 1949; repr. New York: Russell and Russell, 1962), 37–123.

of the text, there was no possibility of later variants' having authorial value, short of the discovery of additional manuscript evidence pre-dating what was already located within the stemma, in which case analysis would properly locate it there. The editor of modern vernacular printed texts has thus had two alternatives: to base an edition either on the earliest text, the one closest to a (usually) lost authorial original, or on the last one over which the author demonstrably exercised his or her revisional prerogatives.[25] If one chose the first, subsequent authorial revision must be disambiguated from transmissional corruption through collation of later printed texts and included in the critical text as emendation. If the second, the author is deemed to have approved the revised text in its entirety by having acquiesced in its publication, and the task of the editor is that of identifying and removing the more egregious forms of transmissional corruption from the last edition printed in the author's lifetime.

Ironically, what the new bibliography confirmed was how variable was the control the author had over his text as it passed through the print shop, even in the first edition,[26] for it was the acknowledged responsibility of the compositor to punctuate his copy and to spell according to a rough house style, within which variation was permitted to justify his line of type or adjust type-setting to cast-off copy,[27] or simply to accommodate his own orthographic preferences. And, if the author had limited control over the first edition, he had usually none at all over subsequent reprints. Before the Copyright Act of 1709, once the author had sold his manuscript to a printer, he had no further control over it. To accept the last edition in an author's lifetime as the basis for a critical edition, therefore, was to countenance an accumulated mass of non-authorial textual practices (in punctuation, capitalization, font, layout, and orthography) that were a concomitant of reiterated reprinting, in order to recover every possible *verbal* revision the author might have made.

---

[25] The editors of the Columbia Milton, for example, base their text "on the latest edition published in Milton's lifetime, and in the case of writings that did not appear in print during Milton's life, on manuscript copies, or on the earliest edition published after his death" (1:vii).

[26] See Percy Simpson, *Proof-Reading in the Sixteenth, Seventeenth and Eighteenth Centuries* (London: Oxford Univ. Press, 1935; repr. 1970); Thorpe, *Principles*, 131–70; and *Folger Library Hooker*, 1:367–69 and 2:xlii–xlvii.

[27] See Joseph Moxon, *Mechanick Exercises on the Whole Art of Printing, 1683–4*, ed. Herbert Davis and Harry Carter (Oxford: Clarendon Press, 1958; 2nd ed., 1962), 193, 215; 204–5.

One response to this dilemma was to follow one's base text with maximum fidelity; that is, in effect, to follow a "best text" editorial philosophy. In McKerrow's *Nashe* the "Note on the Treatment of the Text," specifies that "the spelling of the copy-text . . . has been followed exactly except as regards evident misprints. . . . I have been as sparing as possible of alteration, and have allowed a number of forms to stand which would perhaps have been corrected by the original printer if he had noticed them—. . . ."[28] Moreover, such fidelity to "copy-text" was a deliberate response to the use of variants from unauthoritative later editions as the basis for emending texts eclectically, as earlier eighteenth- and nineteenth-century editors had done.

After McKerrow's *Nashe* (and Grierson's *Donne*), scholarly editions of Renaissance texts of necessity become old-spelling texts.[29] The choice of one's "copy-text" thus became all the more important because it determined, by default, so much of the actual texture of the resulting edition. McKerrow had defined the term functionally: "by which . . . I mean the text used in each particular case as the basis of mine" (*Nashe*, 1:xi). By the time W. W. Greg had come to formulate his "Rationale of Copy-Text" (1950), the term had come to be freighted with a palpably theological significance, although Greg's essay itself is notably *un*dogmatic. Greg divided the authority of the copy-text into authority for "accidentals" (punctuation, orthography, etc.) and that for "substantives" (the words themselves). As in the linear descent characteristic of printed texts, only the earliest print could possibly bear witness—however imperfect—to authorial usage for accidentals, copy-text was regarded as authoritative in this regard, *but for accidentals only*. As to substantives, which the author *might* have revised in subsequent prints, the editor was free to emend the copy-text by reference to evidence of authorial revision recovered by collation. And, because the attempt to disambiguate later variation as either authorial revision or compositorial corruption so often broke down before indifferent variation, copy-text became authoritative in this regard as well.

---

[28] *The Works of Thomas Nashe*, ed. Ronald B. McKerrow (London: A. H. Bullen and Sidgwick & Jackson, 1904–1910; repr., ed. F. P. Wilson, Oxford: Basil Blackwell, 1966), 1:xi.

[29] For the drama, the normative old-spelling editions were those of *The Shakespeare Apocrypha* and Marlowe's *Works* by C. F. Tucker Brooke; see Bowers, "Readability and Regularization in Old-Spelling Texts of Shakespeare," *Huntington Library Quarterly* 50 (Summer 1987): 202 and n. 16.

As sharp as Greg's scholastic razor was for differentiating how the authority of copy-text in printed texts differed from that in texts descending via manuscript transmission, the aim of the Gregian copy-text editor remained identical to that of the Lachmannian critical-text editor: to produce a *critical* edition better than any reprint, however scrupulously accurate, of any individual exemplar. "Better" for both meant closer to what the author wrote in his lost manuscript. The holy grail of authorial inscription might lie just beyond the veil of print, not buried in the mists of time, but it remained both holy *and* absent—perhaps, indeed, holy *because* absent. The power of the "rationale" lay in the way it allowed the editor to be faithful to one's author in both accidentals *and* substantives, a luxury foreclosed to the Lachmannian editor, for whom there was never any possibility of reproducing authorial usage in so-called "accidentals." Accordingly, Jean Robertson modernized the text of her critical edition of *The Countess of Pembroke's Arcadia* (Oxford, 1973), arguing that, "as there is no holograph, there is little point in preserving the idiosyncrasies of one particular scribe" (lxix). Thus, while both kinds of editors use the terms "base text" or "copy-text," they use them in sharply different senses. In Lachmannian theory, the choice of one's base text is arbitrary: it is the single text—often the most complete one— against which all other texts are compared in order to chart textual variation; it may or may not become the "basis" for constructing a critical text, whose accidentals, in any event, would follow the conventions of a modern critical edition of a classical text. Bowers states that the choice of copy-text is similarly indifferent *as to substantives,*[30] but that does not mean its choice is arbitrary or merely a matter of convenience; on the contrary, the editor must demonstrate that a particular copy-text is indeed the closest to the author's "final intentions," and the rationale of its choice becomes the fulcrum for one's editorial lever.

However, an epistemological problem arises: in the absence of the lost authorial manuscript, how can a dead author's intentions be inferred from the meager evidence that has managed to survive the pervasive de-

---

[30] See "Current Theories of Copy-Text, with an Illustration from Dryden," *Modern Philology* 48 (1950): 12–20; repr. in *Essays in Bibliography, Text, and Editing* (Charlottesville: Univ. Press of Virginia, 1975), 277–88; "Multiple Authority: New Problems and Concepts of Copy-Text," *The Library*, 5th ser., 27 (1972): 81–115; repr. *Essays*, 447–87; see also "Greg's 'Rationale of Copy-Text' Revisited," *Studies in Bibliography* 31 (1978): 90–161, and "Mixed Texts and Multiple Authority," *TEXT* 3 (1987): 63–90.

formations of print? Indeed, in the absence of evidence that many Renaissance authors *cared* about the accidental features of their texts, how can we claim that our fidelity to Elizabethan orthography is historically consonant with their lost and unknowable intentions? As authorial intentions in this regard are an artifact of the very analysis one has used to determine them, an inevitable circularity of argument ensues. Thus, where printer's copy survives and can be compared with the book printed from it, one encounters in it a scribal transformation of authorial copy quite as thoroughgoing as the compositor's of *his* copy.[31] Beyond the scribal copy lies the authorial draft, not itself meant for "publication" either in print or manuscript, and not necessarily embodying "final authorial intention," however authorial its provenance.[32] It is precisely these ambiguities and complications that John Pitcher explores below, in his account of editing Samuel Daniel.[33]

Unlike Sidney (who never printed his works nor expected that they would be), Edmund Spenser looked to the medium of print in order to forward his poetic career.[34] Spenser *did* care about spelling, as evidenced by the Chaucerianisms in *The Shepheardes Calender* and the etymological spellings in *The Fairie Queene*.[35] As Spenser himself evidently made an effort to see that his orthographic archaisms were retained by the printer,[36] modern editors of Spenser continue to print his works in their original spelling.[37] Ben Jonson oversaw the production of the

---

[31] See *Folger Library Hooker*, 2:xxiv–xlviii, 512–550.

[32] W. Speed Hill, "The Calculus of Error, or Confessions of a General Editor," *Modern Philology* 75 (1978): 254–58, and "John Donne's *Biathanatos*: Authenticity, Authority, and Context in Three Editions," *John Donne Journal* 6 (1987): 111–18.

[33] The *Folger Library Edition of Richard Hooker* was launched under the aegis of Greg and Bowers in the late 1960s: as many of its texts exist in both manuscript and printed exemplars, orthodox copy-text theory could be and was applied. My "Calculus of Error" (see previous note) details some of the difficulties with that model. Gordon Kipling's account of his editing of *The Recyt of the Ladie Kateryne* likewise nods in the direction of a doctrine of authorial intention, but he acknowledges its problematic character in the *Recyt*.

[34] See J. W. Saunders, "The Stigma of Print: A Note on the Social Bases of Tudor Poetry," *Essays in Criticism* 1 (1951): 139–64; repr. *The Profession of English Letters* (London: Routledge and Kegan Paul; Toronto: Univ. of Toronto Press, 1964), 31–48.

[35] See A. C. Hamilton's discussion of Spenser's language in his edition of *The Faerie Queene* (London and New York: Longman, 1977), 11–18.

[36] *Spenser Encyclopaedia*, s.v., Bibliography, Critical.

[37] A self-conscious exception is the Kellogg-Steele edition of *The Fairie Queene*,

1616 Folio of his *Workes* as the capstone of his self-fashioned literary
career and hence worthy of unremitting authorial control,[38] not only of
substantives but spelling, punctuation, format, font, lay-out, and typography as well.[39] In editions of Milton by Helen Darbishire (1952–55) and
Bernard Wright (1959), the case was made that Milton had a system of
idiosyncratic spelling to which his texts ought to be normalized. Robert
Martin Adams answered Darbishire in 1955,[40] and in 1963 John T.
Shawcross demonstrated that the spellings of Milton's printed editions
were those of his amanuenses or compositors, not of Milton himself.[41]
Accordingly, John Carey and Alastair Fowler's edition of the *Poems*
(1968) modernizes the spelling but reproduces the early punctuation,
"though this should not be taken to imply that it is necessarily Milton's"
(xii); Carey and Fowler thus assume that seventeenth-century punctuation is systematic, but not authorial.[42]

Some English Renaissance writers, then, did care about the so-called
accidentals and were in a position to see that their works were printed in
accordance with their wishes.[43] Most, however, were not, and many

---

Books I and II (New York: Odyssey Press, 1965; frequently repr.). "Spenser is the
only major poet of his age whose works have hitherto been unavailable in modern
spelling. Since it is the custom to read the Elizabethan poets with a modern pronunciation, and since, even if it were not the custom to do so, modern spelling is still the
only feasible 'normalization' of the inconsistent and idiosyncratic orthography of
individual sixteenth-century typesetters, little of literary value is to be gained by
perpetuating the spelling of the early editions" (vii).

[38] See *Ben Jonson*, ed. C. H. Herford and Percy and Evelyn Simpson (Oxford:
Clarendon Press, 1925–52), 9:45–51, and David Riggs, *Ben Jonson: A Life* (Cambridge: Harvard Univ. Press, 1989), 220–26.

[39] Jonson was equally scrupulous in supervising the design and printing of the
quartos, as John Jowett shows, below; see also Timothy Murray, *Theatrical Legitimation: Allegories of Genius in Seventeenth-Century England and France* (New York and
Oxford: Oxford Univ. Press, 1987), 39–93, and Jowett, " 'Fall before this Booke':
The 1605 Quarto of *Sejanus*," *TEXT* 4 (1988): 279–95.

[40] *Milton and the Modern Critics* (Ithaca: Cornell Univ. Press, 1955; repr. 1966),
61–76.

[41] "One Aspect of Milton's Spelling: Idle Final 'E'," *PMLA* 78 (1963): 501–10,
and "What We Can Learn from Milton's Spelling," *Huntington Library Quarterly* 26
(1962–63): 351–61.

[42] R. G. Moyles, *The Text of* Paradise Lost: *A Study in Editorial Procedure* (Toronto: Univ. of Toronto Press, 1985), 117, points out that Jonson himself described such
a system in the last chapter, entitled "Of the Distinctions of Sentences," of his *English
Grammar* (written about 1616, published 1640).

[43] In Gregian terminology, punctuation variants that affect meaning are called

affected an aristocratic disdain of such *minutiae*. John Donne's *Biathanatos* survives in a scribal manuscript corrected by Donne himself; the punctuation is therefore authorial. But if it is punctuated according to a system, it is a system very difficult to discern, as well as one that renders reading an already difficult text significantly more so.[44] Shakespeare was dismayingly indifferent to the manner in which his plays appeared in print, although the early poems, *Venus and Adonis* and *Lucrece*, with which Shakespeare launched his *literary* career, were printed much more circumspectly: Rollins suggests that he "not only furnished the printer with a carefully prepared holograph copy but also read the proofs."[45]

Driven by the logic of Greg's "rationale" to choose the earliest printed text (or authorial manuscript, if available) as the basis for their editions,[46] Renaissance copy-text editions are, by definition, old-spelling editions. Apart from the normative influence of McKerrow's *Nashe* and Grierson's *Donne*, the *locus classicus*, repeatedly cited by Bowers, is Greg's "Note on Accidental Characteristics of the Text."[47] G. Thomas Tanselle is similarly emphatic: "the position that the text of a *scholarly* edition of any material can ever be modernized is indefensible."[48] But just as there is an epistemological problem in determining "final authorial intentions," so is there a phenomenological problem in making old-spelling an article of faith in editing Renaissance texts.

In 1945 H. J. Chaytor argued that the manuscript culture of the Middle Ages was an oral culture in which the inscriptions on the codex leaf were read aloud, even to oneself.[49] Following Chaytor, Marshall

---

"semi-substantives"; see Bowers, "The Problem of Semi-Substantive Variants: An Example from the Shakespeare-Fletcher *Henry VIII,*" *Studies in Bibliography* 43 (1990): 80–95.

[44] Hill, "John Donne's *Biathanatos,*" 118–21.

[45] *The Poems*, A New Variorum Edition, ed. Hyder Edward Rollins (Philadelphia & London: J. B. Lippincott Co., 1938), 370.

[46] See Bowers, "Textual Criticism," *The Aims and Methods of Scholarship in Modern Languages and Literatures*, ed. James Thorpe (New York: MLA, 1963), 26–27; "Multiple Authority: New Problems and Concepts of Copy-Text," *The Library*, 5th ser., 27 (1972): 88 (repr. *Essays*, 447–87); and G. Thomas Tanselle, "The Editorial Problem of Final Authorial Intention," *Studies in Bibliography* 29 (1976): 167–211; repr. *Selected Studies in Bibliography* (Charlottesville: Univ. of Virginia Press, 1979), 309–53.

[47] *The Editorial Problem in Shakespeare: A Survey of the Foundations of the Text*, 3rd ed. (Oxford: Clarendon Press, 1954), l–lv.

[48] "The Editing of Historical Documents," *Studies in Bibliography* 31 (1978): 48 (repr., *Selected Studies*, 451–506).

[49] *From Script to Print: An Introduction to Medieval Vernacular Literature* (Cambridge: W. Heffer & Sons, 1945; repr. 1950), 5–21.

McLuhan insisted that only with the invention of printing did the spatial layout and typographic variation possible in print produce a text that was experienced visually rather than acoustically.[50] Direct evidence is lacking (or uncollected) as to exactly when silent reading replaced oral reading. Robert Darnton brackets that "indeterminate point" as between the seventh century ("in some monasteries") and the thirteenth ("certainly in the universities").[51] But earlier in the same essay he asserts that "for most people throughout most of history, books had audiences rather than readers" (169), and nineteenth-century references abound to the reading of novels aloud within family gatherings. If McLuhan is right—that we can use scribal circulation of texts as a proxy for the persistence of an oral culture—the two modes certainly coexist in our period.[52] Just as the circulation of texts by manuscripts continued for two centuries after printing began, so too did earlier habits of the oralization of texts persist along side of the revolutionary visualization of texts wrought by printing.[53] A number of the contributions to this volume find themselves straddling this as yet inadequately unsurveyed divide between oral and visual texts.[54]

To the extent to which oralization of text was the dominant mode of experiencing texts in the English Renaissance, the rationale for the superior authenticity of the old-spelling edition is seriously undermined. As Kellogg and Steele suggest, we do not normally read Spenser (or Shakespeare) as we do Chaucer, in original *pronunciation*. While historical philology can reconstruct how a Renaissance reader would have sounded the words on the page, we ourselves do not do so. Yet a sixteenth- or seventeenth-century reader, even if reading alone, would have transformed written or printed words into speech according to his or her

---

[50] *The Gutenberg Galaxy: The Making of Typographic Man* (Toronto: Univ. of Toronto Press, 1962; repr. 1966), 86–109.

[51] "First Steps Toward a History of Reading," *The Kiss of Lamourette: Reflections in Cultural History* (New York: W. W. Norton, 1990), 185.

[52] Cf. Martin Elsky, *Authorizing Words: Speech, Writing, and Print in the English Renaissance* (Ithaca: Cornell Univ. Press, 1989), 110–46.

[53] See, for example, Ted-Larry Pebworth, "John Donne, Coterie Poetry, and the Text as Performance," *SEL* 29 (1989): 61–75.

[54] See, for example, the essays of Frances Teague, Sara Jayne Steen, and Jean Klene, on the oralization of texts, as well as those of Arthur Marotti, Steven May, Edward Doughtie, and Ernest W. Sullivan, II, on the circulation of manuscript miscellanies. See especially McKenzie, "Speech-Manuscript-Print," cited in n. 3, above.

own phonetic and phonological habits, which are not ours; then as now, readers of poetry vocalize it internally, if not aloud, whatever their dialect. The text would then have been experienced as a sequence of sounds, not of visual symbols (on George Herbert as an exception, see Elsky, 147–168). Compositors of early printed books routinely oralized texts as they set them,[55] and proof was read aloud, not compared ocularly.[56] Oralization is tacitly acknowledged in editions of play-texts, which are usually modernized,[57] but it is no less applicable to the reading of the poems of Spenser or Milton or the sermons of Donne.[58]

4. *Multiple-Version Editions.* When authorial revision is so persistent as to produce recognizably distinct *versions* of the same work (Thorpe, 32–49), the editor may elect to print more than one of them. Tanselle distinguishes between "vertical" and "horizontal" revisions:[59] the former elevate the work into a distinct form, discontinuous with its previous one, and thus call for separate printings; the latter are continuous with it and call for variants referenced to a single text. Hans Gabler and Donald H. Reiman have outlined its emergence as a distinct paradigm of editorial practice.[60] The best Renaissance examples are play-texts: Greg's parallel-text edition of Christopher Marlowe's *Dr. Faustus* (1950), John H.

---

[55] "[T]he *Compositor* . . . first reads so much of his *Copy* as he thinks he can retain in his memory till he have *Composed* it, as commonly is five or six words, or sometimes a Longer Sentence. And having read, he falls a Spelling in his mind; . . ." (Moxon, 204).

[56] Gaskell, *A New Introduction to Bibliography* (Oxford: Clarendon Press, 1972), 112.

[57] See Stanley Wells, *Modernizing Shakespeare's Spelling* (Oxford: Clarendon Press, 1979).

[58] In "The Shock of the Old," a review of *Authenticity and Early Music: A Symposium,* ed. Nicholas Kenyon, in *New York Review of Books* 37.12 (July 19, 1990), Charles Rosen argues that the claim by the proponents of the early music movement for superior "authenticity" rests on the abstraction of a single feature ("authentic sound") of a (musical) performance "from everything that gave it meaning" and investing it, however historical itself, with an ahistorical authority and sufficiency (52): analogously, what is authentically "old" spelling to us was transparently "modern"— and largely indifferent—to a Renaissance reader.

[59] "The Editorial Problem of Final Authorial Intention," *Studies in Bibliography* 29 (1976), § 3; repr. *Selected Studies,* 309–53.

[60] Gabler, "The Synchrony and Diachrony of Texts," *TEXT* 1 (1984, for 1981): 311–17, and Reiman, *Romantic Texts and Contexts* (Columbia: Univ. of Missouri Press, 1987), 167–80.

Smith's of *Bussy D'Ambois* (1987), Michael J. Warren's *The Complete King Lear, 1608–1623* (1989), and Paul Bertram and Bernice W. Kliman's *Three-Text Hamlet* (1991). The model is clearly relevant to the inveterately revising author. Jonson systematically revised the earlier quarto prints of his plays before including them in the 1616 Folio; accordingly Herford and Simpson reprint both Quarto and Folio texts of, for example, *Every Man In His Humour* (1927; vol. 3). Sonnets from Daniel's *Delia* first appeared in the unauthorized 1591 (Newman) edition of Sidney's *Astrophel and Stella*; thereafter they appeared in augmented and revised forms under his own name in 1592 (two editions), 1594, and the 1601 Folio. Shawcross has proposed that, "where multiple authoritative texts exist, a single version of the text is not sufficient for a scholarly edition; rather, significant texts should be offered as the disparate texts that they are.... Variant texts should not be merely recorded in notes that will deemphasize their existence."[61] Many of Milton's and Donne's poems would thus require a form of presentation that does not privilege one version over another, simply because we assume that every poem necessarily goes back to a single authorial form and that all other forms are lesser variants of that authentic original, or because of the economics of publishing multiple versions of the "same" work within a single volume are prohibitive, or because students are putatively unable to absorb a work in multiple forms. Thus, in the new *Donne Variorum*, "where one or more artifacts preserve a poem in a state so extensively revised or changed as to constitute a new version," the editors will "present successive versions in full, with a separate historical collation for each."[62] However, the presiding ideology of the *Donne Variorum* remains author-centered: "Despite the general absence of holograph materials or of printings known to bear the poet's imprimatur,... the goal of our work ..., ideally stated, is to recover and present exactly what Donne wrote." Copy-text is therefore defined as "the earliest, least-corrupted state of the text as preserved in the best witness among the artifacts in which it appears" (Stringer, 8), but it will be reproduced in the form of a conservatively corrected reprint of that "state," not an eclectically con-

---

[61] "Scholarly Editions: Composite Editorial Principles of Single Copy-Texts, Multiple Copy-Texts, Edited Copy-Texts," *TEXT* 4 (1988): 301; Shawcross gave this paper at the RETS Panel at MLA in 1987.

[62] Gary A. Stringer, "General Introduction," *The Donne Variorum*, 10; unpublished draft, 14 December 1989; cf. Pebworth and Sullivan, "Rational Presentation of Multiple Textual Traditions," cited above, n. 20.

structed text, drawing on multiple exemplars.

Inevitably, given the added cost of such specialized editions, not only in publication expense but in research time and consequent foundation subvention, attention will focus on major canonical writers. Were it discovered that Barnabe Barnes had revised his *Parthenophil and Parthenophe* (1593) as assiduously as Daniel did his *Delia*, it is not likely that an edition setting forth Barnes's revisionary zeal would be mounted. Bacon's *Essays* received such treatment in the Arber's *A Harmony of the Essays* (1871, 1895; repr. 1966; cited by Reiman, 173). Nonetheless, Bacon's most recent editor, Michael Kiernan, because "the changes and revisions are so numerous and involved," elected to use the 1625 edition as copy-text and to key those changes to it in order to create "a comprehensive, chronological record of the substantive readings of all extant contemporary manuscripts and of the thirteen editions published during Bacon's lifetime."[63] Kiernan's edition does the immense work of collating for the reader, but it makes it impossible to visualize just how modest an effort the first octavo edition of the *Essayes* was. In McGann's terminology, Kiernan's edition privileges the linguistic over the bibliographical code.[64]

Continuous authorial revision, of the sort to which Richard Burton devoted his life in composing his *Anatomy of Melancholy*, can be accommodated by copy-text editing, so long as composition eventuates in a single continuous work. *The Anatomy* went through five editions (1621, 1624, 1628, 1632, and 1638) in the author's lifetime; a sixth posthumous one (1651/1652) also contains authorial revisions and additions. The whole grew by 46.2% over nineteen years. But as most of Burton's revisions were largely expansions of the existing text, together with the stylistic changes needed to accommodate them, the textual history of *The Anatomy* is happily self-contained. By choosing as copy-text one of its later forms, the editor includes later revisions within the text, not as alternative authorial versions to be treated as entities themselves, but as revisions incorporated within a continuous work in progress by Burton himself, a process that, by the time of the fourth edition, was 97.9% complete. The editors of the new Oxford edition therefore used the 1632 edition as the one whose accidentals are most uniform and as the

---

[63] *The Essayes or Counsels, Civill and Morall* (Cambridge: Harvard Univ. Press; Oxford: Clarendon Press, 1985), cxii–cxiii.

[64] "What is Critical Editing?" *TEXT* 5 (1991): 15–29.

one most carefully proofed by Burton himself. The comparatively
modest 1638 and 1651/52 revisions are inserted as emendations, and the
whole compositional process intelligibly described and economically
referenced in the textual notes.[65]

A fifth prototype is not fully articulated as a working model, nor has
it as yet an authoritative exemplar to point to. It originates, as Arthur
Marotti observes below, in the "cultural materialism ... implicit in the
interpretative practices of the New Historicism" (210), as expressed in
such works as McGann's *Critique* (1983) and D. F. McKenzie's *Bibliography and the Sociology of Texts* (1985). McGann's views especially have
discomfited those who, having operated for a generation under the
authoritative guidance of Greg, Bowers, and Tanselle, had grown to feel
that the excavations of modern textual practice had at last reached bed-
rock and that they could safely build editions that would stand the test of
time.[66] However, they have provoked newer historicists such as
Marotti to call for a literary history (and a concomitant textual program)
that does not privilege the solitary author at the expense of the social
milieu in which he or she wrote. Marotti thus explicitly challenges the
author-centric ideology of earlier editions and the literary history compiled therefrom. He argues that our concern for the intentions of individual authors is an artifact of the print culture to which we are accustomed, that it is exceptional in our period (though those exceptions do
loom rather large: Spenser, Daniel, Milton, and Jonson, for instance), and
that a more socially-based literary history, one that takes into account the
actual practice of manuscript production and circulation, is in order.

McGann's influential *Critique*, however, should be read in conjunction with his 1985 essay, "The Monks and the Giants,"[67] where he argues that in focusing textual criticism exclusively upon the production of
editions, Bowers and his followers have unwittingly contributed to the

---

[65] Ed. Thomas C. Faulkner, Nicolas K. Kiessling, and Rhonda L. Blair (Oxford:
Clarendon Press, 1989), 1:li–liv.

[66] For a sample of current discussion, see Bowers, "Unfinished Business," *TEXT*
4 (1988): 1–11; McGann, "What is Critical Editing?"; T. H. Howard-Hill, "Theory
and Praxis in the Social Approach to Editing" *TEXT* 5 (1991): 31–46 (and McGann,
"A Response ...," ibid., 47–48); and G. Thomas Tanselle, "Textual Criticism and
Literary Sociology," *Studies in Bibliography* 44 (1991): 83–143.

[67] "The Monks and the Giants: Textual and Bibliographical Studies and the
Interpretation of Literary Works," in Jerome J. McGann, ed., *Textual Criticism and
Literary Interpretation* (Chicago: Univ. of Chicago Press, 1985), 180–99.

schism between textual criticism and literary interpretation that afflicts the entire profession. In adapting the methodology of classical and biblical textual scholarship to the very different conditions of editing "national scriptures," McGann argues that the field of view of textual criticism has been unduly narrowed: it is "a field of inquiry ... that does not meet its fate in the completion of a text of an edition of some particular work" (187, 186). Accordingly,

> A proper theory of textual criticism ought to make it clear that we may perform a comprehensive textual and bibliographical study of a work with different ends in view; as part of an editorial operation that will result in the production of an edition; as part of a critical operation for studying the character of that edition; as part of an interpretive operation for incorporating the meaning of the (past) work into a present context. No one of these practical operations is more fundamental than another, and all three depend for their existence on a prior scholarly discipline: textual criticism.
>
> (189)

McGann has thus called for editions that do greater justice to the interdependence of individual artists and the social institutions of which they are a part and to the material nature of literary production and historical distribution over time, in order to supply more fully both the original and the subsequent historical—by which he principally means social—contexts in which all texts are embedded. It is very much this challenge that the entire 1989 panel, *The New Historicism and the Editing of English Renaissance Texts*, chaired by Thomas L. Berger, takes up, allowing Marotti to expand on the earlier views of "Malleable and Fixed Texts" and Margreta de Grazia to take aim at the most fundamental distinction in the Greg-Bowers covenant, that between the "work" and a "text."[68] But Steven May takes a number of New-Historical assertions about courtly poetry to task by reference to the actual contents of four manuscript miscellanies compiled by *bona fide* Elizabethan courtiers. Facts can be very disconcerting.

Relative to the editing of English Renaissance texts, such views have not been unanticipated. Speaking on the 1991 Panel, Edward Doughtie remarked: "On reading Arthur Marotti's article ... I was pleasantly

---

[68] She cites its canonical defense, G. Thomas Tanselle's *A Rationale of Textual Criticism* (Philadelphia: Univ. of Pennsylvania Press, 1989).

surprised to discover that what I had thought of as my old-fashioned edition of an old manuscript was on the cutting edge of—something" (283). In the 1920s and 30s Hyder Rollins edited a series of Elizabethan poetic miscellanies,[69] a form that, like *Tottel's Miscellany*, evolved from prior manuscript collections like *The Arundel-Harington Manuscript of Tudor Poetry*, edited by Ruth Hughey in 1960. Peter Seng, Doughtie himself, Ernest W. Sullivan, and Norman K. Farmer have edited other examples, and a series of facsimile editions of *Seventeenth Century Poetical Miscellanies* is being coordinated by Peter Beal. Such editions of poetical miscellanies, produced irrespective of the "nonauthoritative" texts they contain of canonical and noncanonical authors promiscuously mixed, thus satisfy Marotti's demand for a socially-contextualized editorial program for Renaissance lyric poetry.[70]

Combining aspects of both documentary and multiple-version editions, these editions eschew any attempt to divine authorial intention, the goal both of Lachmannian genealogical analysis and of eclectically constructed copy-text editions. The model for such editions, established by Hyder Rollins, was exploited for manuscript miscellanies by students of William A. Ringler, (for example, Steven May). Pre-Gregian editorial technique has thus been pressed into service for post-Gregian editions in the name of a literary history more sensitive to the material conditions of literary production in early modern England. This should come as no surprise, as no one is more "materialist" than the analytical bibliographer, and it was on the work of such bibliographers (Pollard, Greg, Bowers) that (until quite recently) editors of both dramatic and nondramatic texts

---

[69] *England's Helicon* (1935), *A Gorgeous Gallery of Gallant Inventions* (1926), *A Handful of Pleasant Delights* (1924), *The Paradise of Dainty Devices* (1927), *The Phoenix Nest* (1933), *A Poetical Rhapsody* (1931–32), and *Tottel's Miscellany (1557–1587)*, 2 vols. (1928–29; rev. ed., 1965).

[70] See *John Donne, Coterie Poet* (cited above, n. 13). Gary Taylor has drawn attention to the circulation of individual Shakespeare sonnets in manuscript versions distinct from and prior to their appearance in print in the 1609 quarto; see "Some Manuscripts of Shakespeare's Sonnets," *Bulletin of the John Rylands Library* 68 (1985): 210–46. Stephen Booth, in his widely praised edition of the *Sonnets*, makes no mention of these. In a more overtly ideological vein, Gerald M. MacLean speculates how a socially-based theory of editing would go about "Editing a Discourse, Not an Author," in "What is a Restoration Poem? . . . ," *TEXT* 3 (1985): 319–46.Peter Shillingsburg surveys the issues raised by McGann and McKenzie that confront a would-be "social contract editor" in his "Inquiry into the Social Status of Texts and Modes of Textual Criticism," *Studies in Bibliography* 42 (1989): 55–79.

were nurtured. Similarly materialist are the assumptions of the panelists assembled by Carolyn Kent, a student of Tanselle, the analytical bibliographer *par excellence*, in her panel, *Is Typography Textual?*

Although it seems unlikely that McGann's views will evolve into an editorial model as pragmatically sturdy as the dominant copy-text one, it is quite likely that the day of the critical, or eclectic, edition, with its claim of supplying a text better than any actual texts in existence, and its implicit claim to "definitiveness," has passed or is passing.[71] Indeed, the hegemony of Greg–Bowers–Tanselle regime, focused as it is on "establishing" the text based on "authorial intention," seems now much less persuasive in the face of the "indeterminate text" and the deconstructed author,[72] the attraction of—or even the possibility of—constructing a "critical edition" is now under deep suspicion,[73] and textual fixity as embodied in a unitary, authorially-controlled text is no longer a widely shared goal.[74] Rather, editions of distinct "versions" that better represent the specific circumstances of their original appearance seem more likely.

It is ironic, then, that just as much of the profession professes skepticism about the ideology (or ideologies) of scholarly or critical editing—at least in its copy-text guise—feminist scholars are actively engaged in recovering texts by and about women, scaling the very intentionalist mountain the other side of which their male confrères are descending. Feminist scholarship—defined here as the interest *of* women in editing texts *by* women—shares with cultural materialism a suspicion of the author-centered institutions of literary production that historically have excluded women at every level, first by denying them literacy, then by

---

[71] See my review of *New Directions in Textual Studies* (cited above, n. 3) forthcoming in *TEXT* 6, as well as that of D. C. Greetham, "Enlarging the Text," *Review* 14 (1992): 1–33.

[72] See David Bevington's review of the Wells and Taylor *Oxford Shakespeare*, "Determining the Indeterminate: The Oxford Shakespeare," *Shakespeare Quarterly* 38 (1987): 501–19.

[73] Cf. Derek Pearsall, "Revision and Revisionism in Middle English Editing," forthcoming, *TEXT* 7.

[74] See Stephen Orgel, "Prospero's Wife," *Representing the English Renaissance*, ed. Stephen Greenblatt (Berkeley: Univ. of California Press, 1988), 219–20. Orgel was a speaker at the 1988 Toronto Conference on Editorial Problems, aptly entitled, "Crisis in Editing: Texts of the English Renaissance," which canvassed just such topics (ed. McLeod, AMS Press, forthcoming).

denying those few who achieved it access to the means of publication, and, when the latter was improbably achieved, by sanctions when their "fictions"—for example, those of Lady Mary Wroth's *Urania*—were deemed to hold a mirror up rather too accurately to courtly nature, as Josephine A. Roberts discusses in her essay. Two of the six panels here represented were on editing women writers of our period, as is appropriate when nearly two-thirds of our graduate students are women and when, as Elizabeth Hageman points out, so few texts of women's writings are available for study or classroom use. The intentions of *women* writers are very much in the foreground of feminist scholars, "silenced" for so long by male institutions of literary authorship (see the essays in Roberts's panel, below), and reliable editions of women writers of the Renaissance remain a fundamental *desiderata* in the field. Insofar as the Brown Women's Writers Project is a model for the recovery of women's writing in our period, it corresponds to the earlier cataloguing-collecting-reprinting phase (Arber, Grosart, et al.) in its aims and methods, rather than the critical-editions phase that historically succeeded it. But while the texts it produces are neither critical nor scholarly, their ready availability lays the ground work for such editions. Cultural materialism and feminism, then, "new" as each is as an approach to Renaissance texts represent quite distinct—in some respects, even antithetical—approaches to the editing of these same texts.

The Theory and Practice of Transcription

W. SPEED HILL

I WOULD LIKE TO BEGIN BY QUOTING THE CONCLUSION OF A paper I gave on editing Hooker to the RETS section in San Francisco in 1975:

> I would define the role of an editor in functional [not absolutist] terms; that is, a critical text is an instrument for communicating certain data to a particular audience. That the process of transmission transforms the data I take as axiomatic. So defined, a text will be critical to the degree to which it faithfully transmits those data determined to be of significance to the audience anticipated, making it clear what is transmitted, what suppressed, in full detail, as well as the principles on which this has proceeded. All three terms in this equation—evidence, medium, audience—serve to determine the nature of the final text.[1]

In the decade since that paper was originally delivered, the drive toward the "definitive" text, with its absolutist and ultimately platonic assumptions, has begun to dissipate as editors in the Renaissance have come to grips with the incompatibility of modern expectations of consistency and regularity in the production of texts (accuracy we can still legitimately

---

[1] "The Calculus of Error, or Confessions of a General Editor," *Modern Philology* 78.3 (February 1978): 259–60.

expect) with the historical conditions of production of these texts.[2]
With this in mind, let me comment on the problems of transcription
with reference to the three terms above: evidence, medium, audience.

Evidence

There needs no ghost come from the grave to tell us that data inherent
in a printed text will be transcribed differently than that in a manuscript,
or that an authorial manuscript will contain data different from that in a
scribal one. Texts that survive in printed exemplars represent manuscripts
that have already been transcribed, so that in being faithful to their orthography, punctuation, typography, and capitalization one is simply reproducing the printing conventions of the day. Thus old-spelling texts
cannot be justified by reference to any theory of authorial intention or
desire. There are exceptions. Spenser's orthography is retained in modern
editions because there is ample evidence (1) that he cared about the
spelling—it served to link him with his predecessor Chaucer[3]—and (2)
that he saw his own texts through the press and thus was in a position to
implement that authorial intention. (But did Jonson care about the long
ſ which Herford and Simpson preserve in the Oxford Jonson?) Rather,
old-spelling texts are a convenience to literary scholars (if a modest
inconvenience to students and other scholars), for they subtract one layer
of transformation from the process of transmission and thus put the
scholar-reader at one less remove from an inaccessible or non-extant
original.

A scribal text will generally be treated as a printed text (or a printed
text will be treated as it were another manuscript) and its accidental
features retained item-for-item, normalized to a consistent usage of the
period, or modernized, depending on the context in which the resulting
text appears. In the case of Hooker's scribal manuscripts, because our

---

[2] See especially Jerome J. McGann, *A Critique of Modern Textual Criticism* (Chicago
& London: Univ. of Chicago Press, 1983).

[3] On Spenser's care with language, see "Language and Style," *The Faerie Queene*,
ed. A. C. Hamilton (London and New York: Longman, 1977), 11–18. Spenser was
in London when each of the early editions of *FQ* were printed, but his attendance at
the press was irregular at best; see J. C. Smith, ed., *Spencer's Faerie Queene* (Oxford:
Clarendon Press, 1909; repr. 1964), 1:xiii–xvii. See also, *The Spenser Encyclopaedia*
(Toronto, 1990), s.v. "Bibliography, Critical" (91).

edition is an old–spelling one,[4] we have treated scribal accidentals in the same fashion as printed accidentals, with the obvious adjustments for the kind of irregularities one finds in manuscripts that one does not find in printed texts.

My favorite example is the appearance of three forms of the letter *c* in Benjamin Pullen's manuscript of Hooker's Book V of the *Polity*: one is clearly minuscule, the *c* that looks like a *t* in secretary hand; one is clearly majuscule; the third, which looks like a greek theta, is perfectly ambiguous. It would have been possible to observe the distinction by printing the ambiguous form as a small cap, but as I could detect no *textual* information being conveyed by Pullen's ambiguous *c*—it appeared initially in can as well as in church and even medially, there was no gain in preserving it and a palpable gain in suppressing it: that is, the reduction of extraneous information (nonsignificant data, static) in the resulting text. So, if you want to recover just which *c* is which in Pullen's fair copy of Book V, you will have to call up Bodleian Add. MS. C.165 and look for yourself. The example could be multiplied by any number of individual peculiarities of the various scribal hands that produced the surviving Hooker manuscripts. It was precisely such variations that a print culture strove to suppress. As our edition is the product of a print culture, our text, with stated exceptions, adheres to its conventions.[5]

An authorial manuscript should not, in theory, be treated in a fashion different from a scribal one; for the purposes of the later editor, the author becomes simply the scribe—often not a very good one—of his own text. However, it is not always so treated, because in the Renaissance the authorial manuscript is so scarce that it becomes treated as if it were a relic, not a document. If the use to which the manuscript is to be put is to construct a critical text—a modern artifact, after all—then the authority of its accidental features need have no greater call upon us as editors than any other manuscript (or print witness).[6] An error is an

---

[4] *The Folger Library Edition of the Works of Richard Hooker*, ed. W. Speed Hill and others, 5 vols. (Cambridge: Harvard Univ. Press, 1977–1990); see "Composition and Proofing of the 1597 Folio," 2:xxviii–xl, and "Treatment of Accidentals," 2:xliii–xlviii.

[5] See "The Present Text," *Folger Library Edition*, 2:l–liv.

[6] I have no wish to take on W. W. Greg, whose "The Rationale of Copy-Text" (*Studies in Bibliography*, 3 [1950]: 19–36, repr. in *Collected Papers*, ed. J. C. Maxwell [Oxford: Clarendon Press, 1966]) has exerted such an enormous influence on the editing not only of Renaissance texts but, through Fredson Bowers's espousal of it, on

error, even if it has the authority of the author itself—for example, a
marginal citation that is demonstrably wrong. We can rightly appeal to
the canon of authorial intention here by asking ourselves if, when we
pointed this out to the author, he would approve the correction, by
making the correction and by noting it in the apparatus as an emendation.

What, however, about the authorial corrections embedded within the
text—corrections either of his or her own script or corrections of a
scribe's script? In practice one discriminates among the data in such a
manuscript by asking if it is of *textual* significance. I realize now that this
would be considered begging the question, but in transcribing Pullen's
manuscript of Book V, which had been extensively corrected by Hooker, I took it as my responsibility to *suppress* certain kinds of data as *not
textually relevant*—as interfering with or obscuring the transparency of the
text to a reader. Not every transcriber will agree as to which details are
or are not *textual*; my colleague Laetitia Yeandle, the editor of volume 5
(the *Tractates and Sermons*), whose interests are more paleographic and
archival than mine, has not surprisingly wished to retain more of what I
would deem paleographic data than I did; for example, exactly how and
where a give correction was made, not what the resulting word form
was. Other editors will (or will not) expand manuscript abbreviations.

Medium

By medium, I mean the medium of the end-product of our transcription, typically, a printed volume, set by letterpress or its electronic equivalent. It may, however, be a photographic facsimile with a letterpress
transcription on facing pages, or a type facsimile, such as the Malone
Society prints. As a modern printed volume, it inevitably carries with it

---

the editing of nineteenth-century American texts as well, but I am on record as stat-
ing the "to no small degree . . . an old-spelling text confers on the accidentals of the
adopted copy text a spurious authority" (*Folger Library Edition*, 2:xlviii) and as con-
fessing that Hooker, "if asked," would "scarcely [have understood] what was at issue;
he would certainly not have felt that anything very essential inhered in his personal
orthography, and I suspect he would have been more in sympathy with the modernized texts of Keble, the culmination of a long and honorable tradition, than the old-
spelling ones of our edition, which is so distinct from it, . . ." ("Calculus of Error,"
258). I am prepared to be persuaded that some authors do (or did) care, but only on
an author by author basis. See above, 11–17.

the expectation—especially at the prices it tends to sell for—of accuracy, consistency, and typographic polish. To reproduce within its uniform and unchanging format the vagaries of an Elizabethan manuscript is a violation of our expectations. However, such expectations are themselves subject to change, and there are many whose expectations are, perhaps, the reverse.

The issue tends to come up most acutely in editions of private documents, such as letters, necessarily a more modern concern than an Elizabethan one. Does one reproduce in a text meant to be read in a printed book the accidental variations of a manuscript letter or the draft copy of a sermon? The answer will vary as to whether one considers the collection one of historic documents and its publication a convenience to the modern scholar who lacks access to the originals, or as the publication of literary texts which the author did not himself see through the press.

But even if one is transcribing such material as if it were a document, there are irremediable changes that take place in transcription. Take spacing, for example. Assuming that one uses a typewriter (or a microcomputer/word processor with a typewriter keyboard), one has only the choice between no space (as between letters within a word), a single space (between words), and a double space after the period, etc. The modern typesetter has an infinite gradation of such spaces: hair-space, letter space, en-space, em-space, etc. The compositor—now typically a front-end software program for a computer-driven digital typesetter—will transform whatever the printer's copy reads into an aesthetically pleasing distribution of white space within the line. Fortunately, not much textual meaning inheres in such spaces (I should qualify this, in light of A. R. Braunmuller's[7] remarks, to spaces between letters and words on a line), so their transformation is not ordinarily regretted. Or, take another instance. Pullen's -*ings* routinely consist of three minims, the third of which is dotted; I did not transcribe them as -*nig*, nor did the compositor of the 1597 Folio. Hooker often abbreviates to -*ng*, which we have expanded. But what about the hyphen? Hooker has occasionally inserted one in Pullen's text. Does one transcribe the result as a hyphenated compound, or combine both halves as a single word? I cannot recall Hooker using a hyphenated compound, although he frequently uses one-word compounds such as "churchofficers," and "thoffenders,"

---

[7] See "Accounting for Absence: The Transcription of Space," 47–56, below.

the latter of which usually got set as "th'offenders." As I read Hooker's correction of Pullen, the inserted hyphen is the equivalent of the close-up mark of a modern proof-reader, an instruction to the printer, and the words should be run together in the text. (I have not, however, been able to convince Laetitia Yeandle of this.) One might call this the letter/spirit dilemma in transcription.

Because the production of an edited text is a collaborative effort, the editor typically does not have control of elements of the final text that are the responsibility of the press's designer. However, an awareness of the typographic resources of one's press can be used to advantage. Even though the modern edition is an artifact, it can usefully mimic certain typographic conventions of older editions. We use italic for quotations, just as Hooker's scribe did, printing text in secretary hand as roman. We key marginalia (printed, for economy, at the foot of our text page) to the text by a series of superscribed italic alphabets, as in the Pullen manuscript. Fortunately, we do not have black-letter, though Whitgift's *Defense of the Aunswere to the Admonition, against the Replie of* T. C., printed in 1574 (STC 25430), very usefully uses all three typefaces—black-letter, italic, and roman—to distinguish quotations in English (in roman) and quotations in Latin (italic) from Whitgift and from *his* quotations from Cartwright (black-letter); furthermore, it deploys various font sizes in black-letter to distinguish the original *Admonition* from Whitgift's *Aunswere* from Cartwright's *Replye*. We do occasionally have bold-face, which we *print* as bold-face, and where Hooker uses quotation marks running down the left margin to signal invented or indirect discourse, we have reproduced these, as they clearly were thought of by Hooker as a form of emphasis and appear in Pullen as well as the printed texts.

The problem of consistency in such modern imitations of Renaissance conventions is not a trivial one. Particularly in the sermons and tractates, both Hooker and his antagonist at the Temple, Walter Travers, weave scriptural quotations and allusions into his own text in what is—to a biblical semi-literate and secular modern—an astonishing extent. We have italicized these more systematically than did Hooker or his scribes in any of the surviving prints and manuscripts (which, in the case of these texts, Hooker never intended to publish) and indeed more consistently than Hooker himself did in preparing Book V for the press. There Hooker clearly marked certain passages in secretary to be set in italic (including, rather puzzlingly, passages already in italic), but again not with the consistency that moderns would expect. Hooker's use of scripture varies from allusion to paraphrase to quotation to translation over a continuum with indistinguishable boundaries between authorial discourse and quoted material. It has seemed to us finally more useful for a modern reader to be alerted to the presence of such texts within and behind Hooker's own, at the expense of our being transcriptionally unfaithful to our copy-texts, than to set them forth in the naked non-splendor of their original manuscript forms. Of course, if you wish to restore our italics— and some of them *are* in the original texts—to the bare secretary of the manuscripts, each and every such change is itemized in a textual schedule.

Audience

Which brings me to the final leg of my tripod: audience. Just who reads textual schedules, anyway? *After the volume is published* very few do. The *Polity* is a long work (1,288 pages in our edition), and not many of us have read *it*, much less the textual schedules appended to it. Granted, only in Book VIII is the text so problematic that recourse to the textual notes at the foot of the page is necessary—*not* to reconstruct the text: we have done that for you—but to *test* the reconstruction you are reading. Volume 2 contains the most complete and detailed comparison of the printed text with the printer's copy of a book in the Elizabethan era that I am aware of.[8] But I have yet to run into a bibliographical scholar interested in Elizabethan printing practices who has used it. I argue my case from the example of Randall McLeod, who is studying just this topic, right now (from a copy of Holinshed's *Chronicles* made up from the original marked proof sheets), and if McLeod hasn't used those appendices, I infer that no one else has either.

For whom, then, are such data intended? Unless the text is as genuinely problematic—and there are many Renaissance texts which are— such appendices serve primarily to guarantee that the editor has done his or her job properly. And they are read primarily *before* the actual volume is published: the press's reader will read them; the general editor will read them; the reviewer will read them—at least selectively; and the panel and reviewers of the granting agency who is subvening the edition

---

[8] Compare the examination of Sir John Harington's autograph of Cantos XIV–XLVI of his translation of Ariosto's *Orlando Furioso*, which served as printer's copy, by W. W. Greg, "An Elizabethan Printer and his Copy," *The Library*, 4th ser., 4 (1923): 102–18.

or certifying it will want them there to be read—by someone else! The MLA's own Committee on Scholarly Editions insists that textual apparatus be printed in the volume itself, not simply archived in selected research libraries. I do not mean here to discredit serious textual scholarship or disemploy editors. I am only pointing to the obvious: a major determinant of exactly what data is recorded and how it is reported inheres in the collective specifications of scholarly editions as these are established by publishers, publishers' readers, grants-making agencies, and peer-review panels, whether at NEH or MLA or within one's own department or university. Such data establish the *bona fides* of the editor at least as much as they illuminate the text or facilitate its scholarly study.

I come now, as did one of our great editorial predecessors, Samuel Johnson, to "The Conclusion, in which Nothing is Concluded." Rather than set forth a fixed and invariant decalogue of transcriptional theory and practice—I have edited Hooker, after all, not spoken to God—I offer instead these three benchmarks, which, when you have established *their* elevation, will allow you to determine for yourself what data to record, what to suppress, and in what form to transmit it. Of the three, it is the third—the audience—that is currently most problematic. Editors have lived with the printed and manuscript exemplars of Renaissance texts and with the expectations of a print culture coterminously now for over four centuries. But the current audience for such scholarship is changing so rapidly that its nature and extent can no longer be determined with the same precision that we all look for in the texts we edit or read.

THE GRADUATE CENTER
AND LEHMAN COLLEGE, CUNY

The Receyt of the Ladie Kateryne
and the Practice of Editorial Transcription

GORDON KIPLING

I N OCTOBER AND NOVEMBER OF THE YEAR OF 1501, THE TUDOR
court devised a festival to celebrate the marriage of Henry VII's
eldest son, Prince Arthur, to Katharine of Aragon, daughter of the
Spanish monarchs, Ferdinand and Isabella. Since this marriage was
unusually significant to Henry, representing as it did the successful
culmination of his dynastic and political ambitions, the marriage festival
was designed from the first as a lavish celebration of the Tudor dynasty.
As his contribution to the festival, an anonymous writer compiled,
probably as an official memorial, a detailed account of the event. *The
Receyt of the Ladie Kateryne*[1] chronicles Katharine of Aragon's arrival in

---

[1] The College of Arms manuscript, in its present state, is untitled. The *Receyt*
occupies its own manuscript of 48 leaves, and this has been bound together with
three other originally distinct manuscripts to form College of Arms, MS. 1st M. 13.
Stab holes on the outer margin of fol. 27 (a reversed leaf) suggest that the original
manuscript was stitched together and covered by a fold of vellum or other protective
material. If so, a title may have been written on the cover thus formed. The cover,
in turn, would have been discarded when the *Receyt* manuscript was bound together
with the three other pamphlets to form the College of Arms MS. Supposing the text
did originally have a title, I borrow a phrase from the first lines of the text—*The
Receyt of the Ladie Kateryne*—as the title of my edition: Early English Text Society,
o.s. 296 (Oxford, 1990).

England, her triumphant entry into London, her marriage to Prince
Arthur, the disguisings and tournament held in honor of that marriage,
and Prince Arthur's funeral in Ludlow and Worcester a few months
thereafter. Written immediately after the event (in the regnal year 18
Henry VII, or 1502–1503, according to its author), the *Receyt* incorporates into its narrative verbatim a number of literary and historical documents which the narrator had collected and stitches these together with
a detailed and authoritative eyewitness account of the festival. One thus
finds a copy of the speeches spoken by the pageant actors during
Katharine's royal entry into London, a slightly modified version of the
"device" (written architectural plans) for the pageants, an epithalamium
written for the wedding, and a detailed herald's report of Prince Arthur's
funeral ceremonies.[2] Divided into books and chapters, the narrator-
cum-compiler attempts to cast his historical materials into the form of a
medieval romance, occasionally borrowing prose cadences from Malory
or Lord Berners to describe the actions of Katharine, Arthur, and Henry
VII.

No other contemporary source preserves such a full and vivid account
of the social history, visual arts, and drama in England at the opening of
the sixteenth century. While almost every serious study of early Tudor
history and society in the past century is also indebted to the *Receyt*,[3] the
manuscript has proven especially indispensable for historians of the
drama. Glynne Wickham, for one, regards the narrative as "unquestionably the most important extant document relative to the dramatic records
of the early Tudor period."[4] The *Receyt*, in fact, provides detailed accounts of three of the age's most important forms of courtly and spectac-
ular drama at a time when such accounts are otherwise impossible to
find. First, its account of the magnificent dramatic pageantry for
Katharine of Aragon's triumphal entry into London is unrivaled for its

---

[2] In some cases, independent versions of these documents survive. The pageant
speeches, for example, appear in two London chronicles: Guildhall MS. 3313 (*The
Great Chronicle of London*, ed. A. H. Thoams and I. D. Thornley [London, 1938]) and
British Library, MS. Cotton Vitellius A. XVI. The herald's funeral report also appears
in Sir Thomas Wriothesley's Register of Arms (British Library, MS. Add. 45131) and
in many copies made from the Wriothesley version.

[3] In addition to those works mentioned in n. 5 below, see Wilhelm Busch, *King
Henry VII*, tr. Alice M. Todd (London, 1895); Garrett Mattingly, *Catherine of Aragon*
(Boston, 1941); and S. B. Chrimes, *Henry VII* (London, 1972).

[4] See his MS. "Calendar of contents," dated 1949 and appended to College of
Arms, MS. 1st M. 13.

detail in the history of these shows. Second, the similarly detailed accounts of the four disguisings held at Westminster and Richmond are of necessity cited by every scholar of the English masque from Chambers, Reyher, and Welsford to Anglo, Orgel, and Wickham.[5] Third, its descriptions of the mimetic tournament, with its anticipations of Artesia's tournament in the *Arcadia* and of the Elizabethan Accession Day jousts, constitutes one of the landmarks of Tudor allegory and chivalry.[6] With the single exception of the interlude, which is well documented by a number of texts, the *Receyt* thus provides a complete picture of the state of English court drama at a crucial point in its development.

A manuscript that looms so importantly in our literary, social, and dramatic histories, one would assume, must long ago have appeared in a competent, scholarly edition. But in fact, circumstances have prevented the appearance of such a publication. The manuscript itself, first of all, has remained in the collections of the heralds of the College of Arms since it was written, and until recently, the College library has been uncatalogued and difficult for an outside scholar work in. Unless one knew beforehand that the *Receyt* was in the College and that it occupied fols. 27–74 of MS. 1st M. 13, he would not know what to ask for when he got there, and he would be unlikely to consult the original manuscript at all. Glynne Wickham was almost certainly the first modern scholar from outside the College to consult, describe, and cite the manuscript in a work of historical scholarship. Before that, scholars have had to content themselves with studying three derivative versions of the *Receyt*, the relative reliabilities of which they were unable to judge. There is an early seventeenth-century transcription of part of the text in the British Library (MS. Harley 69), an exceptionally inaccurate, edited and paraphrased version of the Harley manuscript printed as an appendix to Hearne's edition of Leland's *Collectanea* (3rd ed.,1774), and a nineteenth-century edition of the College of Arms manuscript

---

[5] Cf. E. K. Chambers, *The Mediaeval Stage*, 2 vols. (Oxford, 1903), and *The Elizabethan Stage*, 4 vols. (Oxford, 1923); Paul Reyher, *Les Masques Anglais* (Paris, 1909); Enid Welsford, *The Court Masque* (Cambridge, 1927); Sydney Anglo, *Spectacle, Pageantry and Early Tudor Policy* (Oxford, 1969); Glynne Wickham, *Early English Stages*, 4 vols. (London, 1959–); Stephen Orgel, *The Jonsonian Masque* (Cambridge, Mass., 1965). All of these works make extensive use of the descriptions in the *Receyt*, sometimes (as in Reyher) printing long extracts from one or another of the derivative manuscript versions. Only Wickham cites the College of Arms text itself.

[6] Gordon Kipling, *The Triumph of Honour: Burgundian Origins of the Elizabethan Renaissance* (Leiden, 1977), 116–36.

published in the 1808 edition of Grose and Astle's *Antiquarian Repertory.*[7]

This is not the place to detail the inaccuracies of these various transcriptions, but perhaps a brief description of their aims and methods is in order. All of them were produced by heralds in the pursuit of their professional duties or antiquarian interests, and only the last of them made any pretense to verbal fidelity in transcription. The Harley manuscript was thus compiled by a herald who, about 1610, gathered out of the office books of the College of Arms such precedents as would be helpful in fulfilling the ceremonial duties of his office. He mined rather than transcribed the *Receyt*, and in doing so he copied out only those sections of the text which seemed to speak directly to the ceremonial duties of heralds. In effect, he produced a kind of anthology which heavily emphasized court ceremonial and omitted civic and ecclesiastical ceremonial. As a consequence, he omitted from his collection those portions of the text concerned with the Princess's royal entry into London and her marriage at St. Paul's because these ceremonies belonged to the provinces, respectively, of the city fathers and the bishops, not the heralds. Since the text held no particular verbal authority for him, he often edited as he wrote, sometimes condensing what he copied; he corrected grammar, omitted irrelevant passages, and didn't brood much over difficult readings. Whether a particular pageant at a court disguising represented a *towre* or a *trone* made little difference to him.[8] Later in the eighteenth century, Joseph Edmondson, a minor herald with antiquarian tastes, supplied a transcript of this Harley version, rather than the original College of Arms text, to Thomas Hearne, who printed it as an appendix to his edition of Leland's *Collectanea*. In presenting this antiquarian text to the eighteenth-century public, either Edmundson or Hearne attempted to "improve" the style and grammar of the Harley version. The printed text thus condenses, paraphrases, and simplifies the syntax of an already heavily emended copy-text. Not surprisingly, it often manages to garble or omit important passages, so much so that the

---

[7] So many liberties have been taken with the text in these derivative versions that scholars have often found it difficult to ascertain the relationships between these various transcripts and the original College of Arms text. Glynne Wickham typically thinks that the *Collectanea* text was copied directly from MS. 1st M. 13; in fact, it was copied from Harley 69; see *Early English Stages*, 1:404.

[8] He omits such passages as the *Receyt*'s description of the Spanish ropewalker's performance (fol. 64) largely because, one suspects, such events were of little professional interest to heralds.

inadequacies of the *Collectanea* were well appreciated soon after publication. Indeed, because Edmund Lodge, Lancaster Herald, became so upset with Edmundson's work, he decided to publish a complete and reliable transcription of the original College of Arms text in the 1808 edition of the *Antiquarian Repertory*.[9] Unlike his predecessors, Lodge cared very much indeed about transcriptional fidelity, and he certainly tried to produce a complete and careful transcription of his copy-text. As a concession to his readers, he standardized the punctuation and capitalization according to nineteenth-century usage, but he did try to retain the manuscript's original spelling and to preserve abbreviations rather than silently expand them. His printed text even retained the form as well as the substance of his copy-text by keeping the manuscript's paragraphing intact and by printing chapter headings in the style of the original. But even so, Lodge (or perhaps the type-setter) had considerable difficulty in producing an accurate transcription. Although it is the most responsible transcript of all, it suffers from a great variety of transcriptional lapses. Words are misread or dropped; whole lines are omitted; in one place Latin is even mistranscribed as English.[10] Sometimes, in fact, Lodge's edition is so faulty that important passages appear more accurately rendered in the Edmundson-Hearne version.[11] In the end, then, Lodge's version, if more complete than the other two, is about equally unreliable. Nevertheless, because these versions have been widely available to scholars and the original text has not, these three versions—and only these—have had to serve two centuries of scholarship as vital sources of information about historical, social, literary, and dramatic activity at the early Tudor court.

Before congratulating ourselves upon our modern and enlightened editorial methodologies that allow us to put right what our ancestors

---

[9] For the Edmondson version, see John Leland, *De rebus Britannicis collectanea*, ed. Thomas Hearne, 2nd ed. (London, 1770), 5:352–81. According to Lodge, "Edmonson ... was a coach-painter by trade, an antiquary by profession, and a herald by name. Little was to be reasonably expected from selections made by such a person" (*Antiquarian Repertory*, ed. Francis Grose and Thomas Astle, 4 vols. [London, 1807–1809], 2:248). Lodge's own text appears on 248–331.

[10] Lodge thus prints " 'Of me ... trowe ye' " for "O si me inveniat" (*Antiquarian Repertory*, 2:*285). Cf. Wickham, *Early English Stages*, 1:404.

[11] The Lodge text thus omits the information that the men and women performers coupled after dancing separately at one disguising (cf. fol. 55r) and omits as well the separate dancing of the men on another occasion (cf. fol. 59v). The Edmundson version, for all it faults, gets these details right.

have muddled, however, we had better pause to consider the nature of
the manuscript we are attempting to transcribe and edit. If we do so, we
shall find that transcriptional accuracy is a far more elusive and relative
goal than we might at first have imagined. Because of the circumstances
of its authorship and scribal transcription, the text enjoys at best an
ambiguous textual authority. At times it claims the authority of a fair
copy of an authorial original; at other times it betrays all the signs of an
indifferent transcript of a copy somewhat distant from the original.
Before we begin to transcribe, we need to have these complexities
clearly in mind.

To begin with, the text has been transcribed by at least three—and
perhaps four—separate hands, a circumstance suggestive of multiple
scribes creating a derivative text based upon a more authoritative exemplar. The first hand (Scribe A) thus transcribed the main body of the
text, from fol. 29r to fol. 72v, sometimes emending his own work as he
wrote. A second hand (Scribe B1) then finished the job by transcribing
the last four folios of text (73r–74v). Next a third hand (Scribe B2)—or
perhaps the second hand again working less hurriedly[12]—copied the
prologue (fols. 27–28). Finally, a fourth hand (Scribe C) has inserted a
number of words, lines, and even longer passages into the first scribe's
work, either between lines or in the margin.

The nature of Scribe C's contributions is particularly difficult to
ascertain. Often his work seems that of an editor correcting the work of
a scribe against an authoritative copy-text. He thus corrects a number of
scribal errors resulting from eyeskip or transposition.[13] But at the same
time, his work often takes on the characteristics of emendation, revision,
or even original composition. He thus often adds in the margin passages
of considerable importance that cannot easily be identified as the results
of scribal omission. Sometimes, indeed, considerable interruptions in
syntax are required to accommodate these insertions:

> Thus when this goodly werk was approchid unto the Kinges
> presens and sight—*dravyn and conveyd uppone whelys by iij woddosys,*

---

[12] While the hands appear very similar, there are some apparent differences. In
particular, Scribe B1 customarily forms an *h* (usually in *the*) consisting of little more
than two loops, one above the other; Scribe B2, by contrast, generally avoids turning
the bowl of the *h* into a loop by bringing the pen upward and forward from the
descender to the next letter. The differences, however, might well be occasioned by
the effects of haste in the portion of the text contributed by Scribe B1.

[13] See n. 19 below.

ij befor and one behynd, and one eyther syde off the sayde trone ij mer-
maydes, one off them a man myrmayde thother a woman, the man in
harnesse from the wast uppeward, and in every off the sayde mermaydes
a Chyld off the Chapell syngyng ryght suetly and with quaint armoney—
descendid thes viij pleasaunt, disguysid, galauntes men of honour.

(fol. 64v; Scribe C's insertion in italics)

Indeed, Scribe C is as likely to add superfluous and unnecessary qualifications (he tells us that Katharine's retinue was a goodly company "off
countess, baroness, and many other gentlewoman" and elsewhere clarifies
her status pointlessly as Princess "of Espayne") as he is to address important matters of substance. Such corrections as these resemble nothing so
much as the revisions made by Victorian authors in their galley proofs.

In many respects, however, the physical composition of the manuscript points toward some sort of authorial original than to a mere scribal
copy. "Book Five" of the text, for example (the account of Prince
Arthur's funeral), was probably incorporated into the body of the text as
something of an afterthought. Certainly the author of the *Receyt* seems to
have brought his narrative to a close with his own description of Arthur's death at the end of "Book Four." Furthermore, we can establish
that all of Book Five consists merely of an heraldic record of Prince
Arthur's funeral which the author has incorporated into his own work
by means of inserting chapter headings at appropriate places.[14] In fact,
if we examine the physical composition of the manuscript, we can catch
the author in the very act of incorporating this heraldic record into his
treatise. Scribe A thus reflects the author's original intention by finishing
his transcription of Book Four about three-quarters of the way down fol.
67r and then leaving fol. 67v blank. Then we encounter the stub of a
canceled leaf between fols. 67 and 68, which shows that yet another leaf

---

[14] This portion of the manuscript has come down to us in two different textual
traditions, one of them completely independent of the main body of the *Receyt*. The
funeral report is found in a number of heraldic manuscripts, most of them funeral
collections. These all derive from Sir Thomas Wriothesley's Register of Arms (British
Library, MS. Add. 45131, fols. 37–47) and are distinguished by their lack of chapter
divisions. Both the Wriothesley and 1st M. 13 versions are of approximately equal
textual authority, and both descend from a common original. I argue in the full
introduction to my edition that this original was a funeral report compiled by John
Writhe, Garter King of Arms, who was present at the funeral of Prince Arthur. The
author of the *Receyt* merely incorporates Writhe's account into his own narrative by
inserting chapter divisions into Writhe's originally undivided text.

originally intervened between the end of Book Four and the beginning
of Book Five. Since the scribe customarily leaves no blank space at all to
separate one of his "Books" from another, the extraordinary separation
he has allowed here shows that, to his mind at least, he was dealing with
two quite separate texts. Furthermore, the text of the funeral reports
begins with a large, decorated initial letter—by far the most intricately
drawn initial in the entire manuscript. The sudden appearance of such an
intricately drawn initial, therefore, suggests once again that the scribe
thought he was beginning a new text altogether, not merely a new part
of the same text he had been copying all along. If so, we may suspect
that the canceled leaf consisted of a title page to the new text, that it was
removed in order to incorporate the funeral report in the body of the
Receyt, and that the chapter heading ("the furst chaptre of the vth booke
...") was a later addition inserted into the upper margin to disguise the
annexation. The awkwardness of these modifications underlines both the
last-minute nature of this decision and the author's close involvement
with the transcription of the manuscript. To make these modifications
necessary, the author must have made his decision only after the transcription of the funeral report had begun.

The rather brief, "literary" prologue that introduces the text of the
Receyt also seems to be the result of a late inspiration. Since it accurately
outlines the *Receyt's* division "into v partes and small bokes" and specifically mentions "the v [book] of the princes lamentable deth and
buriyng," it could only have been composed after the author made his
decision to incorporate the funeral account into his narrative. Furthermore, it occupies its own exceptional quire of two leaves at the beginning of the manuscript, a circumstance that almost certainly establishes
that the prologue was composed after the copying of the body of the
text began. Otherwise, since the scribe seems to have been transcribing
his text into a series of three identical, sixteen-leaf quires, we would
expect the prologue to occupy the beginning of one of these larger
quires. Finally, that the prologue is copied in a hand different from that
of the body of the text suggests that it must have been transcribed after
Scribe A ceased his labors a mere four folios from the end of the text.

The picture that emerges is that of a scribal fair copy of the author's
rough manuscript, prepared under continuing authorial supervision.
Judging by his clear court script, Scribe A was probably a professional.
Even as he copied the text, however, decisions were being made about
the narrative. Initially, the herald's funeral report was probably included
in the manuscript as a companion piece to the main narrative; belatedly,

this originally separate account was modified and incorporated as "Book Five" of the main narrative. After that was done, the author wrote a prologue and either set it aside to be copied when the main text had been completed or gave it to another scribe to prepare. In the midst of these maneuvers, Scribe A was relieved by Scribe B1, an obviously non-professional copyist, virtually at the end of his task. This scribe completed the last four leaves of the funeral narrative; then either he or a third scribe (B2) completed the job by copying the prologue onto two fresh leaves, which were then appended to the front of the manuscript.

Since the prologue was composed very late in this process, it would be tempting to identify the non-professional hand of Scribe B2, who contributed these leaves to the manuscript, as the hand of the author of the *Receyt*. More compelling evidence of the author's presence appears, however, in the hand of Scribe C, who frequently corrects, emends, or even expands the text as copied by Scribe A. He not only carefully corrects scribal errors, but he inserts passages that seem more like authorial revision than mere correction. He makes no corrections or revisions whatsoever in Book Five, enough though it can be shown that Scribes A and B1 committed a number of copying errors. In short, Scribe C seems interested in correcting or emending only those portions of the text written by the author of the *Receyt*—he takes a more proprietary interest, so to speak, in the *Receyt* proper, but ignores the narrative of a herald which had been merely incorporated into his own text.

If this view is correct, then the College of Arms text would seem to possess a great deal of authority indeed. It almost certainly represents a scribal fair copy of authorial "foul papers," a fair copy, moreover, closely supervised by the author who corrected, revised, and expanded as his scribe copied out the text. In several respects, however, such a view probably overstates the authority of the manuscript. To begin with we must consider that the author's text—his "foul papers"—does not represent wholly original composition. In at least three—and probably four—cases, the author merely incorporates material into his narrative that he has found "ready made" elsewhere. We have thus already seen how he has taken over a herald's funeral report to form a fifth "Book" of his text. Elsewhere he has also certainly appropriated the extensive text of the speeches spoken by the actors from their pageants during Katharine of Aragon's royal entry into London. Elsewhere he has also made an entire chapter of "Book Three" out of a rather turgid epithalamium that some anonymous poet has written. Finally, the lengthy descriptions of the royal entry pageants are probably not original eyewitness accounts but transcriptions of the "devices" (written architectural specifications) supplied to the court by the civic pageant deviser; these he has lightly revised by altering verb tenses to suit a narrative rather than a prescriptive context.[15] Together, this "appropriated" material accounts for all of Book Five, almost all of Book Two, and a chapter of Book Three—nearly 40% of the text. For two of these incorporated texts—the pageant speeches and the funeral report—there exist other independent, substantive texts of at least equal authority to those that appear in the *Receyt* narrative. Take the pageant verses, for example. The *Receyt's* version of these speeches represents at best a court manuscript, made from a fair copy, transcribed in turn from the poet's original. If the author of the *Receyt* himself copied out these verses (rather than simply supplying Scribe A with the hypothetical court copy and instructing him to distribute the verses appropriately in his narrative), then we might

---

[15] For a detailed exposition of this point, see the introduction to the full edition. Here there is space only to point out that the descriptions of the royal entry pageants are different in nature from those of other descriptions of pageants elsewhere (e.g., in the London chronicles). In general, the author of the *Receyt* usually describes pageants by telling us what they represented; in this he follows the usual practice of such reportage. But the manuscript describes how the pageants were made and sometimes suppresses their symbolic meaning. Thus the description of the third pageant indulges in measurements, specifies construction materials, and details decorative schemes. The actors, however, are not described at all. Instead, at the very end of the description, the author tells us that "upon this rehersid sete there sate such persones as their speches shall declare." By contrast, the civic chronicler describes the very same pageant in the more conventional manner; to him the actors are of primary importance, and he is content to pass over the construction of the pageant with a few lines of description. He thus details the names and symbolic significance of the three actors (Job, Boethius, and King Alphonso the Wise), and he notices yet a fourth, nearly overlooked by the author of the *Receyt*: "Raphaell with his goldyn & glyterying wyngis & ffedyrs of many & sundry colours" (College of Arms, MS. 1st. M. 13, fol. 37; *Great Chronicle of London*, 301). The author's description, in fact, resembles nothing so much as a lightly revised version of the pageant designer's "device." As Geoffrey Webb points out, "the part played by drawings, whether plans or elevational designs, in the architecture of the Middle Ages, was, by comparison with modern practice, small." Instead, architects drew up written descriptions, known as "devices," for their projects. "Generally speaking, when a building existed on paper, it existed in words and not in line." For the medieval designer, verbal "devices" served as the "legal documents on which the builder makes his bargain, and by which he is bound" ("The Office of Devisor," in *Fritz Saxl 1890–1948*, ed. D. J. Gordon [London, 1949], 297–98). Certainly the pageant descriptions in the *Receyt* read like architectural devices. Only a slight revision, mostly in the tenses of the verbs, would transform them into the sort of legal "device" familiar to the medieval architect.

well suspect yet another intermediary text, another layer of textual corruption.[16] Meanwhile, copies of the same verses exist in two civic chronicles.[17] Research has established that these copies depend upon the lost *Main City Chronicle*, which in turn must have transcribed its version of the verses from a manuscript circulating among the city actors preparing for their roles in the pageants. This, in turn, depends upon the fair copy of the poet's original, which is the common source of both textual traditions. A similarly complicated textual stemma can be constructed to account for the two distinct textual traditions represented by the surviving texts of the funeral report, which we can establish, with some certainty, to be the work of John Writhe, Garter King of Arms.[18] In all of these cases, the version of the text transcribed in the College of Arms manuscript stands at some considerable distance from the original, and as a consequence it carries far less textual authority. Indeed, many readings from the other substantive texts are manifestly better readings than those to be found in the College of Arms version.

Even if we put aside the matter of relative textual authority, we still have to deal with the transcriptional habits of Scribe A, who copied out the vast majority of the College of Arms manuscript. Indeed, he was only a moderately accurate scribe who seems to have adjusted the accidentals of his copy-text to his own stylistic preferences. Wherever we can check his work against other substantive versions of text, we find that he falls victim to the usual scribal errors, principally word confusion

---

[16] In all likelihood, the *Receyt* text was based upon a copy of the verses presented to the court commissioners, headed by Lord Abergavenny and Sir Reginald Bray, for official approval. This copy apparently lacked the Latin distichs that appear in the version of the text represented in the chronicles. For the Privy Council Order which established Lord Aburgevanny's commission to oversee the civic reception, see College of Arms, MS. 1st M. 13, fol. 5v; for the civic reaction to the heavy-handedness of the court's oversight, see *Great Chronicle of London*, 310, and *Triumph of Honour*, 99 n. 8.

[17] The civic chronicles both include the Latin distichs, and they both place Prelacy's speech in the wrong pageant. This misplacement suggests that the verses came to the scribe of the *Main City Chronicle* in the form of speeches written on separate pieces of paper rather than in a roll or book. Such a format would encourage the misordering and misassigning of speeches. Both of these features point conclusively to the civic provenance of this version. Not only do speeches copied upon separate sheets of paper suggest a text derived from actors' parts, but the preservation of the Latin distichs reflects the city's practical provision for communicating the sense of the show to their non English-speaking guests.

[18] *Receyt*, ed. Kipling, lx–lxii.

(*were/where; how that/brought*), transposition, and eyeskip. Particularly prone to this last category of error, he can be found dropping not only single words and lines of script, but also passages of considerable length.[19] On the other hand, he is an accurate enough scribe to preserve, sometimes side by side, the differing lexical preferences of the various authors of his copy-text, as where a chapter heading, inserted into the funeral report by the author of the *Receyt*, promises a description of the "ensencyng" of Prince Arthur's body, but Writhe's text itself describes how the prelates "sensid" it. Here (as he frequently does elsewhere) the scribe has preserved one of the author's favorite stylistic devices, the addition of *ap-, en-,* and *em-* prefixes wherever possible to make his prose seem more Latinate and hence more portentious. But if he succeeds in reproducing his copy-text's substantives with moderate accuracy, he seems to pay no particular attention to its accidentals. He is particularly cavalier in punctuating his text. Sometimes he supplies virgules, dots, or colons virtually at every clause; sometimes such marks appear seldom and randomly. In either case, the pointing rarely fills any grammatical or phrasal function. Indeed, we can often catch him adjusting the accidentals of his copy-text to his own preferences. Hand C thus habitually spells the word *of* as *off*; Scribe A habitually renders the word in the modern way as *of*. Similarly, Hand C, at least in one instance, uses a thorn; Scribe A never does, and some evidence suggests that when Scribe A found thorns in his copy-text he transliterated them as *th*. He thus occasionally goes too far and mistakes a *y* for a thorn (e.g., "fer in the *contreth* of the west").

Such a variety of texts and scribal practices makes an editor's pursuit of transcriptional accuracy a very difficult occupation indeed. Is he accurate if he merely reproduces the accidentals of the College of Arms text even if he is convinced that these belong only to the scribe and do not represent any of the various authors of the various textual levels? Such an exercise often demonstrates the scribe's difficulties in coping with the rather complicated syntax of his own copy-text, but it cannot

---

[19] On fol. 61v, for example, the scribe's eye skipped from the end of one sentence, "the seid gates," over an intervening passage, to "And when they were departing homward." As he continued to copy, however, he discovered his error. Since he could not rectify his mistake without spoiling the appearance of the page, he merely copied the omitted passage out of order, placing it at the end of the sentence which he was copying when he discovered his error. To correct this disorder, Scribe C then inserted the letters *b, A,* and *c* in the margin to indicate the correct order.

help in eludicating the author's own preferences in accidentals:

> In the Sunday ensueng: the duetie of the Religion of Cristom-
> dome: is: that the seruice and worship of god: shuld be Above all
> othir thynges: wordly especially Maynteyned: And so verily it was:
> aftir the moost excellent solmpnite: A bought the honour of
> almighti god: with prikkyd songe: and Organs: and goodly sere-
> monys in the quere: and Aultirs: and thus was the for non expen-
> did holily: and with great vertue:

Here the editor is faced with the problem that the scribe's pointing does not even pick out phrasal pauses very adequately, nor does it help in clarifying syntactical relationships between the various clauses. And what is the point in preserving the scribe's manifest error (*wordly* for *worldly*)? In this passage, as in many others throughout the text, transcriptional accuracy to the scribe results in an essential misrepresentation of the author's text, and we have no effective way of recovering the author's own text.

Even if we had some way of recovering the author's (rather than the scribe's) accidentals, we would still not be much closer to our ideal. To which text does the editor pretend accuracy anyway? If he is transcribing Book Five (the funeral report), for example, does he follow the College of Arms text or the other substantive version in B.L. MS. Add. 45131? Both are about equally reliable; both are equally distant transcripts of John Writhe's lost original. When our editor finds, in comparing these two texts, that the author of the *Receyt* has inserted chapter titles of his own devising into Writhe's text, does he transcribe them for his own edition or not? If he does so, he must face the fact that they will frequently interrupt Writhe's original paragraphing and require suppressing a few conjunctive words or phrases to make the chapter breaks possible. Thus he has to decide whether he is transcribing Writhe's original text, or Writhe's text as emended by the author. But whichever choice he makes, he will still face the problem that both of his substantive texts include words, phrases, and passages not present in the other, and that some of these have been dropped as the result of scribal error. Does he incorporate these omitted passages into his text, or merely note them in his apparatus? Similarly, does he or does he not transcribe the Latin distichs which are found only in the civic texts of the pageant speeches, not in the College of Arms text? Does he silently emend obvious cases of manifest error? Does he expand abbreviations? The editor cannot escape these choices or their implications. Depending upon his decisions, he will attempt to reconstruct either the scribe's text, the author's text, the various texts of the various incorporated texts, or some sort of frankly composite text that neither scribe nor author would recognize.

I cannot pretend to have answered all these questions to the satisfaction of all possible readers. Indeed, I must admit I have not tried to please all possible readers. I think those primarily interested in sixteenth-century punctuation and word division will have to consult the manuscript anyway, so I have not catered to their rather specialized interests. I suspect most of the *Receyt's* readers will be historians of Tudor society and drama, not literary scholars *per se*. As a consequence, I have adopted a rather liberal policy with respect to the accidentals of my copy-text. I have seen little point in endorsing Scribe A's peculiar choice in accidentals, and I see no way of recovering the author's choices. So I have felt free to silently expand abbreviations, to standardize *i, j, u, v,* to supply editorial punctuation, and, within limits, to supply modern word division.[20] I take as my copy-text the College of Arms manuscript, and I follow the author by inserting chapter titles into John Writhe's funeral report even at the cost of suppressing a few conjunctive phrases here and there as represented in the British Library text. I do this because I am editing the *Receyt* after all, not Writhe's funeral report, and I must necessarily assume that these insertions and suppressions represent deliberate editorial choices on the part of the author. On the other hand, I do insert words, phrases, and lines which I think have been mistakenly dropped from the interpolated texts, either by the author, by Scribe A, or by the scribe who provided the text collected by the author. Such omissions, I conclude, are not the result of deliberate editorial choice but of transcriptional error and as such should be restored to the text. For this reason I will even insert the Latin distichs into the pageant verses because I think the author's copy of those verses mistakenly omitted them.

In the end, I have produced, I judge, a frankly composite text. Neither the author of the *Receyt* or the various scribes would recognize some of its details, perhaps, but it is one, I think, that its readers will find useful and reliable.

UNIVERSITY OF CALIFORNIA,
LOS ANGELES, CALIFORNIA

---

[20] Word division has been generally modernized, except in cases of deliberate elision, particularly in those cases where the author seems to be imitating French habits of dropping a vowel between a definite article and a noun (*thestates*).

Accounting for Absence:
The Transcription of Space

A. R. BRAUNMULLER

SIR BENJAMIN BACKBITE ANTICIPATES THE APPEARANCE OF HIS poems: "a beautiful quarto page, where a neat rivulet of text shall meander through a meadow of margin,"[1] and Henry James attacks Walt Whitman's *Drum-Taps*: "The frequent capitals are the only marks of verse in Mr. Whitman's writing . . . each line starts off by itself, in resolute independence of its companions, without a visible goal."[2] Non-semantic physical attributes—an unjustified right-hand margin, capitals at the start of each line—signal formal properties of the text. In turn, these formal features stipulate conventional relations among writer, text, and reader; they tell us how we are expected to regard the text. *These* texts are poetry, or at least verse, and must be read as such *because* of their margins and their capitals.

Most modern editors are sensitive to the formal features of earlier texts if identical or analogous formal conventions have survived into the present. I would like to suggest that modern editors are not sufficiently sensitive to conventions, specifically conventions of layout or spacing, that have not so survived. Semiotically, transcription restates a coded

---

[1] R. B. Sheridan, *School for Scandal* (1781), Act 1.
[2] *The Nation*, vol. 1, no. 20, Thursday, 16 November 1865, 626.

message in a new code-system, *from* manuscript, for example, *into* the shapes available on a typewriter keyboard or in a computer's set of fonts. Except for inescapable human error, the restatement allegedly changes nothing. Yet we are all aware that much treason occurs in this translation: for example, the occasional italic letter interspersed in a predominantly secretary hand declines into a dully uniform modern type face, and at best the editorial introduction contains a general statement that "the scribe uses italic forms of many capitals and the letters *e* and *r*," or whatever. In printed texts before the late eighteenth century, certain compositorial errors, or apparent errors, can only have come about through the mistaking of inscribed forms that have disappeared completely—the "long" *f*, for example, and many abbreviations, ligatures, and digraphs. So too, and much less obviously, we risk treason when we fail to recognize that space is a sign and part of the code-system we purport to translate for the reader.

Experienced readers are quite flexible when they meet a new sign-system, or variations on an old one, so long as that system appears in deliberately created marks upon the page. If we were not supple, then none of us would have read beyond page three of Russell Hoban's *Riddley Walker,* and few people would so easily adjust to George Bernard Shaw's orthographic quirks. Some systems, it must be admitted, cause more trouble than others. Edward Capell, the great Shakespearean editor of the eighteenth century, introduced a series of signs, some old, some new, including a "particular note of punctuation to distinguish irony," dashes to signal changes of address, double inverted commas for asides, a single-bar cross to indicate something shown to a character, and so forth.[3] Unfortunately, Capell's explanation is not repeated in the major edition where he employed his system, to the continuing confusion of later readers. Even much more ordinary inscribed signs can produce confusion where none was intended: in Samuel Beckett's *Happy Days,* for instance, the stage directions often call for the actress to perform an action and then to repeat it; rather than restate the directed action, Beckett's text merely reads *"Do."* It took me some time—and takes my students some time—to realize that this sign was the common British abbreviation for what a North American calls "Ditto." (The French text more bluntly reads, *"De même."*)

These examples illustrate how difficult inscribed signs may prove. To

---

[3] Capell, *Prolusions; or, select Pieces of antient Poetry* (1760), v.

judge from published transcriptions, we are even less sensitive to space and less flexible in acknowledging and interpreting its appearance, especially in manuscript. Yet Saussure's basic point about the arbitrariness of signs and their combinations surely includes the arbitrariness of the absence of signs. Space filled (a letter, a word) and space not filled (not letter, not word) are at least theoretically the same and similarly capable of expression and solicitous of interpretation. In the editorial world, print bibliographers have come to recognize the importance of what they always knew: textual space is not accidental but deliberate, the result of an intended act, whatever the motivation of that act might be. Charlton Hinman was one of the first to consider the importance of those deliberate acts. Early in his magisterial *Printing and Proof-reading of the First Folio of Shakespeare,* Hinman reminds us that "the 'white' spaces of varying lengths that follow so many Folio verses represent typographical material that was none the less real for not leaving inked impressions in the book."[4] Whether printed or manuscript, most Western languages, unlike classical epigraphy, now conventionally separate one word from another and usually make conventional breaks between syntactically integral units of words (sentences) and ideationally integral units of units (paragraphs or sections), but even so recent a text as the *Beowulf* manuscript "is written continuously like prose" with "[f]ull compounds . . . written as two words . . . other words . . . freely divided" and "separate words . . . run together."[5] Of course, most editors realize that interverbal spacing sometimes has philological or dialectological significance, and we carefully examine an Elizabethan manuscript's treatment of prefixed units like *a* in "a while" and we know that Shakespeare's "you are to blame" may not always record an infinitive.

I would now like to consider some spaces—in print and in manuscript—that need to be transcribed, not ignored. For some of my examples there are explanations, for others only hypotheses. Blanks within the lines of medieval and Renaissance manuscripts sometimes represent deliberate scribal omissions. Explaining how he had been forced to print his *Commentaries* (1578), Edmund Plowden wrote:

> having lent my said Book to a very few of my intimate Friends
> . . . their Clerks and others . . . made such Expedition, by writing
> Day and Night, that in a short Time they had transcribed a great

[4] 2 vols. (1963), 1:35–36.
[5] Fr. Klaeber, ed., *Beowulf,* 3rd ed. (1950), xcvi, xcix.

> Number of Cases ... which Copies at last came to the Hands of
> some of the Printers. . . . But the Cases being transcribed by Clerks
> and other ignorant Persons who did not perfectly understand the
> Matter, the Copies were very corrupt, for in some places a whole
> Line was omitted, and in others one Word was put for another,
> which entirely changed the Sense, and again in other Places Spaces
> were left where the Writers did not understand the Words, and
> divers other Errors and Defects there were, which ... would have
> greatly defaced the Work, and have been a Discredit to me.[6]

Even into the nineteenth century, reports of legal cases appear (in Cob-
bett and Howell's *Complete Collection of State Trials,* for example) with
blanks for words the verbatim reporters failed to hear or note. Plowden
articulates what most editors have long and reasonably suspected, and
few editors nowadays would be tempted to ignore such blanks. Lawyers
and law-reporters presumably left blanks as tokens of honorable ignorance, or to escape censure, but even piratical printers might do the
same. In the unauthorized and unattributed 1628 edition of Francis
Hubert's *Deplorable Life and Death of Edward the Second,* the first line of
stanza 344 (F6a) is followed by *Desunt Nonnulla* and a blank space down
to the second half of what would be—measured by the facing verso—the
fifth line of stanza 346, where the text resumes. Sure enough, the 1629
edition "Now Published by the Author" precisely fills the earlier edition's emptiness. Hubert's authorized edition contains almost 100 stanzas
not in the earlier text; only here (but how carefully!) does that text
represent the absent verses.

Faulty transmission of the text will not, however, account for all the
gaps and spaces in manuscript or print. Scribes might, for example, leave
a blank for an illegible word, or even line, and later return to fill the
space; unusually large inter-verbal or inter-linear spacing, as well as variations in ink or pen, may be the only tangible evidence of such an
event.[7] Of course, this evidence in turn makes one ponder the source(s)
of the word or lines added retrospectively. Some blanks have been attributed to the author: describing Fuller's biography of Shakespeare, S.
Schoenbaum writes: "Although he combed the countryside in quest of
matter for his *Worthies,* he failed to learn the year of Shakespeare's death,

---

[6] 2 vols. (1816), 1:v.

[7] See, among many examples, *The Captive Lady,* Malone Society Reprints (1982),
line 1745.

for which he leaves a poignant blank in his text."[8] When Sir Edward
Coke writes "there is a Bay, called Robin Hoods Bay, in the River of
⸻ in Yorkshire," the blank is so unusual in this text that it may not
represent a uniquely illegible word; rather, it may testify to Coke's
ignorance or to a deliberate omission for some other, unknown, reason.[9]

The printer's difficulties with his copy seem to explain some typographical oddities in the 1640 Jonson folio. In *Pleasure Reconciled to Virtue*
(performed 1618), two of the songs have typographical surprises:

Just to the⸻you move your limbs,

Goe choose among – – – – But with a minde

It should be such should envie draw,
    but – – – – – overcome it.[10]

A Ralph Crane transcript of this masque, edited with two facsimiles in
Herford and Simpson's *Ben Jonson,* volume 7, survives at Chatsworth.
This MS fills in the first and third spaces:

iust to ye tune you moue your limbes

It should be such shold envy draw,
    but euer ouercome-it.[11]

The second example, unlike its fellows, scans perfectly well, and the long
rule appears as a dash in the MS. I include this example to illustrate the
apparent (and lamentable) fact that the compositor neither had nor
adopted a consistent code for marking omissions: in the first example he
used a rule; in the third, a series of dashes; in the second, dashes serve as
conventional punctuation. Consequently, the reader-transcriber must dis-

---

[8] *Shakespeare and Others* (1985), 175.

[9] *The Third Institute of the Laws of England* (1644), chap. 90 (2D1). Robin Hood's
Bay is on the North Sea rather than a river, although a rivulet, King's Beck, flows
through it.

[10] *The Workes of Benjamin Jonson The second Volume* (1640): the first example is "O
more, and more, this was so well," line 17; the second and third are lines 5 and 18
of "It followes now you are to prove" (E2b–E3).

[11] Stephen Orgel, who kindly pointed out this example to me, suggests that the
compositor might have read his copy as "ouer ouercome it," then diagnosed ditto-
graphy and decided to mark the omission.

tinguish omission from punctuation.

In Tudor–Stuart drama, compositors sometimes set blank space (rather than types that left an inked impression) to mark various kinds of textual lacunae. Twice in Dekker's *Patient Grissil* (printed 1603), the printer has enclosed word-length blanks within parentheses:

> signe I (   ), this legge [12]
> the corporation cannot be (   ) sirra (4.2.166–67)

Fredson Bowers thought the first of these "round brackets apparently signif[ies] an indecent movement," but Cyrus Hoy notes that this hypothesis will not explain the second example, and he observes, "The text surrounding the brackets in both passages seems corrupt, and I suspect that in both cases the round brackets signify the printer's inability to deal with indecipherable copy."[13] A wittier use of blank space appears in the corrected quarto of George Chapman's *All Fools* (1605), a play determined to make its audience as well as its characters the butt of one or another ribald folly. Customarily seeking approbation, the Epilogue to the uncorrected quarto concludes: "We can but bring you meate, and set you stooles, / And to our best cheere say, you all are welcome" (K1b, italic in original). Unusually enough, the corrected quarto—arguably overseen by Chapman himself—inserts rather than removes a blank: "We can but bring you meate, and set you stooles, / And to our best cheere say, you all are (   ) welcome" (K1b, italic as before). This inserted emptiness clearly invites the reader to make a couplet rhyming "stools" and . . . "fools": the audience, like the characters, "all are fools" and not "welcome" at all.

Space not only represents a deliberate compositorial act, it may testify to an antecedent act of censorship. In Thomas Middleton's *The Family of Love* (1608), for instance, Mistress Purge inquires, "And what do they sweare by now their mony is gone[?]"; Club replies,

> Why by(   )and God refuse them (B1b)

Dyce cautiously suggested that the blank represented "some expression which the printer was afraid to insert,"[14] but it almost certainly repre-

---

[12] 3.2.49 in *Dramatic Works*, ed. Fredson Bowers, 4 vols. (1953–61), vol. 1, quoted hereafter.

[13] See Bowers, 1:292, and Cyrus Hoy, *Introductions, Notes, and Commentaries to . . . Dramatic Works of Thomas Dekker*, 4 vols. (1980), 1:164.

[14] Quoted in A.H. Bullen, ed., *A Collection of Old English Plays*, 4 vols. (1882–85), 3:24.

sents an oath, censored in obedience to the 1606 Act to Restrain Abuses of Players.[15] Many pre-1606 plays were censored thus, but no other text that I know reproduces a blank for the omitted oath; that *The Family of Love* does so may mean the censorship took place while the quarto was being composed in the printer's shop, when there was no one available to provide a substitute phrase within the Act.[16] As a final example, consider John Marston's *The Malcontent* (1604), where the first quarto's three issues reveal both censorship and typographical subversion. In the first issue of the quarto ("QA," so-called), Pietro asks Malevole, "And sir whence come you now?"

> *Mal.* From the publick place of much dissimulation;
> the Church.
> *Piet.* What didst there? (B1b)

A few copies of this issue survive in which "the Church" has been cut out with a knife and, consequently, a blank line left in the text-block. A subsequent printing ("QA corrected") closes up the wound, but leaves the original punctuation intact: ". . . dissimulation; / What didst there?" The second issue ("QB") lacks the offending words, but fixes the punctuation and defiantly draws attention to the censorship by setting space: "the publick place of much dissimulation. (   )." The third issue ("QC") restores QA's words but retains the tell-tale parentheses and confuses the punctuation: "the publick place of much dissimulation, (the Church.)"

So far I have mentioned inter-verbal and inter-linear spaces in manuscript and print; I would like to conclude with some wider open spaces that commonly appear in holograph letters of the sixteenth and seventeenth centuries. As I hope will be clear, the spatial arrangement of a letter's text conveys, or may convey, a great deal. William Fulwood's *The Enimie of Idlenesse* (1568) was a very popular guide to letter-writing, as well as one of the earliest:

> The second [of "three necessary points"] is the Subscription, which must be don according to the estate of the writer, and

---

[15] In his very untrustworthy edition (1979) of the play for Nottingham Drama Texts, Simon Shepherd explains the parenthetical gap as "either a censored oath or an invitation to the actor's imagination."

[16] W. W. Greg, *The Editorial Problem in Shakespeare*, 3rd ed. (1954), xxxii, points out that "we do not even know whether this purgation [of oaths] was effected by the prompter in the 'book' or by the folio editor [i.e., in preparation for printing]."

the qualities of the person to whome we write: For to our su-
periors we must write at the right syde in the nether ende of
the paper.... And to our equalles we may write towards the
midst of the paper.... To our inferiors we may write on high
at the left hand.... (A8)[17]

Fulwood describes a three-fold, two-dimensional social matrix: the position of the subscription left-to-right and top-to-bottom conveys the
writer's sense of his social relation with the recipient—and possibly his
suasive purposes in writing the letter. A modern transcription that nor-
malizes this spacing (and many, many do) denies us this information and
keeps us ignorant of the sign-system. A similar but less elaborate system
seems later to have come to govern the placement of the salutation. *The
Rules of Civility* (1671, translated from Antonine de Courtin, *Nouveau
traité de civilité* of the same year) advises the writer: "after *my Lord, Sir,* or
Madam, which is usually writ at the top, before we come to the body of
the Letter; we are to leave a space or blank, greater or lesser, according
to the quality of the person to whom we write" (136–37).[18] Letters
written according to this formula can be exceedingly prodigal of paper—
the very conspicuous consumption "showing reverence and esteem" (as
de Courtin has it) meant to impress the recipient with his or her own
worth. A modern, penny-pinching press might hesitate to reproduce
such letters edited on a 1:1 scale, but the transcriber can certainly inform
readers of the facts, even if the press deprives us of the experience.
Transcriber and reader need to be alert to this spatial snobbery (or
ridicule), and editors certainly should consider developing some formula,
perhaps one based upon the usual spacing between lines of text, to
represent these signifying spaces.

---

[17] Similar advice appears in the other important early letter-writing guide, Angel
Day's *The English Secretary* (quoted below). Jean Robertson, in *The Art of Letter
Writing: An Essay on the Handbooks Published in England* (1942), 15, mistakenly says
that Fulwood writes about the "*super*scription" [i.e., the salutation], although there's
a protocol for that, too (again, see below).

[18] De Courtin also mentions the ceremonial placement of the subscription (138).
Alan Roper alludes to this text when discussing a newly-recovered letter by John
Dryden in *The Clark Newsletter*, no. 5 (Fall, 1983), 2; Professor Roper also drew my
attention to Ernest W. Sullivan, II's reference to an unpublished paper by Christina
Marsden Gillis on the significance of the subscription's location: see Sullivan, "The
Problem of Text in Familiar Letters," *PBSA* 75 (1981): 123 n. 8. I have not read
Gillis's paper.

These positional subtleties also make at least one dramatic scene a great deal more comprehensible. In the "pre-quel" to *The Spanish Tragedy*, *The First Part of Hieronimo* (printed 1605), which may or may not be by Kyd, Hieronimo dictates to Horatio a riddling letter addressed to Don Andrea and warning of Lorenzo's treachery. Hieronimo first complains,

> What, fold paper that way to a noble man?
> To Don Andrea, Spain's ambassador?
> Fie! I am ashamed to see it.[19]

Contemporary letter-writing guides, of course, discuss the correct folding of the paper. At the end of the letter, for which the guides also list numerous acceptable closing phrases, Hieronimo dictates

> Thus hoping you will not be murdered, and you can choose, especially being warned beforehand, I take my leave.
>
> (vi.79–81)

Repeatedly, he orders

> boy Horatio, write "leave" bending in the hams like an old courtier—"Thy assured friend," say, " 'gainst Lorenzo and the devil, little Hieronimo, Marshal" (63–65)

> Horatio, hast thou written "leave" bending in the hams enough, like a gentleman usher? 'Sfoot, no, Horatio; thou hast made him straddle too much like a Frenchman: for shame, put his legs closer, though it be painful. (82–85)

For Hieronimo the subscription is a hieroglyphic of humility; the physical shaping of the letters of *leave* conveys as much as, perhaps more than, the semantic content of the word. In making this bawdy and humorous claim, however, Hieronimo may be hyperbolic, but he isn't untraditional. Angel Day's *The English Secretary* warns "the unskilfull herein, that"

> writing to anie person of account, by howe much the more excellent hee is in calling from him in whose behalfe the letter is framed, by so much the lower, shall the subscription thereunto belonging, in any wise be placed.
>
> And if the state of honour of him to whome the Letter shall be

---

[19] Scene vi, lines 4–6, in the edition by A. S. Cairncross (1967), quoted hereafter.

directed doe require so much, the verie lowest margent of paper
shall do no more but beare it, so be it the space bee seemelie for
the name, and the roome fairre enough to comprehend it....[20]

Day's imagery—"the very lowest margent," the "seemelie" location, the
"roome fairre enough"—implies a system of translation from the spatial
to the social, even from the epistolary to the petitionary. The "lowly"
writer places his name in the "lowest" position, while ensuring that the
location does not inadvertently insult the recipient.

Since I began by quoting Henry James's review of *Drum-Taps*, let me
conclude with another quotation: "Every tragic event," he writes,
"collects about it a number of persons who delight to dwell upon its
superficial points—of minds which are bullied by the *accidents* of the
affair" (626). Transcription is no tragic event, but the spacing of a text
may not be a superficial and it is certainly not an accidental point.

UNIVERSITY OF CALIFORNIA
LOS ANGELES, CALIFORNIA

---

[20] The book first appeared in 1586; I quote from the edition, "Newly revised and
corrected," of 1599, C4.

Editing Daniel

JOHN PITCHER

N O ONE WILL DEMUR, I THINK, AT THE SUGGESTION THAT even if a textual question is old, and seemingly unanswered, it may be worth asking again. Dame Helen Gardner—who as far as I know never edited Shakespeare, nor wrote about his text—recently posed the entirely pertinent, and I think unanswered question, why didn't Shakespeare collect his plays and have them printed? Two centuries ago Dr. Johnson asked himself the same thing, of course, but he came up with an answer which leaves us with a Shakespeare thicker-skinned and more indifferent to reputation than many of us can now accept. In the *Preface*, he concluded that Shakespeare did not regard his works as "worthy of posterity," nor "levied any ideal tribute upon future times, or had any further prospect, than of present popularity and present profit. When his plays had been acted, his hope was at an end; he solicited no addition of honour from the reader." But, *pace* Johnson, there is evidence, in and out of the plays, that Shakespeare was a good deal more concerned than this about what his contemporaries were thinking of him, and what posterity might. In 1982, having asked this old question afresh (in her book, *In Defence of the Imagination*), Dame Helen suggested two alternative explanations. First, that as a man of the theater, Shakespeare may have "thought of the plays he had written as essentially scripts for performances, to live on, if they lived at all, through the interpretations of actors, and that he simply did not envisage a time would ever come in which people would read plays as they read and pored over poems, histories, and sermons." This sounds reasonable enough until we recall that by the late 1590s people were already reading Shakespeare's plays in the unauthorized quartos, and that there are signs that certain Jacobeans chose to read them as books rather than see them in productions. Are we to believe that Shakespeare was entirely unaware of this? Dame Helen's second explanation—and here she arrives at a position not far from Dr. Johnson's—is that Shakespeare may have been "truly indifferent to the idea of future fame," and that he took "the reward he wanted in the exercise of his genius and the success of his plays on stage and was content with that." It may be so, but her corollary to this, that his genius was *incompatible* with the tasks of revising and rewriting "what was obscure or carelessly phrased," is every day contradicted by the findings of the textual revisionists. As Dame Helen understood it, the "very idea of Shakespeare, like Jonson, editing his own works is inconceivable," but perhaps the new Oxford edition will eventually make us doubt even this.

One part of this question seems to have eluded Dame Helen, and that is, just how *sensitive to print* was Shakespeare? Because Dame Helen was a great student of Donne, she knew that in the English Renaissance it was not thought fitting for an aristocrat or gentleman to descend to printing his work (any more than he could roll back his sleeves and begin to carve, chisel, or mold in clay), but it did not occur to her that for a Jacobean writer to commit a play to print—or to refuse to—may have been an artistic as well as a social decision. She does not ask whether Shakespeare resisted the opportunity to print his plays simply because their passage into books, and into silent reading, away from the stage, might be in some ways inimical to his own creative and financial interests. Certainly he could have made money from the sale of a collected edition, but perhaps he guessed—and if he did, quite acutely—that his plays in print would be *literature,* letters in type addressing themselves entirely (as Coleridge would have it) to the imaginative faculty. What effects an edition of past plays might have on future productions at the Globe, and what audiences might want, and even how his writing might have to change in response, could well have been matters of concern to Shakespeare. We can add such questions to our textual probing without any sense of being perverse because we know more generally that the consequences of print were to be felt in every other area of contemporary European life. The historians of the Renaissance book and printing press have described the revolutions in religion, science, and power that print brought about, and it cannot be extravagant to think that there might be changes in aesthetic consciousness and expectation when poetic dramas, formerly enacted in public space, were rendered as printed texts speaking privately to the mind. More contentious would be any claim that contemporary writers, Shakespeare among them, were consciously aware of these changes, and that they responded to them in any way perceptible to us now. For Shakespeare, I know of no evidence which could settle this issue definitively either way, but for another poet of the English Renaissance, Samuel Daniel, there is indeed considerable evidence from which we may deduce *his* sensitivity to print.

The first sign of this is in a small but important omission. In the past five years, I have, according to my count, received replies from four hundred libraries, well over half of which have recorded early (that is, pre-1640) editions of Daniel's verse and prose among their holdings. The search for copies was extensive because Daniel's books exist in so many different states and bindings, and combinations of contents, that only a large sample could give one an accurate notion of what the original editions comprised at the press, and in the bookshop owned by Simon Waterson (who published almost all of Daniel's works). The replies, often generously accompanied by catalogue cards, turned up over three hundred books, two dozen separate editions (if we include editions of the prose history), and, in some cases, a list of sixty or more copies of a single book. Yet in all these books, in so far as I can judge from questionnaires, printed descriptions, and photocopies of title-pages, there is not a single inscription written in by Daniel himself. There is a copy of one book where an owner notes on the title-page that he received it from Daniel, and there is another book to which Daniel attached an autograph letter, thanking the owner (Sir Thomas Egerton) for his kindnesses, and presenting the book to him—but not once have I found any sign of the poet adding by hand anything but the very smallest of corrections to the text (and then only in two copies). Instead, there are instances, but again not many, where Daniel has inserted in a book a unique leaf, on which are printed his dedicatory or congratulatory verses. It will not do to make *too* much of evidence of this kind, but it is worth asking why none of these copies contain, say, an autograph sonnet. When he presented a manuscript of his play, *Hymen's Triumph*, to Jean, Countess of Roxborough, at whose wedding it was performed in 1614, he there added a short poem in his own hand, which refers to their friendship and her kindness to him. This poem was not included in the printed edition of the play (1615), which is dedicated to Queen Anne.

Is all of this to be accounted for as a matter of circumstance—this manuscript has survived, where perhaps printed texts with manuscript verses
have not—or is there something more significant here, a hint that Daniel
may have been observing a distinction between print and script, between
the book and the manuscript, between the public and private utterance?
Taken by itself, the absence of Daniel's handwriting in his books can
mean nothing as large as this, but in 1607, in a collected edition which
he entitled *Certaine Small Workes*, he was to be much more explicit about
his unease at being in print.

The 1607 edition opens with a newly-written poem addressed to the
Reader. In this, as Daniel himself acknowledges, he is not writing at his
best, even though what he is saying is worth attending to. At the end of
the poem, after admitting that his "accent" and "measures" may seem
old-fashioned to "new ears," he makes some curious and hitherto un-
explained remarks about retracting what he has published in earlier editions. "Would to God," he writes,

> that nothing falty were
> But only that poore accent in my verse
> Or that I could all other recknings cleere
> Wherwith my heart stands charg'd, or might revers
> The errors of my iudgment passed here
> Or elswhere, in my bookes, and vnrehearce
> What I haue vainely said, or haue addrest
> Vnto neglect mistaken in the rest.
>   Which I do hope to liue yet to retract
> And craue that England neuer will take note
> That it was mine. Ile disavow mine act,
> And wish it may for euer be forgot,
> I trust the world will not of me exact
> Against my will, that hath all els I wrote,
> I will aske nothing therein for my paine
> But onely to haue in mine owne againe.

Some of these tropes are recognizably from Daniel's earliest days, as he
must have intended. Poverty, charges, reckonings, errors of judgment,
neglect—this is the lexicon of expense and exposure with which the
Delia sonnets had begun fifteen years earlier. In those poems, though, he
could still claim, if only in the person of a betrayed lover, that his verse
respected neither "Thames nor Theaters," nor sought to be "knowne
vnto the Great," blotting his papers for them with "mercynary lines,

with seruile pen." His silence and privacy, only broken open because of Delia's denial of him, was yet recoverable. In 1592, he could still go home to Somerset and become an obscure provincial again:

> *Avon* shall be my Thames, and she my Song;
> Ile sound her name the Ryuer all along.

Spenser for one detected a touch of coyness and self-preening in this (it is tempting to see his refrain for the *Prothalamion*, "Sweete *Themmes* runne softly, till I end my Song," as a robust, metropolitan response to this couplet), and he urged Daniel to stop fluttering on the ground like a fledgling and write a tragedy. But years later, in 1607, and twenty editions on, Daniel could no longer go home, nor plead his youth, nor obliterate his mistakes. What he had said in books could not be re-versed (we notice the pun), nor cleared, nor unrehearsed. Such, at least, is his position in that penultimate stanza to the Reader, with its final, self-accusing and punning phrase "mistaken in the rest." Yet in the concluding stanza, when the last thing we looked for was hope, Daniel makes a return upon himself. If he lives, so we are told, he will recant and disavow his mistakes, and either conceal these with the world's indulgence, or simply take them out of circulation (final couplets).

As is often the case with Daniel's later verse, this passage at first looks prosy, and slightly spiritless, with its only strengths in the manner and the facility across the rhyme. But beneath these contradictory conclusions, and a surface of intimate but unsteady confession, the emotions are much less balanced and trimmed than the phrasing. Through these lines, rehearsed and acted, Daniel is getting at what it is like to be on show, to be opened and representing oneself. He *knows* that books are an indelible record of his views, printed in the public mind,

> The errors of my iudgment passed here
> Or elswhere, in my bookes,

but still he hopes to be able to retract them, have them back in, unpledge himself from them: he trusts that England will not hold on to them, note them, remember them. This will seem wildly impossible, even on a figurative level, until we recognize that Daniel is treading water between script and print. He is imagining, in a moment of great vulnerability, that he can treat his books, which are mass-produced printed sheets, as if they were manuscripts, which are scribal documents, costly in time to write out, and limited to a small readership. Write a poem and circulate it in manuscript to patrons and friends (as Daniel did), and you *can* retract the copies, and alter, correct or destroy them. Print a thousand or more books of your poems and everyone, high or low, has a permanent account (hence Daniel's vocabulary of expenditure) of your opinions. There is nothing remarkable about seeing the difference between books and papers, but it *is* unusual for a Jacobean poet to interpret print as a burden, as an order of public memory which can only deal in finalities: the public *will* of necessity *exact* (another pun) against his *will*. By 1607, Daniel is sensitive to print not because he is a snob who would prefer to be nestling down cozily with his patrons in Wilton or Wanstead, rather than being read by the masses, but because for him, or at least for part of him, poetry should not reach that point of exactitude, that conclusiveness demanded by the book.

Some of Daniel's anxiety about print is disinterested, or at least results from his reading of history. In his analysis of the twinned effects of print and gunpowder on European history, he had observed that it was "instamped characters" and the press which had shattered the balance of power held by the small states of medieval Europe. Print was a real force in a real political world. But, as we may guess, his unease about the finality of printed texts may also have expressed another, more personal fear. Perhaps, despite what he wanted to believe, poetry could not be regarded as a medium which transcended historical periods—perhaps it was all too precisely located in specific forms and moments. If so, it was not print which was the menace—rendering poetry in indelible, and exact physical terms—but poetry itself. This may appear to be an issue for literary rather than textual criticism, but this is not so. With Daniel, before we can choose which texts we will edit—autograph manuscript or printed folio—and which variants we will record, and what that record will constitute, we must turn aside to examine how his tropes themselves contest the fixity of his work.

Chief among these tropes, and ones which can be traced throughout his writing in verse, are the figures of water and property. Neither of these, to say the least, is peculiar to Daniel, although their development in his work, and what they measure, is much more unusual. Consider, for example, his early conceit that the sonnets to Delia are a poor river, "charg'd with streames of zeal," flowing back to the ocean of her beauty. The river, as we saw above, may be real enough (the Thames, or the Avon in Somerset), and the ocean too can be refigured either as, in one sonnet, the waters around Britain, dividing the island "from the world," or, in another, as the tides of devotion by which to judge his never-ebbing tears for Delia:

> Th'Ocean neuer did attende more duely,
> Vppon his Soueraignes course, the nights pale Queene:
> Nor paide the impost of his waues more truely,
> Then mine to her in truth haue euer beene.

Both of these oceans are highly literary—this last one alludes to Ralegh's courtship of Elizabeth, the knight's pale queen, and the other, where Britain is separated from the world, to the Virgilian tag, *toto divisos orbe Britannos* (*Eclogues,* i.66). Poetry in *Delia* is identified as fluid and capable of transformation, and as an element which unites and restores (streams to oceans and even, allusively, Daniel to fellow poets). But the waters of writing and printing do not ebb or abate as the years pass, and by the time of *Musophilus* (1599), they are beginning to flood, to be a "swelling tide,"

> And streame of words that now doth rise so hie
> Aboue the vsuall banks, and spreads so wide
> Ouer the borders of antiquitie.

This is Musophilus's image, with which he tries to assure Philocosmus that everything is still calm and safe from inundation, even when the ancient limits to knowledge, the pillars of Hercules, have been passed through on the way out to "that immense and boundlesse Ocean / Of Natures riches." By 1603, however, when Daniel commends Florio for his translation of Montaigne's *Essaies*, there is *"no end of words,"*

> *nor any bound*
> *Set to conceipt, the* Ocean *without shore.*
> *As if man labour'd with himselfe to be*
> *As infinite in writing as in intents.*

The ocean here is not a trope for inestimable beauty, or protection, or never-ceasing service (as in the *Delia* sonnets), but an image of minds overwhelmed by books—minds that *"with the presse of writings seeme opprest."* Even the construction of Babel—the major Renaissance trope for the folly of language—is affected by these liquids: in Daniel's poem, human mistakes and confusion are said to *dissolve* this "Towre *of wit."* Yet the buildings are here to stay in Daniel's poems. Just when the waters of knowledge become less confined to the ancient river courses, and celebrations of service, and they swell into seas of printed confusion, so then the poet refers more and more to his poems as lodgings, rooms, dwellings, buildings, frames—solid things, made and repairable, which are his property.

Nothing of what I say is intended to blur the differences between Daniel's poems, or to underestimate the influence on them of, say, Christian stoical thought (where the body is often imaged as a structure of defense against storms or oceans of misery). In Daniel, these tropes are indeed discrete and function differently, and they are derived from various sources, but they are also *indices* within the poetry: what they point to are his changing notions about sung, and written, and printed words. Verses that went as tributes (and tributaries) to a fathomless, remote lady were still sonnets, or "little songs," and it was possible for him to hide them, and go home to sound her name all along a local river. Years afterwards, amidst a spate of printed libels, or "little books," Daniel represents his poems as things that he can let out, demolish, or refurbish like a builder. In 1607, the *poems* are his home, a mass of printed words which he labors endlessly to maintain. The difference is between poetry as a natural flowing from one source to another, and poetry as a made dwelling, pressed into place. This change of view, sketched in so hurriedly here, may be of some interest to social historians of Elizabethan writing, but to an editor of Daniel it is of unrivaled importance.

We can see this at once if we look at the choices an editor must make when preparing a text of Daniel's *Panegyrike Congratulatorie*. This was his first poem of the Jacobean reign, written in March and April of 1603, only days after King James had been proclaimed Elizabeth's successor. On his journey from Edinburgh to London the new king was entertained in the homes of various members of the nobility and gentry, and on 23 April he arrived in Rutland to stay with Sir John Harington of Exton at his house in Burley. Harington was the father of Lucy, Countess of Bedford, and it was probably through her that Daniel was invited to write and deliver a poem to the king while he was at Burley. Daniel seized the opportunity of the date, St. George's Day, and the Scottish king's ancestry (his great-grandmother was Henry VII's daughter, Margaret), to congratulate James on bringing about a greater union of England and Scotland than anyone could ever have hoped for:

> what ioy
> What cheere, what triumphes, and what deere account
> Is held of thy renoune this blessed day
> A day w^c wee and ours must ever count
> Our solemne festiuall.

The text here is taken from a manuscript in the Royal collection in the

British Library. In this, Daniel has transcribed and signed the poem in his small but elegant italic hand. Given the manuscript's provenance, and what we can learn from the printed texts of the *Panegyrike* (that it was "deliuered to the Kings most excellent maiesty at *Burleigh Harrington*"), it seems reasonable to suppose that Daniel himself presented this particular manuscript to the king on 23 April. But what does "deliuered" mean here? Did he simply hand over the *Panegyrike*, for James to read or to have read to him later, or (as seems more likely) did he declaim it himself there and then? This distinction matters, because if we can regard the manuscript as the poet's reading-copy, written out attractively to serve also as a gift, then we can make sense of his punctuation. Contemporary authors, scribes, and readers were by no means as fussy as we are about punctuation, but the pointing in this passage (two commas in five verses and thirty words) is light even by their standards. In some of the stanzas there is even less punctuation, and what there is is more concerned with establishing the rhythm and pauses than with assisting the grammar. None of this will surprise us (anyone who has edited personal papers will know how erratic an author's punctuation can be), but our knowledge of the occasion at Burley should make us hesitate before we use the manuscript text as the basis of an edition. One orthodoxy would have it that an editor should strip away as much as possible of the accidents of print—the compositorial accretion, in effect—so that we may arrive at the author's spellings and punctuation, and (where appropriate) even his layout of the page. Yet when we have no need to do this with the *Panegyrike*—because we have Daniel's autograph manuscript—we find that the evidence directs us to a specific performance, probably never repeated, where the audience may have never *seen* the text at all.

The printed versions of the poem are longer by a third than the manuscript text, and appear with a group of six verse epistles addressed to members of the English aristocracy. The first edition (1603, in two issues) is a folio, and the second (1603) an octavo: all subsequent texts are reprints. The Folio is printed on high quality paper, with the same typeface, ornaments, and layout as Daniel's collected edition, the 1601/2 *Works* Folio. The *Panegyrike* Folio was evidently designed to be bound separately, but also to complement and be added to copies of this *Works* edition, for either sale or presentation. The relationship between the texts is a straightforward one, so far as revisions and additions are concerned, and can be expressed like this (where it is assumed that Daniel's foul papers did not serve as printer's copy):

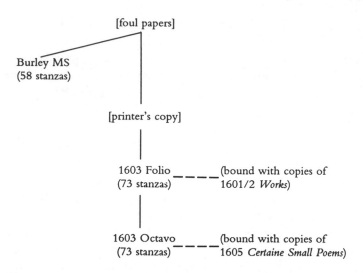

Which of these texts, then, should be the basis of a critical edition of the *Panegyrike*? Perhaps it should be a hybrid, with the Burley MS serving for the first fifty-eight stanzas (incorporating Octavo verbal revisions, with these normalized to the spelling and punctuation of the manuscript), and the Octavo for the last fifteen (where again the spellings etc. must be made to conform with Burley's). In the textual apparatus one would then record Folio readings replaced in the Octavo, and list all the Folio and Octavo punctuation lost in normalizing the poem to the style in Burley.

Even if we were unaware of Daniel's sensitivity to print, and of his increasing sense of poems as fixed objects in books, this choice of a hybrid *Panegyrike* might strike us as fatuous. Were it to be completely successful—where the layers of print had all been scraped away—we would have come closer to Burley, perhaps, but only at the expense of the Folio edition. This last, it must be emphasized, was designed specifically to match the Folio *Works*, which itself was a very grand book, printed in considerable numbers and intended for Daniel's patrons as well as the public. To choose the hybrid, Burley and Octavo, in preference to the Folio (with Octavo revisions) and to normalize to authorial spellings, etc., is at best to fabricate an essentialist *Panegyrike*, to make up an object which never existed, but which (so it might be claimed) is truer to the spirit of Daniel. Perhaps it will be said that because the hybrid is closer than the Folio to printer's copy, it is closer to Daniel— but which Daniel? The poet who declaimed congratulatory verses before

King James, and whose misjudgments, in manuscript, might be forgotten or retracted (he made one that day at Burley, and put it right in the Folio)? Or the poet who confronted print (at least at this point in his career) by making its objectification, its indelible characters, as prominent and as attractive as possible in the Folio?

The case for the Folio *Panegyrike* rests in the first instance on the quality of production, and the thinking behind Daniel's *Works* Folio of 1601. If we consider Sonnet 50 in the *Delia* sequence, we can see at once that, as a job of printing, 1601 is very good indeed:

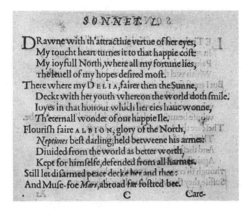

Sonnet L, *Delia*, from Samuel Daniel's Folio *Works* (1601).

Valentine Simmes, who was the printer for both the *Works* and *Pane-gyrike* Folios, was not always the darling of the Stationers' Company, or the censors, but here at least he seems to have done what he was told. Names such as Delia and Albion are set in small caps, while those of classical figures, Neptune and Mars, are rendered in italics. The conventions are applied rigorously throughout *Delia*, although the names Petrarch and Laura, in Sonnet 40, obviously perplexed the compositor, who set them in italic. Elsewhere in the *Works*, there is a similar attention to names, layout of the page, broad margins, and an uncluttered and rather striking lineation. Simmes's bibliographer has described it as one of his best books. The publisher who commissioned Simmes was Simon Waterson, a highly reputable Stationer, who was later to serve as a Warden for the Company. He was also a close friend of Daniel's, and they had begun their careers together (Daniel's first book, in 1585, was

Waterson's first publication). The question to be asked is whether Daniel had sufficient interest in this edition, and influence over Waterson, to have been allowed to determine the type of book the *Works* Folio would be.

One indication of Daniel's interest is in the title of the book. After Spenser's death in 1599, Daniel was regarded by many as his poetic successor—not in style, of course, but in rank of achievement, and in his promise. In 1601, for Daniel to publish an edition of his *Works*—almost a thing unheard of from a living English poet—was to make an explicit claim on that succession. The Folio has a dedication in verse to Queen Elizabeth, and it is followed by an epic on those English civil wars which would lead, if Daniel could but complete it, to the accession of Henry VII and the Tudor dynasty. After that, there was a tragedy about Cleopatra, and a verse letter written by her rival, Octavia—ladies who had each lost Antony, but whose anguish had been set against the grand scale of ancient empires. The subjects were large enough, and, in the case of *Musophilus,* demandingly innovative. It must have looked as though the edition would be profitable as well, because, as Daniel tells us, it was Waterson who had "called vpon" him "for a new impression" of his "workes, with some additions to the ciuill warres"—and this was barely two years after his first collected edition, the *Poeticall Essayes.* Daniel's poetry would sell, and it was highly regarded: this much he must have known. What payment he received for the *Works* can only be guessed at, but part of the deal was that the poet should receive a number of copies printed on large, very high quality paper, and that the royal arms title-page for these would bear the date "1601." The copies for sale would be smaller, printed on good but not particularly expensive papers, and they would be dated "1602." Otherwise, there would be no differences between the issues. The ratio of 1601 to 1602 imprints, in those copies which have survived, is about one to five, but it is doubtful whether Waterson would have been as generous as this figure suggests.

If we review the evidence—the poet's reputation around 1600, Waterson's request for a new edition, and the division of the Folio into two issues—it seems quite possible that Daniel would have had some say in the physical appearance of the book (perhaps even choosing the typographical conventions and page sizes). When, eighteen months later, the *Panegyrike* was published—a poem with which Daniel had greeted the new monarch's accession, ahead of even Jonson—he and Waterson chose to go back to Simmes for a folio which would match the big pages, clear lines, and typeface of the *Works.* So significant was this new book, *Works* and *Panegyrike* bound together, that in 1605, when Daniel ventured to present a copy of it to the Bodleian Library in Oxford, his offer was accepted. This really is quite staggering, since Sir Thomas Bodley's contempt for books in English, let alone English verse, made him unwilling to receive anything that was not written in a classical or foreign language. Almost as surprising, the Bodleian copy has a special poem, printed on conjugate leaves (a unique cancel which replaces the original dedication to Queen Elizabeth), in which Daniel, following Horace, celebrates the library's store of knowledge as the true riches that can be handed on to heirs.

Enough has been said by now to establish that these Folios were of the utmost interest and concern to Daniel, even several years after they had been published. When he corrected them, he went to the extent of using tiny, printed one-letter pasteovers, and he kept his manuscript alterations in them to the very minimum. When he wanted to present a copy of the *Works* to a countess, a new bride, he had Simmes print off a sonnet and new title-page, on unique leaves, and insert them before the *Delia* sequence. When the *Panegyrike* Folio had been in print for well over two years, he added printed leaves (a title-page and a prose dedication) to the copies he had about him. This emphasis on print, if I have interpreted his tropes correctly, was to cause him difficulties later on, but this should not deflect us from accepting that this Folio is the most valuable, and *authorized* Daniel texts we have. This is true, even against the high authority of the Burley MS: to print that instead of the Folio would be to ignore everything we have deduced about Daniel's attitudes towards these editions. In the absence of the author's correspondence, his publisher's bills, and a marked-up printer's copy (documents which survive only rarely from this period) we can do nothing *but* deduce such views. Yet we cannot excuse ourselves for inaction (that is, choose an orthodox approach) by saying that the evidence is only circumstantial. There is a strong presumption that Daniel wanted his poems and plays to look as they do in these *Works* and *Panegyrike* Folios. He would probably not have wanted every punctuation mark in the position that it is (although elsewhere he can be alarmingly indifferent to details like these), and he certainly corrects mistakes where these are clear to him, but, broadly speaking, he does seem to have endorsed the Folios as they stand. In the Oxford Daniel, therefore, the *Panegyrike Congratulatorie* will be an edited version of the Folio text, which incorporates revisions from the Octavo, and which corrects readings and punctuation wherever the Burley MS, Octavo, or modern editors point to an unassailably more

convincing text. Where the manuscript varies from the Folio in substantives, the differences will be recorded in the footnote apparatus, along
with those Folio readings replaced in the Octavo text. So as not to lose
whatever performance element there may be in the Burley MS, there
will also be a complete record of where it differs in punctuation from the
Folio.

The 1601 *Works* is the edition into which all of Daniel's writing from
the 1590s funnels: *Delia, Rosamond,* and *Cleopatra* (six editions before
1599), the *Civil Wars* (MSS, 1595 and 1599), and the later poems, *Musophilus* and *Octavia* (first published in the 1599 *Poeticall Essayes*). By the
time he came to revise and collect them for the *Works*, some of these
poems had already appeared in four different printed versions. After
1601, in a series of smaller collections, Daniel was to alter the texts still
further, and indeed only *Delia* and *Octavia* are in their final authorial
versions in the *Works*. So exhausting was his urge to revise and complete
that until around 1610 Daniel seems to have had little time and energy
to begin new poems. He was to write five plays and masques for the
Jacobean court, and to start a prose history of medieval England (which
would be another highly-praised and unfinished work), but to the
editions after 1603 he only managed to add two or three new short
poems and a four-hundred line elegy. It should be noted, too, that after
the *Works* there is a marked decline in the quality of presentation and the
accuracy in his collected editions. The 1605 selection, a small octavo, is
quite well printed, but it is in no way comparable to the Folios of 1601
and 1603. And the editions of 1607 and 1611—which contain Daniel's
final revisions of poems such as *Musophilus* and *Rosamond*—are quite
pitiful things, poorly-printed octavos in which the type is badly set, the
cancels and headlines are muddled, and the texts are inaccurate. There is
evidence that Daniel was seriously ill around 1607, and he may have
been away from London when the first of these books was being
prepared (the 1611 edition is almost entirely a reprint of 1607). It is
difficult to believe that he was indifferent to the physical appearance and
accuracy of 1607, since he had worked so hard to revise and recast most
of its contents. This is the edition, after all, in which he addresses that
poem to the Reader and remarks on the durability of mistakes in print.

What must we do, then, with the poems which were revised after
their appearance in the *Works* Folio, but which were subsequently published in demonstrably inferior editions? Should a modern critical edition
retain, slavishly, the 1607 Octavo's blunders in words, titles, and layout,
and its impossible punctuation (which can be shown in many cases to

have nothing to do with Daniel)? Again, I would suggest that an orthodox solution (say, print the first edition, for the quality of its accidentals, and incorporate revisions from the last) will not do for Daniel. Once more, we should make the state of the text in the 1601 *Works* the foundation of an edition, adding later alterations, and editing these, where necessary, to conform with the Folio's spelling and punctuation. This may be a controversial decision, but it is not a foolish or an unwarranted one, because Daniel himself, four centuries ago, did exactly the same thing. When revising *The Tragedy of Cleopatra* for inclusion in the 1607 Octavo, he *collated* the most recent version (1605) against the earlier texts in the *Works*—and then used the 1601 text as printer's copy. In other words, as well as rewriting passages and reorganizing the play, Daniel *edited* a version of *Cleopatra*, choosing 1601 as his copy-text against every other version available to him. The connections between the published texts of *Cleopatra* can be summarized like this (where an asterisk indicates a reprint):

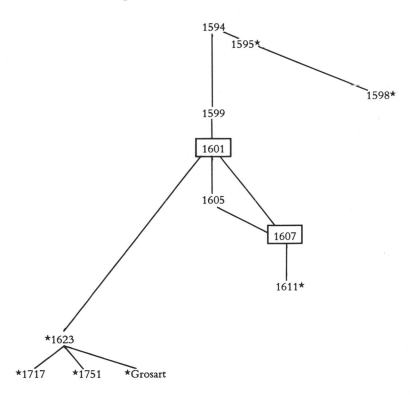

Modern editors, not noticing the links between 1601 and 1607, have concluded that there was an unbroken descent (excluding reprints), 1594–1599–1601–1605–1607, with each text set directly from the preceding one, into which Daniel had incorporated manuscript alterations and insertions. But the pattern of variants makes this explanation untenable for the three texts, 1601, 1605, and 1607. The evidence must be abbreviated here, but three examples, each of which could be multiplied several times over, will clarify the relationship. (There are a number of variants which make it impossible for Daniel to have used any editions other than 1601 and 1605, so 1594–1599 have been ignored for present purposes.)

[A]	V.i.100	To grant her asking, in the best condition.	1601
		To condescend vnto her small petition	1605
		To grant her asking in the best condition.	1607

[B]	IV.ii.95	They cannot pierce the flesh be'ing put vnto it,	1601
		They cannot pierce with them which stands	1605
		They cannot pierce the flesh that them withstands,	1607

[C]	I.i.37	now *1601*] then *1605*] now *1607*
	II.i.180	all vaine *1601*] idle *1605*] all vaine *1607*
	I.i. 121	Yet since *1601*] And my *1605 + 1607*

In Example [A], it is clear that the 1605 revision of 1601 has been rejected or ignored when preparing copy for 1607. In [B], too, the 1605 line has been rejected, but this time because there had been a mistake in the printing. The 1605 compositor, seeing Daniel's revision of 1601, misread the deletions, and set this:

They cannot pierce with them which stands

when what was before him was probably something like

w^c them w^{t}stands
They cannot pierce the flesh [be'ing put vnto it],

It appears that in 1607 Daniel restored the reading he had intended for 1605, but then altered "which" to "that" (a very frequent piece of tinkering in all of his work). Example [C] shows two instances where there is agreement between 1601 and 1607, and one where a 1605 reading was retained in 1607. (Variants like this make it most unlikely that 1607 was set from 1601 independently of 1605.)

Because Daniel revised the play so very much, the editorial problem with *Cleopatra* is a much larger one than the issue of which texts he worked from (important as this is). In the Oxford edition, *Cleopatra* will be printed in parallel-texts, with a near-diplomatic edition of 1601 set against an edited text of 1607. The textual apparatus beneath 1601 will record variants from the editions 1594–1599, 1605, and 1623. Beneath 1607 will be listed variants found in 1611. Presenting *Cleopatra* like this is intended to make possible, for the first time, a comprehensive account of how the play evolved (and where we must place *Antony and Cleopatra* in its evolution), but also to retrace, as elsewhere, the *ingressiveness* of Daniel's middle years, the turning in and turning back which characterizes this period of his work. For a textual critic, following the 1601 *Works* Folio is not the only way of achieving this, but it is a good enough beginning.

ST. JOHN'S COLLEGE
OXFORD

Richard Johnson's Tom a' Lincoln Dramatized: A Jacobean Play in British Library MS. Add. 61745

RICHARD PROUDFOOT

MY SUBJECT IS ANONYMOUS. THE PLAY I AM GOING TO talk about has no title. I propose to borrow one from its narrative source and shall refer to it as *Tom a' Lincoln, or the Red-Rose Knight, Tom* for short. In an earlier and flippant moment of my work on it, I toyed with the anachronistic alternative of *Monty Python and the Fairy Queen*. But the name Tom a' Lincoln had its own teasingly contradictory connotations. The primary reference was to the great bell of Lincoln Cathedral, topical about 1610/11 because it was recast on 3 December 1610 and rehung on 27 January 1611.[1] The name *may* also have been given to a famous bear kept in the Bear Gardens—though the clearest evidence dates from as late as 1677—to which, rather than to the bell, Thomas Nashe *may* refer in the phrase "Thou shouldst heare Tom a Lincolne roare."[2] The hero

---

[1] B. Maxwell, *Studies in Beaumont, Fletcher and Massinger* (Chapel Hill, 1939), 35–36.
[2] Sir S. Lee, "Bearbaiting, Bullbaiting, and Cockfighting," in *Shakespeare's England*, ed. C. T. Onions (Oxford, 1916), 2:432; J. Simons, "A Possible Elucidation of an Obscure Reference in Nashe's *Four Letters Confuted*," *Notes & Queries* 226 (1981):

of our play nicely combines the qualities of anonymity, noise, and belligerence. He too was the product of a recasting of material about 1611.

What I have to present is very much in the nature of a progress report on a current project. As a result, I have both too much and too little to say: too much, because I am still collecting material whose significance is not yet always clear to me; too little, because I have yet to reach any secure conclusions and also because the only informed firsthand account of the play so far published contrives to say so much within its limited compass that much of what I can say must seem like repetition or amplification.[3]

British Library MS. Add. 61745 was acquired at some date after 1974 and was made available for study in the spring of 1982. It had been discovered among the papers of Sir John Coke, secretary of state in the reign of Charles I, at his country home, Melbourne Hall in Derbyshire. The papers in question were apparently transferred to Melbourne Hall in 1634 from Gray's Inn, where Coke's son Thomas was in residence. The longest item in the manuscript is a play text running to eighty-eight pages, but lacking three or more leaves at and near the beginning. The manuscript was offered for sale at Sotheby's in London on 20 November 1973. An extended catalogue description by the late P. J. Croft, Librarian of King's College, Cambridge, identified the play as one of the many unknown works of Thomas Heywood, a prolific dramatist who was, on his own evidence, sole or part author of over two hundred plays. The next stage in the story may be told in the words of Professor M. C. Bradbrook.

> On the 20 November Messrs. Sotheby sold to a New York dealer the manuscript of a hitherto unknown tragicomedy which they described as being by Thomas Heywood. The British Export Licensing Review Committee at a meeting on 11 January 1974 held up the license for two months in case any British institution could raise the price required; if by that date it does not happen the manuscript will presumably come to New York.[4]

The sale fell through: whether because the British Museum matched the bid or because the purchaser, finding cause to question the attribution to

---

521. I am grateful to Dr. Gareth Roberts of the University of Exeter for drawing my attention to these references.

[3] Sotheby's Catalogue, 20 November 1973, 29–35.

[4] M. C. Bradbrook, "A New Jacobean Play from the Inns of Court," *Shakespearean Research and Opportunities* 7–8 (1972/74): 1.

Heywood, withdrew his bid, I do not know. The interest briefly pro-voked at the end of 1973 died down with the disappearance from the public view of the manuscript, said to have been withdrawn from sale by its owner, the Marquess of Lothian. Its subsequent acquisition for the British Library passed unnoted. The play had been read, in 1973, by Mr. Croft and by Dr. Daniel Waley, Keeper of Western Manuscripts at the British Library. The conjectures published in Professor Bradbrook's arti-cle were based, as she took pains to point out, on Croft's catalogue entry and on conversations with Dr. Waley.

In 1973, I was much interested, as General Editor of the Malone So-ciety, to learn of the manuscript and much disappointed when it sank from view again, apparently unsold. On learning, quite accidentally, in the late summer of 1982, that it was available for study in the British Library, I took the earliest opportunity of going to see it. That an un-known Jacobean play should surface from centuries of obscurity was itself exciting: it was a pleasure beyond expectation to find it lively and var-iously entertaining, quite apart from the intriguing puzzles of its author-ship and provenance and its apparently high rate of allusion to or echo-ing of Shakespeare. I asked the British Library and the Council of the Malone Society to let me prepare a transcript for publication by the Malone Society. They agreed and I set to work, slowly. I now have a complete diplomatic transcript of the contents of the manuscript, a fully modernized edited text of the play and a draft of notes on the details of errors and oddities in the manuscript text of the play. What remains to be written is the introduction, which can only be done in London with ready access to the manuscript.

My decision to produce a modernized text (from which most of my quotations will be drawn and whose system of line numbers I shall em-ploy for reference) in parallel with the more familiar Malone Society diplomatic text, may need justification. The nature of the manuscript almost dictated it. The play is apparently of mid-Jacobean date, perhaps the work of a prominent and prolific professional dramatist, but it has survived only in an amateur transcript, made, it is true, with a consider-able degree of efficiency, but made in what would seem to have been unpropitious circumstances and for uncertain purposes. The manuscript has an intrinsic interest that bears little relation to the nature and quality of the text it preserves: study of that text had to begin by releasing it from some of the trammels of its unusual mode of survival.

MS. Add. 61745 is a small quarto book, originally contained in a loose vellum cover. It contains nine gatherings of unequal sizes. Several leaves have been removed from different parts of it, sometimes leaving visible stubs. The play runs from the first gathering to the sixth, ending on the verso of its third leaf. All that remains of gathering 1 is a single leaf: the leaf, or leaves, that preceded it are missing, and with them the play's opening—and its title. Gathering 2 has ten leaves, an irregular number for a quarto gathering, created by the removal of the water-marked half of the innermost of its three sheets. The conjecture that this missing fold may have served as gathering 1 is tempting: certainly the surviving leaf of 1 is watermarked, while the unbroken text of gathering 2 strongly implies that the missing leaves were removed before the in-scription of the text. Gathering 3 originally had eight leaves, of which the third and fifth have been removed, leaving small stubs and causing two gaps in the text. The rest of the play is easier: gatherings 4 (16 leaves), 5 (8 leaves) and 6 (6 leaves, with one watermarked fold re-moved) run consecutively and contain unbroken text.

Peter Croft identified three scribes. In fact, there are five, but his oversight was natural as the second (B) wrote only ten lines and the fifth (E) a mere seven. The three principal hands alternate in various patterns, which can perhaps be best understood as five phases of work.

1   Lines 1–742 alternate between A (3 stints) and C (2 stints), with B's short contribution punctuating A's first stint.
2   Lines 743–1474 alternate between D (2 stints) and A (3 stints, the third including E's seven lines).
3   From line 1474 to line 2078, D, C, and A take turns in se-quence, working for three, and A for two stints.
4   A, who has so far done the lion's share, now gets a short rest, leaving lines 2079–427 to C (3 stints) and D (2 stints).
5   The final phase sees all three back at work. A, C, and D have three stints each between line 2428 and the end of the Epilogue (line 3095). A does the last stint and signs the explicit with his name "Morganus: Evans:".

The continuity of the ink, and possibly the pen, suggests that work went forward on a relay system, used presumably to produce the transcript as quickly as possible. Each of the principal scribes is on for four of the five phases and off for one. The brief presence of B and E implies a desire on A's part not to let the work be interrupted by his absence for even a very few minutes. A's share is by far the greatest, with 1707 lines to C's 826 and D's 544.

The three main hands differ markedly in character and size, but all three show signs of working in haste and under pressure. A is the largest and most formal; C is informal, smaller, and very cursive; D, the smallest of the three, is neat and tidy and gets more into his page than the others, especially in prose passages. All make errors consistent with hasty work: none corrects these, or alters his text, in ways suggestive of an author rather than a transcriber. The number of lines per page varies greatly, from 28 to 42. Early in the manuscript, A averages 30–35 lines per page and C much the same, while D often gets in forty or more. Later, A's pages come to vary greatly as he changes the size of his writing and as he alternates between verse and prose.

The editorial task is initially easy, if laborious. Once sufficiently familiar, none of the hands presents much difficulty. A is clear and consistent; D generally neat, though inclined to vary his letter forms and given to using the same form for *h* and long *f*. C can be harder to decipher because of his imperfectly formed letters, but real puzzles are few and occur most often in conjunction with the play's more outlandish vocabulary. Croft's conclusion, that the scribes "(apart from a few natural and self-evident scribal slips) all three performed their task with great accuracy" is adequately borne out by my experience of the manuscript.

So far I have spoken of the amateur nature of the manuscript. The play it preserves shows at least the formal features of professional work. It is long. The 3095 lines of the diplomatic transcript expand to over 3400 in the edited text, when D's packed pages are relined. Three or more missing leaves imply loss of not less than a further 200 lines of text. Equally suggestive of professionalism are the stage directions, which use the formulae of the professional playhouses; many are extended and circumstantial (as the following examples will demonstrate).

A dumb show.
Enter the Abbess *in haste, with the infant in her arms, and kissing it she lays it down, standing afar off. Enter an old* Shepherd *who, espying the babe, takes it up, greatly rejoicing, and exit. Which done, the* Abbess *with much joy departeth. Then* Time *discovers* Angelica *in her bed awake, weeping and lamenting, with the* King *striving to comfort her. Which done,* Time *draws the curtain, speaking as before.*

(fol. 3b; 165–70)

Enter Caelia, *her hair hanging carelessly, with her babe in her arms, and two* Ladies, *etc.* (fol. 31a; 1968–69)

The directions are generally adequate: only a few necessary directions are missing, and only one passage demands editorial ingenuity to make sense of its action. This puzzle occurs on fol. 7b, where the Clown, Rusticano, has a twenty-three-line speech, apparently designed to cover offstage action by other characters, but then goes on, without a break, to describe his own involvement in the said action. The inconsistency could just be deliberate and the intention farcical, but the absence of exit and re-entry directions for the characters whose absence is implied by the subsequent dialogue prompts the conjecture that the clown's speech, which is wholly irrelevant to the context and wholly self-contained, may have been added without full appreciation of its inconsistency with the accompanying and following action. The role of Rusticano is certainly dominant, and several of his soliloquies could be omitted without detriment to the action.

It is conceivable that the role has been augmented for a particular performance, but even if this is not the case Rusticano contends with Tom himself for prominence. His function as Tom's most faithful follower, companion, and fool ensures his presence throughout, and his racy and salacious prose is a welcome (and blessedly well varied) relief from the play's generally undistinguished and long-winded verse. His is the only role for which no hint is to be found in the primary narrative source, a two-part romance from the fluent pen of Richard Johnson, a versatile and productive popular writer who flourished between 1591 and 1621. The discovery of this play adds a third to the previous record of plays based on Johnson's writings. The other two are Thomas Heywood's *The Four Prentices of London* (written about 1607–16; printed in 1632), which makes some use of Johnson's *The Nine Worthies of London* (1592); and *The Seven Champions of Christendom* (printed in 1638), which dramatizes episodes from Johnson's highly popular romance of the same name, whose two parts were first printed in 1596 and 1597. Its author, like our playwright, invented a dominant clown role to link and unify the episodes of a straggling action.[5] John Kirk, to whom, on the strength of the initials "I. K.," *The Seven Champions* is customarily assigned, is an obscure figure, known only in the 1630s and early 1640s, whose role in the publication of a handful of plays may have been that of supplier of copy rather than author. Thomas Heywood's involvement in the writing of *The Seven Champions* has recently been proposed and

---

[5] J. Kirke, *The Seven Champions of Christendom (1638)*, ed. G. E. Dawson (Cleveland, 1929), xiv–xv.

argued with considerable plausibility by Paul Merchant,[6] who also finds reason to take seriously John Freehafer's suggestion of a date of composition about 1613–14.[7]

The two parts of Richard Johnson's romance, *The most pleasant History of Tom a' Lincoln, that renowned Soldier, the Red-Rose Knight, who for his Valour and Chivalry, was surnamed the Boast of England*, first appeared in print (on the evidence of entries on the Stationers' Register) in 1598/9 and 1607 respectively.[8] The earliest surviving edition calls itself the sixth and is dated 1631. Like all later reprints, of which six are known with dates from 1635 to 1704, this edition contains both parts. Its title-page specifies the contents of each in a paragraph of publisher's blurb: Part 1, "Shewing his Honourable Victories in Forraigne Countries, with his strange Fortunes in the *Fayrie* Land: and how he married the faire *Anglitora*, Daughter to *Prester Iohn*, that renowned Monarke of the World"; Part 2, "Together with the Lives and Deathes of his two famous Sonnes, the *Blacke Knight*, and the *Fayrie Knight*, with divers other memorable accidents, full of delight." The romance, though fairly short, is episodic, depending for its effect more on variety of matter than ingenuity of plotting. Roughly speaking, the seven chapters of Part 1 bring our hero from birth, as the bastard son of King Arthur and a court lady called Angelica, through a humble childhood as supposed son of a shepherd near Lincoln (site of the monastery which conceals Arthur's clandestine amour, clearly derivative from the story of Henry II and fair Rosamund), to his highest point of fortune, marriage to Anglitora. The events of Part 1 leave Tom (as I proposed to call him throughout, rather than the more cumbersome Red-Rose Knight) twice a father. By Caelia, Queen of Fairyland (a figure of deserted love based on Ovidian heroines such as Phyllis and Dido), he has a son whose adventures, as the Fairy Knight, occupy the eighth and last chapter of Part 2. By Anglitora, he has a second son, the Black Knight. Part 1 ends with Tom still blissfully ignorant of the identity of his father and mother. Part 2 starts with Arthur's deathbed confession of his delinquency. Mayhem ensues: the

---

[6] P. Merchant, "Thomas Heywood's hand in *The Seven Champions of Christendom*," *Library*, 5th ser.; 33 (1978): 226–30. I am grateful to Miss Joanna Udall for drawing my attention to this article.

[7] J. Freehafer, "*Shakespeare's Tempest and The Seven Champions*," *Studies in Philology* 66 (1969): 87–103.

[8] R. I., *The Most Pleasant History of Tom a Lincolne*, ed. R. M. S. Hirsch (Columbia, South Carolina, 1978).

widowed Queen exacts gruesome vengeance on Angelica in a passage
that anticipates Act IV of Webster's *Duchess of Malfi*; Anglitora, scorning
her base-born husband, decamps with her son to take up life in foreign
parts as a full-time adulteress. Tom's miseries end in his death at the
hands of Anglitora. Her own death follows soon after—her killer being
her son, playing Orestes to her Clytemnestra. Almost as an afterthought,
the romance ends with the affecting friendship of the half-brothers, the
Black Knight and the Fairy Knight, who end their days in Lincoln,
where they build "a most sumptuous Minster, which to this day re-
maines in great magnificence and glory" (94). Needless to say, the great
bell of Lincoln Cathedral figures in Part 1, as Tom's lavish gift to the
(non-existent?) minster on the occasion of his rural foster-father's death
of grief at his adolescent desertion to become a robber on Barnsdale
Heath. The dying words of this old shepherd, Antonio, give Tom's
subsequent travels such motive as they have:

> from whence thou camest I know not, but sure thy breast har-
> bours the tyranny of some monstrous Tyrant, from whose loynes
> thou art naturally descended. Thou art no fruite of my body for I
> found thee (in thy infancy) lying in the Fields, cast out as a prey
> for rauening Fowles, ready to bee deuowred by hunger-starued
> Dogges: (13)

Tom's travels lead him to and from the court of King Arthur, but the
secret of his parentage is never revealed to him in Part 1.

The play bases its action on the events of Part 1 of Johnson's romance, only twice diverging from them. The Portuguese expedition in
Chapter III becomes in the play an invasion of France (perhaps a topic
allowing of easier stock responses). (It is this episode that it affected by
the loss of two leaves, so that its bearing remains slightly obscure.) Likewise, the play makes no use of the interpolated narrative of Valentine
and Dulcippa used by Johnson to pad out Chapter V (a narrative which
has its own interest as an analogue of the wager plot in *Cymbeline* and its
sources). The play's handling of its source may be not unfairly characterized as a use of the principal episodes of Johnson's romance as pegs on
which to hang a great variety of material that has little or nothing to do
with them. Comic matter, amounting to about a third of the play, is all
of the playwright's invention. This centers on Rusticano, but includes,
for instance, a scene for the four old shepherds who are the fathers of
Tom's group of childhood friends. Many minor characters, among them
Queen Guinevere, Sir Lancelot, and Sir Tristram, seem to owe their

place in the play mainly to their utility as butts or "straight men" for the clown. The chorus, Time, is a further addition: an emblematic figure who combines the person of Time, as used in *The Winter's Tale* and other plays, with functions more closely resembling those of Gower in *Pericles* and Homer in Heywood's four *Ages*. Dumbshows, usually explicated by Time, speed the action. There are three extended songs: one— very overtly erotic—for the ladies of Fairyland in the large set-piece banquet scene; one for Rusticano, on the congenial subject of drink and tobacco; and a song, whose singer is nowhere specified, to celebrate the wedding procession in the final scene. Fights, seductions, and desertions in the original are all written up. The introduction of three mad scenes and two suicides unwarranted by Johnson reflects either parodic intent or a careless generosity to the players. Where Johnson is formal or sentimental, the play veers toward the hectic and the cynical. Sexual virtue proves insecure or easily reversible: parental disappointment leads rapidly and invariably to despair and death. Rusticano's role contains a generous provision of set speeches as well as many dialogues of verbal mistaking, proverb-chopping, or social and linguistic cross-purposes. He is, by turns, salacious, mock-heroic, greedy, drunk, and hungry. He even has a parody of Jacobean sermon rhetoric, a sleep-walking scene in which he imagines himself to be dead, and a sleepy early-morning entry *"with one hose off, the other on, without any breeches"* (fol. 37a; 2419).

Sustained comparison of play with source would take too long, but two passages which have no counterpart in Johnson may suggest something of the distinctive quality of the play. One is the opening speech of "Time as *chorus*":

> I, that have been e'er since the world began;
> I, that was since this orbed ball's creation;
> I, that have seen huge kingdoms' devastations,
> Do here present myself to your still view,
> Old, ancient, changing, ever-running time,
> First clad in gold, next silver, next that, brass,
> And now in iron, inferior to the rest,
> And yet more hard than all. No marvel, then,
> The times are iron now, men scarce deemed men.[9]

---

[9] The manuscript here reads (lines 129–31):
  And nowe in Iron, Inferiour to the rest
  and yet more heard then all/ & soe ye times are now<e>

What cannot learning's art effectuate?
Time long since gone and past it now calls back,
To tell a story of a princely knight,
His birth and fortunes no less strange than rare.

(fols. 2b–3a; 123–35)

Croft quoted this passage as evidence for the playwright's knowledge of
The Winter's Tale, which, indeed, it probably is, especially since the
speech goes on to specify a time-gap of sixteen years between Tom's
birth and his entry into the action of which Johnson makes no mention.
Equally noteworthy, however, is the extended reference to the four ages,
after which Heywood named five plays in the years on either side of
1610, and which receive comparable extended treatment in the prologue
to the third of them, *The Brazen Age* (printed 1613). This choric speech
may give us reasonable expectation of a tragicomic action, which the
ending duly fulfills, though in a tone rather hard to assess.

The penultimate scene dramatizes Tom's return to Arthur's court
after many years of travel in search of his father. The play that has followed a son's search for his unknown father ends with that father's unexpected failure first to remember, then to recognize his son. Worse still,
having failed to spot him under the superficial disguise of the messenger
who announces Tom's approach, Arthur then proceeds to take Rusticano "*disguised like the* Red [Rose Knight]" for the conquering hero
himself (fol. 45a). When Tom's empty seat at the Round Table is noted,
Arthur's reactions are as follows:

The Red Rose Knight? Forgive me, memory.
Hence, dull oblivion of his chivalry!
.... O, lords, 'twas a knight
Blest in success, successful in attempts;
Attempting nothing but he did achieve;
Achieving nothing but with blazed renown;
Renowning honour, honouring his name;
Named never but with praise and endless fame!
His acts are such a Chaos, that I want
Some smoothed-tongue Cicero which might compose

Noe marvayle then/ the times are Iron/ men scarce demd men
The arrangement of the edited text assumes the rhyme "then/men" and an incompe-
tently tidied marginal revision.

And frame them with some methodising style!
For lo, I end beginning all this while.
(fols. 44b–45a; 2934–35, 2944–53)

These lines cue Tom's entry, unrecognized. The superlatives destroy by
inflation a character who is in fact a complete nonentity, a fighter onto
whom others project their own fantasies of honor, beauty, and magna-
nimity.

Though the playwright confined his action to the events of Part 1 of
the romance, he knew Part 2 as well and used the knowledge in one
scene where he chose to alter Johnson's narrative. In both works, Anglitora, daughter of Prester John, elopes with Tom in the clear conviction
that her father will not allow her to marry him. In the romance, Prester
John has already refused his consent, although Tom has won her hand as
the prize proposed for killing a dragon, claiming that "first hee would
loose his Kingdome, before shee should bee the wife of a wandering
Knight" (48). The lovers elope—prematurely, it turns out, as Prester
John, having slept on it, is upset by his rudeness to Tom and changes his
mind. He finds in the morning that his guest has vanished and that his
daughter's chamber is empty, leaving him to face "nothing but relent-
lesse walles, which in vaine hee might speake vnto" (49). He laments for
many days, but gets over it in the end.

The play handles this episode differently. Anglitora, knowing that her
father has vowed never to marry her to a foreigner, elopes without consulting him, contrary to her own stated principle.

If men affect you and you them the like,
If friends do not consent—the match up strike!
Yet first intreat them to consent thereto;
See if they will. If not, wed, bed and do.[10]
Ought man to sell his child as beasts are sold?
Oh, love is never prized with coin or gold;
By wealth, or goods, or substance—oh, not so!
Their fault's the greater that so use to do.
(fol. 36b; 2368–75)

Prester John's reaction likewise differs. On learning of their flight, he

---

[10] So, at least, scribe D's first version: some qualm then led him to confuse the
sequence of events by toning "doe" down to "wooe."

curses Tom and Anglitora, reaching a climax with the lines:

> And can Anglitora prove so ungrate
> Unto her careful parents? Love, farewell:
> Hate, thee I'll entertain! Ye gods, give ear.
> Deformed, mishapen, ugly, stern, abortive,
> Let their ingrateful issue, dastard, brat—
> If ever they have any—prove most hideous;
> Affright the mother at his luckless birth.
> And let him live to prove unto her soul
> As kind as ever she hath been to me.
> Nay, let him live to be her utter ruin.
> Heaven, I pray you hear a little more.
> Let that disloyal knight that raped her hence
> Die by the hands of his now-loved trull.
> Then shall our torments be revenged at full.
>
> (fol. 39b; 2581–93)

(The echoes of *King Lear* here and of *Hamlet* later in the scene would be evidence for any attempt to argue directly parodic intentions and might help to account for the reshaping of the source in this episode.) In the play, Prester John is supplied with a queen, called Bellamy. She responds to the elopement by running mad (as her daughter had done in the previous scene, mistakenly supposing Tom to have succumbed to the dragon). Bellamy's suicide soon follows and is reported to the king:

> *Lord.* My liege, I bring you sole sad news. The queen,
> Distract and senseless, ran o'erthwart the meads,
> Decking her head with cockle, [hem]lock, tares,
> That grow dispersed on the champion plain.
> Mixed tears with smiles, she echoes forth this note,
> As burden to her swan-like mournful song:
> "My daughter, sweet Anglitora, is gone",
> And to a swift-head torrent comes at last,
> Wherein she casts herself—oh, not herself!
> Her garments bare her on the silver stream:
> Meanwhile she, senseless of her misery,
> Sat warbling forth the pleasant'st notes she could.
> Ere help could succour her, she laid her head
> Upon the river's bosom, sank and died.
>
> (fol. 40b; 2647–60)

Next for suicide is Prester John himself: he takes longer about it.

> O let the bases and foundation sink
> Of this terrestrial tripartited globe,
> That everlasting silence may o'erwhelm
> My woeful self in deepest barathrum!
> Why are [ye] so incensed, ye sacred powers,
> To heap your ponderous judgements on my head?
> A poor old man ye see, unapt to bear.
> O strike me with your thunder, let not ire
> Be too secure, thus forcing me to feel
> And see such fatal, vile, disastrous acts.
> Will ye not pity? See, I'll do it myself.
> Behold, ye frowning heavens, I disdain
> To breathe one minute longer in such pain.
>   *He stabs himself, then staggers and speaks.*
> Mount, mount, my soul, and meet thy glorious consort,
> Hovering in the air! And look, the eternal essence
> Spreads itself to embrace thee. Look, it stays.
> Fly, fly, my spirit. See, see, here I have given thee
> Free passage from thy flesh's loathed dungeon.
> Why stayest thou, s[oul]? Thy manumission's bought:
> Thy freedom's purchased with my dearest blood.
> Close eyes, stop ears, tongue cleave unto thy roof!
> Cease, cease, you weak supporters. Prop me not.
> Let all the powers of decaying nature
> Be frozen senseless, stupid, stiff, benumbed.
> Strong heart, resist not; powerful faculties,
> Give way to meagre, lean and grim-faced death.
> Let it of sense, of motion, clean bereave me.
> Frailty, adieu, adieu: thus, thus I leave thee!
>   *Moritur.*
>   (fols. 40b–41a; 2661–88)

In Prester John's curse, the playwright reveals his knowledge of Part 2 of
the romance, in which Anglitora kills Tom and dies in turn at the hands
of her son. Furthermore, the matter of his dying speeches seems to owe
something to a suicidal speech by the Black Knight in Part 2, Chapter 8
(91–92).

What the play does is to take the comitragic pattern of Johnson's
two-part romance and convert it into a version of Part 1 which becomes

tragicomic by the simple expedient of piling up horrors toward a happy
resolution. The marriage of Tom and Anglitora entails the suicide of
Caelia, the Fairy Queen who has a prior claim to Tom, in both romance
and play: the play adds the deaths of Prester John and Bellamy. The
transition to a comic ending after these deaths is effected with shameless
facility by a final use of the chorus.

> Time here might end a truly tragic play,
> But that the Red Rose Knight calls Time away.
> Sour mixed with sweet is good, but only sweet
> Will sooner cl[o]y than when they both do meet.
> Here for to leave you were to dip our pen
> More deep in wormwood than in *mel*: and then
> Time might displease, which rather than he'll do,
> Our subject now shall run no more of woe.
>
> (fol. 43b; 2847–54)

But for all his Chinese recipe for a comic dénouement, the dramatist
strongly implies that the story isn't finished yet—that Tom is still ignorant of his parentage and his fathering of the Fairy Knight. The way is
prepared, or at least left open, for a sequel. This note is sounded by the
song which accompanies the final wedding procession. After four stanzas
of celebration, it ends:

> Brave Arthur, thou dost know thy son,
> Which joys thee much, though thou conceal it:
> But yet, before thy glass [i]s run,
> To his great grief, thou wilt reveal it.
>
> But peace, vain tongue, that babblest so:
> It naught befits this sacred mirth.
> Go on, go on, and as they go,
> Be joyful, heaven: be frolic, earth!
>
> (fol. 46a; 3054–60)

In the manuscript, the last stanza is separated from the others by a horizontal line, perhaps suggesting an intention to omit it on some occasion
of performance (a suggestion which *may* be reinforced by the presence,
in the right margin, of a smudged "d," possibly signifying "delete").
Certainly these two stanzas seem strangely at odds with the overall spirit
of festivity in the ending of the surviving text of the play.

   We are left with three questions to which no secure answer can yet be proposed. Is this play an example, or a parody, of romantic tragicomedy? Was the surviving text expressly adapted for performance on some particular occasion? Was a sequel envisaged, or indeed written? I have no further evidence relating to the third question, but cannot forbear from noting the non-existence of a play or masque called *The Fairy Knight*, by Dekker and Ford, licensed on 11 June 1624. The others may offer more room for exploration. In summary, one may say of the play's adaptation of its source that a passive, almost slavish, following of the main events of the romance goes hand in hand with a radical shift in tone, most apparent in the emphasis given to the clown. This may well reflect the assumed taste of an audience quite unlike the literate female readership at which Johnson's romance would seem, in the manner of "the Homer of women," Robert Greene, to be directed. The play seems to envisage a predominantly male audience, perhaps with a preponderance of younger members. The self-parodying heroics and adolescent sexual humor alike confirm the plausibility of some connection with the Christmas Revels at one of the Inns of Court. There is strong circumstantial evidence for such a connection. Peter Croft confirmed the suggestion implicit in the provenance of the manuscript by identifying scribe A, "Morganus: Evans:," as the son and heir of John Evans of Lantwit Major, county Glamorgan, gentleman, who entered Gray's Inn as a student on 7 June 1607. The identification is confirmed by personal memoranda relating to the affairs of the father's estate in the later portion of the manuscript.

The connection of the play with Gray's Inn seems established. Found among papers that originated there and subscribed by a student of the Inn who was at least its principal copyist, it also bears many specific traces of appropriateness to a Christmas Revel at the Inn. Most overt is the epilogue, in which the player of Rusticano offers the play and its performers, with sustained legal imagery, for judgement by the "courteous hearers."

> Thus is the marriage finished and our play,
> But whether well or ill, we dare not say.
> Self-'ccusing conscience soon would "guilty" cry,
> But that's against self-loving policy.
> First we must be convicted, then confess
> Our skilless art, our artless guiltiness.
> The bar's the stage; the men arraigned, we;
> Your censures are our judges. Oh, let them be
> Mild, gentle, gracious, not too strict, too sour,

> Too full of piercing gall. Oh, do not lower
> At these, our weak endeavours, but let love
> Go hand in hand with judgement.
> .... Wherefore, courteous hearers,
> Our author and the actors here have sent me
> To know what you determine. Yea, th[e]y swear
> Poor Rusticano all the blame shall bear,
> Because he was so foolish, at the upshot,
> To wear his master's habit and to come
> So unexpected in his leader's room—
> Which, as they think, is most distasteful to you.
>   (fol. 46b; 3063–74, 3081–88)

Legal jokes are sprinkled throughout the text: mistaking of "termers" for "turners" (fol. 8b; 478); quotation or distortion of Latin legal tags; more questionably—in the view advocated by Professor Bradbrook—covert satire on Lincoln's Inn, such as the whole story of Tom a' Lincoln could easily invite. While finding little in the text to support the allegation of satire against Lincoln's Inn, I am tempted to conjecture that two subsidiary characters in the play might owe something to personal satire within Gray's Inn—but I readily admit that the notion is highly fanciful. On the last page of the manuscript, Morgan Evans lists "my bookes & such things I leaft behinde mee in my study at my goinge home, wich I Committed to the Custidy of Sir Walwine" (fol. 63b). Croft wrote: "'Sir Walwyn' may refer to Thomas Walwyn, matriculated from Clare College, Cambridge, Michaelmas 1579, admitted to Gray's Inn 28 Oct. 1584." An odd detail of the adaptation of the source is the apparently unmotivated replacement of Sir Triamore by Sir Gawain or, as the play spells his name, "Gallowine." Personal allusion to Thomas Walwyn, a senior member of the Inn, could be imagined as the explanation. Similarly, the jokes against Lancelot—too unattractive as a marriage prospect for Angelica in the opening scene, later mocked by the clown as "lancelout" (fols. 2a–b, 30a)—could be accounted for as student humor, conceivably directed at Lancelot Lovelace, reader at Gray's Inn in 1609.[11]

My next conjecture is, I trust, less hazardous. In the 1630s, Thomas Heywood dedicated the printed texts of two of his plays to members of Gray's Inn. John Othowe (or Athow), dedicatee of *1 Fair Maid of the*

---

[11] Joseph Foster, *The Register of Admissions to Gray's Inn, 1521–1889* (London, 1889), 59.

West (1632), was admitted on 16 February 1608; Thomas Hammon(d), to whom Heywood dedicated both *2 Fair Maid of the West* and *1 The Iron Age*, also in 1632, entered the Inn on 29 October 1611. Both remained there throughout their careers. This connection between two play-loving members of Gray's Inn (of the same generation as Morgan Evans) and one putative author of *Tom a' Lincoln* may be—indeed probably is—wholly coincidental. Certainly no detail in the play yet suggests reference to Athow or Hammond. Nor have I yet had the opportunity of discovering whether or not their handwriting survives in any document at Gray's Inn or elsewhere. I cannot therefore dramatically reveal that they are scribes C and D. What is certain is Heywood's long-term friendship with Athow and Hammond, a fact that can only strengthen any hypothesis requiring the playwright's involvement in dramatic activity at Gray's Inn.

I have not yet given the attention he deserves to Morgan Evans, the one clearly identified party in the story. Professor Bradbrook rightly insisted that Croft's argument for Heywood's authorship faced one major obstacle. The transcript of the play ends with a Latin explicit or colophon.

> finis Deo soli gloria
> Quam perfecta manent, strenuo perfecta labore
> Metra quid exornat? lima, litura, labor

Miss Bradbrook comments: "The couplet contains one false quantity (stĕnuo, which should be strēnuo) and makes an obvious allusion to Horace, *Ars Poetica* 290–294. It may be translated, if *quam* is read as *quae*, 'What adorns the measures that have been completed, made perfect by strenuous toil? Polishing, erasure (the "blot"), more toil: . . .'[12] The lines of Horace alluded to come in a passage in which Latin poets are praised for leaving the example of the Greeks to "sing of deeds at home, whether they have put native tragedies or native comedies upon the stage."[13] Horace then qualifies the praise with this complaint against the laziness of poets.

> si non offenderet unum
> quemque poetarum limae labor et mora. vos, o
> Pompilius sanguis, carmen reprehendite quod non

---

[12] M. C. Bradbrook, 4.

[13] Horace, *Ars Poetica*, ed. and trans. H. R. Fairclough, Loeb Classical Library (1926), 474–75.

> multa dies et multa litura coercuit atque
> praesectum deciens non castigavit ad unguem.
>
> (290–94)

... were it not that her poets, one and all, cannot brook the toil
and tedium of the file. Do you, O sons of Pompilius, condemn a
poem which many a day and many a blot has not restrained and
refined ten times over the test of the close-cut nail.

The commendation of poetic labor in Evans's couplet, whether his applause
is self- or other-directed, seems somewhat misplaced at the end of a text
remarkable for the lack of polish in its verse. It is tempting to read the
couplet—false quantity and all—as the naive self-congratulation of an amateur writer who has done remarkably well in many ways, if hardly by
Horatian standards. However, though it may seem less likely that the couplet should have originated with a professional poet and have been merely
transcribed by Evans, the clear error, *quam* for *quae*, with which it starts is
more easily explained as an error of transcription than of composition.

Evans makes another, less ambiguous, contribution to study of the
play. His memoranda in the latter part of the manuscript include three
dated items which afford a plausible *terminus ad quem* for the transcription
and therefore the composition of *Tom a' Lincoln*. Short beginnings of
translations from "Merthines Prophysyes" and "Merthines destinies" for
1616 and 1619 respectively appear on fols. 50a and 51a (separated, on
fol. 51b, by a record of six payments for "strabeeres"—presumably
strawberries). On fol. 61b is a memorandum about a tenancy dated 8
September 1619. It is reasonable to deduce that the transcript of *Tom*
dates from before 1616 and that the use of the remaining portion of the
manuscript book came later. The *terminus a quo* for composition is firmly
fixed as 1607 by the play's use of the second part of Johnson's romance,
printed in that year. Probable allusion to *The Winter's Tale, The Tempest*
and perhaps *Cymbeline* would push it forward to 1611.

It is now time to turn to the other name so far attached, more con-
jecturally, to the play, that of Thomas Heywood. *Tom a' Lincoln* indeed
displays characteristics familiar in some of Heywood's plays, though by
no means exclusive to them. The mixture of heroic/erotic romance matter with low comedy and clowning had a long history, extending back
at least to the 1570s, if not to the first half of the sixteenth century.
From the mid-1590s, Heywood was a notable practitioner in the mode.
Like the author of *Tom*, Heywood, in his romantic plays, prefers plot

complication and narrative variety to any sustained analytic treatment of character or theme; he likes comic set-pieces and freely uses other characters as mere foils for his clowns; his patriotic British reflex has a hair-trigger; he uses songs freely and frequently; he has a penchant for grieving fathers and mad scenes and other climaxes of extravagant rhetorical passion; the matter of his clowns' speeches is largely made up of food, drink, sex, and on occasion, tobacco. A resourceful parodist would have found plenty to work on here, were it not that some features of Heywood's plays, notably their scenes of verbally inflated passion, have already almost the quality of self-parody. In drama of this kind, the line between "straight" and parodic intent is often hard to draw.

In the context of such general congruity, three other features of the play may have more substance as potential evidence for Heywood's hand in it. Croft rightly indicated that a notable scene in *Tom* directly imitates a scene in Heywood's *The Rape of Lucrece* (printed 1608). He did not observe that two further plays of his contain scenes which also bear remarkable resemblance to it. The scenes in *The Brazen Age* (1613) in which Venus attempts the seduction of Adonis contain merely some parallels of word and action, but the scene of Psyche's spying on the sleeping Cupid in his last play, *Love's Mistress* (1636), repeats and adapts the same pattern of action and thus deserves to be considered more closely. The three similar scenes are all bedroom scenes. Each starts with an apostrophe to night and proceeds to the discovery and awakening of the sleeper. The paradigm is clearly the rape sequence in Shakespeare's *Lucrece*, perhaps reinforced, in its theatrical dimension, by the opening of the final scene of *Othello*. Here are the openings of the three scenes, in chronological order of composition.

1   *Enter Sextus with his sword drawne and a Taper light.*
         Sex. Night be as secret as thou art close, as close
      as thou art black and darke, thou ominous Queene
      Of Tenebrouse silence, make this fatall hower,
      as true to Rape as thou hast made it kinde
      To murder and harshe mischiefe: Cinthea maske thy
         cheeke,
      And all you sparkling Elamentall fires,
      Choke vp your beauties in prodigious fogges,
      Or be extinct in some thick vaparous clowde,
      Least you beholde my practise: I am bound

Vpon a black aduenture, on a deede
That must wound vertue, and make beautie bleede.
    . . .

                          Lucr. discouered in her bed.
                    (*The Rape of Lucrece*, 1608, G1)

2   Enter Caelia the fayrie Queene in her night attyre
              Cae: Murders blacke mother, rapines midwife
         Lusts infernall temptresse, guyde to fowlest sinne
         fountaine of all enormous actions. night
         horrid: infernall, derne, & ominous night
         Run not, o Run not wth thy swarfy steeds
         To fast a course: but driue light farre from hence
         what ist that hates the light but blacke offence
         and I abhorre it, goying now to tempt
         chastest Hyppolitus to hell bread lust
         To thoughts most impious actions most vniust
         bright Cynthia thou doest maske thy watry face
         blushing to viewe me lust-polluted Queene
         thy handmaides glittering starres doe rowle themselves
         invelopt in some fog or vaporous cloud.
         & blushing at my thoughts themselves thus shrowd
         yet I must one, thus gods & men wth stood
         my minds one fire, lusts heate inflames my bloud
            . . .

                    shee goes to yᵉ Red & awaks him,
                      (fol. 25b; 1564–81, 1589–90)

3   *Enter* Psiche *in night-attire, with a Lampe and a Raysor.*
              Psi. Times eldest daughter Night, mother of ease,
         Thou gentle nurse, that with sweet lulabies,
         Care-waking hearts to gentle slumber charm'st;
         Thou smooth-cheek't negro night, the black-ey'd
              Queene,
         That rid'st about the world on the soft backs
         Of downy ravens sleeke and sable plumes,
         And from thy Charriot, silent darkenesse flings;
         In which man, beast, and bird, inueloped,
         Takes their repose and rest; *Psiche* intreats thee,
         Noe Iarre nor sound betray her bold attempt:
                    Cup. discovered sleeping on a Bed.

> Soft silken vaile that curtaines in my doubt,
> Give way to these white hands, these jealous eyes,
> Sharpe knife prepar'd for a red sacrifice;
> Bright lampe conduct me to my love or hate,
> Make mee this night blest, or infortunate:
> (*Love's Mistress*, 1636, F2)

Are the similarities between this passage from *Tom* and the Heywood scenes such as to urge common authorship? If not, then it is at least hard to avoid the conclusion that the author of *Tom* was consciously imitating or parodying the rape scene from *The Rape of Lucrece*.

An odd detail of the second stage direction in the passage from *Tom* is that Scribe C originally wrote "bed," then altered it to "Red." That this scene requires a practicable bed, just as much as the other two, is made clear two lines later, when Tom *"pulls his sword from the bolster,"* thus supplying the phallic symbol obligatory in such scenes. Where the scene in *The Rape of Lucrece* ends with Sextus's bearing Lucrece off and that in *Love's Mistress* with Cupid's punishing Psyche's curiosity by disappearing from her, the scene in our play shifts far and suddenly from the initial bashful outrage of Tom to the following conclusion.

> *Caelia* I am unready, yet most ready too.
>
> > *She leaps into the bed.*
>
> *Tom* Fie, we have spoke too much, let['s] something do.
> *Caelia* I am undone, yet nothing have we done.
> *Tom* I trust we shall by rising of the sun.
> *Caelia* Knights' tongues are swift, their weapons very slow.
> *Tom* You lie too open. Guard yourself below.
> *Caelia* I little fear your forces.
> *Tom*   With my dart,
> I'll pierce your target, framed by finest art.
>   *Caelia* But draw the curtains. For should those here see
> Our simple skill, ashamed we should be.
> > (fol. 26b; 1647–57)

The overtness of this sexual dialogue has many analogues in Heywood, conveniently anthologized in his *The Escapes of Jupiter*, in which he turned the erotic episodes of his *Golden Age* and *Silver Age* into a self-subsistent action. But no known play of Heywood's quite matches what follows. The discreet withdrawal of the lovers leaves the stage clear for Rusticano.

Here's a coil, with all my heart! I am an arrant rogue, but all the
British knights—except myself—are close in bed with the ladies.
Here two men and one lady; here three men—twelve lasses; here
one and one by each; insomuch that their beds make more noise
than any four creaking wheels of any dungcart in Lincoln. They
exclude me for a wrangler. I can get no room amongst them. I
warrant you, we shall have many lusty British lads got tonight. O,
what brave spirits have those wenches! I'll warrant you one of
them will tire four our best knights. Heigh ho! I wonder what kin
this rascally sleep is to hunger? I cannot believe but 'tis his son, it
makes a man gape and yawn so. But see, I have talked so long 'tis
fair day all abroad and gaffer Phoebus is mounting his cart to go to
his work. By'rlady, he is a very early husband. Nay, there is never
a whistling carter in Oxfordshire shall drive so far in a whole day
as he will do in one hour. For his horses as far surpass theirs as
buttermilk doth whey, or chalk cheese. Well, by this time some
be quite tired, and I'll go creep into some warm place. It will
never grieve an hungry man, to cloy his appetite, to take another
man's leavings. *Jejunus stomachus raro vulgaria temnit*: and, by my
faith, I have stomach to any of the ladies. But suppose that all the
knights should be tired with their long journeys? The wenches
should all set upon me. S'foot, then I were clean undone. Howsoever, I'll venture—for faint heart never used fair lady!

                                                  (fols. 26b–27a; 1659–80)

   Croft rightly drew attention to Heywood's notorious use of outlandish Latinate vocabulary and urged the presence of some of his odd words
in *Tom* as further evidence for his authorship. Vocabulary, though, may
be equivocal evidence in a case of uncertain authorship. First of all, Heywood had no monopoly of his odd words, many of which are found
also, in lower concentration, in the works of other writers of the period.
The presence of "infract," "infortunity" or "trisulked" (perhaps in error
for "trisullk") may indeed result from his authorship, but could as well
stem from imitation or parody. The contexts in which such words occur
often suggest deliberate effects of overinflated and therefore bathetic rant.
Equally, *Tom* contains a number of odd words which seem not to be
paralleled in Heywood. Four words, all from the speeches of Rusticano,
may serve as illustrations. Two occur together:

   Who came to the Queen of Fairies with thee? Rusticano. Who
   was drunk there for company with thee? Rusticano. Who

mischiefed and metagrabolised four ladies' collosodiums in one
night? Rusticano.   (fol. 32a–b; 2068–71)

"Metagrabolise" and "collosodium" are odd words indeed. OED traces
the former to Rabelais, citing Urquhart's translation (1653) for its first
example: "Consider, *Domine*, I have been these eighteen dayes in *meta-
grabolising* this brave speech."[14] The French original is as follows: "Aui-
sez, *Domine*, il y a dix-huict iours que ie suis à metagrabouliser ceste
belle harangue."[15] A marginal gloss in the British Library copy (given
by Ben Jonson to Thomas Skinner in 1628 and marked with Jonson's
own extensive marginalia) reads "excogitare." "Grabolise" is evidently
cognate with "garble." The only cue to "collosodium" I have yet found
is in another obscure romantic play, *Guy of Warwick* (printed 1661). The
clown, Philip Sparrow, having been pinched on the buttock by fairies,
exclaims "do you call these Fairies, a vengeance on them, they have
ticked my Collefodiums ifaith" (C1). "Collosodium" and "collefodium"
are alike unknown to OED, but I take them to be the same word,
mildly grabolised by either Scribe C or the compositor of *Guy*. On re-
checking the manuscript, it now seems to me quite uncertain whether
the crucial letters are, as I originally believed, "oso," or "efo." In favor
of my original reading, "collosodium," it could be claimed that a "col-
losal," "sedium" or "sodium" is adequately self-explanatory for an ample
buttock.[16]

In addition to these comic words and the Latin inkhornisms, the play
uses a few words that appear to represent the vocabulary of Rusticano's
Lincolnshire. Among these are "phraise" and "kadumbeld." Contexts
define the former as a dish of eggs and butter made in Lincolnshire and
the latter as a jocular synonym for tipsy. So far I can offer no convincing
etymology for either, although the word "Froyse," used by John Taylor
in a catalogue of food in *The Great Eater of Kent*,[17] sounds like a variant
form of "phraise," while Rusticano's confusion of the word with
"phrase" may recall Bardolph's puzzlement about "word" and

---

[14] F. Rabelais, *The First Book of the Works of M'. Francis Rabelais*, trans. T.
Urquhart (1653), Book I, chapter 19, p. 83.

[15] *Les Oeuvres de M. François Rabelais* (Lyon, 1599), 56.

[16] I gratefully acknowledge etymological suggestions from my colleague Dr. Jane
Roberts of King's College London.

[17] (1630), C1.

"phrase."[18] The case of "kadumbeld" is different: too many possibilities are raised by a wide range of apt senses of the root "cad-" in combination with either "dumb" or "humble."

One small orthographic detail may carry greater weight. Investigators of the Heywood canon have long acknowledged, with gratitude, his habit of spelling one common word in a highly distinctive and uncommon way.[19] The affirmative "ay(e)" was generally spelled "I" in the late sixteenth and early seventeenth centuries. Heywood habitually spelled it "ey." Though OED lists this form as current from the seventeenth century to the nineteenth, its only early example is from Heywood's *Royal King and Loyal Subject* (1637). The form occurs in his autograph manuscripts. It is also to be found, more or less frequently in relation to compositorial tolerance of it, in most of his printed plays. Sometimes it creates confusion and is mistakenly set as the noun or verb "eye." Scribe C of *Tom* had trouble with a passage in one of Anglitora's mad speeches. (Square brackets indicate deletion, angle brackets uncertain letters.)

> thou squint-eyed minion (ile /wingd with revenge/
> beg leaue [wh<o>] of Ioue, to mount beyond the starrs
> venus & thee Ile hale from yo[r] bright carres
> for [he] shee & thee[e] eye both in one Conspire
> to robbe me of the Iewell I desyre
>
> (fol. 33a; 2120–4)

The affirmative in line 2123 is spelled "eye." As he attempted, with evident difficulty, to decipher the line, C seems to have taken the word in his exemplar for "eye," used verbally. I would postulate a copy-form "ey" as the only likely source of what he wrote. Once the possibility of an exemplar in the hand of Heywood is entertained, the extreme frequency of false starts and minor corrections in the transcript becomes more intelligible. Heywood's hand is perfectly legible, with practice, but its extreme cursiveness can cause great trouble until one becomes thoroughly used to it.

The plausibility of Croft's attribution of *Tom* to Heywood is enhanced

---

[18] *2 Henry IV*, 3.2.69–77.

[19] A. Brown, "An edition of the plays of Thomas Heywood," *Renaissance Papers* (1954), 71–76; "Two Notes on Thomas Heywood: I. A spelling of Heywood's," *Modern Language Review* 50 (1955), 497–98; W. W. Greg, *Collected Papers*, ed. J. C. Maxwell (Oxford, 1966), 160 n. 1.

by several of the facts that I have recorded. Heywood elsewhere drew on the writings of Richard Johnson for source material, certainly for one play, perhaps for two. His plays between about 1607 and 1612 bear a range of general and specific resemblances to *Tom*, among them the use of a chorus and dumbshows in the five *Ages* and elsewhere. The Lincolnshire allusions seem hardly of a kind to sustain Professor Bradbrook's conjecture of Gray's Inn satire against Lincoln's Inn. Indeed they are quite congruous with Croft's view that a Lincolnshire author might be involved (although the play equally refers, for instance, to Oxfordshire and south Yorkshire). Among the least expected "local" passages is an extended and affectionate comic "character" of a country parson, "our Sir John a' Lincoln," occasioned by no more than Rusticano's mistaking of the name Prester John as "priest Sir John" (fol. 30a–b; 1924–59). Thomas Heywood was the son of a Lincolnshire priest.

Obstacles to the attribution are principally three: the apparently parodic nature of much of *Tom* (though there is no reason why a man may not choose to parody himself); the clumsy and repetitive quality of much of the verse (especially by contrast with the achievement of the comic prose); above all, the strong implication of the explicit that Morgan Evans was more than merely a transcriber. The quality of the writing need not be too much of a problem. Heywood was both fluent and prolific. His notorious reference to "two hundred and twenty" plays "in which I haue had either an entire hand, or at the least a maine finger"[20] (which translates into an annual output of five or six plays over a forty-year career that included the writing of voluminous nondramatic works) certainly implies that some of his plays may have received less care than others. If *Tom* were accepted as his, two further references to his activities as a playwright might gain in interest and in particularity of reference. These lines from the Prologue to *Royal King and Loyal Subject* would gain in point if Heywood were associated with a play whose matter includes "Faiery Elves."

no History

> We have left unrifled, our Pens have beene dipt
> As well in opening each hid Manuscript,
> As tracts more vulgar, whether read, or sung
> In our domesticke, or more forraigne tongue:

---

[20] *The English Traveller* (1633), A3.

Of Faiery Elves, Nymphs of the Sea, and Land;
The Lawnes and Groves, no number can be scan'd
Which we have not given feet to, . . .   (A3)

Likewise, the quality of writing in *Tom* might be easier to reconcile with
his more polished performances were we prepared to lend credence to
Francis Kirkman's derogatory characterization of Heywood's prolific
output:

he not only Acted almost every day, but also obliged himself to
write a sheet every day, for several years together; but many of his
Playes being composed loosely in Taverns, occasions them to be
so mean; that except his *Loves Mistress*, and, next to that, his *Ages*,
I have but small esteem for any others.[21]

That *Tom a' Lincoln*, while exploiting the straight sex, violence and
low comedy characteristic of late Elizabethan dramatic romance, is also
parodic in intent is at least a tempting conjecture, rendered plausible by
several details of the play's handling of its source. Whether this parodic
quality is more congruous with authorship by a professional exponent of
the genre parodied or by a witty student or students can hardly be determined until a study-text of the play is available in print.[22] I have
suggested some grounds for supporting each of these views. What is
certain is that the play's handling of popular dramatic forms reveals some
awareness of the intrinsic absurdity of some features of these forms.
Though lacking the sophistication of Beaumont's *The Knight of the
Burning Pestle*, *Tom a' Lincoln* is founded on a wide knowledge of the
dramatic repertoire of the early years of the seventeenth century and
derives much of its energy from the appreciative impartiality with which
its smiles alike at Heywood, Shakespeare, and presumably others, harder
to identify.

I have deliberately not dwelled on the allusions to or echoes of
Shakespeare. They cover a wide range of plays and extend from stray

---

[21] Catalogue of English printed plays appended to Corneille's *Nicomède* (1671),
"Advertisement to the Reader," in W. W. Greg, *Bibliography of English Printed Drama
to the Restoration*, vol. 3 (1957), 1353.

[22] *Tom a Lincoln*, ed. G. R. Proudfoot, The Malone Society (Oxford, 1992),
prints such a text and the other contents of the manuscript. This lecture, delivered at
the Newberry Library in January 1986, is the basis for some sections of the introduction to the edition.

verbal debts such as "night-tripping fairies"[23] to the more extended reminiscences of *Hamlet, King Lear,* and *The Winter's Tale* which my quotations have exemplified. I think that Peter Croft may have overstated the debt to *The Winter's Tale* and would like to close by suggesting that the farcical disguises and absurd prophecy which effect the dénouement are at least as likely to poke fun at *Cymbeline.*

KING'S COLLEGE
LONDON

---

[23] *Tom,* fol. 4a; 201; *1 Henry IV,* 1.1.87.

Did *Shakespeare Have Any Sisters?* Editing Texts by Englishwomen of the Renaissance and Reformation

ELIZABETH H. HAGEMAN

OME YEARS AGO, WHILE I WAS TEACHING A COURSE IN SEVEN-
teenth-century literature, I received in the mail notice of a
new, enlarged version of Witherspoon and Warnke's *Seventeenth Century Prose and Poetry*. More naive then than I am now,
I eagerly sent for a copy, happily assuming that it would solve my problems in trying to find and then to teach literature by women who wrote
in the age of John Donne, Sir John Suckling, and John Milton. For
although I had managed to find, in the University of New Hampshire
library, a few pieces by Margaret Cavendish, Katherine Philips, and Anne
Finch, neither my students nor I knew how to read them. Looking at
those snippets of writing beside "The Canonization," "Why so Pale and
Wan, Fond Lover," and *Areopagitica* was a discouraging business. Perhaps
it was true, as we had learned from Virginia Woolf, that Shakespeare had
no literary sisters, that Renaissance women, inhibited by a complex of
cultural constraints, did not know how to write—that those who tried to
substitute pen for needle *were* inarticulate—that without *real* educations
and thus without the skills necessary to feel the anxiety of influence,
Renaissance women should not have been expected to have participated

in the literary life of their age.[1] But Witherspoon and Warnke, I read in the ad from Harcourt Brace Jovanovich, were providing a new text informed by recent critical theories. There, I thought, I would find writings by seventeenth-century women and some help in reading them.

What I in fact found in the 1982 version of *Seventeenth Century Prose and Poetry* was exactly what had been printed in the 1963 edition I already owned: one poem by one woman writer. On page 994 Katherine Philips, who lived from 1631/32 to 1664, was said to be "the first Englishwoman to write poetry of real value." "Her acquaintances," I read, "included such distinguished names as Cowley, Cartwright, Vaughan, and Jeremy Taylor. . . . The poem 'To my Excellent Lucasia' is typical of [her] verse in its Platonism, its metaphysical conceits, and its attenuated prettiness."

Hardened by that experience, I was somewhat less disappointed three years later to find very few women from early modern Europe represented in Gilbert and Gubar's 1985 *Norton Anthology of Literature by Women*.[2] My expectations soon fell so low that I was delighted to find *four* women included in the sixteenth-century portion of the 1986 edition of the *Norton Anthology of English Literature*[3] and mildly amused to see in the seventeenth-century pages of that book only Anne Haklett and Dorothy Osborne. One sample of Katherine Philips's Platonism, metaphysical conceits, and attenuated prettiness would be, it seems, of some mild interest to juniors and seniors studying the seventeenth century; it might be helpful for women's studies people—Gilbert and Gubar print the

---

[1] The classic statement of the impossibility of women participating in the literary life of Renaissance England is of course Virginia Woolf, *A Room of One's Own* (New York and London: Harcourt Brace Jovanovich, 1929; repr. 1957). See also Walter Ong, "Latin Language Study as a Renaissance Puberty Rite," *Studies in Philology* 56 (1959): 103–24, and Josephine Donovan, "The Silence Broken," in *Women and Language in Literature and Society*, ed. Sally McDonnell-Ginet, Ruth Borker, and Nelly Furman (New York: Praeger, 1980), 205–18.

[2] Sandra M. Gilbert and Susan Gubar's 2,390 pages of texts include 87 pages of works by British and American women born before 1640. The English women writers in those 87 pages are Julian of Norwich; Margery Kempe; Elizabeth I; Mary Sidney, Countess of Pembroke; Aemelia Lanier; Margaret Cavendish, Duchess of Newcastle; Jane Lead, and Katherine Philips. Anne Bradstreet and Mary Rowlandson represent America.

[3] The four women writers in the sixteenth-century section of the fifth edition of *The Norton Anthology of English Literature*, vol. 1 (New York and London: W. W. Norton, 1986) are Mary Sidney, Countess of Pembroke; Elizabeth I; Lady Mary Wroth; and Aemelia Lanier.

same poem as did Witherspoon and Warnke; but even "To my Excellent Lucasia" is not, one would judge from the evidence of the *Norton Anthology of English Literature*, essential reading for students in sophomore survey courses.

But I do not wish to complain about textbooks; I want to open a discussion of the experiences some of us have had as we have attempted to fill the gaps in the story of the Renaissance and Reformation by providing texts by women writers. What *I* have found is that my work, which was focused on the hapless Katherine Philips,[4] has led me to restructure my understanding of the English sixteenth and seventeenth centuries. Now that I know some of its women writers, the male writers look different to me than they used to, and I have modified my ideas about women's "place" in our period.

Not unlike editors of writers such as Shakespeare and Donne, editors of women writers have set out to find and collate all available manuscript and printed texts of our authors, to evaluate and emend textual cruxes, to write notes identifying literary, religious, political, and biographical allusions within our author's texts, and to compose introductory essays indicating the significance of the works we have edited. We have found that there were more women writers than we had expected in our period, we have discovered errors of fact and judgment in earlier scholarship, and we have learned to take pleasure in texts that hitherto seemed opaque. We are beginning to find, if you will, Judith, Joan, and Mary Shakespeare, and they are, we have discovered, writers worth knowing.[5]

---

[4] See my "Katherine Philips: the Matchless Orinda," in *Woman Writers of the Renaissance and Reformation*, ed. Katharina M. Wilson (Athens, Georgia: Univ. of Georgia Press, 1987), 566–608.

[5] Patricia Gartenberg and Nena Thames Whittemore list works by some 56 women in "A Checklist of English Women in Print, 1475–1640," *Bulletin of Bibliography and Magazine Notes* 34 (1977): 1–13. Patricia Crawford provides a "Provisional Checklist of Women's Published Writings 1600–1700" in *Women in English Society, 1500–1800*, ed. Mary Prior (London and New York, 1985), 232–64. For recent work on women writers of Tudor England, see my bibliographical essay in *English Literature Renaissance* 14 (1984): 409–25 and Josephine A. Roberts's work on Mary Sidney, Countess of Pembroke, ibid., 426–39. I treat women writers of the early and mid-seventeenth century in a companion piece in *English Literary Renaissance* 18 (1988): 138–67. All these bibliographies are updated and reprinted in *Women in the Renaissance: Selected Essays from "English Literary Renaissance,"* ed. Kirby Farrell, Elizabeth H. Hageman, and Arthur F. Kinney (Amherst, Mass.: Univ. of Massachusetts Press, 1990). Several anthologies, most notably Betty Travitsky, *The Paradise of Women: Writings by Englishwomen of the Renaissance* (Westport, CT: Greenwood Press,

Shakespeare's sisters are not always as happily self-confident in their protofeminism as we might like. In diaries and letters, as well as in more public writings, they reveal what it feels like to be part of what anthropologists call a "muted" group.[6] They were sometimes demoralized, sometimes angry at their culture's labeling them "weaker vessels." Knowing that they "should" be chaste, silent, and obedient, they used some of their learning to translate into English texts their husbands, fathers, and brothers thought important.[7] They sometimes reinforced, but sometimes modified the ideology of their day in advice books to their children; and sometimes they were active, even threatening, participants in England's most prestigious literary circles. Their writing sometimes reflects, sometimes builds on, their literary and cultural milieu: they, like their male contemporaries, call upon the resources of kind that Rosalie Colie discussed in 1972 in her wonderful book by that name.[8] They do different things with literary genres than do their male counterparts because their individual experiences are different from theirs; in fact, much of their most interesting writing is in genres different from

---

1981), print excerpts by women from our period. Recent rediscoveries of women writers of early modern England, it should be noted, were anticipated earlier in this century, especially by Ruth Willard Hughey, "Cultural Interests of Women in England, from 1524–1640, Indicated in the Writings of the Women," Ph.D. diss. Cornell Univ., 1932, and Charlotte Kohler, "The Elizabethan Woman of Letters: The Extent of Her Literary Activity," Ph.D. diss. Univ. of Virginia, 1936.

[6] For one application of Shirley and Edwin Ardner's theory of "muted groups" to criticism of writing by women, see Elaine Showalter, "Feminist Criticism in the Wilderness," in *Writing and Sexual Difference*, ed. Elizabeth Abel (Chicago: Univ. of Chicago Press, 1982), 9–35.

[7] The essays in *Silent But for the Word: Tudor Women as Patrons, Translators, and Writers of Religious Works*, ed. Margaret Patterson Hannay (Kent, Ohio: Kent State Univ. Press, 1985) treat the various ways in which sixteenth-century women writers worked within and against the confines of the Christian ideology of their day. In *The Whole Duty of a Woman: Female Writers in Seventeenth Century England* (New York: Doubleday, 1985), Angeline Goreau stresses the hegemonic power of Renaissance and Reformation ideas about female modesty.

[8] Colie writes about women's participation in literary history only in an aside when she suggests "in an era of women's lib, a category apparently inconceivable to Roda-Roda, *eine Frau allein*" who might write "in the high style, a volume of confessional poetry; in the middle style, a cookbook; in the low style, a narrative of successful call-girling. Which is to say: though there are generic conventions all right, they are also metastable": Rosalie L. Colie, *The Resources of Kind: Genre-Theory in the Renaissance,* ed. Barbara K. Lewalski (Berkeley: Univ. of California Press, 1973), 30.

those chosen by now-famous male writers of the age.[9] Our learning to read those women's works has been enhanced by our knowing something about the modes of analysis anthropologists, cultural and social historians, psychologists, and other disciplines have contributed to literary studies[10] and by our liberating ourselves from the assumption that Renaissance and Reformation women always were as quietly docile as their culture wanted them to be.[11]

Indeed, one surprising discovery is how many Renaissance women were noisy, rather than quiet writers. Works that had not yet seen print were circulated in manuscript form, given to friends—even, in the case of Katherine Philips, to members of the royal family—and seen by their contemporaries as competition for men like Edmund Waller or Jeremy Taylor. The nineteenth-century critic Edmund Gosse believed that Taylor introduced Philips to London literary circles.[12] But contradicting that myth, which is predicated on the notion that Taylor's importance was greater than Philips's, are the facts that Philips's London acquaintances were well-established before Taylor's reference to her in his essay

---

[9] See Sandra K. Fischer, "Elizabeth Cary and Tyranny," in *Silent But for the Word* (n. 7, above), for the observation that "Such marginal genres as religious writings, translations, and closet drama in a sense afford vicarious action: the writing itself, whether or not disseminated and read, becomes a philosophically justified enactment of the author's life" (228).

[10] Among the most influential works from other academic disciplines are Nancy Chodorow, *The Reproduction of Mothering: Psychoanalysis and the Sociology of Gender* (Berkeley: Univ. of California Press, 1978), and Carol Gilligan, *In a Different Voice: Psychological Theory and Women's Development* (Cambridge, Mass.: Harvard Univ. Press, 1982). *New French Feminisms*, ed. Elaine Marks and Isabella de Courtivron (Amherst, Mass.: Univ. of Massachusetts Press, 1980), provides a useful collection of translations of writers such as Luce Irigaray, Julia Kristeva, and Hélène Cixous; Ann Rosalind Jones, "Writing the Body: Toward an Understanding of *l'Écriture feminine*," in *The New Feminist Criticism: Essays on Women, Literature, and Theory*, ed. Elaine Showalter (New York: Pantheon Books, 1985), 361–77, argues that we must combine new feminist theories of language and psychology with a solid awareness that women's writing is "a conscious response to socioliterary realities, rather than . . . an overflow of one woman's unmediated communication with her body."

[11] Natalie Zemon Davis, *Society and Culture in Early Modern France: Eight Essays* (Stanford, Calif.: Stanford Univ. Press, 1975), esp. "Woman on Top," 124–51, has been especially helpful in this regard. See also Ann Rosalind Jones, "Assimilation with a Difference: Renaissance Women Poets and Literary Influence," *Yale French Studies* 62 (1981): 135–53.

[12] "The Matchless Orinda," in his *Seventeenth-Century Studies* (London: William Heinemann, 1897), 240.

on friendship (that they grew, in fact, out of schoolgirl friendships) and that Taylor's essay, our only evidence of his interest in Philips, argues that true friendship is an altogether different thing from the "friendship, gratitude, and strictest love" that Philips says she hopes her sister-in-law will enjoy with her new husband or the meeting of souls that she celebrates in her various poems on female friendship. In fact, I would argue that Taylor's essay, masked as a polite response to questions put to him by Philips, is a patronizing counterargument to her poems.[13] If Taylor is an important writer, surely the woman who caused him to write his essay on friendship is important too.

But before—and perhaps even ultimately instead of—compiling lists of important women writers and/or important (or even representative) pieces of women's prose and poetry, we must read—and allow our students to read—the WHOLE of women's writings. Philips, it turns out, wrote—in addition to the friendship poems for which she was and is best known—a variety of kinds of poems: epithalamia, verse letters to her husband, poems celebrating other poets, political encomia, and elegies. A collection of her letters, printed in the eighteenth century, is available for study, as are manuscripts letters, diaries, and memoirs by a number of other Renaissance women. Those more private pieces reveal other aspects of women's lives—including their sense of the power and uses of the written word.[14] Similarly, in Philips's requests of her friend and literary "manager" Sir Charles Cotterell, we can catch glimpses of a seventeenth-century mind solving problems, working within and against cultural rules, giving rhetorical, even fictional shape and meaning to her life, describing her own work and criticizing her literary rivals.

Three years ago, Gary Waller argued that if we want to hear the voices of Renaissance women, we must learn to listen for "the voices of silence." Waller's point—if I understand him correctly—is that rather than patronize women writers, we must learn to read what they wrote, to "hear" their voices, to understand not only Lady Mary Wroth but also "Anne Wentworth and Anna Trapnell, neither of whose work would be noted in a conventional literary history."[15] Although I agree

---

[13] On this point, see my "Katherine Philips: The Matchless Orinda," n. 4, above.

[14] In "Women's Published Writings 1600–1700," in *Women in English Society 1500–1800* (n. 5, above), Patricia Crawford notes how many women writers' "own statements suggest that they were forced to write for publication because they knew that their experiences as women were different from those of men" (212).

[15] "Struggling into Discourse: The Emergence of Renaissance Women's Writing," in *Silent But for the Word* (n. 7, above), 253.

with much of Waller's argument, I would not reject, as he seems to want to do, aristocratic and middle-class women who are "[subjected] to a language which emphasizes the women's role as empty, passive, helpless."[16] I would argue that we have only begun to hear the voices of Margaret More, Catherine Parr, Elizabeth I, Lady Mary Sidney, Lady Mary Wroth, Aemelia Lanier, Katherine Philips, Anne Wentworth, Anna Trapnell, and the many other women of the Renaissance and Reformation whose writing does survive. When that writing is given proper and full attention, we will see that "conventional literary history" has been deeply flawed by omissions and misunderstandings. The more authentic literary history we will then create will be quite different—and far more interesting—in its shape and scope.

UNIVERSITY OF NEW HAMPSHIRE

---

[16] Waller, 249.

Life and Letters: Editing the Writing of Margaret Roper

ELIZABETH MCCUTCHEON

HER LONGEST WORK IS VIRTUALLY FORGOTTEN TODAY, although it had almost no precedent when it first appeared, in 1524.[1] Much of her other writing has disappeared. Even so, Margaret More Roper continues to be known as a brilliant exemplar of the learned woman and an affecting instance of daughterly devotion.[2] Neither image may seem surprising. The "learned lady" is a new Renaissance type, for which Margaret Roper is a prototype in England, and we have often—too often—seen Renaissance women only through their fathers, husbands, or sons.[3] But the relationship

---

[1] John A. Gee, "Margaret Roper's English Version of Erasmus' *Precatio Dominica* and the Apprenticeship Behind Early Tudor Translation," *The Review of English Studies* 13 (1937): 259–61, shows just how unprecedented its publication was; cf. n. 11, below.

[2] To name just one recent instance: Judy Chicago's exhibition, *The Dinner Party*, includes Margaret Roper's name on the "Heritage Floor" that, with the thirty-nine place settings above it, celebrates the achievements of women throughout history. This exhibition—not as yet permanently housed, so far as I know—was first shown at the San Francisco Museum of Modern Art in 1979; since then it has toured the world, appearing in London in the spring of 1985.

[3] The tradition is encapsulated in George Ballard, *Memoirs of Several Ladies of Great Britain, Who Have Been Celebrated for Their Writings or Skills in the Learned Languages*

between father and daughter was so close, Thomas More so famous, and his execution on Tower Hill in 1535 so tragic, that it is peculiarly hard to see Margaret Roper for herself—especially since Thomas More oversaw her education, her writing is almost inextricably connected with his life or with a larger humanist circle, and commentary, largely biographical, has been shaped by an interest in her father's life and reputation.[4]

To what extent can we reread a familiar story with Margaret Roper as our focus? More particularly, what did she write? In what context? What different purposes did her works serve? And what Margaret or Margarets do we hear? These are some of the questions that I found myself asking as I edited her writing for Katharina Wilson's anthology, *Women Writers of the Renaissance and Reformation*. I want to return to them now, discussing Margaret Roper as a test case for the many other Renaissance women whose writings consist primarily of translations and/or letters—women like her daughter, Mary Basset; Lady Anne Bacon; Lady Lumley; and Lady Elizabeth Wolley, lady-in-waiting to Queen Elizabeth I, whose life and letters I am continuing to work with.

Let me address specific textual questions briefly. I was not attempting to find or establish new texts but to present Margaret Roper's life and virtually unknown texts (that at first sight might have little appeal to a twentieth-century audience) to undergraduates and other potential readers.[5] This audience also helps to explain my choice of works. I

Arts and Sciences (Oxford, 1752), which commemorates English women with claims to membership in the "republic of letters" (v). For a provocative discussion of the second point, see Minna F. Weinstein, "Reconstructing Our Past: Reflections on Tudor Women," *International Journal of Women's Studies* 1–2 (1978): 133–35.

[4] E. E. Reynolds points out some of these problems in his biography, *Margaret Roper: Eldest Daughter of St. Thomas More* (New York, 1960), ix. There is another problem, too; those who wrote about her in the sixteenth century were so concerned with defending her virtue (and the virtue of the learned woman, in general) that much that would individualize her has been irretrievably lost. For more on her education and relationships between it and her writing, see Elizabeth McCutcheon, "The Education of Thomas More's Daughters: Concepts and Praxis," in *East Meets West: Homage to Edgar C. Knowlton, Jr.*, ed. Roger L. Hadlich and J. D. Ellsworth (Honolulu, 1988), 193–207.

[5] I based the selections from the *Devout Treatise upon the "Pater Noster"* on DeMolen's diplomatic reprint of the British Library copy in Richard L. DeMolen, ed., *Erasmus of Rotterdam: A Quincentennial Symposium* (New York, 1971), 93–124, 139–46, and errata; the reprint of the Yale University copy edited by Germain Marc'hadour in *Moreana* 7 (1965): 9–64 and *Moreana* 13 (1967): 5–24; and then the

emphasized her English writings and included a generous selection from Richard Hyrde's preface to her translation, partly because it is the first Renaissance document in English to argue the case for the new learning for women,[6] and partly because it represents Margaret Roper as a writer. Additionally, I was bound to follow the general editorial rules, modernizing punctuation and spelling and replacing archaic and obsolete words (indicating the original by notes). In fact, I refined these rules. In substituting familiar words for obsolete ones, for example, I used words which circulated in the sixteenth century, so as to preserve some part of the Renaissance ambiance. And, after working closely with the texts, I decided that certain words, notably "quod" and "ye," were such distinctive markers that they should not be changed. But my work required me to be as much an historian, biographer, psychologist, stylist, and literary detective as a textual critic.

Unfortunately we have only a small part of what Margaret Roper wrote. Extant works include two Latin letters to Erasmus (one a holograph); the *Pater Noster,* an English translation of Erasmus's devotional treatise on the Lord's Prayer; and two letters written in English to her father in the Tower. A long letter (really a dialogue in epistolary form) that is addressed to her step-sister, Lady Alington, constitutes an apologetic for More's refusal to swear to the oath of succession; it has been attributed to Margaret and to her father. Her many other letters are lost, although More cites a few lines from one he received in the Tower (*Correspondence,* 545). Lost, too, are a number of other works, some of them obviously apprentice pieces; Stapleton (an early biographer of More) saw Greek and Latin prose and verse and mentions her treatise on the Four Last Things, written in friendly competition with her father, although only his treatment, unfinished, was published.[7] This precipitates a question for which there is no easy answer: to what extent do we have her work because of serendipity, chance, and/or the conscious decision

---

microfilm copy of the 1526 edition: Reel 27 in the *STC* series. Citations included in the present essay are from DeMolen. I based the letters upon Thomas More, *The Correspondence of Sir Thomas More,* ed. Elizabeth Frances Rogers (Princeton, 1947), also consulting Scolar's facsimile reprint, *The Workes of Sir Thomas More Knyght,* with an introduction by K. J. Wilson (1557; repr. London, 1978), and St. Thomas More, *Selected Letters,* ed. Elizabeth Frances Rogers (New Haven, Conn., 1961).

[6] See Foster Watson, *Lives and the Renascence Education of Women* (London, 1912), 14.

[7] Thomas Stapleton, *The Life and Illustrious Martyrdom of Sir Thomas More,* trans. Philip E. Hallett, ed. E. E. Reynolds (Sussex, 1966), 103–4, 106–7.

of More, Margaret Roper, others in the family circle, or early editors?

Only one of her writings had a large circulation during her lifetime—the *Pater Noster*, which went through three editions, although no copy of the first is extant and the new *STC* lists just three copies altogether.[8] Like many later works by Tudor women, it appeared quasi-anonymously; the author, but not the translator, was identified by name. But the attribution is confirmed by a case involving the regulation of the book trade in 1525–26,[9] and Hyrde's preface also hints at the identity of the "yong vertuous and well lerned gentylwoman of .xix. yere of age" the title-page describes.

We can only guess at the circumstances surrounding the Englishing. One editor has suggested that Roper was returning the honor Erasmus had paid her the year before when he dedicated his commentary on Prudentius to her, in honor of the birth of her first child.[10] It must represent a continuation of her own studies and interests, too; her translation heightens the relationship between parent and child, making Erasmus's work more intimate and personal in this and other ways.

But why was the *Pater Noster* published, when just a year before Thomas More had addressed her as one who expected an audience of two—her husband and her father—and singled out her modesty, which did not "seek for the praise of the public, nor value it overmuch," even if she received it (*Selected Letters*, 155)? This note of mingled pride and regret, "the almost incredible novelty" of the idea of publication,[11] and Margaret's youth suggest that More himself played an important part in the decision to publish, although Hyrde, a family tutor, speaks of the "laboure" that he had "about the printing." Clearly the More circle was impressed. Hyrde points out how the gentlewoman expressed "lyuely the latyn" and calls attention to her erudition and her elegance in both Latin

---

[8] For more on the dating problem and the editions, see E. J. Devereux, *Renaissance English Translations of Erasmus: A Bibliography to 1700* (Toronto, 1983), 176–78, and "Some Lost English Translations of Erasmus," *The Library*, 5th ser., 17 (1962): 256–57.

[9] Discussed in A. W. Reed, "The Regulation of the Book Trade before the Proclamation of 1538," *Transactions of the Bibliographical Society* 15 (1917–19): 166–67.

[10] DeMolen, 93.

[11] Stapleton, 106. The larger context is important; unaware that anything by Margaret Roper had been published, Stapleton argues: "She had produced works which fully deserved to be published and read by all, although the bashfulness of her sex, or her humility, or the almost incredible novelty of the thing (as More hints) never allowed her to consent to publication" (105–6).

and English (*Devout Treatise*, 103), and More addressed his daughter as a fellow writer with a style of her own in the letter I have already cited. There were other issues, too. Thomas Berthelet, the printer of the second edition of the *Pater Noster*, published Gentien Hervet's translation of an Erasmian sermon at about the same time, evidence for James McConica's argument that the *Pater Noster* was part of a "broader campaign" to disseminate Erasmian piety in English.[12] And Hyrde himself emphasizes gender-related issues, using the work as concrete proof of the fruit of the new learning for women and encouraging other women, including the translator's young cousin, Frances Staverton, to emulate so excellent a model.

The circumstances behind the correspondence between Margaret Roper and her father are both simpler and more complex. Certainly her letters are expressions of tender affection. They are also political acts, although documentation is hard to come by, for obvious reasons. Here, however, the anthology's concern with women's lives *and* their writing served me well. I was able to review the available evidence, including Tudor biographies and More's letters to his daughter. It seems likely that some of her letters were designed to allow access to her father; More made Margaret his representative sometime after he was in prison (*Correspondence*, 511). Moreover, the correspondence between them clearly allowed him to record his view of conversations, interrogations, and attempts at intimidation. Significantly, the government had its suspicions about Margaret Roper's role, then and later. She answered the Council's charge that she had retained her father's books and writings by claiming that, published works aside, she had only "a very few *personal* letters, which she humbly begged to be allowed to keep for her own consolation" (Stapleton, 193; my emphasis).[13] William Roper's life of More, which includes conversations between More and Margaret Roper, further substantiates a political consciousness only hinted at in her extant letters to her father. Thus we need to balance what Robert Bolt called

---

[12] See John A. Gee, "Hervet's English translation, With Its Appended Glossary of Erasmus' *De Immensa Dei Misericordia*," *Philological Quarterly* 15 (1936): 136–52; and James Kelsey McConica, *English Humanists and Reformation Politics* (Oxford, 1965), 67.

[13] For other evidence see E. E. Reynolds, *Margaret Roper*, 103; and *Letters and Papers, Foreign and Domestic, of the Reign of Henry VIII*, ed. J. S. Brewer, J. Gairdner, and R. Brodie, 21 vols. (1862–1910; repr. Vaduz, 1965), 13:267. Richard Marius, *Thomas More: A Biography* (New York, 1984), 503, assesses the political implications of the correspondence between More and Margaret Roper.

her "ardent moral fineness" and "reserved stillness" (in *A Man for All Seasons*)[14] against a toughness and shrewdness of will, a sensitivity to the finest social and political nuance, and the vivacity and vitality that emerge primarily in the dialogue-letter addressed to Lady Alington.

The circumstances behind this letter are extraordinarily elusive. When it was first printed, in 1557, the headnote pointed out that "it is not certainely knowen" whether Margaret Roper wrote it or More wrote it in her name (*Correspondence*, 514). Its drama and dialogue seem Morean, and several commentators have surmised that the letter is mostly (or wholly) More's. But surprisingly little has been done on the question of its authorship, despite the intrinsic importance of the work.[15] In including passages from it in the anthology, then, I stressed its psychological and biographical value; the questions Margaret asks (she plays the part of Eve, albeit her role is transformed) humanize More and amplify our sense of Margaret and her many roles. I hope to return to this letter, analyzing its rhetorical strategies and stylistic mannerisms vis-à-vis More's writing and Margaret Roper's. We may never be able to settle the authorship question or wholly distinguish the individual contributions of More and Margaret Roper (if the letter was jointly conceived and/or composed): evidence has been deliberately concealed or otherwise lost and father and daughter worked closely together for many years.[16] But opening the question of who wrote it—More, Margaret Roper, or both—could let us sort out the many different factors that affect what we

---

[14] Robert Bolt, *A Man for All Seasons* (New York, 1960), xxi. For further discussion of Margaret Roper's posthumous reputation, see my chapter, "Margaret More Roper: The Learned Woman in Tudor England," in *Women Writers of the Renaissance and Reformation*, ed. Katharina M. Wilson (Athens, Georgia, 1987), 449–80.

[15] Brief but provocative remarks about the authorship of this dialogue-letter include R. W. Chambers in Nicholas Harpsfield, *The Life and Death of Sr. Thomas Moore*, ed. Elsie V. Hitchcock and R. W. Chambers, Early English Text Society Original Series 186 (Oxford, 1932), clxii; Marius, 466–71; Louis L. Martz, "Thomas More: The Tower Works," in *St. Thomas More: Action and Contemplation*, ed. Richard S. Sylvester (New Haven, Conn., 1972), 63–66; Reynolds, 76; and Richard S. Sylvester, "Conscience and Consciousness: Thomas More," in *The Author in His Work: Essays on a Problem in Criticism*, ed. Louis L. Martz and Aubrey Williams (New Haven, Conn., 1978), 169–72. The longest single study of the letter is Walter Gordon's fine essay, "Tragic Perspective in Thomas More's Dialogue with Margaret in the Tower," *Cithara* 17 (1978): 3–12.

[16] See Marius, 476; Sylvester, "Conscience and Consciousness," 174 n. 30, points out that More "incorporated a complete sentence from one of Margaret's letters into his final English prayer."

call "authorship" and be more specific about the characteristics of the prose that we know Margaret Roper wrote.[17] In this and other ways we need to take more seriously the claims that Richard Hyrde made on her behalf in 1524,[18] seeing Margaret Roper as a woman of letters whose extant work, fragmented though it is, foreshadows the literary production of other Renaissance women.

UNIVERSITY OF HAWAII

---

[17] Two recent studies have discussed the style of the *Pater Noster:* Rita M. Verbrugge, "Margaret More Roper's Personal Expression in the *Devout Treatise upon the Pater Noster,"* in *Silent But for the Word: Tudor Women as Patrons, Translators, and Writers of Religious Works*, ed. Margaret P. Hannay (Kent, Ohio, 1985), 30–42; and Elizabeth McCutcheon, "Margaret More Roper's Translation of Erasmus' *Precatio Dominica,"* in *Acta Conventus Neo-Latini Guelpherbytani: Proceedings of the Sixth International Congress for Neo-Latin Studies*, ed. Stella Revard, Fidel Rädle, and Mario A. Di Cesare (Binghamton, 1988), 659–66.

[18] Not until later in the century did women make such claims on their own behalf. In her edition of *First Feminists: British Women Writers: 1578–1799* (Bloomington, 1985), Moira Ferguson includes Margaret Tyler's dedication to the Lord Thomas Howard of her translation of a Spanish romance (1578), pointing out that it contains "the first explicitly feminist argument published by a woman that I have found in English" (52). See, too, the title-page to Elizabeth Weston's *Parthenicon* (Prague, n.d.), with its representation of a woman in Elizabethan dress who brandishes a very large quill pen in one hand and holds a large book in the other. Weston is discussed in Ballard, 243–47; the *Parthenicon*, which includes letters that she exchanged with other humanists and poets, was probably published around 1605.

Provenance and Propaganda as
Editorial Stumbling Blocks

FRANCES TEAGUE

T HE NEWEST EDITION OF THE NORTON ANTHOLOGY IN-
cludes Queen Elizabeth for the first time, printing two of her
six known poems. The bibliography in the back directs readers to editions of all her poems, all her translations, all her
prayers, and *some* of her speeches.[1] Yet Queen Elizabeth is one of history's greatest women. Her oratory contributed to that importance—not
her private poems, translations, or prayers; her speeches both help us understand English history and have literary merit. Nonetheless, her oratory
is often omitted in anthologies of Renaissance literature or women writers. Why? One reason is this: although George P. Rice has edited
selections from her addresses, he is not always careful about the texts he
uses. In *Elizabeth I and Her Parliaments*, J. E. Neale does include scrupulously edited texts for her Parliamentary speeches, but excludes other
oratory, such as the Tilbury speech.[2]

---

[1] M. H. Abrams, et al., eds., *The Norton Anthology of English Literature* (New
York: Norton, 1986), 1:973–74, 2553. Since giving this paper I have published a
considerably expanded version in *Gloriana's Face*, ed. S. Ceresano and M. Wynne-
Davies (Hemel Hempstead: Harvester Wheatsheaf, 1992), 63–78.

[2] In her discussion of Elizabeth's rhetoric, Allison Heisch ("Queen Elizabeth I:
Parliamentary Rhetoric and the Exercise of Power," *Signs* 1 [1975]: 31–55) says that

In short, her speeches are excluded because no reliable edition of this important body of prose exists. Further, the texts available may be glossed by untrustworthy accounts that distort our image of Elizabeth. We may mistake effective propaganda for spontaneous sincerity or regard the text of a speech as well-established when its provenance is in fact doubtful. I could illustrate my points with an embarrassing array of examples. Let me instead discuss only one, Elizabeth's address to the troops at Tilbury. Here is part of what she said:

> ... I am come amongst you, as you see, at this time, not for my recreation and disport, but being resolved in the midst and heat of the battle to live or die amongst you all, to lay down, for my God and for my kingdom and for my people, my honor and my blood, even in the dust. I know I have the body but of a weak and feeble woman, but I have the heart and stomach of a king—and of a king of England too—and think foul scorn that Parma, or Spain, or any prince of Europe should dare to invade the borders of my realm. To which, rather than any dishonor shall grow by me, I myself will take up arms, I myself will be your general, judge, and rewarder of every one of your virtues in the field. I know already for your forwardness you have deserved rewards and crowns; and we do assure you, in the word of a prince, they shall be duly paid you.[3]

The dramatic moment and splendor of the language may obscure what happened. We imagine a nation in great peril and a warrior queen, who was welcomed by her soldiers' cheering her and her plan to lead her troops "In the midst and heat of the battle," but this imagined picture is false.[4]

---

she has done an unpublished edition of the Parliamentary speeches (31). My thanks to Elizabeth Hageman for directing my attention to this article. J. E. Neale, *Elizabeth I and her Parliaments,* 2 vols. (New York: St. Martin's Press, 1958); Neale, *Queen Elizabeth I* (New York: Jonathan Cape, 1934); Neale, "The Sayings of Queen Elizabeth," *History,* n.s., 10 (1925): 212–33. George P. Rice, *The Public Speaking of Queen Elizabeth* (New York, 1951: repr. New York: AMS, 1966).

[3] The text is from *Cabala* (anon., London, 1651; seen on microfilm); I have normalized capitalization and punctuation.

[4] My account of the historical events draws principally on Miller Christy ("Queen Elizabeth's Visit to Tilbury in 1588," *EHR* 34 [1919]: 43–61) and Winifried Schleiner ("*Divina Virago*: Queen Elizabeth as an Amazon," *Studies in Philology* 75 [1978]: 163–180) as well as Neale's works (n. 1).

Although no one then knew it, the Armada had been chased away and England was out of danger. The queen did not, in any case, intend to fight herself. Instead she spoke to raise the spirits of her army, an end she achieved, according to William Camden: "Incredible it is how much she encouraged the Hearts of her Captains and Souldiers by her Presence and Speech to them"[5] Some historians, more cynical than Camden, now think that the real reason Elizabeth's appearance encouraged her troops was her promise to pay the soldiers promptly. To some extent, her welcome was lukewarm. Leicester, the Tilbury commander, was initially reluctant for Elizabeth to come near the coast, though he was certainly willing to have her visit the camp. When she reviewed the troops, he tried to persuade her to have a heavy bodyguard in case anyone tried to assassinate her.

Finally, she may not have spoken the words I quoted. Indeed, she may not have spoken at all to the men in her army. One eyewitness of her visit (Mendoza) says nothing of her speech, while a second (Aske) summarizes what she said in verse. Her chaplain, Dr. Leonel Sharp, said her message was written down and read to the troops by officers and himself. The text of the speech was not published until 1651, sixty-three years after the speech was given, in a book that claims Dr. Sharp sent it to the Duke of Buckingham in a letter. One can make sense of the conflicting accounts by arguing this way: Elizabeth gave her own speech. Not everyone could hear her because the army was about 200,000 men, so that her words were later repeated to the troops by the officers who received a copy of what she said from her chaplain, Dr. Sharp. Imprisoned in the 1620s, Sharp sent his copy of the queen's speech to the Duke of Buckingham to ingratiate himself; Buckingham evidently gave it to the anonymous collector of letters for the book, *Cabala* (1651), where the speech first appeared. The problems lie not in our inability to construct plausible explanations, but in the need for such explanations. One could, after all, argue that Sharp invented the text to help himself or that the collector of the *Cabala* falsified the letter knowing that no one could ever prove the forgery. Despite the multiple accounts of Elizabeth's visit to the Tilbury camp, no one can prove that she spoke the words we have. A conscientious editor must first decide whether the speech is authentic, as most historians believe, and then whether to accept the *Cabala* version as copy text.

---

[5] William Camden, *The History of . . . Princess Elizabeth,* ed. Wallace T. Mc-Caffrey (Chicago: Univ. Chicago Press, 1970).

An editor who accepts the speech must also consider its authorial intention: is it expedient public relations, or is it a sincere and impulsive expression of royal love? Posing the question in this form, of course, creates a false disjunctive, for almost certainly Elizabeth was neither too hot nor too cold blooded when she spoke at Tilbury. But considering these extremes does highlight some common errors made in dealing with Elizabeth's oratory, errors growing out of modern misconceptions about her character and abilities. The first mistake is, thank heavens, disappearing: that of asking, "*Did* Elizabeth write any of her own speeches?" Yes. Although William Cecil often edited what she wrote, he wrote only a few speeches for her delivery and those are well-identified, thanks to Neale. Such a question not only offends by its sexism, but also reveals ignorance of Elizabeth's achievements. After all, the woman spoke nine languages; translated Petrarch, Boethius, and Plutarch; and ran a country. The notion that she was incapable of writing her own speeches needs to be put to rest. A second mistake is that of sentimentality. No one would deny that the cult of Elizabeth existed, but to see her speeches solely in terms of that cult distorts them. This passage from a 1959 history book provides an example:

> Perhaps an objective observer would have seen no more than a battered, rather scraggy spinster in the middle fifties perched on a fat horse, her teeth black, her red wig slightly askew, dangling a toy sword and wearing an absurd little piece of parade armor like something out of a theatrical property box. But that was not what her subjects saw, dazzled as they were by more than the sun on the silver breastplate or the moisture in their eyes. They saw Judith and Esther, Gloriana and Belphoebe, Diana the virgin huntress and Minerva the wise protectress, and best of all, their own beloved queen and mistress, come in this hour of danger, in all simplicity to trust herself among them.[6]

This account creates a curious fiction about the events at Tilbury. To begin with, it suggests that sensible people in the twentieth century would regard Elizabeth as a foolish scarecrow and her soldiers as servile cretins. Further, it overstresses the patriotic aspect of the trip to Tilbury. Both patriotism and morale raising were factors in Elizabeth's visit: she

---

[6] Schleiner quotes this passage, 168; it is from Garrett Mattingly's *The Armada* (London: Jonathan Cape, 1959), 349.

did love her troops, but she also knew how to motivate them. If we accept such a misconception of Elizabeth's speech, we overlook the amount of rhetorical manipulation that took place.

Conversely, it does us little good to be over-clever in our reading of the speech and its influence on later events. Recent critics have sometimes suggested that the English were well aware of Elizabeth's Tilbury appearance and disliked it because they hated the idea of an Amazon queen, a maiden warrior. I have heard it suggested that Shakespeare's Joan la Pucelle is a rejection of that Amazon figure, and hence a rejection of Elizabeth's Tilbury appearance; another scholar suggests that the Amazon, Hippolyta, must submit to and marry Theseus in *A Midsummer Night's Dream* because English society was growing restive about Elizabeth's sterile reign.[7] Both interpretations are predicated on our ability to see at a distance tensions and social disjunctions of which Renaissance commentators were unaware. Yet how can we see what the consequences of an event so poorly recorded? If Elizabeth's appearance as Amazon had such an influence, what are we to reply to the third scholar who remarks, "If the references to Elizabeth as an Amazon are few, the main reason may be that she preferred the reputation of a peaceful ruler." When one goes back to the original sources, as an editor must, one learns that we simply do not know what happened at Tilbury, much less how much influence it had.

My point is perhaps too obvious: women writers of the Renaissance were extraordinary and editing their work requires extraordinary care. We must always go back to our original sources and can accept nothing on faith. In particular, we must be cautious in examining the provenance of such women's texts and in considering how a contemporary audience might have understood them.

UNIVERSITY OF GEORGIA

---

[7] The former is Leah Marcus, who has since published her ideas in *Puzzling Shakespeare*; the latter is, of course, Louis Montrose ("Shaping Fantasies: Figurations of Gender and Power in Elizabethan Culture," *Representations* 12 [1983]: 61–94) in his fascinating reading of *A Midsummer Night's Dream*. The third scholar is Winifried Schleiner, cited above in n. 4, 179.

Lady Mary Wroth's Urania:
A Response to Jacobean Censorship

JOSEPHINE A. ROBERTS

W HEN LADY MARY WROTH'S PROSE ROMANCE, *THE Countess of Mountgomery's Urania*, was first published in 1621, it unleashed a storm of criticism from powerful noblemen, who claimed that the author had presented thinly-veiled accounts of their private lives under the guise of fiction. One of the most outspoken critics was Edward Denny, Baron of Waltham, who wrote a bitter poem in revenge against Lady Wroth, whom he described as a "hermaphrodite," and charged her with slander in an angry series of letters that eventually reached the hands of James I.[1] For her own part, Lady Wroth boldly answered the charges by denying any malicious intent and by turning Denny's verses back against him, so that her rhymes match his, word for word. Yet despite her demonstration of courage, the author recognized the severity of the situation and quickly began contacting powerful allies for help. She wrote to William Feilding,

---

[1] For a more detailed account of the controversy surrounding the publication of the *Urania*, see my introduction to *The Poems of Lady Mary Wroth* (Baton Rouge: Louisiana State Univ. Press, 1983), 31–37. See also John J. O'Connor, "James Hay and the *Countess of Montgomery's Urania*," *Notes and Queries* 200 (1955): 150–52, and Paul Salzman, "Contemporary References in Mary Wroth's *Urania*," *Review of English Studies* 29 (1978): 178–81.

first earl of Denbigh, enclosing copies of the correspondence with Denny
and the poems, in hope that through his influence with James, he might
"make all well with his Majestie."[2] She eventually wrote to the duke of
Buckingham to assure him that she never meant her book to offend and
that she had already stopped the sale of it. She requested the "king's warrant" to retrieve those copies of the book that had already been sold. There
is no evidence that any warrant was ever granted or that further official
action was taken against Lady Wroth, but the fear of reprisal was so great
that she declared in the letter to Buckingham that she had never intended
to publish her *Urania* and that the copies were sold against her will.[3]

The publishing history of the *Urania* offers very mixed evidence concerning the author's involvement in bringing the work to press. The book
was entered in the Stationers' Register on July 13, 1621, but it contains no
dedicatory epistles, poems, or prefatory material, an omission that is significant in a book written by and dedicated to a prominent courtier. The text
of the romance begins on signature B1, which suggests that the printer expected some preliminary material that he did not later receive. It is unclear
to what extent the author fully assented to the publication of her work, but
she did admit sending Buckingham his own personal copy, and the illustration for the title page was chosen by someone who was well acquainted
with the nature of her romance.[4]

Contemporary readers were quick to detect the allusions to court per-
sonalities and scandals, as revealed by Sir Aston Cokayne's description of
the *Urania*: "repleat/ with elegancies, but too full of heat."[5] The correspondent John Chamberlain commented on the author's audacity in taking
"great libertie or rather licence to traduce whom she please," but warned
that while she may think she "daunces in a net," she risks falling to disaster.[6]

---

[2] Lady Mary Wroth to Sir William Feilding, *Historical Manuscripts Commission*,
Denbigh, V, p. 3; Denbigh MS. C 48/2 (March, 1622).

[3] Lady Mary Wroth to the Duke of Buckingham, *Historical Manuscripts Commission*, 2nd report, item 392, p. 60; Bodleian Library MS. Add. D.111, fol. 173 (Dec.
15, 1621).

[4] The title page of *Urania* is reproduced in *Poems*, 76. The engraver was the
Dutch artist, Simon van de Passe, who executed portraits of members of the Sidney-
Pembroke circle, as well as the royal family. For a bibliographical account of the 1621
volume, see Graham Parry, "Lady Mary Wroth's *Urania*," *Proceedings of the Leeds
Philosophical and Literary Society* 16 (1975): 51–60.

[5] *Poems of Sir Aston Cokayne* (London, 1662), Wing C4897, 20.

[6] *The Letters of John Chamberlain*, ed. Norman E. McClure, 2 vols. (Philadelphia:
American Philosophical Society, 1939), 2:427.

One indication of the extent of Lady Wroth's daring is her treatment of highly sensitive court affairs, such as the murder of Sir Thomas Overbury—a scandal of such proportions that it stunned the entire Jacobean court. Lady Wroth presents a thinly disguised account of an unnamed gentlewoman, who describes in the first person how she fell in love with "this King of ungratefulness and cruelty," Robert Carr, the earl of Somerset.[7] She is outraged to discover that Carr has revealed their affair to a gentleman friend (Sir Thomas Overbury) and vows to take revenge against anyone who would so cruelly abuse her. Lady Wroth's account stops short of showing the actual murder of Sir Thomas Overbury in 1613, but she supplies ample evidence of Frances Howard's emotional turmoil and ruthless desperation. Her account is distinguished by the use of the first-person to explore her motivations and to present a sympathetic portrayal of her as a victim of passion and betrayal. In contrast to the predominant view of Howard as a satanic figure (especially in the numerous broadside ballads published concerning the Overbury affair), Lady Wroth provides a strikingly different perspective, one which involves a satiric exposure of the treachery and instability of court life. It is appropriate that in the fictional version Howard's anger is directed against the "King" (Carr), rather than Overbury himself.

Lady Wroth's bold examination of Jacobean court affairs was by no means restrained by the controversy over the publication of her book. In fact, she continued to write a second part of the romance, nearly 240,000 words in length, which survives in a unique manuscript at the Newberry Library.[8] Although never published, this second part raises a series of significant questions concerning the effects of the censorship of the first half. To what extent does the unpublished work reveal an attempt to moderate the degree of satiric exposure? Does the author alter her satiric strategy and methods in the second part? In the face of hostile authority, does Lady Wroth ultimately show signs of what Annabel Patterson has described as "self-censorship"?[9]

---

[7] Edward Le Comte first called attention to the portrayal of the Overbury affair in the *Urania* in *The Notorious Lady Essex* (New York: Dial, 1969), 213. For historical background concerning the Overbury scandal, see William McElwee, *The Murder of Sir Thomas Overbury* (New York: Oxford Univ. Press, 1952).

[8] Newberry Library, Case MS. FY 1565.W95.

[9] Annabel Patterson, *Censorship and Interpretation: The Conditions of Writing and Reading in Early Modern England* (Madison: Univ. of Wisconsin Press, 1984).

Although the second part of the *Urania* picks up in mid-sentence where the published section had broken off, there are early indications of the author's shift away from the major characters that had dominated the original work. She creates an entirely new second generation of characters, the children of the first, who are much less easily identifiable as actual persons in the manner of the *roman à clef.* Indeed, Lady Wroth seems in the second part to avoid satiric exposure of individuals, in favor of a broader, more inclusive critique of Jacobean society.[10] She emphasizes an uneasy transition from an older, disillusioned and immorally complacent society to an inexperienced and untested, yet promising new generation.

The second part reveals a far more deeply troubled and disordered world, where human expectations and hopes are constantly thwarted. Lady Wroth drastically alters the design of the plot by overturning the expected marriage between the two leading figures, Pamphilia and Amphilanthus, whose union was promised at the end of the 1621 version. Instead, these characters undergo painful disillusionment and remain alienated from one another throughout most of the Newberry manuscript. Pamphilia, who had remained constant to the unfaithful Amphilanthus throughout part one, abruptly dissolves her own vows and marries the Tartarian king. Even more significantly, she casts aside her symbolic role as a virgin queen, an emblematic figure of Elizabeth I.[11] As Pamphilia breaks away from the strict code of moral constancy that governed her behavior in the past, she begins to overthrow established conventions and comes to a greater understanding of her own roles. After her husband's death, she arrives at a revolutionary model of male-female relations as "youke fellows, noe superior, nor commaunding power butt in love betweene united harts" (II. fol. 51). Similarly, Amphilanthus resolves at the end of the Newberry manuscript to discover a new social role in which he will become "a new man as new borne, new fram'd and noe thing as I was before" (II. fol. 52). Even so, the unpublished continuation never actually describes their ultimate reconciliation.

The Newberry manuscript also probes some of the larger social prob-

---

[10] Carolyn Ruth Swift has analyzed Wroth's "feminine consciousness in conflict with societal values" in "Feminine Identity in Lady Mary Wroth's Romance *Urania*," *English Literary Renaissance* 14 (1984): 328–46.

[11] Elaine V. Beilin, " 'The Onely Perfect Vertue': Constancy in Mary Wroth's *Pamphilia to Amphilanthus*," *Spenser Studies* 2 (1981): 241.

lems created by the shifting structure of Jacobean society, whereby older hierarchies were rapidly dissolving in a more mobile, materialistic, and fragmented culture. In the unpublished continuation, Lady Wroth treats such specific social issues as the role of parental consent in marriage, the legal validity of the *de praesenti* contract, and the economic plight of the widow.

But apart from Lady Wroth's concern with refashioning social roles and institutions, her most radical critique of Jacobean society is supplied through the creation of a new ruling class. In the Newberry manuscript, the two most important figures of the second generation are the illegitimate children, Andromarko, who is the natural son of Polarchos, and the Faire Design, whose father is never named, but who will succeed Amphilanthus as a supreme champion and is described as "the blessing of this new age" (II. fol. 40). In the face of a disintegrating social structure, Lady Wroth creates an anti-dynastic challenge to the old order, wherein merit and ability become more important than either rank or wealth.

As these few examples from the Newberry manuscript suggest, the effect of censorship on Lady Wroth's fiction may have been far more powerful than the authorities had any reason to expect. Instead of being silenced, the author launched into a far more ambitious and probing examination of social issues than she had attempted before. It is true that she moves away from the satiric treatment of individuals, but in her continuation she offers a far more global and critical treatment of Jacobean society than had appeared in the published *Urania*.

LOUISIANA STATE UNIVERSITY

Notions in Garrison:
The Seventeenth-Century Commonplace Book

PETER BEAL

Adventure not all thy learning in one bottom, but divide it be-
twixt thy Memory and thy Note-books ... A Common-place-
book contains many Notions in garison, whence the owner may
draw out an army into the field on competent warning.

S O WROTE THOMAS FULLER IN 1642.[1] HE WAS EXTOLLING THE
virtues of keeping commonplace books: first because they were
an aid to memory, secondly because they were a way of preserving learning and of putting it to effective use. To judge from
the many examples of surviving commonplace books—a number which
must represent only a tiny fraction of those once in existence—it may be
supposed that many of Fuller's contemporaries shared his view. The period has justly been described as embodying a "notebook culture," for the
practice of keeping notebooks and commonplace books in general was
one of the most widespread activities of the educated classes in contemporary England.

They took various forms. The commonplace book proper, according

---

[1] *The Holy State and the Profane State*, 3:175–76.

to the Oxford English Dictionary, is "a book in which 'commonplaces' or passages important for reference were collected, usually under general heads; hence, a book in which one records passages or matters to be especially remembered or referred to, with or without arrangement." Here is the rub: "*with or without arrangement*." Hence the loose application of the term "commonplace book" both then and now to cover different kinds of compilation. Besides the term "notebook" itself— applied to any kind of memorandum book, whatever the nature of the entries—the related terms one tends to come across most often are "tables" and "table book." This usually means some kind of unbound notebook or pocket book which could be carried around and used for jotting down on the spot things to be remembered. Shakespeare's Sonnet 122, which begins "Thy gift, thy tables, are within my brain," is about the receipt of a table book from his friend and turns upon the conceit that he has no need of "tables" or "tallies" to remember *him* (or *her*). Table books could also evidently be treated as more formal vehicles for original compositions, as is suggested by references such as Henry King's poem "Upon a Table-book presented to a Lady," where he encourages her to plant and people herself the "empty regions" of her "Little Book": "... You have roome/ Here both the Scribe and Authour to become."[2] And table books also seem to have been used on occasions as sketch books. Dekker tells his readers that his *Guls Horn-Booke* "is a Table wherein are drawne sundry Pictures." At the same time a lengthy poem by Jasper Mayne extols the virtues of "Mrs Anne Kinges table booke of pictures," which contained skillful drawings of "sprightly dames."[3] These last references suggest that table books might sometimes be used rather like "*libri amicorum*," a species of album, sometimes illustrated, which had become fashionable in the sixteenth century, particularly in Protestant Germany, and which was the forerunner of the later autograph album. A "pocket book" or "pocket manuscript" was any kind of notebook or manuscript carried around on the person, the same sort of thing as a "*vademecum*." Anything entered into these might well be *retained* in this form: thus, in one of his manuscript songbooks we find the composer Edward Lowe noting: "the rest of ye words are in my pocket Manuscript."[4] The term "*adversaria*" was applied to any kind

---

[2] *The Poems of Henry King*, ed. Margaret Crum (Oxford, 1965), 154.

[3] BL, MS. Add. 33998, fols. 57–58.

[4] BL, MS. Add. 29396, fol. 76.

of memorandum book, large or small, in which undigested matter was recorded just as it occurred, without any conscious arrangement, just like what merchants called a "waste book." The term "coucher" was similar except that it was usually applied to particularly large books which were left on desks or tables for the same kind of use as ledgers or registers. Then there is the term "miscellany" or "miscellanies"—meaning any kind of compilation or anthology comprising works, or extracts from works, by different authors. I shall say more about this particular variety later on.

An essential feature of any kind of manuscript commonplace book was that it was, initially at any rate, a *private* compilation, intended for use only by the compiler himself or by a strictly limited circle of family or friends. This means, of course, besides all else, that every commonplace book is a unique document, a unique witness to the tastes, values, and thinking of a specific person or group. Compilers of commonplace books and miscellanies could sometimes copy portions—even large sections—from other people's compilations. There is evidence of multiple compilations: that some miscellanies were passed around and made common use of within restricted circles—such as in a single family or among a group of students or courtiers. There is even evidence of a certain professional duplication of certain examples, which, for one reason or another, came into the hands of professional scriveners. Yet I know of no example of two commonplace books being an exact duplication of one another. Somehow, inevitably, the personality of the writer or compiler will interpose, varying his selection, changing or annotating the text or adding further material. This means, so far as textual editors are concerned, that no individual text within a commonplace book can safely be viewed as an independent entity, divorced from the collection in which it occurs and considered without regard to the habits of the compiler himself. Commonplace books were invariably compiled not so much for the sake of faithfully transmitting literary texts as for the use of the *compiler*.

The importance which some owners evidently attached to such things is seen, for example, in certain bequests. For instance, Edward Pudsey gave strict instructions in his will, in 1613, that all his books should be "safe kept" for his son Edward, "especiallye," he said, "my note books."[5] One of these "note books"—which includes almost the earliest

---

[5] See Juliet Mary Gowan, "An Edition of Edward Pudsey's Commonplace Book" (unpub. M.Phil., Univ. of London, 1967).

known manuscript extracts from plays by Shakespeare—is still preserved. [6]
In 1639 the Suffolk draper and amateur calligrapher Thomas Fella made
similarly strict provisions for the delivery to his grandson of "all my
written bookes of precidents which are of my owne writing ... and my
other englishe bookes and written bookes."[7] Many other surviving
commonplace books and miscellanies contain prefatory inscriptions
which bear witness to the pride certain compilers took in their efforts
and achievements. If one example may serve to illustrate this, let us take
the prefatory verses in the commonplace book of Judge John Saffin, who
was born in 1632 in Devon and died in 1710 in Massachusetts:

> Here's Miscellanies in this Book compris'd
> of Theologie, Law, History, Epitomis'd:
> and various Subjects gather'd, some D[e]vis'd;
> by the Compiler, both in Prose, and verse,
> w[hi]ch he did sometimes write: sometimes Reherse:
> O what a pleasure tis, and Sweet Delight,
> to read, to Contemplate, and sometimes write. . . .[8]

Many inscriptions which could be cited convey a common impression:
that the compilations in question were not merely ephemeral productions but were seriously valued by their owners, regarded as monuments
to their own personal taste and learning, and bequeathed to others as
sources of both pleasure and usefulness.

The key concept, I would suggest, is "usefulness." It could, I believe,
be argued that not only were commonplace books widely used: they
constituted the primary intellectual tool for organizing knowledge and
thought among the intelligentsia of the seventeenth and probably also the
sixteenth centuries.

In what I would venture to call its *purest* or most *classic* form, the
commonplace book is essentially an educational aid. Just as the notebook
or table book was an *aide-memoire*, the commonplace book was a practical aid to study: a means by which someone systematically stored a large
amount of miscellaneous learning or information which was felt to be
both worth remembering and of practical application. The importance of

---

[6] Divided between Bodleian, MS. Eng. poet. d.3, and Shakespeare Birthplace
Trust Record Office, ER 82.

[7] See J. L. Nevinson, "Lively Drawings of a Suffolk Scrivener," *Country Life
Annual, 1964*, 156–58.

[8] See *John Saffin his Book*, ed. Caroline Hazard (New York, 1928), 1.

what were known as "commonplaces" was a tenet of Renaissance
Humanist thinking and derived directly from classical teaching. For
Aristotle, for instance, the proper treatment and classification of "topics"
was one of the fundamentals of the science of rhetoric. "Topics," he
said, could be "applied alike to Law, Physics, Politics, and many other
sciences that differ in kind." "Specific" topics were "propositions peculiar to each class of things"; "universal" were "those common to all
alike."[9] Expounding Aristotle's rhetorical system later, Cicero defined a
"topic" as "the place [or *locus*] of an argument,"[10] and he said, "Those
arguments which can be transferred to many cases, we call common
places" [*loci communes*].[11] "Commonplaces" in classical rhetoric were
therefore generally applicable ideas, precepts, images or similes which
pointed or illustrated universal truths and could be used to adorn and
enhance formal argument and exposition. Summarizing these views,
Bacon observed that the "ancient writers of rhetoric" taught that "plead-
ers," or orators, "should have the Places whereof they have most contin-
ual use ready handled in all the variety that may be."[12]

The extent to which people in the Renaissance period took this kind
of "commonplace" seriously is illustrated by the almost universal taste
for such things as proverbs, maxims, apothegms, aphorisms and *sententiae*—literary forms which were felt to encapsulate, briefly and pithily,
universal perceptions and wisdom about human experience, both public
and private. It is as if people believed, or wanted to believe, that human
knowledge could be adequately reduced to brief essentials, that it could
all be epitomized almost by a mechanical, even ritualistic, process of
distillation.

The prevalence of this taste has, of course, often been remarked
upon. It manifested itself in a multitude of activities. On the one hand,
there was the production of huge printed *florilegia*, or compendia of
proverbs and *sententiae* (such as the multi-lingual *florilegia* of Jan Gruter,
for example, or the encyclopedic *Florilegium locum communium* of Tobias
Magirus). On the other hand, there was the practice of certain authors
and printers to have anything approaching a *sententia* in their work

---

[9] *The Art of Rhetoric*, I.ii.20–22 (John Henry Freese's edition [1926], 31).

[10] *Topica*, II.8 (H. M. Hubbell's edition [1949], 386–87).

[11] *De Inventione*, II.xv.48 (Hubbell, 208–9).

[12] *The Works of Francis Bacon*, ed. James Spedding, et al., 14 vols. (London, 1857–
74), 3:390.

deliberately highlighted for special attention by the use of italics, inverted commas, pointing hands in the margin, or other markings. These markings are, as G. K. Hunter has noted,[13] clues to the seriousness and pretensions of the works in question: thus, for instance, we see Chapman highlighting numerous passages in his tragedies and translations but none in his comedies, while Sir John Davies does the same in his deeply philosophical poem *Nosce Teipsum* but not in his popular *Orchestra*. Printers highlighted sententious passages as if to show that they were worthy of being recorded for their own sake and therefore of being copied into commonplace books (if, indeed, they were not drawn from commonplace books in the first place). Presumably the same spirit motivated those innumerable contemporary readers who have left in printed books their manuscript annotations and underlinings to mark off passages of special note.

If commonplace books were taken seriously and regarded as useful tools, it follows that some attention had to be paid to the system by which they were compiled. This, in some ways, is the heart of the matter. The arrangement determined the use to which the information could be put; in any case, if someone took great trouble to store that information, he had to be able to retrieve it; otherwise it was worthless. This question was addressed earlier in the Renaissance period by those European scholars who played key roles in the revival of classical learning and, consequently, of classical rhetoric. In his great study *The Classical Heritage* (1954), R. R. Bolgar has summarized the ideas of various fifteenth- and early sixteenth-century thinkers who encouraged students to use notebooks. One, for instance, Luis Vives, wrote:

> Make a book of blank leaves of a proper size. Divide it into certain topics.... In one, jot down the names of subjects of daily converse: the mind, body, our occupations, games, clothes, divisions of time, dwellings, foods; in another, idioms or *formulae docendi*; in another, *sententiae*; in another, proverbs; in another, difficult passages from authors; in another, matters which seem worthy of note to thy teacher or thyself.[14]

---

[13] G. K. Hunter, "The Marking of *Sententiae* in Elizabethan Printed Plays, Poems, and Romances," *The Library*, 5th ser., 6 (1951–52): 171–88.

[14] Bolgar, 273.

Erasmus [handwritten]

The most influential writer of all in this regard was Erasmus. In his *De copia verborum*, first published in 1513, he gives a detailed account of how students might improve their vocabulary and eloquence by the use of suitably arranged notebooks. Each notebook was to be divided into sections under certain headings, which were themselves divided into subheadings, all chosen according to a system. Thus the main headings would relate to what he called "stock themes"—such as the various virtues and vices, love and hate, youth and old age, and so on. Each of these would subdivide logically: thus "Faith" would subdivide into "Faith towards God" and "Faith towards Man" and then these would again subdivide into such categories as "Loyalty to Friends," "Loyalty to Masters," "Loyalty to Enemies," and so forth. Armed with notebooks more or less pre-arranged into this kind of classification system, the student was therefore prepared for a particular kind of reading: that is to say, to read literature in an essentially extrapolatory manner, for purposes of selective recording and memorizing. Erasmus, in fact, encouraged the student to go through the entire corpus of classical literature in this way at least once in his lifetime. Bolgar has observed that this notebook method allowed people to encompass and digest classical literature and learning and that without it "the Humanist contribution to European culture would have lost much of its importance."[15]

Examples could be given of how the kind of principles advocated by Erasmus was put into practice by other scholars in specific subjects: most notably, theology. The Protestant martyrologist John Foxe, for instance, published his *Locorum communium* in 1557. This comprises around a thousand pages, largely blank but for the occasional theological heading followed by a brief list of subdivisions: so, under the general classification "Praedicamentum substantiae. Locus 1," the heading "Creator" is followed by a brief summary of attributes: "Deus solus et unus, natura universalis et prima causa . . . infinita, foelicitas, summum bonum, fons et autor boni." These headings appear in a deliberate theological sequence, but not in alphabetical order. It is thus a skeleton commonplace book, arranged for the guidance of the compiler, in which he is expected to enter in the appropriate places matter from his reading relating to all the fundamentals of the Christian religion. This is a means not only of collecting and retaining this information, but also of ordering his actual thinking, as if he were addressing, so to speak, a series of questions and

cf fol 5 of F V.b.198 [handwritten]

---

[15] Bolgar, 300.

fol 4

propositions, or "*Praedicamenti,*" such as he might face in academic disputations.

Among English writers clearly the outstanding advocate for the usefulness of commonplace books in general was Francis Bacon. In a passage—which, incidentally, is quoted at the beginning of one of the huge surviving commonplace books of John Evelyn[16]—Bacon declared: "I hold the entry of Common-places to be a matter of great use and effect in studying; as that which assureth copiè [copiousness] of invention and contracteth judgment to a strength." He wrote again, elsewhere: "I hold Collections under Heads & Common Places of far more profit, and use; because they have in them a kind of Observacion; without the which neither long Life breeds Experience, nor great Reading great Knowledge." However, with an eye to the strictly systematic compilations favored by Erasmus and his followers, as well as to the massive digests of classical learning which were published as a result of them, Bacon added qualifications. If there was a fault in the practice of keeping commonplace books, he thought, it lay in normal compilation *methods*. "This is true," he emphasized, "that of the *methods* of common-places that I have seen, there is none of any sufficient worth; all of them carrying merely the face of a *school*, and not of a *world*; and referring to vulgar matters and pedantical divisions without all life or respect to action." The normal "Patterns" for commonplace books were made, he said, either by "young Students" or else by "common Book-makers that follow an Alphabet, & fill the Index with many idle Heads enough to make him that shall follow their Pattern, to fill his paper-Book as full of idle marks." Commonplace books could only be truly useful if the compiler were truly judicious in his choice of "the Heads, under which all things are reduced; of the Books, out of which they are to be taken; and above all things, of the Notes themselves, that shall be set down." Although he thought that some books ("the meaner sort") might be "read by deputy, and extracts made of them by others," Bacon stressed how essential it was that a scholar should compile his commonplace book himself, for "in general one Man's Notes will little profit another, because one man's Conceit doth so much differ from another's." So here again was a practical reason for consciously restricting their circulation. One exception to this principle in Bacon's own practice is recorded in an autograph list of some of his own notebooks. "The principall use of this

---

[16] Christ Church, Oxford, Evelyn MS. 54.

Bacon

book," he records of one of them, "is to receyve such parts and passages of Authors as I shall note and underline in the bookes themselves to be wrytten foorth by a servant and so collected into this book." A man of means might, therefore, be excused not from the obligation of reading for himself, but simply from the mechanical task of transferring passages to a written notebook.[17]

Interestingly, Bacon's remarks counteract what he implies was a common prejudice against commonplace books, "as causing," he said, "a retardation of reading, and some sloth or relaxation of memory." A sense of what he meant by this is supplied by Sir Henry Wotton in his *Aphorisms of Education* of about 1630. Wotton attacked what he felt was the common over-use of "epitomes" and "thrifty Compendiums" of learning. These "are helpful to the memory, and of good private use," he said, but "show a short course to those who are contented to know a little, and a sure way to such whose care is not to understand much."[18] There was also the charge occasionally implied by writers that people kept commonplace books in order to plagiarize other people's ideas as a counterbalance to their own lack of originality. As Swift said in *A Tale of a Tub*: "What though his head be empty, provided his commonplace book be full."

In a passage I quoted earlier, Thomas Fuller too defended commonplace books against such detractors. "I know some have a Common-place against Common-place books," he said, "and yet perchance will privately make use of what publickly they declaim against." But he too emphasized the importance of a system: "Marshall thy notions into a handsome method," he said.

Some specific advice about the use of commonplace books is found in the late 1640s in unpublished letters by John Cosin, later Bishop of Durham. Writing from exile in France to a fellow Royalist, Christopher, Lord Hatton, Cosin gave detailed recommendations about the "paper Bookes" which should be used for covering the subjects of theology and history. Theological headings, he suggested, should be taken from Daniel Tilenus's *Syntagmatis*. (First published in 1607, Tilenus's book comprised a three-part series of theological arguments arranged under a total of 170

---

[17] For quotations from Bacon given here, see Spedding, 3:398; 9:23–25; 11:60; 12:253; and Vernon F. Snow, "Francis Bacon's Advice to Fulke Greville on Research Techniques," *Huntington Library Quarterly* 23 (1959–60): 369–78.

[18] Wotton, *A Philosophical Survey of Education . . . and The Aphorisms of Education*, ed. H. S. Kermode (London, 1938), 23.

headings.) "A Blank leaf or Two" should be "left after euery Generall Head," he said, with a separate paper book devoted to "choyce & difficult Places of ye Scripture." Paper books for history should be divided under only two headings—"Secular & Ecclesiastical"—"& let yo[u]r method," he said, "be nothing but Chronologie." The entire span of history, he thought, could be covered by twenty-two paper books, each comprising four quires of paper. The first, in four parts, would be sufficient for history BC (that is, the Assyrian, Persian, Greek and Roman periods). Then a separate volume was to be devoted to each century AD up to the end of the fifteenth century, with two leaves allocated to each individual year, with the exception of the first two centuries AD which would fit into one volume with one leaf per year. From 1500 to 1650 each volume would cover a period of twenty-five years, with eight leaves allocated to each year. The final volume would be an index to the whole. Cosin's views show again how a highly intelligent scholar could take commonplace books seriously enough to work out his own "method" for particular subjects. It is characteristic too that he shared his "method" only on a private and personal basis with an aristocratic friend, in this case a fellow Royalist. He even recommends that Hatton borrow a copy of Tilenus's book from another member of their tightly-knit circle, the Royalist diplomat Sir Richard Browne.[19]

It was not until later in the century that a truly extensive explanation of commonplace-book method in general was published, and even then it was in restricted form. It came from no less a philosopher than John Locke. In his *Essay Concerning Human Understanding* Locke expressed the view that "Nothing can contribute more to obviate the inconvenience and difficulties attending a vacant or wandering mind, than the arrangement and regular dispersal of our thoughts in a well ordered and copious common-place book." In 1686, in the French *Bibliothèque Universelle*, Locke explained in detail a peculiar system he had personally devised and used for the past twenty-five years: that is to say, since about the time of the Restoration. This essay was first published in an English translation, in his posthumous works in 1706, as *A New Method of a Common-Place Book*. In brief, he recommended taking a "paper book" of any size. The first two facing pages would form the index to the headings: the key to the whole system. These two pages should be divided into twenty-five

---

[19] Bodleian, MS. Bodley 878, fols. 5 and 30. I am obliged to Hilton Kelliher for drawing my attention to these manuscripts.

squares. Each square would contain a capital letter of the alphabet, but omitting the letters J, K, V, W, and Y (which Locke regarded as unnecessary) and putting Q at the end after Z. Except for Q, which need only be followed by u, the capital letter in each of the squares should be followed—in descending order, one to a line—by the five vowels, a, e, i, o, and u. This two-page index would effectively cover all the headings scattered throughout the volume, the key idea being the first letter and the first vowel of each heading. Thus the numbers of the pages containing entries under the heading "Epistola" would be noted in the index in the square with the capital E and after the subdivision i; the pages carrying the heading "Adversaria" would be indexed under Ae, and so on. On the pages with the actual entries Locke recommended that each new heading should begin on the verso of a leaf, since then you could have two facing pages immediately for each heading. As the facing pages became filled up you could move on to the next available blank verso— noting at the bottom margin of the filled page a v (meaning *verte* or "turn over") if you carried straight over, or else the relevant page number of the continuation if the next suitable blank verso was later on in the volume. At the top left margin of the continuation you would also note the number of the page you had continued from. When you had gone through the book once doing this you could then go through again using up any blank pages with a second layer of entries.

This may sound complicated, but like all systems, it is easier to operate than to explain. In effect, it meant that you could enter notes in a single book under a very extensive number of headings, arranged not alphabetically but simply as they occurred, and which could be located very quickly by reference to an index no more than two pages in length. The index comprised 100 classifications; if you added a second vowel— so that the heading "Epistola," for instance, was recorded under Eio— you could increase the number of classifications to 500. In practice Locke found that this was not necessary—100 was quite sufficient, especially if you used different commonplace books for different subjects. Locke suggested that the headings themselves should be in a single language throughout (preferably Latin) to avoid confusion, while individual entries, recording extracts from books, should include the name of the author, title of book, size of volume, date and place of publication, and then one other piece of information. Both the total number of pages in the volume and the particular page on which the extract occurs should be recorded, one written over a line above the other, like a fraction. Thus, "p. $\frac{259}{626}$" means that the passage occurs on page 259 in a volume of 626 pages. This information might be useful since it gave some indication of the whereabouts of the particular passage in relation to the whole if one happened to resort to a different edition of the work.

Locke's "Method" was, curiously enough, the single most influential—not to say, most commercially exploited—system to be devised. It was widely adopted, particularly in the later eighteenth and nineteenth centuries. In 1770, for instance, John Bell published his "Common Place Book Form'd generally upon the Principles Recommended and Practised by Mr Locke." His book, he said loquaciously, was "not solely for the Divine, the Lawyer, the Poet, Philosopher, or Historian" but also for "the use and emolument of the man of business ... for men of fortune as well as study; for the Traveller; the Trader, and in short for all those who would form a system of useful and agreeable knowledge, in a manner peculiar to themselves, while they are following their accustomed pursuits, either of profit or pleasure." You could buy Bell's commonplace book in a folio edition—a deluxe "Library" edition, so to speak—for £1 5s (with the option of additional quires at 2s each) and also in a cheaper octavo edition, which might, if you wished, serve as a "pocket book" or "a Waste Book to the general Repository." Various other stationers and booksellers followed Bell's lead for at least the next seventy years. *The Literary Diary; or, Complete Common-Place Book* of 1816, for instance, was allegedly a simpler version of Locke's prototype, while, about the 1840s, Walker and Edwards of London published *A New Commonplace Book being an Improvement on ... Mr. Locke.*

Is it a coincidence that this commercialization of the commonplace book should occur when, it might be thought, the heyday of the genre was largely over? To my mind it follows a typical process in this respect. Granted the potential usefulness of commonplace books to *everyone*, and the widespread search for the most satisfactory *method* of compilation, their essential value is somehow lost—their sense of specialness is somehow felt to be dispersed—when a uniform method becomes freely available to all and sundry and commonplace books are compiled not simply by gentlemen scholars but, in Bell's words, also by "the man of business ... the Trader" and the like. It is also as if, with rare exceptions, the publisher steps in only when the fashion for the genre in private manuscript form has largely run its course.

This point is paralleled by the development of miscellanies, particularly the verse miscellany. These—I would suggest—were very much associated with the commonplace book mentality and represent, so to

miscellanies

speak, the "pleasurable" rather than strictly "useful" side of the genre. Verse miscellanies—what are indeed sometimes loosely called "poetical commonplace books"—were compiled as a means of retaining for future use a large body of witty material—and of what is often called "fugitive" verse—which might otherwise be lost or scattered. If we recall Bacon's observation that one man's notes will little profit another, it is probably true to say that verse tended to have and retain much greater currency than prose, and for this reason alone might have been felt more worth collecting. These compilations are not generally arranged in any systematic order, although very occasionally a rudimentary attempt is made to group poems roughly according to subject or type. There are traces of the "commonplace-book" habit, I think, in some of the titles or headings given to poems, which often tend to specify the subject more explicitly in such a way as to highlight the general theme which the poem illustrates. Thus Donne's elegy "The Anagram" might be headed *Donne* "In praise of an old woman"; his "The Autumnal" might be headed "In commendation of declining beauty," and so on. When "commonplace book" titles of this kind are rendered by the compiler in Latin—so that Donne's "The Expiration," for instance, is headed "Valedictio Amoris"—it is even more likely that the text is academic in origin.

The limited circulation of these manuscripts within restricted spheres meant, again, that there was a sense of something special about having these verses—a mild sense of privilege, which would not have applied if the poems had been published and therefore available to everyone. We find Drayton, in the preface to *Poly-Olbion* in 1612, railing against this fashion. "Verses," he said, "are wholly deduc't to Chambers, and nothing esteem'd in this lunatique Age, but what is kept in Cabinets, and must only passe by Transcription." The fashion for producing large collections of such verse seems to have been at its height from about 1620 until the Civil War period. One possible reason why it flourished in these years was that, with only a few notable exceptions, the vast majority of original verse produced in this period was Royalist in character. If verse miscellanies seem to peter out somewhat during the Civil War, this may partly reflect the fortunes of the Royalist cause, for as Abraham Cowley said, in the preface to his unfinished epic *The Civil War*, there was little point in making "Lawrels for the Conquered." Most surviving examples were evidently produced by young gentlemen, although there is evidence that they were occasionally kept by women. For instance, Constance Fowler (the daughter of Sir Walter Aston of Tixall, Staffordshire) told her brother Herbert in 1639: "send me some

uerses for I want some good ones to put in my booke."[20] The main
centers of poetical transmission were the main centers of poetical
creation. These seem to have been the Universities of Oxford and Cambridge and, to a lesser extent, the Inns of Court to which so many
university graduates subsequently proceeded. Some of the most distinguished poets of the period were Cambridge men—George Herbert,
Milton, Herrick, Cowley, Crashaw, Randolph, Cleveland, Dryden and
others—and a number of verse miscellanies were certainly produced at
Cambridge. Nevertheless, to judge from the number of surviving examples, it seems that Oxford—Christ Church in particular—was an especially flourishing center for the writing and circulation of verse. Their
poets at this time included such people as Richard Corbett, William
Strode, George Morley, Henry King, William Cartwright, Martin
Lluellyn, Brian Duppa, Jasper Mayne, and Jeramiel Terrent, as well as
Ben Jonson, who was a temporary Resident at Christ Church and was
honored with an M.A. degree there in 1619. If there is a single dominant factor in the flourishing of verse at this time, it is perhaps that so
many poets—including a traditionally large intake of students into both
Christ Church, Oxford, and Trinity College, Cambridge—came from
Westminster School, where the composition of verse is known to have
been particularly encouraged under a succession of notable headmasters.

It is probably not coincidence that, after the great printed miscellanies
of the Elizabethan period, the publication of verse miscellanies does not
seem to have picked up again until the 1640s and 1650s—with a succession of publications such as *The Academy of Complements, Wits Recreations,
Wits Interpreter, Parnassus Biceps,* and many others. It is as if publishers
were free to make verse public only *after* it had ceased to be the province
of select coteries, when the fashion for verse miscellanies had already in
a sense become stale and when the centers where they had particularly
flourished had been somewhat disrupted. It is also with some of the
published miscellanies of the Commonwealth period that verse miscellanies begin to lose their specifically academic character, that they become
no longer an offshoot of the student's commonplace-book habit, but
become straightforward anthologies: they thereby anticipate the production of a particular kind of verse miscellany which met new social needs,
that is, the professionally produced *Poems upon Affairs of State* which
proliferated after the Restoration.

---

[20] BL, MS. Add. 36452, fol. 30v.

Do we know which authors were in the habit of keeping commonplace books or miscellanies and how their writings might have been influenced by them? Some notable writers kept them, we know, because examples still survive. Bacon, for instance, I have mentioned. Several of his memorandum books still exist, in which he jotted down ideas, personal observations and notes on work in progress, and in one of these—his *Comentarius solutus*—he lists his various "paper books" and their specific uses. One paper book, for instance, would be used, he says, "like a Marchant's wast booke where to enter all maner of remembrance of matter ... w[i]thout any maner of restraint"; another would contain "Kalenders or Titles of things ... for better help of memory and judgm[en]t" and "things of most pr[e]sent use"; and yet others would be what he calls formal "title bookes" wherein selected matter from the other notebooks might be copied, partly by a servant, "in order, and under fitt Titles."[21] Bacon's list is a reminder that—for him, at least—the commonplace book method was a *process*, involving a series of paper books, each performing specific functions, leading not only to the ordering, but also to the refinement of material. It might be wondered whether the short, pithy, Baconian essay would ever have developed quite the way it did but for this method, as well as for his habit of preserving so many maxims, apothegms, and other snippets of wisdom and succinct perception in commonplace books.

One of Milton's commonplace books is still preserved: a compendium of extracts from various authors, ancient and modern, arranged in three sections—covering ethics, economics, and politics.[22] This was apparently along the lines of the educational treatise *De regimine principum* by the thirteenth-century theologian Egidio Colonna. Other commonplace books still survive compiled by Locke[23] and by writers such as John Evelyn,[24] George Villiers, second Duke of Buckingham,[25] and George Savile, first Marquess of Halifax,[26] all of which might profitably be discussed in detail. Yet other writers are known from report to have

---

[21] Spedding, 11:59–62.

[22] BL, MS. Add. 36354: see A. J. Horwood's facsimile Edition (1876) and the Columbia edition of the *Works*, vol. 18 (1938).

[23] See, e.g., Lord King, *Life of Locke* (1830), 2:75–105.

[24] Evelyn Papers at Christ Church, Oxford.

[25] See Christine Phipps's edition, 1985.

[26] Finch Papers in Leicestershire Record Office and Devonshire Collections at Chatsworth.

kept commonplace books even though examples no longer exist. Just
before his death John Donne, for instance, gave Henry King "all his Ser-
mon-Notes, and his other Papers, containing an Extract of near Fifteen
hundred Authors."[27] The younger John Donne, in his own will (1662),
refers to this gift as comprising "all those Papers which are of Authors
Analysed by my Father; many of which he [Henry King] hath already
receiv'd with his Common-Place Book."[28] The use of commonplace
books by some other authors has been inferred by modern scholars from
the nature of their writings. It seems fairly clear, for instance, that
Webster and Chapman made great use of them: that they kept commonplace books full of quotations, *sententiae*, images, metaphors and other
ideas, both derived and original, which could readily be mined during
the process of composition. Their plays are mosaics of quotations and
figures of speech which seem to have been incorporated—or, to use Dr.
Bradbrook's term, "bonded"—into the final compositions.[29] Other
playwrights besides may have made less extensive use of commonplace
books. Ben Jonson's well-known *Timber: or, Discoveries*, for instance, is
little more than a patchwork of quotations from classical and Renaissance
literature, intermingled with some original comments, and is evidently
based on some kind of commonplace book if not virtually amounting to
one in itself. Whether Shakespeare ever distilled his reading into commonplace books, or used any systematic method of recording ideas and
images as they occurred to him, is less evident from his writings and we
can only speculate.

Did the commonplace book have any future after the seventeenth
century? Clearly people continued to keep commonplace books of
various kinds throughout the eighteenth and nineteenth-centuries. If
they tend to be less interesting to scholars today than those of an earlier
period, perhaps it is because they belong less to a flourishing manuscript
culture and because most of what they contain is trivial and ephemeral
material copied largely from contemporary printed sources. Even then,
a serious commonplace-book methodology is occasionally encountered.
Robert Southey, for instance, had a highly developed system of transferring
passages from his extensive reading matter to notebooks, all "classified

---

[27] Henry King, *Poems*, ed. J. Hannah (1843), lxix–lxxvi.

[28] See Geoffrey Keynes, *A Bibliography of Dr. John Donne*, 4th ed. (1973), 251.

[29] M. C. Bradbrook, *John Webster Citizen and Dramatist* (1980), *passim*; see also R.
W. Dent, *John Webster's Borrowing* (1960), and Frank L. Schoell, "G. Chapman's
Commonplace Book," *Modern Philology* 17 (1919): 199–218.

and arranged" for his use.[30] Yet a compiler like Southey was the exception. For most Victorians, particularly for young people, the commonplace book had degenerated to a plaything, to a species of album or scrapbook, in which things were as likely to be glued as to be written or drawn, and "scraps"—meaning small, colored, cut-out pictures and designs—were actually sold by stationers specifically for the purpose of filling children's scrapbooks.

Has the commonplace book any legacy today? Well, consider this: a combined diary, address book and memorandum book, all in a loose-leaf binder which can be modified or expanded at will, and with compartments for much else besides: a portable planner, not to mention a prestige item which confers executive status on the owner, and a store of instantly available information by which the user can organize his or her busy life; therefore something upon which he or she might well develop considerable dependency. In 1638, commenting on poetasters of the period, Richard West wrote:

> Their Braines lye all in Notes; Lord! how they'd looke
> If they should chance to loose their Table-book![31]

Perhaps we could paraphrase this today and say:

> Their brains lie all in memos! How they'd act
> If they should chance to lose their Filofax!

SOTHEBY'S
LONDON

---

[30] *Life and Correspondence of Robert Southey*, ed. C. C. Southey (1850), 6:17–18. *Southey's Commonplace Book*, edited by John Wood Warter, was published in two volumes in 1849–50.

[31] Commendatory poem in Thomas Randolph's *Poems* (Oxford, 1638).

From Illustrated Epigram to Emblem:
The Canonization of
a Typographical Arrangement

BERNHARD F. SCHOLZ

T HE HOLD WHICH CONCEPTS OF GENRE HAD ON WRITERS and readers of the Renaissance and the Baroque is a fact almost too well-known to bear restating. "Literary invention"—both "finding" and "making" during that period was, as Rosalie Colie suggested a number of years ago, "largely generic."[1] Being a work of literature, one could put it slightly anachronistically, was tantamount to being able to satisfy certain generic norms. Yet a glance at the literary production of those centuries quickly reveals that despite the enabling and constraining role played by the notion of genre, many more types of text were productive than official poetics was able to dream of. And while a strictly constructionist tendency in the wake of Aristotle's *Poetics* would insist on recognizing sharp differences between literary kinds, there apparently existed a complementary tendency to disregard the constructionist project of a Scaliger or a Castelvetro and to allow, even encourage, deviations from strictly defined kinds, transforma-

---

[1] Rosalie L. Colie, *The Resources of Kind: Genre-Theory in the Renaissance* (Berkeley: Univ. of California Press, 1973), 17.

tions of canonized genres, and mixing of forms. But those deviant forms were only out on a suspended generic sentence, so to speak. So great, apparently, was the pressure exerted by the dominant constructionist discourse on kinds that sooner or later they, too, were assigned their proper place in one of the ever expanding genre classifications. "The fact," in Colie's words, "that the *concept* of generic form was taken for granted [was] more important than any definition of a specific generic norm could ever be."[2] Literary production, if it was to be dealt with conceptually, had to be inserted into the logical space of a type of discourse which insisted on analyzing and constructing it along generic lines, along the lines of literary kinds, and not, as yet, along historical lines.

The pressure and the impact of this kind-oriented discourse on literature can still be gleaned from the prefaces and the title pages of a number of sixteenth and seventeenth century emblem books, as well as from numerous poetological treatises in which elaborate attempts were made at locating the emblem in at times grotesquely intricate schemes of classification. Careful study of a significant number of these documents during the last two decades has shown beyond doubt that while Andrea Alciato, the *emblematum pater et princeps*, himself never used the expression "*emblema*" except as a name for his collection of mostly ekphrastic epigrams, his followers and imitators, in compliance with the dominant kind-oriented discourse on literature, felt the need to clarify their use of that expression as a genre term again and again. Daniel Russell's claim about the use of the term "*emblème*" in sixteenth century France *grosso modo* also applies to the use of that term and its calques and synonyms in other vernaculars in which emblem books were written: the term "emblem" "came slowly to refer to a combination of picture and text designated to enhance the presentation of a moral lesson after having first referred to only one or the other of the two parts of such compositions."[3]

Completely adequate as it is as a statement about the development of the *use* of the *term* "*emblème*," Russell's formulation nevertheless raises a problem. "Such compositions"? The emblem as a two-part "composition"? The ease with which we move from the phrase "a *combination* of picture and text" to the phrase "the two parts of such *compositions*," i.e.,

---

[2] Colie, 12.
[3] Daniel S. Russell, "The Term 'emblème' in Sixteenth-Century France," *Neophilologus* 59 (1975): 347.

the readiness with which, in the case of an emblem, we treat these two phrases as nearly synonymous, can only be explained on the basis of the assumption of a peculiar reading and viewing convention which governs the way in which we habitually approach the word-image combination called "emblem." In accordance with that convention we expect textual coherence not only on the syntactic and the semantic level, but also on the level of the textual *gestalt*: as anybody who has paged through a number of illustrated books presented to us as "emblem books" will agree, we are most willing to call a word-image combination an emblem when only one such combination is printed on a single page, with motto, icon, and epigram preferably arranged in vertical order. In that case we will be satisfied that we have before us what Peter M. Daly recently called an "emblem book in the strict sense, that is, the tight three-part form introduced by Alciato."[4]

But there's the rub. From everything we know about the circumstances surrounding the publication of the first edition of Alciato's *Emblemata*, we can be quite sure that Alciato himself had no three-part form or two-part composition in mind when he wrote his epigrams. Rather, the Augsburg printer Heinrich Steyner, in what looks like an unauthorized step, supplemented Alciato's epigrams with a woodcut each, and that for commercial rather than aesthetic reasons.[5] The question which needs to be raised is therefore: how did a combination of an epigram and a woodcut as it was to be found in the first edition of the *Emblemata*, the *Emblematum liber*, as it is now commonly called, eventually turn into a composition, i.e., into a structured, bounded whole? How did what started out as a typographical arrangement on the level of *parole* eventually come to be viewed as textual on the level of *langue*? How, in other words, did what started out as a one-time combination of texts belonging to the genre of the epigram with "texts" belonging to the genre of illustration eventually become a definitional feature of a new genre called "emblem"? Or do we have to take a step back and ask: did a specific textual *gestalt* ever really become a generic feature of the emblem?

---

[4] Peter M. Daly, "Introduction," *The English Emblem Tradition 1*, Index Emblematicus, ed. Peter M. Daly et al. (Toronto: Univ. of Toronto Press, 1988), x.

[5] See F. W. G. Leeman, *Alciatus' Emblemata. Denkbeelden en voorbeelden* (Groningen, 1984). For an overview of the history of research on the circumstances of the publication of the first emblem book, see my "The 1531 Augsburg Edition of Alciato's *Emblemata*: A Survey of Research," in *Emblematica: An Interdisciplinary Journal for Emblem Studies* 5.2 (1991): 213–54.

The *Emblematum liber* of 1531, it needs to be stressed, does not permit associating the tripartite combination of motto, icon, and epigram with the notion of a somehow self-contained tripartite *gestalt*. Although Steyner always placed a woodcut between the titles and the texts of Alciato's epigrams, thereby turning those titles into titles of the combination of image and text, he nowhere made an attempt at either typographically separating two three-part combinations following upon each other, or at arranging the three parts of such a combination on a single page. Instead, as even a brief glance at the *Emblematum liber* suggests, a page could be headed by either a motto or a woodcut or an epigram; it could even begin in the middle of the text of an epigram for which there was not sufficient room on the preceding page. Steyner, it appears, had a type page of approximately thirty-four lines to fill, and fill it he did, without any obvious regard for the layout of the page itself. What nevertheless turns the combinations of titles, pictures and poems printed on the pages of the *Emblematum liber* into parts of textual wholes, and what allows the reader/viewer to decide which texts and which woodcuts go together, are certain linguistic properties of the texts such as deictic and referential expressions, and, more importantly perhaps, co-reference of texts and pictures: the texts denote specific objects "from nature or from history," and the adjacent woodcuts depict the same objects. Thanks to the recurrence of these features, the titles, pictures, and epigrams of the *Emblematum liber* are perceived as arranged in groups of three. Add to this the fact that Steyner always adheres to the vertically arranged sequence of title, woodcut, and epigram, and it becomes possible to claim that in the *Emblematum liber* of 1531 a vertical sequential arrangement is established as a textual feature by means of repetition. But, significantly, this semantically and syntactically achieved grouping is as yet not matched by a perceptual *gestalt*. Semantic and syntactic closure there may be; perceptual closure, if I may coin that expression, is not to be found.

In the 1534 Paris edition of the *Emblemata*, the *Emblematum libellus*, as it is known today, the edition by Christian Wechel of which Alciato appears to have approved, that perceptual gestalt is indeed realized: every three-part combination of motto, icon, and epigram occupies one single type page, thus allowing for a reading/viewing of the illustrated *Emblemata* in which those combinations of word and image are not only held together linguistically and by means of co-reference, but also by what the gestalt psychologists would call a *"good gestalt."* Textual coherence, in other words, apart from being achieved linguistically, is now achieved perceptually as well.

But was it perceived as such by the first readers of the *Emblematum libellus*? And would an early reader, studying copies of both the 1531 and the 1534 editions, have noted the different looks of Wechel's edition except in terms of layout, or, depending on the size of his own purse, waste of paper or proof of affluence? As with the *Emblematum liber* of 1531 there are, unfortunately, no extant documents which might allow us to prove or to disprove conclusively that the original readers of the *Emblematum libellus* did indeed view the perceptual gestalt of the three-part combination of motto, icon and epigram as textual, and hence as potentially generic. But arguing backwards from the stage in the development of the definition of the emblem marked by Daly's notion of the emblem as a "tight three-part form," and Russell's synonymous use of "combination" and "composition," we are, I believe, entitled to claim that Christian Wechel's Paris edition of 1534 was the first one which offered the possibility of entering a specific surface gestalt into the range of the defining features of the emblem. Steyner's 1531 edition, on the other hand, can be seen as the archetype of later emblem books and iconographical compilations in which the perceptual gestalt of the emblematic three-part combination is neither textual nor generic.

Looking through the emblem books of Alciato's early imitators, one will soon become convinced that the pattern established by the typography of the 1534 Paris edition recurs much more frequently than that of the 1531 Augsburg edition. That may be due to conscious imitation, but we certainly should not rule out the possibility that the one-emblem-per-page solution may have recommended itself on aesthetic grounds, too. As for the English emblem tradition, Whitney's *Emblemes* of 1586, Peacham's *Minerva Britanna* of 1612, Wither's *Collection of Emblems* of 1634/35, and Quarles's *Emblemes* of 1639, to name but the most prominent examples, all follow the pattern set by the 1534 Paris edition. The picture is similar for other national traditions of emblem writing.

The wide acceptance of the typographical arrangement initiated by Wechel's edition did, however, leave room for other arrangements. Thus the second German translation of the *Emblemata* by Jeremias Held, published in Frankfurt on the Main in 1566, is clearly based on the Paris 1534 edition as far as the choice of pictures and as far as the state of Alciato's texts are concerned. In Held's layout German translations are placed directly after (under) Alciato's Latin epigrams, but no attempt is made at maintaining the one-emblem-per-page pattern. Instead, as in the 1531 edition, the texts often run over to the following page, with the following three-part combination plus German translation beginning lower on the page, and likewise running over. Here then, one is tempt-ed to say, was a viewer/reader who, as a printer, had obviously seen Wechel's typographical innovation but who had not seen the perceptual closure of each individual three-part combination achieved by it. And if he had seen it, he obviously didn't find it worth imitating. The first Ger-man translation by Wolfgang Hunger, published by Christian Wechel himself in 1542, had retained the perceptual integrity of the typographi-cal arrangement of the 1534 edition, printing the German texts on facing pages. Christian Wechel, we are entitled to surmise, wished to retain the sense of a tripartite whole which he had established with his edition of the *Emblemata*; in *his* bilingual edition the German translations literally remain outside the perceptually closed Alciatian texts.

Why Held's translation, published some thirty years after the *Emble-matum libellus* and some twenty-five years after Hunger's translation, should abandon the typographical arrangement pioneered by Wechel, although it was clearly based on one or both of Wechel's editions, can no longer be ascertained. Perhaps we have to look for a possible explana-tion in the fact that the title page of the 1567 translation identifies Alciato's *Emblemata* as a *"Kunstbuch,"* a book of samples for painters, goldsmiths, silk embroiderers, and sculptors.[6] As producers of specimens of what has become known in recent years as "applied emblematics," craftsmen like these would not primarily have been interested in the perceptual gestalt of the bookish three-part combination of motto, icon, and epigram. For them the fact that, as Alciato himself had put it in his treatise on the signification of words,[7] "things at times can signify" may have been what counted, and that the *Emblemata* contained a whole host of descriptions and depiction of such signifying things, backed by the authority of as famous an author as the great jurist from Milan. Add to this that there are emblem books in which the mottos and the icon occupy a whole page, and the epigram a facing one, and that in others, as in John Bunyan's *Book for Boys and Girls* (London, 1686) the pictures are not graphically executed, and the conclusion cannot be avoided that the typographical arrangement inaugurated by Wechel's 1534 edition of the *Emblemata*, though it was frequently imitated, was never ranked

---

[6] For a detailed discussion of Hunger's translation, see Ingrid Höpel, *Emblem und Sinnbild: Vom Kunstbuch zum Erbauungsbuch* (Frankfurt/M.: Athenäum, 1984).

[7] See Hessel Miedema, "The Term Emblema in Alciati," *Journal of the Warburg and Courtauld Institutes* 31 (1968): 234–50.

among the necessary conditions for calling a specific three-part combination of text and woodcut an emblem.

This wavering with respect to the textual gestalt of the emblem should not, however, come as a surprise: whenever a place was found for the new emblem genre in the literary classifications of the sixteenth and seventeenth century, it was in the context of a discourse on kinds which specified that the emblem should be distinguished from as close a relative as the device by subject matter rather than by surface form. In more modern terms: attempts at assigning the emblem its proper place in those genre classifications focus on the emblematic *signifié* and its moral/religious/political uses, rather than on the perceptual characteristics of the emblematic *signifiant*. And though it remains correct to claim that the term "emblem" eventually came to refer to the two-part combination of picture and text, that claim has to be supplemented by the observation that the bi-mediality of the *denotatum* of that term was never expressly thematized. Typical instances of this concentration on the emblematic *signifié* and its uses are the numerous attempts at distinguishing between the emblem and the device by decreeing that, while both should present norms and maxims of right action, the device should relate these to an individual bearer, while the emblem should generalize them. Thus we read in Thomas Blount's translation of Henry Estienne's treatise on the making of devices that the difference between emblems and devices

> is taken from this, that the words of the *Embleme* may demonstrate things universall, and hold the rank of morall precepts, which may as well serve for all the world as for the proper author of the Embleme. This generall application of the motto, is a great error of a *Devise*, which ought to be particular, and the words thereof proper and suitable to the person onely, in whose favor the Devise is made.[8]

Estienne's grouping of the emblem and the device with hieroglyphs, symbols, aenigmas, sentences, parables, reverses of medals, coats of arms, blazons, cyphers, and rebuses, which repeats earlier Italian attempts at grouping, likewise takes the presence of the visual element for granted and does not involve an attempt at distinguishing between the members of this group by means of an analysis of the salient differences in the relations and the arrangements of word and image.

---

[8] Henri Estienne, *L'Art de faire les devises* (Paris, 1645), trans. Thomas Blount (London, 1646).

The perceptual *gestalt* of the emblem, i.e., the typographical arrangement of the three-part combination of motto, icon, and epigram in relation to the type page, thus remained theoretically under-determined
throughout the roughly two and a half centuries during which emblems
were produced in great numbers. Should we then adopt the view that
"during much of its history the emblem was not ... perceived as a distinct form at all," and that therefore the emblem should better be understood as "simply a way of presenting or communicating moral commonplaces, doctrinal principles, political propaganda, alchemical recipes
or even philosophical ideas through the combination of a discursive text
with a pseudo-ideogrammatic code of a non-linguistic nature?"[9]

Having seen how a subject-oriented discourse on kinds of the sort
which dominated sixteenth and seventeenth century discussions on the
emblem apparently did not permit raising the question of surface
form,[10] we should be warned not to allow our own dominant discourse
on kinds to settle *a priori* the issue of the perceptual gestalt of the emblem. As far as the emblem is concerned—and I suspect that the situation
is not different for other genres either—the issue of form does not
reduce to the alternative of "having a distinct form" or "not having a
distinct form at all." The emblem, we saw, emerged out of concrete imitations of either the 1531 Augsburg or the 1534 Paris edition of Alciato's illustrated *Emblemata*. It did so, we must keep in mind, under the
conditions of a poetics of *imitatio*, a poetics, that is, which, while it ex-
tolled the virtues of imitation, variation, and emulation, rejected replication. Thus instead of expecting to find a distinct form of the emblem as
far as typography is concerned, and finding our expectations thwarted,
we should perhaps better speak of an "emergent" form of the emblem,
a continuing movement toward form kept in check by the constraints of
the poetics of *imitatio*.[11] As an emergent rather than an ideally distinct

---

[9] Daniel S. Russell, *The Emblem and Device in France*, (Lexington, Ky.: French
Forum Publishers, 1985), 163ff.

[10] For a detailed discussion of sixteenth- and seventeenth-century discourse on the
emblem, see my *Emblematice Scribere: Historical and Systematic Studies in Emblem Literature* (Leiden: E. J. Brill, forthcoming).

[11] On the poetics of *imitatio,* see Thomas M. Greene, *The Light in Troy: Imitation
and Discovery in Renaissance Poetry* (New Haven: Yale Univ. Press, 1982). I borrow the
notion of an "emergent" form from Paul J. Hopper, "Discourse Analysis: Grammar
and Critical Theory in the 1980s," *Profession 88* (The Modern Language Association),
18–24. An extended discussion on the emblem as "emergent form" can be found in
my forthcoming *Emblematice Scribere*.

form, the emblem can be described in terms of a process of permanent structuration and re-structuration, which was controlled (rather remotely, at times) by the typographical archetypes of the first two editions of the *Emblemata*, by the constraints concerning subject and use articulated in the prefaces and on the title pages of emblem books, and, last but not least, by the rules of the poetics of *imitatio* that specified degrees of resemblance and difference. In the field of forces created by these three factors, the perceptual gestalt of the emblem remained unspecified. But that does not mean, we now understand, that that gestalt was understood as a completely arbitrary feature of the emblem.

A seemingly paradoxical consequence follows from this discussion of the typographical features of the texts of the emblem genre: not having a distinct form may have been the manner in which the emblem had a distinct form. Are we then still entitled to claim that in the emblem a specific typographical arrangement became textual? The answer, I believe, can be affirmative, as long as we keep in mind that the grammar of the emblematic text did not exist *a priori*, but was under constant re-negotiation as long as the emblem genre was productive.[12]

GRONINGEN UNIVERSITY

---

[12] The same would seem to be true *mutatis mutandis* of the essay, yet another genre which had its origin in a specific Renaissance text.

Malleable and Fixed Texts: Manuscript and Printed Miscellanies and the Transmission of Lyric Poetry in the English Renaissance

ARTHUR F. MAROTTI

I
N THE POSTHUMOUS (AND ANONYMOUS) SECOND EDITION OF the poems of Richard Corbett, one of the most-transcribed poets in the manuscript miscellanies of the seventeenth century, the printer says in his note to the reader: "I heere offer to thy view, a Collection of certaine peices of poetry, which haue *flowne* from hand to hand, theses [*sic*] many yeares, in *private* papers, but were neuer *Fixed*, for the *publique* eie of the world to looke upon, til now."[1] From the time of Richard Tottel's famous *Miscellany* (1557) through most of the seventeenth century, enterprising stationers and printers appropriated verse that was circulating in manuscript and translated it into print, arresting typographically those processes of change characteristic of manuscript transmission, but introducing new alterations by the editorial, composi-

---

[1] *Poemata Stromata* (London, 1648), A2r–A2v, quoted in Edwin Wolf, 2nd, *The Textual Importance of Manuscript Commonplace Books of 1620–1660* (Charlottesville, Va.: Bibliographical Soc. of the Univ. of Virginia, 1949), 15.

torial, and mechanical conditions of the publishing process. A single literary history might embrace both manuscript-circulated and printed literature, but it should not obscure the very different characters of literary texts in these two systems of literary transmission. I would like therefore to consider some of these features, especially with reference to manuscript and printed miscellanies of the English Renaissance.

First, however, I would like to dissociate what I am doing from the usual textual and bibliographical program for dealing with the relationship of manuscripts to printed texts—one that is informed by a textual "idealism" that effectively eradicates those interesting socioliterary processes in which texts are historically embedded. I agree with such revisionist textual scholars and bibliographers as Jerome McGann, Randall McLeod, and D. F. McKenzie that what is needed now is a more sociological and cultural-materialist approach to textuality.[2] I would extend McKenzie's recent definition of bibliography as "the sociology of texts" to textual scholarship,[3] arguing that it is time to make that discipline less author-centered and to value as interesting elements of texts' socioliterary history some of those very "corruptions" and "errors" it has been the aim of traditional scholarship to purge.

In manuscript circulation texts were inherently malleable, escaping authorial control to enter a social world in which recipients casually transcribed, revised, supplemented, and answered them, not particularly worried about changing an authorial "original." In fact, some authors expected and welcomed the changes that recipients of their works brought to them, acknowledging the possibility that modern textual scholarship has been reluctant to admit, that texts might (accidentally or deliberately) be improved by individuals other than the original writers.[4]

---

[2] See, for example, Jerome J. McGann, *A Critique of Modern Textual Criticism* (Chicago: Univ. of Chicago Press, 1983); Randall McLeod, "UnEditing Shakespeare," *Sub-Stance* 33/34 (1982): 26–55; and D. F. McKenzie, *Bibliography and the Sociology of Texts*, The Panizzi Lectures, 1985 (London: The British Library, 1986).

[3] *Sociology of Texts*, 5. McKenzie assumes just such a broad scope for his definition, calling bibliography "the discipline that studies texts as recorded forms, and the processes of their transmission, including their production and reception" (4).

[4] Edwin Wolf remarks: "The words of a poet were not sacrosanct in his own day; corruptions are common, but it may be that some ... poetry was actually improved in the stream of transmission" (3). J. W. Saunders, "From Manuscript to Print: A Note on the Circulation of Poetic MSS in the Sixteenth Century," *Proceedings of the Leeds Philosophical and Literary Society* 6.8 (1951): 524, notes, for example, that George Whetstone "left his poems dispersed among learned friends and expected

In print, however, texts were typographically fixed as objects within a set of publishing conventions and printing house practices, their final form presented often as the result of authorial and/or editorial "perfecting" or "correcting": print cultivated the notion of an "authorized" text—with or without the cooperation of authors.[5] But, of course, in *both* systems texts remained malleable, especially so in the first two centuries of print, when the copies from which texts were typographically set were often, by modern standards, "bad texts," were seldom corrected by authors and usually proof-read only by printing-house employees, were set by different compositors with varying habits of spelling and punctuation, and continued to be reproduced in different forms in both manuscript and print. It is useful, nonetheless, to contrast the situation of texts in manuscript transmission and in print, especially since the changes brought about by the latter, in effect, created the modern definition of literature and most of the assumptions of textual and bibliographical scholars that still prevail.[6]

Lyric poetry is an interesting genre to study in terms of the dynamics of literary transmission in Renaissance, for, as the last form to be separated from the world of the socially occasional and incorporated in the institution of literature developing within print culture, it existed for an unusually long time in the two overlapping systems of transmission. It

---

them 'at theyr leasure to polish' the work, should he fail to return from abroad."

[5] In print culture both publishers and authors began to express concern for the correctness of the texts being printed—a contrast to the more casual attitude toward texts in the manuscript system. In the preface to the first (unauthorized) edition of Sidney's "Astrophil and Stella" (1591), a quarto augmented with verse by Campion, Daniel, and Greville, Thomas Newman tried to add prestige to his enterprise by claiming to be concerned about the accuracy of his (corrupt) texts. In publishing the full edition of his *Delia* (1592), Samuel Daniel partly justified his enterprise by asserting that the "uncorrected" (A2r) texts Newman printed in that volume needed fixing. Herrick wrote in "His Request to Julia" that he would rather have his poems burned than printed "not perfected" (*Hesperides* #59, in *The Complete Poetry of Robert Herrick*, ed. J. Max Patrick [Garden City, N.Y., 1963], 32).

[6] In my discussion of the impact of print culture on literature, I am especially indebted to the following: Elizabeth Eisenstein, *The Printing Press as an Agent of Change: Communications and Cultural Transformations in Early-Modern Europe*, 2 vols., (Cambridge: Cambridge Univ. Press, 1979); Richard Newton, "Making Books from Leaves: Poets Become Editors," in *Print and Culture in the Renaissance*, ed. Gerald P. Tyson and Sylvia S. Wagonheim (Newark: Univ. of Delaware Press, 1986), 246–64; Richard Helgerson, *Self-Crowned Laureates: Spenser, Milton, and the Literary System* (Berkeley: Univ. of California Press, 1983); and Timothy Murray, *Theatrical Legitimation: Allegories of Genius in Seventeenth-Century England and France* (New York: Oxford Univ. Press, 1987).

was recorded, preserved, and passed on in manuscript in single (usually bifolia) sheets,[7] in individual quires and in manuscript "books." Verse was collected in manuscripts or bound manuscript volumes by private individuals (infrequently the authors themselves) or by members of social or family circles at the university, the Inns of Court, the Court, and the great houses. These texts include both (organized or haphazard) poetical anthologies and catch-all miscellanies containing such other material as prose letters, medical recipes, household accounts, school exercises, and journal writing. Since the various surviving manuscripts containing lyric poetry often preserve copies of poems that did not find their way into print in their own time or in the century or more following their composition, they have, of course, been valued by modern textual scholarship, though, at the same time, most of the texts they contain have been accorded little "authority." They have been examined selectively by textual scholars, but the time has come, as Peter Beal has suggested, for us to subject these fascinating social-historical documents to a more broadly-based analysis.[8]

The practices of poetical anthologizing in the sixteenth and seventeenth century printed miscellanies and augmented editions of single authors were closely related to those of the manuscript tradition, but, of course, both technological and sociocultural differences developed between the two media that had an impact on the character of the texts being collected and on the roles of authors, editors or collectors, and readers. In my discussion, I shall concentrate on some of the material differences between the two media, but such a focus is inseparable from a discussion of larger issues.

Some of the differences between the material features of manuscript-circulated and printed poetry are crucial, if obvious. Each scripted copy of a poem is unique in appearance, while printed texts are designed for exact replication. Handwriting, using individual versions of stylized secretary, italic, and hybrid scripts, was individualized. John Ramsey has an account of his life at the beginning of his manuscript miscellany in which he explains that he was wounded in his right hand in a duel: in the volume his handwriting changes dramatically from secretary script—pre-

---

[7] On this point, see Germaine Warkentin, "Sidney's *Certain Sonnets:* Speculations on the Evolution of the Text," *The Library,* 6th ser., 2 (1980): 434–36.

[8] *Index of English Literary Manuscripts,* ed. Peter Beal (London: Mansell, 1980), 1:248–49.

sumably written with the right hand before his injury—to italic script done with the left hand, and finally palsy changes the writing still further.[9] Some manuscripts contain practice writing by children, who were set to copy texts by parents and tutors, often many times over.[10] Especially since women usually were taught to use italic, rather than secretary, hands (although men too by the early seventeenth century chose italic or hybrid secretary-italic forms),[11] there are gender markers in some manuscript collections or portions of them. For example, there is an answer poem in BL MS. Egerton 2711 to Wyatt's "Madame withouten many Wordes" probably written, Richard Harrier suggests, by a woman in the late sixteenth or early seventeenth century.[12] Sir John Harington's daughters Frances and Ellina transcribed poems in italic script in BL MS. Add. 36529.[13] Handwritten texts could be treasured for their personal associations. Sir Stephen Powle wrote, for example, in his commonplace book after the text of Tichborne's poem, "My prime of youth is but a frost of cares," "Written by him sealfe. 3. dayes before his exequution: I haue the originall written with his owne hande."[14]

---

[9] Bod. MS. Douce 280. For an interesting recent discussion of handwriting and individual character, see Jonathan Goldberg, "Hamlet's Hand," *Shakespeare Quarterly* 39 (1988): 307–27.

[10] See Janet Backhouse, "An Elizabethan Schoolboy's Exercise Book," *Bodleian Library Record* 9 (1978): 323–32.

[11] Citing Martin Billingsley, who notes in *The Pens Excellencie* that the italic hand was taught to women because it was the easiest script, Giles E. Dawson and Laetitia Kennedy-Skipton (*Elizabethan Handwriting, 1500–1650, A Manual* [New York, 1960], 10) point out that the mass of contemporary manuscript evidence indicates that women almost invariably used this hand.

[12] *The Canon of Sir Thomas Wyatt's Poetry* (Cambridge, Mass.: Harvard Univ. Press, 1975), 12.

[13] *The Arundel-Harington Manuscript of Tudor Poetry*, ed. Ruth Hughey, 2 vols. (Columbus: Ohio State Univ. Press, 1960), 1:41.

[14] Bod. MS. Tanner 169, fol. 79r. Peter Beal cites (in Edmund Blunden's translation) Donne's Latin poem to Dr. Andrews revealing that poet's preference for manuscripts over printed volumes:

> What Printing-presses yield we think good store,
> But what is writ by hand we reverence more:
> A Book that with this printing-blood is dyed
> On shelves for dust and moth is set aside,
> But if't be penned it wins a sacred grace
> And with the ancient Fathers takes its place
> . . . .   (Beal, 1:245)

While the scribe's work physically resembles the author's transcribing of his text, the compositor's setting of type, a mirror image of the printed page, is a markedly different process: in the first case the line between transcription and composition can be blurred, whereas compositors, checked by printing-house proof-readers (and sometimes by authors), were supposed to reproduce the "copies" they were given, although they were free to spell and punctuate in their own ways. When whole poems, lines, or words are deleted in manuscripts, their traces remain: for example, BL MS. Egerton 2421 has several poems crossed out, including a popular bawdy poem here called "A Venerous discourse"[15] but, since the transcriber/editor did not actually cut the texts from the manuscript, they are still part of the collection. Obviously, those features editorially removed before publication disappear from sight.

In contrast to script, type fonts—Gothic or black letter, roman, italic, etc.—regularized visible language.[16] The texts of poems in Tottel's *Miscellany* (1557), *A Handefull of Pleasant Delites* (1566?), *The Paradise of Dainty Devices* (1576), *A Gorgeous Gallery of Gallant Inventions* (1578), *Brittons Bowre of Delights* (1591), and *The Arbor of Amorous Devices* (1597) were in black-letter, though italic or roman fonts were used for titles and names; *The Phoenix Nest* (1593), *England's Helicon* (1600), and *A Poetical Rhapsody* (1602) imitated the new practice of printing verse in roman type.[17] Such a shift anticipated a similar movement in handwriting from secretary to italic script.[18] In print, abbreviations were eventually ex-

---

[15] This poem, beginning "Nay pish, nay phue," survives in many other manuscript versions. In his useful annotated edition of Bod. MS. Rawl. Poet. 85 ("John Finet's Miscellany" [Diss. Washington Univ., 1960], 109), Laurence Cummings cites sixteen manuscripts and one printed version, that in the late anthology, *Sportive Wit* (1656).

[16] Beginning with Gutenberg, of course, typefaces bore an interesting relation to different forms of handwriting, from late medieval manuscript hands on forward. See Philip Gaskell, *A New Introduction to Bibliography* (New York: Oxford Univ. Press, 1972), 16–33. In the seventeenth century, a quaintly script-like typeface is used on some title pages of books or for frontispiece poetry—see, for example, the title page of Herbert's *The Temple*, the Walton poem under the engraving of Donne in the 1635 edition of that author, or Milton's sarcastic Greek poem under Marshall's strange engraving in the 1645 edition of his poems, on which see Gary Spear, "Reading Before the Lines," 187–193, below.

[17] *Bel-vedere* (1600), a commonplace book collection of poetical citations, distinguishes the strung-together quotes from one another by alternating roman and italic print. Most of the lyric poetry printed in the 1590s was in roman type.

[18] See Dawson and Kennedy-Skipton, 9–13.

panded, punctuation was much heavier, the superscripted characters of manuscript writing descended to the level line. The mixing of various kinds and sizes of type fonts, along with the use of woodcuts, plates and ornaments, allowed for some of the forms of aesthetic and intellectual expressiveness that characterized medieval, but not contemporary, manuscripts.

Lineation and page-layout operate differently in manuscript and printed texts. Especially when the manuscript-transcriber is an amateur, the lines are apt to be irregular rather than rectilinear, though some manuscripts have lined or folded pages and many have ruled margins. In his commendatory epistle to Thomas Watson's *'EKATOMPATHIA* (1582), John Lyly calls attention to the difference between "crooked" handwritten love poems and the perfectly aligned printed texts, explaining that he is reluctant to publish his own love lyrics because in print they would lose some of the expressiveness of scripted verse: ". . . seeing you have used mee so friendly, as to make me acquainted with your passions, I will shortly make you pryuie to mine, which I would be loth the printer should see, for that my fancies being neuer so crooked he would put them in streight lines, unfit for my humor, necessarie for his art, who setteth down, blinde, in as many letters as seeing" (A5v). In Gascoigne's "Dan Bartholomew of Bathe" the lover complains when his mistress prefers printed poems to his handwritten ones: "The rymes which pleased thee were all in print / And mine were ragged, hard for to be red."[19]

In manuscripts, scribes could alter the size of their handwriting to fit poems into available spaces. There was less flexibility in published volumes. The exigencies of page-size and type-size, for example, forced the printer of Googe's *Eglogs, Epytaphes, and Sonettes* (1563) to break seven-foot, hexameter, and pentameter lines after the fourth foot and to set each line as two.[20] This constraint operated as late as John Donne Jr.'s mistakenly presented 1660 "edition" of the poems of Pembroke and Rudyerd (a belatedly published poetical miscellany); in it each of the six- and seven-foot lines of poulter's measure used in Dyer's famous manuscript-circulated poem, "He that mirth hath lost," is printed as two.[21]

---

[19] *George Gascoigne's "A Hundreth Sundrie Flowres,"* ed. C.T. Prouty, Univ. of Missouri Studies, 17.2 (1942; repr. Columbia: Univ. of Missouri Press, 1970), 212.

[20] A facsimile reproduction with an introduction by Frank B. Fieler (Gainesville, Fla.: Scholars' Facsimiles & Reprints, 1968), xii.

[21] This is the first printing of Dyer's well-known poem. Bod. MS. Rawl. Poet.

Although some professionally-transcribed manuscripts of verse include rudimentary forms of ornamentation and attempt to lay poems out on the page with some sense of aesthetic design,[22] generally there is a marked difference between the iconicity of ornamented or unornamented texts in printed editions and the appearance of the same texts in manuscript collections where their physical appearance does not call attention to them as aesthetic objects. In an authorial manuscript to be used to produce an edition of his poem on Baron Chicester, Christopher Brooke included a note to the printer giving instructions for the aesthetic presentation of his verse in the printed edition: "Let this Poem be printed wth a Margent of / black aboue and beneath; and but 12 or / 14 lynes on a side at the most; the / distinctions *duely* observed; and some / Iudicious man to correct the Proofes / by the Copie / C: B:."[23] Often the final gatherings in printed editions left room for augmenting the verse of a single poet with the work of others, while the practice of collecting verse in blank books, for example, often produced empty spaces throughout a manuscript, into which texts could be copied later.

While each printed book had pages of uniform size (most poetical texts appearing in quarto or octavo), bound manuscripts sometimes included different-sized papers or quires. In physical format manuscript collections differed from printed ones in other ways: for example, some manuscript volumes are transcribed from the end as well as the beginning,[24] most have different hands or sizes of writing, and some utilize double columns or sideways transcription. While printed texts were produced in a relatively short time, manuscript collections typically took

---

85 also has a version of this work lineated in the same way (fols. 109r–112v).

[22] Bod. MS. Rawl. Poet. 31, a vellum-bound, carefully-ordered text in the hand of a professional scribe, inserts ornamental divisions between its poems, as does BL MS. Add. 22118. BL MS. Add. 33998, a professionally transcribed anthology, boxes the title of each poem and the names of the authors of those pieces that are ascribed. Some manuscripts retain features of older calligraphically-produced manuscript documents: BL MS. Egerton 2642, for example, a miscellany containing a book of heraldry as well as funeral verse, epitaphs, moral, satiric, and epigrammatic poetry from the 1570s and 1580s, is a rubricated manuscript.

[23] BL MS. Egerton 2405, fol. 1r. This manuscript also contains a much longer note "To the Gentlemen that shall licence/ this Poem for the Presse," defending the satirical elements in his poem and the rightness of his motives, ending with instructions "to take out or dash [this letter] wth y^{or} pen, Lest the Printer should be so grosse to print it wth the rest" (fol. 25r).

[24] For example, Bod. MS. Eng. Poet. e. 14 has its material run from the start on fols. 1–76 and, inversely and in reverse, from the end from fols. 101v through 76v.

shape over an extended period, in some cases as much as two centuries.[25]

While verse in printed texts is frozen, in the system of manuscript transmission poems could easily elicit revisions, corrections, supplements, or answer poems, since they were part of an ongoing social discourse. Even an authorial holograph was not immune to alteration: Wyatt's collection of his own verse in BL MS. Egerton 2711, for example, contains not only that poet's own revisions of his work but also the alterations introduced by Nicholas Grimald and other sixteenth-century correctors.[26] Bodleian MS. Eng. Poet. e.14, for example, includes a supplement to Sir Henry Wotton's "You meaner beauties of the night" labeled "Two other Staves added by Another" (fol. 68v). Poems like Ralegh's "The Lie" and Marlowe's "The Passionate Shepherd" attracted answer poems that became part of the line of manuscript transmission.[27] In the manuscript environment the roles of author, scribe, and reader overlap: in a poem written in a lady's table book, Henry King, for example, invited her to be "both the Scribe and Author."[28] In print culture such functions are more sharply distinguished. While printers were not usually composers of verse,[29] compilers of manuscripts often added their own poems to the commonplace book miscellanies or poetical anthologies they made: John Harington of Stepney (The Arundel-Harington MS), John Finet (Bod. MS. Rawl. Poet. 85), John Lilliat (Bod. MS. Rawl. Poet. 148),[30] Lewison Fitzjames (Bod. MS. Add. B.97), John Ramsey

---

[25] For example, BL MS. Add. 30982 runs from the early Jacobean era through the late seventeenth century.

[26] See Hughey, 1:44–45. Harrier says of one of the poems in the Egerton Manuscript that shows considerable revision ("What rage is this?") that it is "a remarkable specimen of a poem in the process of being written" (3).

[27] For an interesting treatment of Richard Latewar's interstanzaic answer poem to the former, see Josef Höltgen, "Richard Latewar, Elizabethan Poet and Divine," *Anglia*, 89 (1971): 417–38; on the latter poem, see Suzanne Woods, " 'The Passionate Sheepheard' and 'The Nimphs Reply,' A Study of Transmission," *Huntington Library Quarterly* 34 (1970): 25–33.

[28] Quoted in Margaret Crum, "Notes on the Physical Characteristics of Some Manuscripts of the Poems of Donne and Henry King," *The Library*, 5th ser., 16 (1961): 121.

[29] Hyder Rollins, however, notes that Thomas Proctor wrote verse for the miscellany he edited, pointing out that other editors felt free to do the same (*A Gorgeous Gallery of Gallant Inventions [1578]*, ed. Hyder E. Rollins [Cambridge, Mass.: Harvard Univ. Press, 1926], xix).

[30] For an edition of this manuscript, see *"Liber Lilliati": Elizabethan Verse and Song*

(Bod. MS. Douce 280), and Nicholas Burghe (Bod. MS. Ashmole 38), for example, all took the opportunity of recording their own verse in the collections they assembled.

Manuscript lyrics were closer to performance, serving as scripts for reading aloud or texts to be sung; printed lyrics, even those found in such miscellanies as *The Paradise of Dainty Devices,* whose texts were meant to be sung to the reader's choice of songs in common meters, move away from both speech and song to become objects of (silent or oral) private reading. In both manuscript and printed forms, song lyrics are incomplete texts, requiring the performer's knowledge of appropriate tunes, but in the manuscript system of transmission that was closer to the immediate social conditions of composition, the proper coupling of text and music could more easily be assumed; printed lyrics, except those in books of songs, airs, or madrigals, were on their way to becoming de-musicalized verse.[31]

The contrast between the two systems, however, is not as sharp as it appears at first glance. Since, for example, the spelling and punctuation habits of compositors as well as such material constraints as those imposed by type-fonts with kerned letters[32] affected the form of the printed text, considerable alterations to texts occurred in the printing process: D. F. McKenzie's recent argument that "accidentals" are substantive acknowledges this fact.[33] In addition, since compositors set type by memorizing each line, like manuscript scribes (some of whom were working entirely from memory rather than from written copies), they introduced new textual changes every time type was set.[34] And, of course, the

---

(Bodleian MS Rawlinson Poetry 148), ed. Edward Doughtie (Newark: Univ. of Delaware, 1985).

[31] For an excellent recent discussion of the relations of lyric poetry to music, see Winifred Maynard, *Elizabethan Lyric Poetry and Its Music* (Oxford: Clarendon Press, 1986). Maynard's argument (21–37) that *The Paradise of Dainty Devices* was the most popular of the Elizabethan miscellanies because its lyrics continued to be sung to available tunes seems convincing.

[32] See Randall McLeod, "Spellbound: Typography and the Concept of Old-Spelling Editions," *Renaissance and Reformation*, n.s., 1 (1979): 50–65, repr. in *Play-Texts in Old Spelling: Papers from the Glendon Conference,* ed. G. B. Shand and Raymond C. Shady (New York: AMS Press, 1984), 81–96.

[33] "Typography and Meaning: The Case of William Congreve," in *The Book and the Book Trade in Eighteenth-Century Europe*, Proceedings of the Fifth Wolfenbutteler Symposium, November 1–3, 1977, ed. Giles Barber and Bernhard Fabian (Hamburg: Dr. Ernest Hauswedell & Co., 1981), 81–125.

[34] As Hyder Rollins observed on the basis of his extensive study of Tudor

economically-mandated practice of binding uncorrected or partially corrected sheets meant that, as every student of the Shakespeare First Folio knows, different copies of the same edition of a work often varied greatly.

There were some interesting connections between the media of manuscript and print. For instance, printed texts often returned to the system of manuscript transmission: BL MS. Harl. 6910 and BL MS. Add. 18044 transcribed texts from printed editions[35]—a not-surprising phenomenon in an age in which keepers of commonplace books continually copied published material. Also features of poetry publications affected the habits of deploying verse in manuscript collections: for example, the arrangement by genre that particularly suited printed editions also appears in certain seventeenth-century manuscript collections.[36] Some manuscripts contain tables of contents and first-line indices. The practice of entitling poems and of ascribing them to particular authors belonged more properly to the print medium and spilled over into the system of manuscript transmission. One even finds an example in a manuscript collection of using another feature of the print format, the running head: BL MS. Harl. 4955 uses "Beniamin Johnson" in the section in which that poet's work is gathered; BL MS. Harl. 6910 employs the running title of "Poesyes" in a section of the collection gathering ring posies.[37] Bodleian MS. Malone 23, which looks like an anthology transcribed as a presentation volume to a social superior, records the titles of poems in boldface italic, demonstrating the influence of the repertory of typography. Although one might expect the appearance of printed editions of the verse of a particular author to have established the texts that were read, the lines of manuscript transmission, in the cases of such poets as Donne and Herrick, retained variant versions of their work (as though the printed texts had no especial authority, or, more to the point, as

---

poetical miscellanies, editions subsequent to a first one of printed work were usually more textually corrupt (*A Poetical Rhapsody, 1602–1621*, ed. Hyder Edward Rollins, 2 vols. [Cambridge, Mass.: Harvard Univ. Press 1931], 2:77–78).

[35] For the former, see Katherine K. Gottschalk, "Discoveries concerning British Library MS. Harley 6910," *Modern Philology* 77 (1979–80): 121–31; the latter manuscript is entitled "Collections out of seuerall Authors by Marmaduke Rauden Eboriencis 1662 Hodsden."

[36] For example, Folger MS. V.a.103, an anthology begun early in the Caroline era, arranges poems under the following headings: "Epitaphs Laudatory," "Epitaphs Merry and Satyricall," "Love Sonnets," "Panegyricks," "Satyrs," and "Miscellanea."

[37] See Gottschalk, 125.

though the issue of authoritative texts meant little). In fact, a certain casual attitude about the accuracy of texts carried over from the system of manuscript transmission into print culture. Few authors corrected proofs of their works, and a writer like Jonson, who carefully monitored the printing of his texts, was the exception rather than the rule. King James, for example, wrote in the preface to *His Maiesties poetical exercises at vacant houres* (1591) that he didn't have time to correct the copyist's errors.[38] As interesting cases of mixing media, there are some surviving examples of the gathering of manuscript and printed texts in the same bound volume.[39]

If we look at the manuscript and printed miscellanies of the Tudor era, there are interesting connections between some of them as collections of verse. Some printed texts are transpositions of manuscript miscellanies into typographic form: Tottel's *Miscellany* strongly resembles those sections of the Arundel-Harington manuscript contemporaneously transcribed under the direction of John Harington of Stepney,[40] and *The Paradise of Dainty Devices* is based on the commonplace book of Richard Edwards.[41] Conversely, some personal anthologies show a high degree of "editorial" sophistication and care. Literary connoisseurship developed within both manuscript culture and print culture simultaneously, each influenced by the other.

Many individual poems, in their own time, existed in both manu-

---

[38] He remarks: "... being of riper years, my burden is so great and continuall, without anie intermission, that when my ingyne and age could, my affaires and fasherie will not permit mee, to re-mark the wrong orthography committed by the copiars of my unlegible and ragged hand, far les to amend my proper errours" (*The Poems of James VI. of Scotland*, ed. James Craigie [Edinburgh: Blackwood, 1955], 1:98).

[39] Bod. MS. Eng. Poet. f.10 includes printed pages—for example, after fol. 5v, the title page of a book printed at Oxford and, after fol. 54, a printed table of all the English kings through Charles I; conversely, there is a volume in the British Library in which several poetical pamphlets are collected, followed by 16 folios on which are transcribed 35 poems, 34 numbered after the first: BL Dept. of Printed Books C.39.A.37, containing *Publii Ovidii Nasonis De arte amandi or The Art of Love* (Amsterdam, n.d.); *The Rape of Lucrece. by M^r. William Shakespeare* (London, 1624); *The Scourge of Venus: or the Wanton Lady. With the Rare Birth of "Adonis ... by H.A."* (London, 1614); *Alcilia. Philoparthens louing folly. Wherunto is added "Pigmalions" Image: with The Loue of "Amos" and "Laura"* (London, 1619); and *The First and Second part of "The Remedy of Loue: Written by Sir Thomas Overbury Knight"* (London, 1620).

[40] See Hughey, 1:66.

[41] See *The Paradise of Dainty Devices, 1576–1606*, ed. Hyder E. Rollins (Cambridge, Mass.: Harvard Univ. Press, 1927), xiii.

script and printed collections: in some cases publishers only reproduced one form of a text that continued to be changed and rewritten in a still vital manuscript tradition, no one version assuming primacy. Edward Dyer's poem "The lowest trees have tops" is one such example. Not only did verbal changes continue to appear in the various versions, but transcribers and competitors also felt compelled to compose answers and, in at least one case, a supplement to it. Although it was published anonymously in Francis Davison's *A Poetical Rhapsody* (1602), and in John Dowland's *Third and Last Booke of Songs or Airs* (1603), in the absence of those minimal controls that would have been exercised by the contemporary publication of this author's collected verse, the poem proliferated in manuscript, accumulating variants textual scholars regard as "corruptions" of an unavailable original text that the two printed versions are assumed to approximate. In Davison's volume, the last Elizabethan poetical anthology, the lyric appears as follows:

> The lowest Trees haue tops, the Ante her gall,
> The flie her splene, the little sparkes their heate:
> The slender haires cast shadowes, though but small,
> And Bees haue stings, although they be not great:
> Seas haue their sourse, & so haue shallow springs,
> And loue is loue, in Beggars, as in Kings.
>
> Where riuers smoothest run, deepe are the foords,
> The Diall stirres, yet none perceiues it mooue:
> The firmest faith is in the fewest wordes,
> The Turtles cannot sing, and yet they loue:
> True Hartes haue eyes, & eares, no tongs to speake,
> They heare, & see, and sigh, and then they breake.

> *Incerto*[42]

Since the poem, as Rollins observed, "is made up almost entirely of proverbs and commonplaces,"[43] there were unusual pressures at work in manuscript transmission to change features of the text as transcribers easily confused the lines of the lyric with their own store of familiar sayings. Add to this the possibility of changes introduced by the practice

---

[42] Changing only the long ſ, I reproduce Rollins' conservative text (*Poetical Rhapsody*, 1:186).

[43] *Poetical Rhapsody*, 2:168.

of memorial transcription[44] and you have an extreme case of textual malleability.

Variations found in the twenty manuscript and three printed versions of this poem include the transposition of the two stanzas (BL MS. Harl. 6910), the insertion of an additional stanza in the middle (Folger MS. V.a.162; Bod. MS. Malone 19; Bod. MS. Tanner 169), and the addition of an eight-line supplement written by someone Ruth Hughey suggests "was making use of the poem for personal reasons."[45] Verbal variations include what look like misreadings of a transcribed source text—e.g., "course" for "source" and "hollowes" for "shallowes" in line 5—as well as misremembered words or phrases possibly occurring in the process of memorial transcription—e.g., "smallest" for "lowest" and "shrubs" for "trees" in line 1, "riuers" for "waters" and "floods" for "fordes" in line 7, and "fairest" for "firmest," "loue" for "fayth," and "clearest" or "sweetest" for "fewest" in line 9.[46] While it might be an editor's nightmare, this poem should be a cultural historian's delight—in its intertextual complexity and socioliterary vicissitudes, it is a collaborative social production, as open a text as one could imagine.

There are other examples one could cite of poems that existed simultaneously in the two systems of literary transmission in as interestingly varied forms—such as Ralegh's "The Lie," a work whose publication in the second edition of *A Poetical Rhapsody* (1608) did not halt the process by which the text continued to change and develop.[47] But inevitably such fruitful textual malleability was drastically reduced as print culture grew stronger and more authors, like Jonson, Herrick, and Pope, grew fussy about the form their texts took in print. Despite the sloppy editorial practices, compositorial inconsistencies, and poor proof-reading that characterized the print industry, texts were bound to be stabilized as objects within the literary institution embodied in print culture. But this process took place very slowly and not without the loss of some of those

---

[44] See J. B. Leishman, " 'You Meaner Beauties of the Night,' A Study in Transmission and Transmogrification," *The Library*, 4th ser., 26 (1945): 99–101.

[45] 2:308.

[46] See the textual variants printed in Rollins, *Poetical Rhapsody*, 2:164–67, Hughey, 2:307–8, and *Lyrics from English Airs, 1596–1622*, ed. Edward Doughtie (Cambridge, Mass.: Harvard Univ. Press, 1970), 520.

[47] See Rollins, *Poetical Rhapsody*, 2:218–21, and *The Poems of Sir Walter Ralegh*, ed. Agnes M. C. Latham (1951; repr. Cambridge, Mass.: Harvard Univ. Press, 1962), 128–38.

valuable marks of human intervention that manifested themselves so clearly in the old environment of manuscript transmission.

WAYNE STATE UNIVERSITY

Jonson's Authorization of Type in Sejanus and Other Early Quartos

JOHN JOWETT

TEXTUAL CRITICS STUDY THE INKED IMPRESSIONS OF TYPE faces upon paper as part of their investigations into the transmission of particular texts. Typography therefore has a specialized capacity to signify; it frequently discloses the subtle signatures of print workers, stories of disaster, setback, delays, difficulties overcome—the daily odyssey of book production. Any signs of compositorial activity, miscalculations in casting off, censorship, forced insertions, and the like that are obvious to the more casual reader are shortfalls against an ideal of perfection and invisibility. Book producers routinely aspired to meet this ideal or something like it; it is only the latter-day textual critic, with his or her sophisticated instruments of reading and specialized discourse, who is able to interpret these obscure aspects of typographical signification.

I am interested here in other kinds of typographical signals, those that are marked with intentionality and perceptible to the non-specializing reader. Through them, specific editions act as unique mediations between an author and historically defined groups of readers. It usually falls to the publisher or editor to take up and modify the work's history of reception. When Hugh Perry, original publisher of Henry Chettle's *Tragedy of Hoffman*, gave the play to the reading public in 1631, he

described it as "without a father to own it." In Perry's suggestive extension of the usual metaphor, the unregenerate stage work underwent a
"new birth," whereby the publisher himself brought it, after its passage
over the stage "with good applause," into the world of "arts and learning." By 1631 the author could be absent by default—not, as in earlier
printed drama, by convention. Performability was the virtue advertised
on the title pages of plays printed in the 1560s and 70s; the text's origins
lay in stage enactment; the author's function was redundant and his
person usually unnamed. For a distinct contrast we must turn to plays
announced as translations: the Englished Seneca of John Studley and
Thomas Newton, both proclaimed as Cambridge students, or Gascoigne's translations presented to the students of Gray's Inn. Translators
merited naming; their workplace could be identified with the study, for
the texts' origins and verbal integrity mattered.

A symptomatic change came in 1594, when Lodge, Greene, Marlowe, and Nashe burst onto the title pages. They were all university wits.
But Jonson's first published play, *Every Man Out of His Humour* (published in 1600), stands apart from all previously printed drama. This is
appropriate, for the play is itself a kind of personal manifesto, and, moreover, a theorized stage work alienated from its audience by the "Grex."
The title page proclaims the writer with an emphasis such that his
presence is felt as the very hand behind the usually neutral and anonymous wording; "The Comical Satire of EVERY MAN OUT OF HIS
HUMOUR. *AS IT WAS FIRST COMPOSED* by the AUTHOR B.
J. *Containing more than hath been Publicly Spoken or Acted*. With the several
Character of every Person. *Non aliena meo presi pede / si proprius stes / Te
capient magus / & decies repetita placebunt*." As the child is father of man,
the text brings forth its author. "B. J." tumbles onto the title page be-
gotten in a tautology: "composed by the author"; neither term had previously been seen on the title page of a play. In the Horatian motto
Jonson even manages, by the sleight of hand of quotation, to insert the
first-person pronoun, "meo," into the title page's traditionally third-
person space. And so, even though it does not belong to the same fiction
as the play, the very title page becomes textual in the particular sense of
being subjected to an author function.

Jonson suggests on this title page that the play was cut for performance and/or revised and expanded for publication. It was always a selling
point to advertise theatrical "new additions," but the gambit of offering
a *non*-theatrical text is peculiarly Jonsonian. He will do the same, with
renewed emphasis, in bringing *Sejanus* into print. His programmatic ele-

vation of public plays into authored works, beginning with his very first printed text, involves a forceful declaration of the author's interest in the typography. Except in the cases of *Every Man In His Humour*, which was brought to the press by the theater company, and the collaborative *Eastward Ho!*, his hands are on the very forceps that give the text new birth. Jonson has appropriated functions of the stationer and printer, harnessing for himself the work of the compositor to establish the equivalent of a house style and standard which bear his own distinctive hallmark— or, to sustain the obstetrical metaphor, birthmark.

As he scorns the common auditors, Jonson often implies that they miss a predetermined meaning. But his very efforts to preserve this meaning intact take him along diverging paths towards stage platform and stationer's shop. Ironically, he becomes committed to highly specific and diversified manifestations of the text. That fixed and stable entity, the "underlying" text, is each time marked by its absence. In this situation the performance text can have no theoretical priority over the printed book: each is a distinct phenomenon emerging from that center whose presence is deferred because it is, as a text, incomplete. The antipolysemous printed text has to admit that it too is supplemented and different. And the book itself cannot be regarded as a neutral framework for an embodied text which arrives in it from elsewhere, for it has itself been textualized. Details of orthography, typography, and page design are ostentatiously presented to be noticed and "read." Jonson makes the books overtly "printerly"; the type becomes (so to speak) a token.

Jonson's idiosyncrasy in matters of spelling and punctuation is apparent from the beginning. His punctuation, of course, responds to nuances of meaning, and as such works upon the text so as to stabilize its interpretation. However, it does not aim at the modern ideal whereby the pointing is most successful where it is least noticed. It is precisely noticeable and "printerly." Similar considerations apply to the spelling, which, in that it is regularized, tends to consolidate word boundaries and the semantic units they enclose, but by its inclusion of distinctive and pseudo-classical forms, becomes another element in the page's typological presence.

What later became Jonson's highly characteristic use of classically "massed" stage directions and, in more restricted circumstances, marginal annotation, was not characteristic of the four quartos published in 1600– 1601. Marginal notes are used sparingly in *Poetaster* (published 1602), though less freely than in the Folio text where stage directions are printed marginally. The formality of the 1600–1602 quartos lies in the conspicuous Roman type used to mark acts and scenes. In the plays of classical setting, *Poetaster* and *Cynthia's Revels*, "Enter" is omitted from entries; in the latter text the names are separated with stops rather than commas.

It is no accident that *Poetaster*, Jonson's first play set in the reign of Tiberius, should anticipate *Sejanus* (published 1605) in using annotations in the printed text. In each case the turn away from the semblance of acted drama converges with the text's validation in classical works. In validating the work within history, the marginal notes also question its mimetic operation: in what way does a representation of ancient Rome represent aspects of the world as Jonson and his readers knew it? Whereas a total denial of any correspondence would leave the work pointless, Jonson must deny any one-to-one equivalence between characters or situations to avoid the accusation of slander. As Envy says in the prologue to *Poetaster*, "I am prevented; all my hopes are crossed, / Checked, and abated ... Rome! Rome! O my vexed soul! / How might I enforce this to the present state?" The immediate humor is at the expense of Envy, Rome and the present state being given as different; but contextually the lines make the audience expect a correspondence, provokingly uncertain in extent yet certain in its presence.

Both plays got their author in trouble with the authorities; both quartos include in their authorial texts statements that the plays were taken as defamatory and that the published text has required alteration. In *Poetaster* Jonson claims to have been "restrained ... by authority" from printing his Apology from the Author; in *Sejanus* Jonson blames the marginal notes themselves on "those common torturers that bring all wit to the rack" and have enforced him to show his "integrity in the story." In each case the ground is more discreetly negotiated in the 1616 Folio. The begrudging afterword to *Poetaster* has been replaced by the dramatic epilogue in which Jonson famously explains his technique as "To spare the persons, and to speak the vices"; in *Sejanus* the marginal notes and the explanatory address "To the Reader" have been dropped—along with much of the commendatory verse and the Quarto's defensive but implausible addendum to the Argument, in which, as we shall see, the person of the king requires a special sparing.

What Jonson presents to his reader in the Quarto of *Sejanus* is far from a typical play-text with a border of annotation. I have already mentioned the establishment of "neoclassical" entries and scene divisions in earlier Jonson quartos; *Sejanus* is the first to develop them to a consistently and even exaggeratedly austere classicism, and the first to print all the character names at the head of scenes in capitals (the effect can be seen in Illustration 1). It is by far the most extreme in its quantities of prefatory matter, its inscriptional effects, and its excessively formalized orthography. The physical make-up of the book consistently interferes between text and reader, to the extent that the book may be seen as a "greater" text, itself layered, which holds, qualifies, or quotes the "inner." And the address "To the Reader" in the "outer" text asserts that the "inner" text itself has been revised and so sets at an obscure distance the original collaborative work that was performed on stage.

Repression of the stage play is just one part of a larger endeavor to intensify and narrow the reader's response to the "inner" text. Accusations of mere eccentricity will be tempered when the dangers of Jonson's situation are taken into account. The stage play had been regarded, not surprisingly, as a subversive work. According to Drummond, Jonson had been called before the Privy Council to answer charges relating to it and to his Catholicism. Jonson's Catholic background came to official attention once again as a consequence of the Gunpowder Plot: in November of 1605 (the year *Sejanus* was published) the Privy Council commissioned him as a minor government spy against those associated with the conspiracy. Earlier in the year he had spent time in prison, not for his religious beliefs but for his part in the anti-Scottish *Eastward Ho!*. Though already established as the Court's leading writer of masques, Jonson was besieged with danger and no doubt crossed with conflicting loyalties. Hence, presumably, the admonition printed after the Argument:

> This do we advance as a mark of terror to all traitors and treasons; to show how just the heavens are in pouring and thundering down a weighty vengeance on their unnatural intents, even to the worst princes; much more to those for guard of whose piety and virtue the angels are in continual watch, and God himself miraculous working.

This is not a convincing account of the play. In its substance alone it sits very uneasily below the Argument. The appearance of the printed page indicates, whether accurately or fictively, that the coda was added on the spur of the moment after the book's layout had been determined. I am suggesting a convergence between the apparently prior requirement to add extra material—here the coda I quoted above—and Jonson's use of overtly reshaped page layout as a literary and even socio-political polemic in its own right. Whereas the seven-line coda is printed in pica type, the thirty-one lines of the Argument proper appear in much smaller long-primer. The Argument is thus in a smaller typeface than any other part of the book except for the marginal notes themselves. This gives the impression that the type size of the Argument has been reduced specifically to fit the coda on the same page. A simple calculation proves that this is logistically plausible. If the Argument without the coda had been set in pica, it would have comfortably fitted the single page. My concern here is to note, not a sequence of events as such, but that the visible impression of such a sequence is given. The page layout signals it, whether fictively or not. It clearly bespeaks authorial anxiety, though whether this anxiety was a biographical occurrence is again beyond the horizon of my study.

The marginal notes to *Sejanus* are another deeply ambiguous denial of any intention towards political satire. Their typographical appearance as a distinct block of print seemingly defends the matter within (again, see Illustration 1). The type on the page gives a physical representation of the way the notes metaphorically frame the play and offer a mediation between it and the reader. The dramatic work has entered a new literary environment which is expressed in type through the conventions of page layout. Compared with the more usual play quarto, in which the distribution of space on the page still owes something to the layout of the theatrical manuscript, the shape of type-masses on the *Sejanus* page has been fundamentally altered. The theatrical manuscript's four vertical columns have to be squeezed to fit the page size of the normative quarto: the speech-prefix column is replaced by indents from the left-hand margin, and the fourth column, extending right from the end of verse-lines, is considerably reduced, so that long verse-lines reach or even overflow the right-hand margin. That play quarto remains visibly variegated between verse and prose; the speech units are distinctly marked off from each other; stage directions in italic type are interspersed through the dialogue with relative frequency; and white spaces intrude from both left and right margins to break the text into units of dramatic articulation. None of this is true of *Sejanus*. Prose is reserved for special inscriptional effects; theatrical stage directions are not to be found; new speeches are not indented; and the verse-line, where split between speakers, is printed on a single type-line, preserving the metrical unit at the expense of the theatrical speech unit. The flanking notes confine the dramatic text to a particularly narrow column; the play is presented as an elongated but solid and relatively unbroken oblong of type. The layout is again a polemic in its own right.

SEIANVS.

ACTVS PRIMVS.

SABINVS. SILIVS. NATTA. LATIARIS. CORDVS.
SATRIVS. ARRVNTIVS. EVDEMVS.
HATERIVS. &c.

SAB. HAile [a] *Caius Silius*. SIL. [b] *Titius Sabinus*, Hayle.
Yo'are rarely met in Court! SAB. Therfore, well met.
SIL. 'Tis true : Indeed, this Place is not our Sphære.
SAB. No *Silius*, we are no good Inginers;
We want the fine Artes, and their thriuing vse
Should make vs grac'd, or fauor'd of the Times :
We haue no shift of Faces, no cleft Tongues,
No soft, and glutinous bodies, that can sticke,
Like Snailes, on painted walls; or, on our brests,
Creepe vp, to fall, from that proud height, to which
We did by [c] slauerie, not by seruice, clime.
We are no guilty men, and then no Great;
We haue nor place in Court, Office in state,
That we [d] can say, we owe vnto our Crimes;
We burne with no [e] black secrets, which can make
Vs deare to the pale Authors; or liue fear'd
Of their still waking iealosies, to raise
Our selues a Fortune, by subuerting theirs.
We stand not in the lines, that do aduance
To that so courted point. SIL. But yonder leane
A paire that doe. (SAB. Good Cossen [f] *Latiaris*.)
SIL. [g] *Satrius Secundus*, and [h] *Pinnarius Natta*,
The great *Seianus* Clients; There be two,
Know more, then honest Councells : whose close brests
Were they rip'd vp to light, it would be found
A poore, and idle sinne, to which their Trunkes
Had not bene made fit Organs : These can lie,
Flatter, and sweare, forsweare, depraue, [i] informe,
Smile, and betray; make guilty men; then beg

B   The

[a] *De Caio*
Silio. vid.
Tacit. Lipſ.
edit. 4°.
Anna. lib. I.
pag. 1. *lib.*
pag. 28.
& 33.
[b] *De Titio*
Sabino. vid
Tac. lib. 4.
pag. 79.
[c] *Tac. An-*
nal. lib I.
pag. 2.
[d] *Iuuenal.*
Sat. I, *ver.*
75.
[e] *Et Sat.* 3.
ver. 49. *&c.*
[f] *De Latia-*
ri, cõſ. Tac.
Annal. lib. 4
pag. 94. *&*
Dicn. Step.
edit. fol. lib.
58, *pag.*
711.
[g] *De Satrio*
Secundo, &
[h] *Pinnario*
Natta.
Leg Ta-
cit. Annal.
lib. 4. *pag.*
83.
Et de Sa-
trio, conſ.
Senec. cõ-
ſol, ad Mar-
ciam.
[i] *Vid. Sen.*
de Benef.
lib. 3 *cap.*
26.

Signature B1r, Ben Jonson's *Sejanus His Fall* (1605),
(reproduced by permission of the Folger Shakespeare Library).

A third example of textually significant layout may be found on sigs. K3v–4, where the play represents Sejanus' ritual appeal to the goddess Fortune for oracular knowledge of his future. One may suspect that the sententia marked immediately before the entry on K3v and the exceptional mid-scene entry itself are just two initial excuses for the kind of typographical display in which these pages freely indulge (see Illustration 2). A tendency that runs right through the Quarto here becomes acute: the sacrifice of textual clarity in favor of typographic virtuosity. In, for instance, the first type-line of K4, type in capitals puzzlingly invades the dialogue, undercutting the formal distinction between dialogue and speech prefix. In the second line the speech is printed in italic. What distinction is being made between capitals and lower case, or between either and italic? Do these different type-styles denote varying degrees of textual authority? Perhaps arbitrarily, the impression is given of different strata of text citing or expanding upon each other. In the third type-line after the entry on K3v, the stage direction (here a misleading term) is similarly split into two distinct levels: a presumptively archaic "TUB. TIB." in capitals as if to replicate an inscriptional source, and the glossarial explanation on the same line, in lower case with conventional capital initials, "These sound, while the *Flamen* washeth." This gloss in turn receives extensive comment in a marginal note labeled "d." The formula is repeated, but more expansively and intelligibly, on the opposite page (see Illustration 2). What we witness here is not a record of dramatic action. The original ritual is itself re-enacted, so to speak, not on the stage but in typography. Jonson's annotations, nowhere more excessive, can be seen, as always, to validate facts, but more particularly they here endorse the ceremonial decorum of the events they gesturally enclose. It can be no accident that it is precisely when ordinary dialogue is suspended that the marginal notes make their repeated incursions into the space of the play text. They become a customary vessel in which the ritual is physically, typographically, held. All this will be scandalously emptied when Sejanus, calling religion a blind mistress or a juggling mystery, throws the priest's wares scorned on the earth. Italicization of "blind mistress," "mystery," and "religion" picks out the dangerous juggling with words. A maze of possibilities stands between this moment and Jonson's interrogation on his *Sejanus* and his papistry.

Later in Act 5 the device of Tiberius' letter to the Senate, on which the play's dénouement hangs, is another occasion for some extravagantly formal inscriptional effects (see Illustration 3). Though for dramatic purposes the contents of the letter exist only in speech, Jonson seizes on the

SEIANVS.

PRAE. ᵃFAVOR IT WITH YOVR TONGVES.
MIN. *Be prefent, and propitious to our vowes.*

cœtus à præconibus fauere iubebatur. id eft bona verba fari. Talis enim altera huius for-mulæ interpretatio apud Briff. lib. 1.ex:at. Oui. lib. 1. Faft. Linguis animifq; fauete. Et Metam.lib.15.—piumque AEneadæ præftant & mente, & voce fauorem.

ᵃ *Quibus, in claufu, populus vel*

TVBICINES. TIBICINES.

While they found againe, the *Flamen* ᵇ takes of the Honey, with his finger, and tafts ; then minifters to all the reft : fo of the ᶜ Milke, in an earthen veffell, he deales about; which done he fprinkleth, vpon the Altar, Milke ; then impofeth the Ho-ney; and kindleth his Gummes, and after cenfing about the Altar, placeth his Cenfer thereon , into which they ᵈ put fe-uerall branches of Poppy , and the mufique ceafing , fay all,

ᵇ *Vocaba-tur hic Ri-tus Libatio. lege. Rofin. Ant.lib.3. Bar. Briffo. de form.lib. 1. Stuchi-um. de Sa-*

ᵉ *Accept our Offring, and be plea'd great* Goddeffe.

crif. Ft Lil. Synt 17. ᶜ *Jn facris Fortunæ lacte , non vino libabant.* ijfdem Teft. *Talia facrificia ᵃbiva, & vᵣφᴅᴅια dicta. Hoc eft fobria, & vino carentia.* ᵈ *Hoc reddere erat, & litare, id eft propiziare, & votum impetrare : fecundum* Nonium Marcellum. *Litare etiam* Mac. *lib.3. cap. 5. explicat, facrificio facto placare numen. In quo fenf. leg. apud* Plaut. Suet. Senec. &c. ᵉ *Solennis formula, in donis cuius numini offerrendis.*

TER. See, fee, the Image ftirres. SAT. And turnes away.
NAT. *Fortune* ᶠ auerts her face. FLA Auert you *Gods*
The prodigie. Still ! ftill ! Some pious Rite
We haue neglected . Yet ! Heau'n be appeaf'd.
And be all tokens falfe, or void, that fpeake
Thy prefent wrath. SEI. Be thou dumbe, fcrupu'lous Prieft:
And gather vp thy felfe, with thefe thy wares,
Which I, in fpight of thy *blind Miftreffe*, or
Thy iugling *myftery, Religion*, throw
Thus, fcorned on the earth. Nay, hold thy looke
Auerted, till I woe thee turne againe;
And thou fhalt ftand, to all pofterity,
Th'eternall game, and laughter, with thy neck
Writh'd to thy taile, like a ridiculous Cat:

ᶠ Leg. Dio. Rom Hift. lib. 58. pag. 717. de hoc facrificio.

Auoid

Signature K4r, Ben Jonson's *Sejanus His Fall* (1605),
(reproduced by permission of the Folger Shakespeare Library).

SEIANVS.

San. I, and get more. Lat. More Office, and more Titles.　*Dio. ibid.*]
Pom. I will not loofe the part, I hope to fhare
In thefe his Fortunes, for my *Patrimony.*
Lat. See how *Arruntius* fits, and *Lepidus.*
Tri. Let 'hem alone, they will be markt anone.
Sen. Ile doe, with others. Sen. So will I. Sen. And I.
Men grow not in the State, but as they are planted
Warme in his fauors. Cot. Noble *Seianus.*
Hat. Honor'd *Seianus.* Lat. Worthy and great *Seianus.*
Arr. Gods! how the Spunges open, and take in!
And fhut againe! Looke, looke! Is not he bleft
That gets a feate in eye-reach of him? more,
That comes in eare, or tongue-reach? O but moft,
Can claw his fubtle elbow, or with a buzze
Flieblow his eares. Praet. Proclaime the *Senates* peace;
And giue laft fummons by the Edict. Prae. Silence.
In name of Caesar, and the Senate. Silence.

aMEMMIVS REGVLVS. and. FVLCINIVS.　*a Vid. Brif-*
TRIO. CONSVL'S. THESE. PRESENT. KALENDES. OF. IVNE. VVITH.　*fonium : de*
THE. FIRST. LIGHT. SHALL. HOLD. A. SENATE. IN. THE. TEMPLE.　*formul.*
OF. bAPOLLO. PALATINE. ALL. THAT. ARE. FATHERS. AND.　*lib.2.* *Et Lipfiun*
ARE. REGISTRED. FATHERS. THAT. HAVE. RIGHT. OF. ENTRING.　*Sat.Menip.*
THE. SENATE. VVE. VVARNE. OR. COMMAVND. YOV. BE. FREQVENT-　*b Palatinus,*
LY. PRESENT. TAKE. KNOVVLEDGE. THE. BVSINESSE. IS. THE. COM-　*à monte*
MON. VVEALTHES. VVHOSOEVER. IS. ABSENT. HIS. FINE. OR. MVLCT.　*Palatino,*
VVILL. BE. TAKEN. HIS. EXCVSE. VVILL. NOT. BE. TAKEN.　*dictus.*

Tri. Note, who are abfent, and record their names.　*e Solemnis*
Reg. cFathers Conscript. may VVHAT I AM TO VTTER,　*praefatio*
Tvrne good and happy for the common VVealth.　*Confulum*
And thou Apollo, in whofe holy Houfe　*in relatie-*
We here are met, Infpire vs all, with truth,　*nibus.*
And liberty of Cenfure to our thought.　*Dio. pag.*
The Maieftie of great *Tiberius Cafar*　*718.*
Propounds to this graue *Senate*, the beftowing
Vpon the man he loues, honour'd *Seianus,*
The d *tribuniciall* dignity. and power;　*d Vid. Suet.*
Here are his Letters, figned with his fignet:　*Tib. cap.65*
　　　　M　　　　　　　　　　　　　　　　　What

Signature M1r, Ben Jonson's *Sejanus His Fall* (1605),
(reproduced by permission of the Folger Shakespeare Library).

medium of print in order to reproduce the letter's supposed graphic features in all their *Romanitas*: most notably its upper-case lettering and use of points to separate words. Here Jonson moves beyond the tabulation of sources, beyond the purely literary technique of modified implantation, to give, as it were, a type facsimile of a key document that has been incorporated into the text. There could be no clearer mandate to regard the text as an object whose physical attributes are themselves invested with textuality.

Elsewhere I have examined this strange and extraordinary quarto in the light of the play's oppositional qualities, the practical risks of publication, and the apparent contradictions in Jonson's ideological stances.[1] Another critical line of enquiry would be to describe the text as mannerist, as regards both its typographical features—its problematization of historical space in the physical space of page layout, its ostentatious stylization of classical effects—and its verbal features of tone, imagery, and structure. In either case the implications are far-reaching, and they emphasize the need for the reader of *Sejanus* to take into account the Quarto's typography. Needless to say, I am not satisfied by the common editorial position which regards the Quarto as superseded by the 1616 Folio text. I suspect, with Greg and Bowers, that an eclectic text should properly be Quarto-based, but the whole thrust of my argument is against an eclectic text in the first place. If we must prioritize one printing, which should it be? Each is of such high authority that the purely textual sense of that word ceases to be sole arbiter. But in the Folio, though it is essentially a modified reprint, the most distinctive features of the Quarto are weakened, abandoned, or dispersed. The Quarto is in various senses more textually significant; it is also more culturally significant, more Jonsonian, more interesting.

But if this is so, how is the Quarto to be assimilated by us and our contemporaries? One could go some distance with a modernized text supplemented by, say, ten photographic facsimiles of Quarto pages. It seems to me a serious mistake, however, to drive a wedge between a sanitized text, which has had forced on it the semblance of a typical Renaissance dramatic work, and the typography of the original edition. That typography would have become extraneous, even incompatible with the text as read. The photographs would be consigned to the role

---

[1] " 'Fall before this Booke': The 1605 Quarto of *Sejanus*," *TEXT* 4 (1988): 279–95.

of illustration; they would be redundant to most readings of the play. There is a problem here that is intrinsic to the medium of photography. If a page presents what is manifestly a photograph, it will always be perceived as an illustration of a distant object; it cannot actually *be* the text. This limitation even applies to complete photographic facsimiles on the lines of the Oxford Shakespeare Quartos. The economics of publishing run strongly in favor of such reproductions, but they can only supply an image for specialized use: even among textual critics they are commonly avoided as reading texts. Strictly speaking, the conflict between physical artifact and verbal text cannot be resolved. In the case of *Sejanus* the most practical solution is perhaps a type facsimile of the kind familiar in the publications of the Malone Society. Making a virtue of necessity, I suggest that the imprint of a type would be best represented in edited form by another independently originated type. Photography as a technology may certainly be exploited, but without producing that artifact we call a photograph; instead it will result in the black-and-white image which demands "read me."

I see no need to reproduce misprints and errors, or even to correct within the conservatism of Malone Society guidelines. It is in the nature of the task that extensive conflation with secondary texts will not take place, and in the nature of this particular text that extensive correction will not be necessary.

Jonson was editor of his own texts, and editorial treatment of his texts should do justice to him in that capacity as well as in the role of pure author. As I have suggested, the boundaries between these activities can prove illusory. No one showed a keener appreciation than Jonson that each textual manifestation, in performance or print, was a distinctly socialized entity. As the editor in turn addresses a specific audience, he or she should beware of silencing the textuality of Jonson's own editing.

UNIVERSITY OF GLASGOW

Reading Before the Lines: Typography, Iconography, and the Author in Milton's 1645 Frontispiece

GARY SPEAR

OR THE PURPOSES OF THIS ESSAY, I AM GOING TO EXPAND the definition of "typography" to mean not just the setting of type and the arrangement of printed materials, but the production of a finished text, which would sometimes include, in the seventeenth century, an engraved frontispiece depicting the author facing the title page of the work. The particular frontispiece in question is that found at the beginning of Milton's first published collection of poems, the 1645 volume entitled *Poems of Mr. John Milton, Both English and Latin*. My essay is an attempt to understand this engraving not as an ornament extraneous to the text as its position "before the lines" would place it, but rather as a textual place where the materiality of authority and authorial identity appear as the *effects of the material circumstances* of textual production. The repositioning of prefatory materials, elevating them from the status of ornament to the status of text, partakes of a desire to render typographical practices themselves crucial to our reinterpretation of such standard topics from literary history as the emergence of authorial identity and the monumentalizing of literary figures within a literary canon. Milton's image is of unique interest in this respect, since the engraving that figures forth the Messianic birth of a new prophetic, poetic presence images as well a powerful struggle over the nature of poetic authority. These tensions become particularly apparent when we realize that the frontispiece and title page operate to deconstruct the very poetic authority that it is their explicit purpose to represent. The engraving of Milton, the verse contributed by Milton to go under the engraving, and the claims of authorial identity posited by the printer on the title page all represent differing conceptions of the author. Typography and textuality converge in interesting ways even before we hear Milton's first vatic utterances in "The Nativity Ode," for the very questions that the frontispiece was commissioned to resolve, the question of "*who* is the author*,*" elides interestingly into another, more urgent question of identity: "*what* is an author?"[1] The visual representation of the author here, far from stabilizing his identity, provides us with a powerful emblem of the contradictory enterprise of constructing and contesting authorial identity.

This conflict represents on a very basic level of material practice the collaborative nature of literary production and the degree to which issues of authorship are bound up with typographical practices. This complicity is all but ignored by contemporary critics of Milton's first volume. Louis Martz's discussion of the frontispiece and the organizational strategy of the collection is fairly representative:

> Here is the picture of a youthful poet, free from adult cares, sometimes wandering along, amusing himself. . . . It is clear, from many indications, that Milton has designed his book with great care to create this impression. The entire volume strives to create a tribute to a youthful era now past—not only the poet's own youth, but a state of mind, a point of view, ways of writing, ways of living, an old culture and outlook now shattered by the pressures of maturity and by the actions of political man. Even the frontispiece, by William Marshall, attempts to set this theme.[2]

---

[1] The question "What is an Author?" necessarily invokes Foucault's classic essay of the same title collected in Josue V. Harari, ed., *Textual Strategies* (Ithaca: Cornell Univ. Press, 1979), 141–60, although this essay takes the question in a different direction by positing the essential, mediating functions of seventeenth-century print culture.

[2] Louis Martz, "The Rising Poet, 1645," in Joseph H. Summers, ed., *The Lyric and Dramatic Milton: Selected Papers from the English Institute* (New York: Columbia Univ. Press, 1965), 5.

Martz's formalist imperative compels him to see all of the features of the text including the frontispiece as related, coherent, whole. Underlying this is the figure of Milton the author as completely autonomous: "Milton designed his book with care." That Martz grants Milton a full sense of agency and hence of authority only highlights the extent to which material practices become subsumed beneath the conception of authorship required by conventional literary history. Even more recent revisionist accounts still operate with the same types of assumptions in place: the idea that the production of a public *persona* is an enterprise completely under the control of the author himself. Thus Richard Helgerson, in an important study of the problematics of poetic authority, sees the frontispiece as appearing because of Milton's tacit approval and, thus, representing Milton's "brazen" determination to grasp laureate status for himself.[3]

My point here is not that the conditions of textual production have hitherto gone unremarked upon. Numerous accounts present interesting, even tantalizing, possibilities, yet they all see the frontispiece as having largely ornamental, and hence secondarily critical, value. In the process of monumentalizing and reaffirming the canonical status of Milton, details of typography are often seen as extraneous to the greater issues of literary history and criticism. My argument in providing the typographical aspects of the text with a reading interrogates this sense of authorial autonomy and problematizes the question of an author's claim on his own literary property (especially urgent questions in an age before the protections of copyright), by seeing other types of authority granted and affirmed by the material and commercial relations of seventeenth-century print culture.

"Who is the author?" William Marshall's engraving provides us with one answer. Marshall himself was an important producer of literary identities, since he provided frontispieces for works by Donne, Jonson, Shirley, and later his most famous work, the engraving to *Eikon Basilike*, the alleged final words of Charles I published posthumously in 1649. His prestige endows Milton with courtly associations, and his representation secures those associations by depicting Milton in an academic gown and posed according to the stance in aristocratic portraiture as developed by Van Dyck at the court of Charles I. The courtly reinscription of pastoral

---

[3] Richard Helgerson, *Self-Crowned Laureates: Spenser, Jonson, Milton, and the Literary System* (Berkeley: Univ. of California Press, 1983), 254.

Frontispiece of Milton's 1645 *Poems*
(reproduced by permission of the Wesleyan University Library).

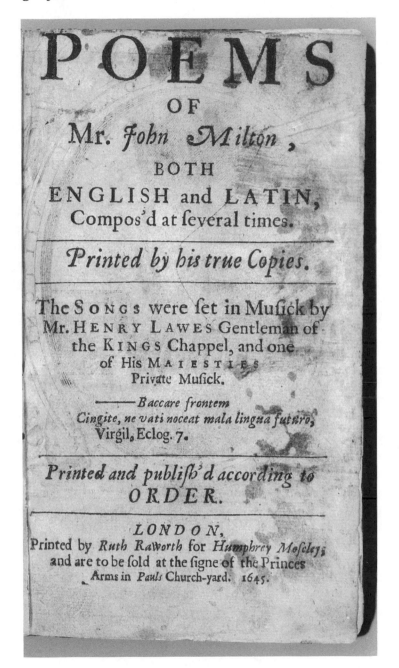

Title page of Milton's 1645 *Poems*
(reproduced by permission of the Wesleyan University Library).

life is alive in the background scene which depicts shepherds in their stylized, conventional activities of composing verse and debating. The image is enclosed by an oval frame which labels its subject as "John Milton, the English Author at the age of 21." The choice to represent Milton at the age of twenty-one (when in 1645, he was not twenty-one but thirty-one), relates the image of Milton to the date of the composition of the first poem in the collection, "On the Morning of Christ's Nativity," written in 1629. As others have noticed, this arrangement suggests the "birth" of a new prophetic voice by associating the "nativity" of the author through the "Nativity Ode" with the incarnation of Christ. The positioning of the figure before the draped window, the place of the hand in the folds of an academic gown, and the depiction of Milton in clothes ornamented with ruffs and lace all point to an image that Marshall was no doubt commissioned to create—the image of Milton as the last poet in a literary vogue, the Cavalier mode. Though few of the poems in this volume would substantiate this association, Marshall's "Milton" is a academic, courtly poet.

"Who is the author?" According to Humphrey Moseley, the stationer, Milton is the poetic heir to the popularity of the Royalist poet, Edmund Waller. Moseley writes: "But howsoever ther opinion is spent upon these, that incouragement I have already received for the most ingenious men in their clear and courteous entertainment of Mr. Wallers late choice Peeces, hath made me adventure into the world presenting it with these ever-green, and not to be blasted Laurels." "Laurels," one might add, that are prominent in Marshall's engravings of Jonson and Donne, but tellingly absent in his engraving of Milton. Waller's poems were nearly contemporaneous with Milton's first volume of poems and were a great commercial success (before Waller's implication in a Royalist plot against Parliament). While it might be unfair to see Moseley's flattery as governed solely by the desire for profit, his praise does seem strategic, and that strategy rests upon producing an "identity" for the burgeoning talent, one with particular commercial potential for an aristocratic, Royalist audience who might form a readership for Milton's verse. In a way, Milton had already constituted this readership when he remarked upon the excellence of his own unpublished poetry three years earlier in *The Reason of Church Government*, and vowed, perhaps too soon, to abandon the writing of poetry for the assumption of a career as a political writer.

The Greek epigram registers Milton's attempt to assert his own identity in this arena of authorial creation by disavowing the representation that serves as the "public entry" (a frontispiece was originally an architectural term for the façade of a building) to his work. His reasons for criticism are themselves something of a mystery. They could be as simple as the reasons Aubrey records in the *Brief Lives*—the portrait just does not look like Milton at the age of twenty-one. If Aubrey is reporting the truth, Milton was disturbed about this picture until the end of his life, being by nature preoccupied as he was by with his youthful beauty. But the Greek epigram points to a larger dilemma of representing authorial character. Milton so disapproved of the engraving that he had Moseley pass on to Marshall an epigram in Greek to be copied underneath his engraving. Since apparently neither Moseley nor Marshall could translate it, Marshall ended up merely copying the character of the epigram without realizing the critical thrust of the message. Translated, the epigram reads:

> Looking at the form of its original [i.e., at Milton], you might say, perhaps, that this likeness had been drawn by the hand of a novice artist, but friends, since you do not recognize what is depicted here, have a laugh at the caricature of an inept, no-talent scribbler.

The engraving foregrounds a problem of representation and authority. On one level, Milton is, of course, disputing the likeness of the engraving—with its crude features and bulbous nose—to its original subject. Yet, the implications of the epigram are much more important, for the Greek word "*dusmimeta*," literally, a "bad figure," translated above as "caricature," has a double meaning. It can mean "bad representation," or it can mean "that which is *difficult* to represent." Taken in this second sense, Milton's disputation strikes a much deeper chord by according his own literary productions as being a clearer likeness of the ineffable, indescribable essence of the "author." The epigram then operates as a strategic disavowal of the authority of "type" by diverting the reader's attention from the material conditions of typography to the poems themselves as places where authority and authorship are present.

The "reading" of a visual image takes us back into the textual questions of typography by raising questions that are brushed aside when typography is seen as the vulgar handmaiden to critical analysis. This representation of authorship in the 1645 *Poems* points to the larger issues of how cultural identity is constructed through the mediations of print culture. This discussion points in two directions that prefigure the actual literary experience of the poems themselves. First, it shows the extent to which public identity was not always within the author's control. Milton's texts, even at this early stage of his literary development, do not always anticipate their reception.

Second, it points to the ways in which authorial identity was in some fundamental ways a textual and cultural construct—an idea that allows us to approach the questions of typography and textuality as parts of an emerging literary and political marketplace.

WESLEYAN UNIVERSITY

The New Historicism and the Editing of English Renaissance Texts

THOMAS L. BERGER

WHEN I PROPOSED THIS SESSION TWO YEARS AGO, THE New Historicism could be said to be "new." That is no longer the case, but much of what the New Historicists have said and are saying remains provocative and fascinating. Much of what the New Historicists have said and are saying about contexts for literature applies directly to the tasks we undertake, or pretend to undertake, when we edit texts. Contexts of texts matter. They matter a whole lot.

I once met a woman who worked for *The New Yorker*. One of her tasks was to read each issue before it went to press. But she wasn't a proofreader. Rather, I guess you could call her a disaster reader. For example, she had to make sure that if on one page there was a touching poem about someone dying of cancer, there had better not be a particularly gruesome Charles Addams cartoon on the facing page. Similarly, Omaha Steaks advertisements were not to be placed in side columns next to stories about world hunger. Things like that. But suppose she failed, as indeed she tells me she did, often with hilarious and ghastly results. How are we to read that poem if the Addams cartoon is indeed present on the facing page? Do we read that poem differently when that poem appears in the author's *Collected Works*? I think we probably do.

Let me give you an instance or two a bit closer to home. In the preliminaries, the front matter, to Shakespeare's First Folio (1623), the title page announces that what is contained within are "Comedies, Histories, Tragedies," not "Works." "Works," after all, were what Ben Jonson called his collection of 1616, and he took a good deal of abuse for it:

> Pray tell me *Ben*, where doth the mystery lurke,
> What others call a play you call a worke.

The remainder of that preliminary material—the dedications, the address to the reader, the commendatory poems, even the table of contents—authorizes and legitimizes the volume, so much so that in the last leaf of the preliminaries, before the text "proper" begins, the "Comedies, Histories, and Tragedies" of the title page become for the first time "The Workes of William Shakespeare, containing all his Comedies, Histories, and Tragedies." The process of legitimization is complete. Shakespeare's plays have become, like Jonson's, "*Works.*" There is more. This final page also offers "The Names of the Principall Actors in all these Playes." Not only have the plays themselves become legitimized as "*Works*" but so too has the theater itself, with its "Principall Actors."

Charlton Hinman's facsimile of the folio (1968) is the tool I used to leaf through the preliminaries of the First Folio, and a marvelous tool it is. One of the many important things that Hinman gave us in the facsimile is his through line numbering system. Every play has its own through line numbering, and thus there now exists, as there never had before, a convenient system for referring specifically and accurately to a line, a word, or a piece of type in the text of the First Folio. Well, almost. Although each of the plays has its own through line numbers, in the preliminaries there is nary a line number to be found. As the front matter is not "text," quite literally, it does not count. The front matter, the material which authorizes and legitimizes the texts which follow, doesn't matter at all. It's not part of the "text."

Let me move on to two other pages of Hinman's most useful facsimile. At the end of *Measure for Measure* (102) are included "The Names of All the Actors." Here Lucio is called a "fantastique," as he is nowhere else in the play. The list is not lined in Hinman's facsimile; it is not, after all, text. Nor do the words describing the characters appear in Marvin Spevack's *Harvard Concordance* (1973). How can they? As they appear unlined in the *Riverside Shakespeare* (1974), they cannot be concorded. They do not exist. This seems a pity, especially when one considers that Lucio is very much onstage when Isabella says

> But man, proud man,
> Dress'd in little brief authority
> Most ignorant of what he's most assur'd—
> His glassy essence—like an angry ape
> Plays such fantastic tricks before high heaven
> As makes the angels weep; who, with our spleens,
> Would all themselves laugh mortal.
>
> (2.2.118–124)

"The Actors Names" at the end of Folio *2 Henry IV* (422) go un-lined by Hinman as well. Those names, and the descriptions following them, are cast into some sort of textual limbo. Poins, Falstaff, Pistol, Bardolph, Peto, and the Page are described as "Irregular Humourists," oxymoronic perhaps, but delightful. The word "humourist" does not, nay cannot, appear in the *Harvard Concordance*, for it is not part of the "text."

The speakers whose papers are printed below share my concerns about texts, about what texts can tell us, about editorial methodology and practice, and about the ways in which editors of texts often impose themselves most on the texts they edit when they intend not to impose themselves at all.

ST. LAWRENCE UNIVERSITY

What is a Work? What is a Document?

MARGRETA DE GRAZIA

THE DISTINCTION BETWEEN A WORK AND A DOCUMENT appears quite obvious. A work has an author, a document does not. A work is subject to critical interpretation, a document is not. A work is usually intended for publication, a document is not. A work is fictional, a document factual. The distinction between the two has been fundamental to disciplinary boundaries: literary studies deals with works; historical studies with documents. Even within literary studies itself, there has been a division of labor that depends upon it, especially during the approximately twenty-year period when formalist criticism prevailed: literary historians established background through documents while literary critics interpreted works.

It will be the claim of this paper that, in the area of Renaissance or Shakespeare studies at least, this distinction is approaching collapse. In the currently prevailing interpretive and editorial practices, the two are blurring into one another: works are becoming more like documents, documents more like works. Both have folded into the comprehensive terms of *texts* or *discourses* or *narratives*. This strikes me as a change worth noting, and I will begin to do so with a consideration of the essay that first made me aware of it: an essay written in 1808 by the Shakespearean editor still renowned for his work with documents: Edmund Malone. Malone indefatigably sought out documents, transcribed them, reproduced them (a few in the newly devised form of facsimile), glossed the plays with them, and was the first to write a documentary history of the stage and a documentary biography of Shakespeare.[1] His editions of Shakespeare (the ten volumes of his 1790 edition and the twenty-one of the 1821 edition completed by Boswell), served as archives in which the relevant documents were classified, stored, and preserved.[2]

In the essay "An Account of the Incidents from which The Title and Part of the Story of Shakespeare's Tempest Were Derived; and its True Date Ascertained," Malone was also the first to collect and discuss the documents pertaining to the Virginia Company's 1609 expedition to the New World, the accounts that have figured so prominently in recent New Historicist readings of the *Tempest*—readings, that is, that view colonialism as "the articulatory principle of [the play's] diversity."[3] What interested me about the essay was how Malone could possess the relevant historical documents and yet never consider the possibility that the play itself might also be involved in colonialist speculation.[4] (To ask this question of Malone was, of course, to ask the question of every subsequent reader of the play who, possessing the documents, basically ignored them.) Perhaps this was asking too much of Malone: locked in Enlightenment ideology from which imperialism drew so much of its justification, how could he anticipate the post-colonial position that allows us to see the play's embroilment in issues of power and oppression? How could someone who termed himself an "antiquarian" possibly be expected to hold a "New Historicist" point of view?

On the other hand, Malone does show himself astutely aware of the centrality of "the colonial projects that took place at this period" (388), "the subject of discourse" that could not but have caught Shakespeare's

---

[1] For Malone's extensive collection and use of documents, see Margreta de Grazia, *Shakespeare 'Verbatim': The Reproduction of Authenticity and the 1790 Apparatus* (Oxford: Oxford Univ. Press, 1990), chap. 3, "Situating Shakespeare in an Historical Period."

[2] *The Plays and Poems of William Shakespeare*, 10 vols. (1790; facs. repr. New York: AMS Press, 1968) and 21 vols. (1821; facs. repr. New York: AMS Press, 1966).

[3] Francis Barker and Peter Hulme, " 'Nymphs and reapers heavily vanish': The Discursive Con-texts of *The Tempest*," in *Alternative Shakespeares*, ed. John Drakakis (London and New York: Methuen, 1985), 191. Malone's essay, first published in 1808, was reprinted in vol. 15 of the 1821 *Plays and Poems*, 379–419.

[4] Malone lists ten other pamphlets published between 1609–12 besides Silas Jourdain's "A Discovery of the Bermudas, otherwise called the Isle of Divells" (1610) and William Strachey's "The Proceedings of the English Colonie in Virginia" (1612) and believes the list "far from being complete" (389–90).

attention, especially when his patron and dedicatee, Southampton, had himself supported an expedition to Virginia. "Men's thoughts indeed were then so strongly directed towards the new world, that the successes and miscarriages of the several adventurers who sent there could not but have been a very general topick of conversation" (388–89). His description of the accounts he identifies with Shakespeare's "archetype" (386) reveals his own consciousness of how crucial it was for the Virginia company to control information in order to keep investors interested. The circulation of "sundry false rumours, and despightful speeches" did "deterre and keepe backe the hands and helpe of many well-disposed men" (401); to counteract them, numerous pamphlets were published "to dissipate the gloom and despondency and to shew the practicability and probable advantages of settling a colony in Virginia" (409). Yet, for Malone, while the play had taken its name from the 1609 tempest off the Virginia coast that separated the governor's ship from the rest of the fleet and drove it to the island of Bermuda, and while it made numerous covert allusions to the 1609 expedition (the unexpected safety of the lost ship, the sailors' abandoning ship, qualities of the isle, and so forth), it remained entirely independent of the period's "colonial projects." For the play had transmuted the historical facts beyond recognition: "a single disastrous event" was "converted by the magical hand of Shakespeare almost into a Fairy Tale" (419). The literary work abided in a world of its own, resistant to the incursions of its topical source as documented by Jourdain's eyewitness and Strachey's authoritative pamphlets.

What Malone's essay demonstrates is how historical documentation can work to sequester the play from rather than involve it in historical process. In his essay, works remain separate from documents, literature from history; just as they do physically in his editions where the documents are confined to the prolegomena, appendices, and footnotes while the works belong to the contents proper; the works are emended, modernized, and annotated, while the documents are simply transcribed or in a few cases reproduced by facsimile. For Malone, the value of the historical discovery is that it enables him "to ascertain precisely the time of [the *Tempest*'s] composition" (396). Knowing the date of the seastorm and calculating the time when news of it would reach Shakespeare, he situates the play not in global history, but in Shakespeare's unique history, that is, the history of his artistic development, his chronology. Prior to his discovery of the pamphlets, Malone had attempted to date the only topical reference he had found in the play—Trinculo's observation that in England, "when they will not give a doit to relieve a lame beggar, they will lay out ten to see a dead Indian"—by seeking out records of when in Shakespeare's London a dead Indian had been exhibited.[5]

It is, I think, the collapse of this distinction between work and document that sets New Historicist readings into motion. The dramatic work can then be drawn into the same discursive fabric as the historical document, the performance of the King's Men with the transactions of the Virginia Company. In the chapter on the *Tempest* in his most recent book, Stephen Greenblatt ranges from Latimer's exemplum of a woman charged with murdering her own child, to an eyewitness report of a royal reprieve of several condemned conspirators, to the Virginia Company's account of the storm and its aftermath, before he reaches the *Tempest* itself, and then concludes with an entry about the Mowa tribesmen from H. M. Stanley's notebook: "I want to close with a story," he concludes.[6] Indeed hi*story* for Greenblatt is mainly comprised of stories, homologous stories that can be paratactically juxtaposed. No discrimination need be made between testimony, eyewitness account, official report, letter, play, journal entry: all qualify as social practices demonstrating the same strategy, in the case of the *Tempest* chapter, of "salutary anxiety": of bringing subjects to the point of anxiety and then releasing them through gratitude, obedience, and love. Each of the book's four major chapters begins with a record of some kind: with a "notorious police *report* of 1593," "an unusual *story*" Montaigne recorded in his travel journal, an *account* based on sworn statements of a series of exorcisms between the spring of 1585 and the summer of 1586, a *sermon* that "*tells of something* that happened many years before in Cambridge." The authenticity of the documents (a crucial consideration for Malone) is never at issue. No longer is it necessary to ask whether the accounts are factual or fictional, for all collapse into the intermediary category of the *anecdote*. What draws the stories, narratives, texts together is their subscription to the same taxonomy. They are uniformly cultural practices ("textual traces") through which the negotiation and exchange of what Greenblatt terms "social energy" has taken place (6). Though in his introduction he claims that literary representations are "more intense ...

---

[5] "An Attempt to Ascertain the Order in which The Plays of Shakspeare Were Written," *The Plays and Poems* (1790), 1:382, and "An Account," 387–88.

[6] *Shakespearean Negotiations: The Circulation of Social Energy in Renaissance England* (Berkeley and Los Angeles: Univ. of Calif. Press, 1988), 161.

than other textual traces left by the dead" (1), in practice he accords all narratives equal status as the objects of his discourse analysis.[7]

Turning now to textual criticism, the distinction between work and document has until recently been primary. In a series of recently published lectures, G. Thomas Tanselle has warned of "the failure to recognize at the outset the basic distinction between texts of works and texts of documents."[8] "The texts of verbal documents are not the texts of works" (70). Quite simply, a text of a work, unlike that of a document, does not exist in any concrete or physical form: it is an abstract linguistic entity that does not "exist in paper or in sounds" (19); in pure and unadulterated form it exists (or existed) only in the mind or intention of the author. The pieces of paper on which a work was scripted or printed "convey" the work but do not preserve it as they do documents. The work must be extracted from these vessel-like documents, reconstituted on the basis of the recorded evidence by the "active recreation" (42) of both editors and interpreters. The distinction mandates two different editorial activities: a document should be *reproduced* as accurately as possible by way of diplomatic text or facsimile transcription; a work, however, needs to be *reconstructed* by a critical edition, comprised of different documents, admitting the further alterations of a historically informed and critically sensitive editor.

The 1986 Oxford edition of Shakespeare throws into question Tanselle's traditional distinction between work and document by deciding to recover and present "the play as it appeared when performed" rather than what "Shakespeare originally wrote."[9] Once committed to the "texts of Shakespeare's plays as they were acted in the London playhouses" (xxxvii) rather than as they existed in Shakespeare's mind, the distinction cannot so easily be maintained. In theory, at least, the Oxford edition has admitted into the *Works* the theatrical interpolations that would have formerly been considered non-authorial playhouse documents. Such a policy allows for the inclusion of changes, additions, deletions originating not necessarily in Shakespeare's mind but possibly in

---

[7] See, however, Edward Pechter, who calls Greenblatt to task for effectively subordinating the literary text to social history, "The New Historicism and Its Discontents: Politicizing Renaissance Drama," *PMLA* 102 (May, 1987): 292–303.

[8] G. Thomas Tanselle, *A Rationale of Textual Criticism* (Philadelphia: Univ. of Pennsylvania Press, 1989), 35.

[9] *William Shakespeare: The Complete Works*, gen. eds. Stanley Wells and Gary Taylor (Oxford: Oxford Univ. Press, 1986), xxxiii.

theatrical practices: in the Master of Revels' expurgations, for example, another playwright's revisions, an actor's interjections, an excerpt from an earlier text. It is because the edition commits itself to the plays in performance that its editors can "draw more liberally than most previous editors on the reported texts," the so-called "bad quartos" that appear to be records of performances (documents) rather than transcripts of Shakespeare's intentions (works). An even more flagrant dissolution of Tanselle's work/document distinction is the Oxford edition's printing of two discrete *King Lears*: the 1608 Quarto *History* and the 1623 Folio *Tragedy*. Since the end of the eighteenth century (not coincidentally—since Malone's edition),[10] the quarto and Folio *Lears* had the status of documents that were conflated in order to produce the work Shakespeare had in mind. But with the Oxford edition, the two former documents are each raised to the status of works, independent entries in *The Complete Works*. After this precedent, is there anything in principle to prevent the texts of the five other multiple-text plays from dropping their documentary status and becoming works in their own right?

With these two examples, I hope to have suggested that New Historicist and New Textualist practices share an indifference to a distinction that was once basic. What makes this indifference all the more remarkable is its compatibility with formulations of a relatively new and burgeoning area of literary study, and one to which both approaches have been largely (though not universally) inimical: theory.[11] I am thinking of Roland Barthes' dissolution of Work into Text or of Paul de Man's insistence that appeals to disciplines outside literature (whether history, anthropology, linguistics, etc.) are simply appeals to other texts, that all analysis of cultural and historical forms is limited by the same impasses of textuality that function in formal literature: "The bases for historical knowledge are not empirical facts but written texts."[12] Such conflations

---

[10] Steven Urkowitz, " 'The Base Shall to th'Legitimate': The Growth of an Editorial Tradition," *The Division of the Kingdom: Shakespeare's Two Versions of 'King Lear'*, ed. Gary Taylor and Michael Warren (Oxford: Clarendon Press, 1983), 37–41.

[11] For a critique of New Historicism's theoretical reticence, see Jonathan Crewe, *Hidden Designs: The Critical Profession and Renaissance Literature* (New York and London: Methuen, 1986), 73–82. For a demonstration of textual criticism's mistrust of theory, see Lee Patterson, "The Logic of Textual Criticism and the Way of Genius," *Textual Criticism and Literary Interpretation*, ed. Jerome J. McGann (Chicago: Univ. of Chicago Press, 1985), 89.

[12] Roland Barthes, "The Death of the Author," in *Image, Music, Text*, trans. Stephen Heath (New York: Hill & Wang, 1977), 142–43. Paul de Man, *Blindness and*

of the rhetorical and empirical have come from historians as well as critics, from Hayden White, for example, and Natalie Davis, especially in her most recent book, whose very title could also apply to this paper: *Fiction in the Archives.*[13]

In post-structuralist theory, New Historicism, and New Textualism, the motive impelling the conflation of work and document seems to me the same. It is the recognition that a single authorial consciousness, however expansive and diversified, may not be sufficient to account for the complexity and anomalies of texts, perhaps Renaissance texts in particular. Both Greenblatt and the Oxford editors find it necessary to pluralize, complicate, and disperse the once unitary authorial source. In his introduction, Greenblatt, seeking an explanation for the enduring vitality of Shakespeare's plays, turns first to what he terms a confrontation between "a total artist and a totalizing society" (2) but then turns away from that postulated "numinous literary authority" (3) and its attendant formalist textual analysis to propose instead that "we begin by taking seriously the collective production of literary pleasure and interest" (4). The search for originary authorial creation is thus replaced with "a subtle elusive set of exchanges, a network of trades and trade-offs, a jostling of competing representations, a negotiation between joint-stock companies" (7). The corollary in textual studies to Greenblatt's "circulation of social energy" might be located in the Oxford edition's preference for theatrical prompt-book over authorial foul-papers: a preference for what it terms a "socialized" text over a "private" one.[14] Although, as has been pointed out, the edition is not always consistent in this preference, it would in theory include the changes undergone before and during production by hands other than Shakespeare's.[15] In both the preparation and

---

Insight: Essays in the Rhetoric of Contemporary Criticism, 2d ed. rev., *Theory and History of Literature,* (Minneapolis, 1983), 7:165.

[13] Hayden V. White, *Metahistory* (Baltimore: Johns Hopkins Univ. Press, 1973) and *Tropics of Discourse* (Baltimore: Johns Hopkins Univ. Press, 1978).

[14] This distinction is discussed in *William Shakespeare: A Textual Companion,* Stanley Wells and Gary Taylor, et al. (Oxford: Clarendon Press, 1987), 15–16. On the institutional practices and social determinants contributing to authorship, see Jerome J. McGann, *A Critique of Modern Textual Criticism,* 1985, and D. F. McKenzie, *Bibliography and the Sociology of Texts,* The Panizzi Lectures, 1985 (London: The British Library, 1986).

[15] Jonathan Goldberg, "The Commodity of Names: 'Falstaff' and 'Oldcastle' in *1 Henry IV,*" *Reconfiguring the Renaissance,* ed. Jonathan Crewe (*Bucknell Review* 35 [1992]: 76–88).

interpretation of Shakespeare's plays, then, the author is no longer the exclusive source of either the text itself or its hermeneutic possibilities.

As Michel Foucault has pointed out in his now canonical essay whose title "What is an Author?" is echoed by my own, we have no theory of the work.[16] Our notion of the work is dependent on our notion of authorship: the characteristics we assign to it are not intrinsic to a text, but rather are dependent on the interpretative operations dictated by our more or less psychologized and experiential understanding of authorship. I would like to propose that our notion of a document is similarly dependent on our notion of authorship: quite simply, a document is a non-authored text. As Foucault has also pointed out, the identification of the author figure with a sovereign generative but regulatory consciousness is an Enlightenment construction, the hermeneutic counterpart of "the sovereignty of the subject" as well as "the twin figures of anthropology and humanism" that preside over our organization of knowledge into disciplines.[17] I would like to propose that our definition of the document is also an Enlightenment product, as its pervasive presence in Malone's scholarship would suggest. Furthermore, I would like to propose that the work/document dichotomy is essential to protecting the aesthetic from the contingent, literature from history. By relegating history to Shakespeare's sources, by limiting its interventions to topical allusions, by keeping it in the background, Shakespeare studies protect Shakespeare from coming into contact with the historical contingency. As we have seen, Malone uses documents to fasten the work more tightly to the author rather than to put it in touch with history: he uses them to identify topical allusions that signal what historical event or personage Shakespeare had in mind; he uses them to determine dates of composition that enable him to arrange the works on a personal temporal trajectory that abstracts them altogether from the historical events they register.[18]

That the work/document distinction is no longer respected among some of our more prominent preparers and readers of Shakespeare

---

[16] *Textual Strategies*, ed. Josue V. Harari (Ithaca: Cornell Univ. Press, 1979), 143–44.

[17] *The Archaeology of Knowledge and The Discourse on Language*, trans. A. M. Sheridan (New York: Pantheon Books, 1972), 35.

[18] For a discussion on how chronology abstracted Shakespeare's "development" or "progress" from history, see de Grazia, *Shakespeare Verbatim*, chap. 4, "Individuating Shakespeare."

should not, I think, lead to the conclusion that all texts should be treated indiscriminately. On the contrary, what I hope my argument has suggested is the inadequacy of the dichotomies supporting the distinction: fiction/fact, subjective/objective, literary/historical are oppositions to which Renaissance textual materials cannot readily conform. This is not to say that all textual materials are the same, but rather that it cannot be assumed that an author lies behind works anymore than that the past lies behind documents. We may need, therefore, to formulate new questions to ask of its textual materials, questions more attentive to their extraordinary heterogeneity. It may be more appropriate now to query the relationships among their uses of language that cannot be restricted to the categories of the fictional and the factual.[19] The Enlightenment taxonomy upholding the illusion of authorial autonomy appears no longer to be serving our needs. Nor can it accommodate the anomalies and instabilities of sixteenth- and seventeenth-century textual materials.[20]

UNIVERSITY OF PENNSYLVANIA

---

[19] In his essay "Rethinking Intellectual History and Reading Texts," in *Rethinking Intellectual History: Texts Contexts Language* (Ithaca: Cornell Univ. Press, 1983), Dominick LaCapra suggests an approach to "worklike" and "documentary" materials that would break down the dichotomy in order to discriminate more finely among uses of language and their relation: "On the approach I am suggesting, [J. L. Austin's terms] the constative and the performative are best seen not as generic types or sets of speech acts ('realms of discourse') but as more or less pronounced aspects of speech acts (or texts) that may be conceptually elaborated into analytic distinctions, ideal types, or heuristic fictions" (30 n. 4).

[20] On the inapplicability of post-Enlightenment bibliographic method to the disuniformity of Elizabethan theatrical documents, see Marion Trousdale, "A Second Look at Critical Bibliography and the Acting of Plays," *Shakespeare Quarterly* 42 (Spring, 1990).

Manuscript, Print, and the English Renaissance Lyric

ARTHUR F. MAROTTI

I N CONSIDERING THE RELEVANCE OF THE NEW HISTORICISM TO textual editing (and to the broadly conceived field of bibliography), I was struck by the vigor and intelligence of the debate already underway among textual editors and bibliographers, who have been responding especially to the challenges posed by the work of such scholars as Jerome J. McGann and D. F. McKenzie.[1] McGann's expanded program for textual criticism and editing is one that includes analyses of "the original textual moment," "secondary moments of textual production and reproduction," and of the "immediate moment of textual criticism."[2] In editing, this entails the employment of sociocen-

---

[1] See, especially, McGann's *A Critique of Modern Textual Criticism* (Chicago and London: Univ. of Chicago Press, 1983) and *The Beauty of Inflections: Literary Investigations in Historical Method and Theory* (Oxford: Clarendon Press, 1985), Part II, "Textual Studies and Practical Criticism," 67–132, and D. F. McKenzie, *Bibliography and the Sociology of Texts*, The Panizzi Lectures, 1985 (London: The British Library, 1986). In his recent analysis of the relationship of textual and literary theory, D. C. Greetham has outlined some of the critical issues at stake between a traditional author-centered approach to textual study and what he calls the newer " 'social' school of textual criticism" ("Textual and Literary Theory: Redrawing the Matrix," *Studies in Bibliography* 42 [1989]: 11).

[2] *The Beauty of Inflections*, 82–83.

tric as well as author-centered approaches to texts, the extension of the
field of textual reconstruction to those non-authorial variants that emerge
within the material conditions of textual transmission—that is, to textual
elements regarded as "corruptions" by the strict rules of traditional
editing practices. Combined with McKenzie's redefinition of bibliography as "the sociology of texts," this socially-based project can be regarded as yet another manifestation of a cultural materialism that is implicit
in the interpretative practices of the New Historicism. Although the
methods of author-centered editing and of analytic bibliography continue
their usefulness, the idealism and scientism of both enterprises are gradually being replaced by a more social-historical conception of editing and
bibliography, one which foregrounds the *interpretative* work of editors and
bibliographers, thus facilitating communication with scholars and critics
for whom editing and bibliography were unknown territories or arcane
practices.

In the 1989 issue of *Studies in Bibliography*, Peter Shillingsburg ex-
amines the implications of the "social theory of texts," envisioning an
approach that concentrates on "the importance of the entire bio-socio-
economic context in *determining* the work of art,"[3] one that demands an
abandonment of the principle of authorial authority that was at the center of traditional textual criticism. Although Shillingsburg is obviously
intrigued by the approach to textuality that is socially-based (both for
production and reception), he expresses a serious concern that this might
not lead to a responsible editing of texts. He assumes that producing a
standard edition, attempting to clear texts of their historical "corruptions," reaching the most "authoritative," authorially-sanctioned form is
still the necessary (if only the pragmatically necessary) goal of editing. His
concept of a critical edition, however, differs sharply from that of
McGann, who conceives of such an artifact as facilitating what he calls
"radial reading," "a process by which the entire sociohistory of the
work—from its originary moments of production through all its subsequent reproductive adventures—is postulated as the ultimate goal of critical self-consciousness. That the goal is in fact an unreachable one is
clear. A practical move toward its attainment is essential to the critical enterprise, however."[4] Ted-Larry Pebworth's and Ernest W. Sullivan, II's

---

[3] "An Inquiry into the Social Status of Texts and Modes of Textual Criticism,"
Studies in Bibliography 42 (1989): 55, 67.

[4] In a review of McKenzie's *Bibliography and the Sociology of Texts*, McGann argues

recent suggestions for the "Rational Presentation of Multiple Textual Traditions"[5] would encourage such "radial reading" by printing alternate versions—or whole lines from alternate versions—of poems. Their assumptions, however, remain the author-centric ones of traditional textual criticism, and textual variants interest them only when they are "authoritative," that is, different "semiotic entities"[6] created by authorial revision.

What if, however, the process were taken one step further and textual scholars were to value more highly important alternate versions of poems created within the process of literary transmission, that is, to edit poems in sociocentric rather than in author-centric ways? Would the methods of traditional textual editing and analytic bibliography be utilized and supplemented, or, as some specialists seem to fear, rejected and discarded? Would the result of sociocentric editing be a wild proliferation of scholarly editions, no one of which would serve as a standard one?

In the case of English Renaissance poetry there are already some models of sociocentric, or at least of bibliographically rather than authorially-focused, editing that might be followed—for example, Hyder Rollins's editions of sixteenth-century poetical miscellanies.[7] Some scholars who have edited particular important manuscript collections have obviously imitated Rollins: Ruth Hughey for the Arundel-Harington MS, Peter Seng for British Library MS. Cotton Vespasian A.25, Edward Doughtie for Bodleian MS. Rawlinson Poetical 148, and Ernest L. Sul-

---

that "What we call scholarship is the territory where radial types of reading are constantly put into practice. Critical editions ... are typically structured so as to enforce spatial and radial reading processes along with the linear process. One does not simply move through such an edition, starting at the beginning and then proceeding on page by sequential page. Rather one moves around the edition, jumping from the reading text to the apparatus, perhaps from one of these to the notes or to an appendix, perhaps then back to some part of the front matter which may be relevant, and so forth. The edition also typically drives one to other books and acts of reading, ancillary or related materials which have to be drawn into the reading process in order to expand and enrich the textual and the reading field" ("Theory of Texts," *London Review of Books*, 18 Feb. 1988, 21).

[5] *Papers of the Bibliographical Society of America* 83 (1989): 43–60.

[6] "Rational Presentation," 44.

[7] See, for example, *Tottel's Miscellany (1557–1587)*, 2 vols. (1928; repr. Cambridge, Mass.: Harvard Univ. Press, 1966); *The Paradise of Dainty Devices* (1576–1606) (Cambridge, Mass.: Harvard Univ. Press, 1927); and *A Poetical Rhapsody, 1602–1621*, 2 vols. (Cambridge, Mass.: Harvard Univ. Press, 1931).

livan, II, for the two Dalhousie MSS.[8] Except for Hughey's valuable, but somewhat isolated work (which she conducted from the late '30s through the late '50s), these projects are relatively recent ones. Most of the dissertation editions of Rosenbach Library manuscript poetical commonplace books done under the direction of M. A. Shaaber and of British manuscript anthologies done under that of William Ringler have not yet reached print (except by way of scholarly articles excerpted from them)—even though texts such as Laurence Cummings's edition of Bodleian MS. Rawlinson Poetical MS. 85, like Steven May's edition of Cambridge Univ. MS. Dd.5.75, are resources that ought to interest contemporary historical scholars.[9]

Clearly, manuscript miscellanies (containing various kinds of writing in verse and prose) and manuscript poetical anthologies are crucial to the New Historicist or cultural materialist study of English Renaissance verse. They represent the meeting ground of literary production and social practices: or, to be more accurate, they demonstrate that literary production, reproduction, and reception are all socially mediated, the resulting texts demanding attention in their own right and not just as legitimate or illegitimate variants from authorial archetypes. Author-centric editing has done these documents a great disservice, though the textual introductions to some editions, such as those in Ringler's *Sidney*, the

---

[8] See *The Arundel-Harington Manuscript of Tudor Poetry*, ed. Ruth Hughey, 2 vols. (Columbus: Ohio State Univ. Press, 1960); *Tudor Songs and Ballads From MS Cotton Vespasian A–25*, ed. Peter J. Seng (Cambridge, Mass.: Harvard Univ. Press, 1978); *Liber Lilliati: Elizabethan Verse and Song (Bodleian MS Rawlinson Poetry 148)*, ed. Edward Doughtie; and *The First and Second Dalhousie Manuscripts: Poems and Prose by John Donne and Others, A Facsimile Edition*, ed. Ernest W. Sullivan, II (Columbia: Univ. of Missouri Press, 1988). Cf. also "Poems from a Seventeenth-Century Manuscript with the Hand of *Robert Herrick*," ed. Norman K. Farmer, Jr., *The Texas Quarterly*, Supplement to vol. 16 (1973): 121–85.

[9] See Howard H. Thompson, "An Edition of Two Seventeenth-Century Manuscript Poetical Miscellanies" (Diss., Univ. of Pennsylvania, 1959); David Coleman Redding, "Robert Bishop's Commonplace Book: An Edition of a Seventeenth-Century Miscellany" (Diss., Univ. of Pennsylvania, 1960); James Lee Sanderson, "An Edition of an Early Seventeenth-Century Manuscript Collection of Poems (Rosenbach MS. 186)" (Diss., Univ. of Pennsylvania, 1960); Laurence Cummings, "John Finet's Miscellany" (Diss., Washington Univ., 1960); Steven W. May, "Henry Stanford's Anthology: An Edition of Cambridge University Library Manuscript Dd.5.75" (Diss., Univ. of Chicago, 1968, now published by Garland Press); Katherine K. Gottschalk, "British Museum Manuscript Harley 6910: An Edition" (Diss., Univ. of Chicago, 1974).

Krueger/Nemser *Davies*, and Dunlap's *Carew*,[10] have called attention to them. By and large, however, the descriptions of these miscellanies and anthologies have been sketchy (if not, as in the case of the Gardner and Milgate editions of Donne, downright misleading).[11] Fuller descriptions and editions of these documents are overdue. Instead of treating the texts they contain as more or less "corrupt," from the point of view of idealistic, author-centered editing, we should value them for their historical particularity. And we should more regularly extend the single-poem focus to groups of poems and juxtapositions of authors: Harold Love's notion of the "rolling archetype"—that is, the flexible method of compiling groups of manuscript poems in different configurations—is useful as a sociocentric focus.[12]

Some doctoral dissertations that closely examine important manuscript collections of verse have not had the attention they deserve: I have in mind L. G. Black's study of late sixteenth-century miscellanies and Mary Hobbs's discussion of mid-seventeenth-century collections in her edition of the Stoughton MS.[13] Peter Beal's *Index of English Literary Manuscripts*,

---

[10] *The Poems of Sir Philip Sidney*, ed. William A. Ringler, Jr. (Oxford: Clarendon Press, 1962); *The Poems of Sir John Davies*, ed. Robert Krueger, with Introduction and Commentary by the Editor and Ruby Nemser (Oxford: Clarendon Press, 1975); *The Poems of Thomas Carew with his Masque "Coelum Britannicum,"* ed. Rhodes Dunlap (Oxford: Clarendon Press, 1949).

[11] See *The Divine Poems of John Donne*, ed. Helen Gardner, 2nd ed. (Oxford: Clarendon Press, 1978); John Donne, *The Elegies and The Songs and Sonnets*, ed. Helen Gardner (Oxford: Clarendon Press, 1965); John Donne, *The Epithalamions, Anniversaries, and Epicedes*, ed. W. Milgate (Oxford: Clarendon Press, 1978); and John Donne, *The Satires, Epigrams and Verse Letters*, ed. W. Milgate (Oxford: Clarendon Press, 1967). For an illuminating discussion of the inbuilt biases of Donne's Oxford editors, see Ted-Larry Pebworth, "Manuscript Poems and Print Assumptions: Donne and His Modern Editors," *John Donne Journal* 3 (1984): 1–21.

[12] "Scribal Texts and Literary Communities: The Rochester Circle and Osborn b. 105," *Studies in Bibliography* 42 (1989): 233. Love's discussion of seventeenth-century group and coterie collecting practices is especially valuable. See also his "Manuscript Versus Print in the Transmission of English Literature, 1600–1700," *Bibliographical Society of Australia and New Zealand* 9 (1985): 95–107, and "Scribal Publication in Seventeenth-Century England," *Transactions of the Cambridge Bibliographical Society* 9.2 (1987): 130–54.

[13] L. G. Black, "Studies in Some Related Manuscript Poetic Miscellanies of the 1580s" (D.Phil. Thesis, Univ. of Oxford, 1970), and Mary Hobbs, "An Edition of the Stoughton Manuscript (an Early Seventeenth-Century Manuscript Poetry Collection in Private Hands Connected with Henry King and Oxford) Seen in Relation to Other Contemporary Poetry and Song Collections" (Diss., Univ. of London, 1973). Cf. Black's "Some Renaissance Children's Verse," *Review of English Studies*, n.s., 24

however, which utilizes such work, has begun to invite more widespread attention to the rich body of manuscript miscellanies and poetical anthologies, which Beal has rightly identified as the most underutilized single resource for the study of sixteenth- and seventeenth-century verse.[14] The new annual Beal co-edits, *English Manuscript Studies, 1100–1700*, and the Harvester microfilm project, which makes British literary manuscripts more readily available to scholars at their home institutions, should stimulate more editions and historical bibliographical studies.[15]

As a new historicist scholar I would suggest that we not just produce conservative critical editions of authors, but also do the following:

1. We should find ways of presenting a wider range of "corrupt" or non-authorial variants in the textual apparatus of single-author editions: their presence need not be justified by imagining the possibility of alternate authorial versions of texts (as in the case of the two *King Lears*) but by their intrinsic historical value.

2. Especially in cases where the identity of an author in the history of reception is the product not only of authenticatable works, but also of dubious and spurious ones as well, we should regularly include the latter in scholarly editions.[16]

3. We should edit the more interesting poetical miscellanies and poetical anthologies as sociologically and historically significant documents, despite their "corrupt" texts, misattributions, and typical lack of aesthetic order.

4. Analogously, either separately or as part of editions of

(1973): 1–16, and Hobbs's "Early Seventeenth-Century Verse Miscellanies and Their Value for Textual Editors," *English Manuscript Studies, 1100–1700*, ed. Peter Beal and Jeremy Griffiths (Oxford and New York: Blackwell, 1989), 1:182–210.

[14] *Index of English Literary Manuscripts*, ed. Peter Beal (London: Mansell, 1980), 1:248–49.

[15] The in-progress Harvester Press project includes microfilms of manuscript collections of sixteenth- and seventeenth-century miscellanies and poetical anthologies from the British Library, the Bodleian, Cambridge University Library, the Victoria and Albert Museum, the Folger Shakespeare Library, and other archives.

[16] In explaining what he means by attention to the "secondary moments of textual production," McGann remarks: "In the critical study of this material certain shifts of emphasis take place. Most obviously, the author is studied as he or she is a critical and historical reconstruction. The heading 'Author,' then, will comprise a range of ideas or concepts of the author which have emerged in the minds of various people and the ideologies of different classes, institutions, and groups" (*The Beauty of Inflections*, 82).

whole manuscripts, we should give more editorial attention to the work of anonymous and non-canonical authors. This would broaden our sense of the literary and help us to see the social embeddedness of poetic texts in an historical period in which "literature" had not yet become segregated from the general social world as a supposedly autonomous institution.

5. We should draw textual editing and historical bibliography more closely together as related activities—not primarily for the purpose of establishing authoritative texts, but rather in order to deepen our understanding of the sociology of literature and of the development of the literary institution within the media of manuscript and print transmission.

In this kind of revised editing program, for example, John Donne's poetic texts would emerge as socially-generated constructs, produced initially in some (only partially recoverable) authorial forms but accessible mainly through the historical *reproductions* encouraged by the system of manuscript transmission into which they were released and continued by the transformative processes of print technology and conventions. So, too, "Donne" as an author would appear to be less an idealized font of creative originality and more an historically-evolving, socially-produced literary identity, the result of "corrupt" as well as "authoritative," spurious and dubious as well as authenticated, texts, original social contexts as well as successive historical acts of recontextualization.

New Historicist and cultural materialist approaches to the study of literature ask that we recognize that a text does not exist without a material embodiment and that the reading and interpretation that activate the text are shaped by its material features. As Roger Chartier has observed, "no text exists outside of the support that enables it to be read; any comprehension of a writing . . . depends on the forms in which it reaches its reader."[17] D. F. McKenzie argues that it is "impossible . . . to divorce the substance of the text on the one hand from the physical form of its presentation on the other."[18] But, of course, such formulations should not shock the traditional bibliographer whose business has been

---

[17] "Texts, Printing, Reading," in *The New Cultural History*, ed. Lynn Hunt (Berkeley: Univ. of California Press, 1989), 161.

[18] "Typography and Meaning: The Case of William Congreve," in *The Book and the Book Trade in Eighteenth-Century Europe*, ed. Giles Barber and Bernhard Fabian (Hamburg: Dr. Ernst Hauswedell & Co., 1981), 82.

the description and analysis of material artifacts—both in print and in manuscript.

I have been arguing that literary works designed for and released into manuscript circulation especially invite sociocentric editing and study. After all, by the rules of this system of transmission, writers, in effect, ceded the property rights to their texts to those who received them along the line of their transmission and assumed that revision, supplementation, answering, and parody would normally occur, even, in some cases, "improvement" to authorial "originals."[19] In such a system, a poet was in a position somewhat analogous to that of a playwright handing a manuscript over to a company of players for production: pens and minds other than his own were free to alter, edit, and excerpt the original text, and the author was, in effect, a collaborator in literary production as well as an original producer of the words that then had their own social vicissitudes out of the writer's control.[20] Even authors like Jonson and Herrick, who exercised a high degree of authorial control over the form and dissemination of their texts in print, knew that circulating their verse in manuscript meant submitting texts to the vagaries of history.

Some authors were, of course, drastically altered in the course of the manuscript and print transmission of their work. Take, for example, the case of Ralegh, whose poems passed into the system of manuscript transmission and were subjected to radical revision and supplementation. The poem beginning "Farewell falce love, thou oracle of lies," for instance, survives in eighteen-, twenty-four, and thirty-line versions, the longest of which first appears in print in Thomas Deloney's *Garland of Good Will* (1631). By conservative textual standards, the 1631 text is a particularly "corrupt" version of the poem, but, in addition to preserving what are probably scribal errors and deliberate changes and additions to an original authorial version, it does contain compositor "errors" that produce some interesting readings—for example, in line thirteen, "fortlesse field" for

---

[19] For example, J. W. Saunders, "From Manuscript to Print: A Note on the Circulation of Poetic MSS. in the Sixteenth Century," *Proceedings of the Leeds Philosophical and Literary Society*, 6.8 (1951): 524, notes that the poet George Whetstone "left his poems dispersed among learned friends and expected them 'at theyr leasure to polish' them, should he fail to return from abroad."

[20] See Stephen Orgel, "What is a Text?" *Research Opportunities in Renaissance Drama* 24 (1981), 3–6.

"fortress foiled" of the Dobell MS,[21] which is the sole surviving eighteen-line version of the poem. As the second printed version of the poem (the earlier one consisting of twenty-four lines—in William Byrd's *Psalmes, Sonets, & Songs*, 1588), this text had an undeniable historical impact, and, after all, the third printing of the poem, in the 1660 collection, *Le Prince d'Amour*, reproduces the thirty-line version. Because Ralegh's most recent editor, Michael Rudick, cannot find any evidence that Ralegh himself produced either the twenty-four-line or thirty-line version of the poem, as a conservative textual editor he has little interest in them, though, he does quote the two "spurious" stanzas in his notes. But, if we consider that the "purest," eighteen-line version of the poem only survived in a single manuscript, and the twenty-four and thirty-line versions of the poem were *historically* more important, what is the sense of editing "Ralegh" in a way that denigrates non-authorial variants or that encourages historical erasure in the name of rescuing an authorial image that is allegedly prior to historical vicissitude?[22]

The body of this poet's work also attracted to it the poems of other writers: hence the odd divorce between the Ralegh that a conservative editorial effort produces (a poet of very few authenticatable poems) and the poet "Ralegh" shaped in literary reception and literary history by these as well as by the dubious and spurious poems associated with this author's name. Perhaps, from a social-historical point of view, the latter "Ralegh" is the more important one, the one we should make visible in a scholarly edition. Of course, scholarly editions that print dubious and spurious work along with justifiably ascribed work (Grierson's *Donne*[23] and Ringler's *Sidney* come to mind) implicitly acknowledge the historical value of the former, but the dubious, the spurious, and the corrupt have literally gotten bad press in the scholarly enterprise of editing—subordinated, marginalized, or excluded. Perhaps one of the unacknowledged advantages of facsimile reproductions of early editions that contain

---

[21] For Ralegh's poetry, in the absence of an adequate published standard edition, I have used Michael Rudick, "The Poems of Sir Walter Ralegh: An Edition" (Diss., Univ. of Chicago, 1970).

[22] Ralegh's poem "The Lie" is an even more striking example of a text that changed to an extraordinary degree in the course of its transmission in manuscript and print. Words were changed, stanzas were added and subtracted, the poem was answered by at least one other lyric, and the text published in unusual and special contexts. See Rudick, 205–9.

[23] *The Poems of John Donne*, ed. Herbert J. C. Grierson, 2 vols. (Oxford: Oxford Univ. Press, 1912), 1:401–67.

dubious, spurious, and corrupt texts along with more "authoritative" ones is that the blurring of the lines between them can give modern readers better access to the historically-specific reception of poets' work than do modern critical editions—though, of course, both kinds of reproduction are important scholarly resources.

In the early modern era, especially in the manuscript environment, works were regarded as intrinsically open to supplementation, revision, excerpting, parody, and poetic answering or rejoinder. Manuscript culture encouraged more radical transformation, while print culture developed at least a pretended fidelity to the corrected, perfected text—though, despite the project of humanist philology,[24] nothing like a modern pursuit of textual "purity" was desirable or possible in the early print era. Print culture, in fact, continued many of the processes of transformation of texts that resulted in what modern editors regard as "corruptions": not only did publishers feel free to change the texts they received, as Tottel did in the case of Wyatt's poetry, but also, as Hyder Rollins has pointed out, since every new edition of a book was a resetting of a previous one and proofreading was far from rigorous, errors typically multiplied over time in the printing history of a particular work, a fact demonstrated, for example, in the series of editions of sixteenth-century printed miscellanies.[25]

Although authors such as Jonson and Herrick, who willingly participated in print culture, produced different texts for print than the ones they wrote for manuscript circulation and exercised considerable editorial care in publishing their work, for the most part the printed editions of individual poets have much less textual authority than they have been accorded (and "textual authority" itself is an historically problematic value). Over a quarter of a century ago, L. A. Beaurline lodged exactly this complaint.[26] Nonetheless, modern scholars have undervalued manuscript versions of poets' work or failed to regard them as socioliterarily distinct, suited to their medium of transmission and to the circumstances of reception poets could imagine in this environment. But, even if the printed texts of the work of authors who deliberately readied their work

---

[24] For a recent insightful discussion of the question of textuality in humanist philology, see Stephanie H. Jed, *Chaste Thinking: The Rape of Lucretia and the Birth of Humanism* (Bloomington: Indiana Univ. Press, 1989).

[25] See Rollins, ed., *A Poetical Rhapsody*, 2:77–78.

[26] "An Editorial Experiment: Suckling's *A Sessions of the Poets*," *Studies in Bibliography* 16 (1963): 43–60.

for publication must be accorded a privileged position, there is little to justify the bias toward print that exists in the case of those published texts that were unauthorized—especially given the compositional idiosyncrasies and inconsistencies of printing-houses, the lack of rigorous editorial care, and the practice of binding uncorrected or partially corrected sheets as well as corrected ones in a press run.

The prejudice of modern literary historians and textual scholars in favor of printed texts has had some unfortunate results. For one, it has led to an undervaluing of women's writing. Margaret Ezell has recently observed that literary historians and feminist scholars who attend virtually exclusively to printed texts miss much important work by women authors, particularly those texts that were deliberately designed for coterie manuscript circulation.[27] Literary historians and textual scholars have failed to perceive the importance of authors who were widely circulated in manuscript, but who either were not published or did not loom large in the environment of print. Take the case of two seventeenth-century poets whose work appears in a great many manuscript collections, Richard Corbett and William Strode. Although Corbett's poems were published posthumously in two separate editions, their impact has been greatly underestimated. The editions of 1647 and 1648, the former by the notoriously sloppy and opportunistic John Donne, Jr., the other probably a continental printing differing considerably in content, are very poor productions, hasty gatherings of *part* of Corbett's work, which must be sought more widely in dispersed manuscript anthologies of the period, some hundred of which survive.[28] Strode's case is even more illustrative: Earl Miner's books on the *Metaphysical Mode* and the *Cavalier Mode* in seventeenth-century verse completely ignore both Strode and Corbett.[29] Even Douglas Bush's widely inclusive *English Literature in the Earlier Seventeenth Century, 1600–1660* has next to nothing

---

[27] See Margaret Ezell, " 'To be your daughter in your pen': The Social Functions of Literature in the Writings of Lady Elizabeth Brackley and Lady Jane Cavendish," *Huntington Library Quarterly* 51 (1988): 281–96.

[28] See *Certain Elegant Poems, Written by Dr. Corbet, Bishop of Norwich* (London, 1647) and *Poetica Stromata or A Collection of Sundry Peices in Poetry*, Drawne by the known and approued Hand of R. C. (n.p., 1648). The standard modern edition is *The Poems of Richard Corbett*, ed. J. A. W. Bennett and H. R. Trevor-Roper (Oxford: Clarendon Press, 1955).

[29] See Earl Miner, *The Metaphysical Mode from Donne to Cowley* (Princeton: Princeton Univ. Press, 1969) and *The Cavalier Mode from Jonson to Cotton* (Princeton: Princeton Univ. Press, 1971).

on Strode, claiming that he was "virtually a man of one poem, the gracious little conceit 'I saw faire Cloris walke alone.' "[30] Except for an excellent Oxford B.Litt. thesis editing Strode's work,[31] there is no good modern edition of this writer, although, considering the surviving manuscript evidence, one would judge him, from a social-historical point of view, to be one of the most important seventeenth-century poets. Because textual editors generally feel most comfortable producing modern critical editions of authors whose work appeared in print during their lifetimes or shortly after their deaths, those writers whose work was designed for and was largely confined to the environment of manuscript transmission have, for the most part, received less attention than they deserve. Exceptions, such as the poems of Robert Sidney, really do not disprove the rule: the Clarendon Press edition of this writer was institutionally mandated by the (re)discovery of a large authorial manuscript and by the family connection with Sir Philip Sidney, rather than by a collecting effort involving scattered manuscript documents.[32]

Several years ago I developed an addiction to reading textual introductions of standard critical editions of sixteenth- and seventeenth-century poets. My general purpose was social-historical, and I did learn much from the work of such editors as William Ringler, Helen Gardner, Wesley Milgate, and Rhodes Dunlap. But I was also frustrated in my desire to learn more about the artifacts that these and other textual scholars had examined. Because their purposes were basically those of author-centered textual editing, when they came to manuscripts preserving especially "corrupt" texts or the mixed work of several writers—that is when they dealt with some of the hundreds of manuscript miscellanies and poetical anthologies in which so much of the social history of English Renaissance poetical texts is implicit, their interest in doing historical bibliography was very limited. On the other hand, since bibliographers have largely focused their attention on printed artifacts and

---

[30] Douglas Bush, *English Literature in the Earlier Seventeenth Century, 1600–1660*, 2nd ed. (Oxford: Clarendon Press, 1962), 124.

[31] M. A. Forey, "A Critical Edition of the Poetical Works of William Strode, Excluding the *Floating Island*" (B. Litt. Thesis, Oxford Univ., 1966). The only printed edition of Strode's work is one that fails to draw on the best manuscript sources: *The Poetical Works of William Strode (1600–1645)*, ed. Bertram Dobell (London: Pub. by the Editor, 1907).

[32] See *The Poems of Robert Sidney*, ed. P. J. Croft (Oxford: Clarendon Press, 1984).

only occasionally have written analyses and descriptions of whole manuscripts, I decided to seek out the social history of poetic transmission in the primary texts themselves, examining these documents for my own New Historicist or cultural materialist purposes. I have been helped by Peter Beal's *Index*, the Harvester microfilm catalogue and films, Margaret Crum's first line index of manuscript poetry in the Bodleian Library,[33] library catalogues from the British Library, the Bodleian, Cambridge University Library, and other libraries, scattered descriptions of manuscripts in textual introductions to editions of particular poets, articles in bibliographic journals, and, of course, by the manuscript collections of such libraries as the British Library, the Bodleian, the Huntington, and the Folger. What I am doing is bibliographical in McKenzie's definition of the discipline. But I am convinced that, with their own particular skills and knowledge of the historical and material vicissitudes of texts, textual editors have much to contribute to the project of historical rediscovery being attempted by me and by other scholars. I can only add one more voice encouraging the fruitful interaction of textual and bibliographic scholars with their New Historicist and cultural materialist colleagues.

WAYNE STATE UNIVERSITY

---

[33] *First-Line Index of English Poetry 1500–1800 in Manuscripts of the Bodleian Library Oxford*, ed. Margaret Crum, 2 vols. (New York: MLA, 1969). Hilton Kelliher informs me that the project of computerizing the British Library's handwritten (and incomplete) first-line index is in its early stages.

Work, Document, and Miscellany:
A Response to Professors
de Grazia and Marotti

A. R. BRAUNMULLER

HROUGH SERENDIPITY OR, MORE LIKELY, THE GENIUS OF this session's organizer, the two papers dovetail very nicely, with Margreta de Grazia taking up and taking down the traditional work/document distinction and Arthur Marotti exploring some of the consequences for texts and editions of erasing the linked notions of a "standard edition" and of a text purged of corruption. If this response were like many I have heard at these meetings, I would now launch either an attack on the speakers or, more commonly, an elaborate essay featuring my own research. As the only person on this panel who has actually edited a manuscript as a substantively (in)coherent but physically unified codex rather than as a contingent repository of unideal representations of ideal texts needing recovery, I probably have enough self-complimenting anecdotes to fill my allotted span of your attention.[1] To the dismay of no one except, perhaps, my mother and my

---

[1] See A. R. Braunmuller, *A Seventeenth-Century Letter-Book* (Newark: Univ. of Delaware Press, 1983). My point is simply that this is an edition of an entire manuscript, rather than an edition formed from items that appeared in one or more manuscripts.

publisher (who may not be all that different when viewed from the perspective of the difference between work and document), I will not do that. I would, however, be most interested to know the panelists' views on how private letters (the documents, or texts, or works to which I have devoted some editorial pain) fit or qualify their observations.

I begin with Margreta's paper. The distinction she draws between work and document was not quite so hard and fast even in the Old Historicism, nor indeed in the Renaissance itself.[2] Is it too cheap to say that Lorenzo Valla's founding act of the modern editorial tradition, the destruction of the Donation of Constantine, was a moment when criticism turned a text from document to work? Valla endowed an unambiguous document with a challengeable motive; he gave a monument ulterior purposes. If that's not persuasive, what about the way in which early Stuart Parliaments treated Magna Charta, making it over from a transparent legal document (like a judicial decision in the yearbooks) into a source of endless constitutional debate and, consequently, interpretation? In both examples, the reagent transforming document into work is an exercise of historical relativism, an exercise that curiously turns the usual New Historicist dichotomy between the aesthetic and the contingent on its head: by understanding the pastness of their documents, Valla and the common lawyers make them works not for an age but for a succession of ages. Of course under certain circumstances interpreters will wish the "work" to retain its "documentary" authority, will wish to retranslate it from the extra-temporal realm (once they have interpreted it) back into the contingent moment of their history.

I have time for only two other observations on Margreta's complex argument. One concerns theatrical texts, works, and documents, the other concerns the authored vs. non-authored criterion as a distinction between work and document. The Oxford *Complete Works* is guilty of loose writing in speaking of the texts of Shakespeare's plays as they were acted, since of course the text of a performance can neither be written nor printed—ask anyone who has struggled with Labanotation, or who has tried to reconstruct an historical choreography. Insofar as any written or printed text can record a performance, there's no reason except for faulty definition early in this century for a "good" quarto to be any whit

---

[2] Nor, for that matter is the distinction maintained by our own organization: the index to the Modern Language Association's annual bibliography calls itself a "Document Author Index," an oxymoron in Margreta's terms.

inferior to a bad one as a record of performance, and on that faulty distinction, of course, Random Cloud has erected a cheerful destruction of the difference between good and bad, between work and document in the Oxford editors' inadvertent sense.[3]

Margreta ascribes a motive for conflating work and document to post-structuralists, new textualists, and new historicists: "the recognition that a single authorial consciousness is not sufficient to account for the complexities and anomalies of texts...." The Prince Hal-like financial image is an intriguing one, since by "account for" all those groups may mean "control." These texts are out of control, cannot be assumed to be under a single consciousness's complete sway, or accepted if they are so imagined. One response might be to say that the fault is not in our canonical stars, but in ourselves that we are underminers. Yet if a single author is insufficient to make one given text hold still, then there's no *a priori* reason for any text to hold still, be it *King Lear*, manuscript versions of Ralegh's "Lie," or the variously ascribed and modified texts of famous letters of advice (father to son, tutor to traveling pupil, etc.).[4] Thus, while we all may be tempted to agree with Margreta that she's not arguing that texts should be treated indiscriminately, we should hesitate to agree with her dichotomy between works behind which no author lies and documents behind which something called "the past" lies.

One obvious crossover point between Margreta's and Arthur's papers is Thomas Tansclle's strongly argued defense of authorial intention and hence the immanence of a work versus the transitory mediation of documents. Arthur places before us a socioliterature and its discourses in which authorial intention was that there should be no authorial control. The special, but extremely large and fertile, category of poetical miscellany is one in which an authored text (a "work" in Margreta's terms) is deliberately and meditatedly released into circumstances that are likely to make it a multi-authored text, a text written by so many individuals and contingent circumstances of transmission that it might very well be said to be written by the past (that is, be a "document"). Arthur identifies a moment, a long one, in the transition from oral to written culture where

---

[3] See Random Cloud [a pseudonymous author so entered in the appropriate Document Author Index], "The Marriage of Good and Bad Quartos," *Shakespeare Quarterly* 33 (1982): 421–31.

[4] For the last category (famous letters of advice) and some bibliographical citations, see my "Editing Elizabethan Letters," *TEXT* 1 (1984 for 1981), esp. 189–90.

an argument can be built not on a dichotomy between "work" and "document" so much as one between the utterly solipsistic (the unspoken, unheard, uncirculated, uncopied, unprinted, and above all unread) and whatever the Bakhtinian dialogic opposite might be. This opposite circumstance would be the adult equivalent of the children's party game in which a whispered message is passed in a circle until its utterly changed progeny returns to the "author" or a chain-letter destined, perhaps, to return to its originator bearing the other twelve ways of looking at a blackbird, or a lie, or a nymph, or a seducing shepherd, or the collected and improved discourses of William Strode.

Another way of saying some of this lies in Arthur's third point of advice to editors: that we (or they) recognize the social embeddedness of poetic texts. I entirely agree, but it seems to me that this recognition would once and for all end a tradition that Arthur also seems concerned to retain, if only as an enabling Other—the "standard edition." The principle here seems to be: If they thought it was Donne, so may we, whether or not Donne did it. That naturally lets lots of folks who probably aren't Donne into the Clarendon, or some subsequent edition, of "John Donne," but so what?

One final comment and one final question. The final comment is to observe the economic reciprocity between the idealized, essentialized author and the "standard edition." Arthur speaks of a system of textual transmission in which writers "ceded the property rights to their texts." The implication, it seems to me, is that traditional (New Bibliographical) editorial practice is not only patriarchal in its premises—removing "corruption," revealing the virgin and unsophisticated text—but capitalist as well.[5] By fixing author and text once and for all, we also fixed what belongs to whom and thereby generate all that intellectual labor devoted to the system of "borrowing" and plagiarism among individual entrepreneurial authors. A standard edition is not just a standard of accuracy, completeness, and so forth, it is a statement of net worth, a declaration of possessions.

My final question concerns the way Arthur identifies the members of his category, the poetical miscellanists who freely immerse their texts into the transformative element. He speaks often of texts being designed for manuscript transmission as if that design also meant not merely an ac-

---

[5] See Stephanie H. Jed, *Chaste Thinking: The Rape of Lucretia and the Birth of Humanism* (Bloomington: Indiana Univ. Press, 1989).

ceptance, but even an encouragement, of contingent modification. To say that the miscellanists accepted such modification (emendation, improvement, etc.) as a condition of manuscript circulation is one thing; to say that they liked or sought it is another. I wonder—and it is a question that returns us once more to the issue of authorship as self- or other-constituted—how he knows?

UNIVERSITY OF CALIFORNIA
LOS ANGELES, CALIFORNIA

Behind the Arras:
Editing Renaissance Women's Letters

SARA JAYNE STEEN

L ET ME BEGIN WITH A DISJUNCTION BETWEEN MY ROLE AS A
textual editor and my role as a scholar in the field of Renaissance women. When I became an editor in the 1970s, Renaissance letters on the whole were historical documents, and, as
documents not originally intended for publication, they were to be
treated as artifacts and reproduced as precisely as the difference between
manuscript and print would allow, without change in accidentals or ex-
pansion of abbreviations and with full discussion of the papers and inks
that could not be duplicated. Had those letters been literary works—and
only a few letters were so classified, such as those of Montaigne—then
my responsibility would have been to determine, insofar as I could, the
author's final intent and produce from extant manuscripts and printed
texts a conflated critical text that might never have existed in any single
material form.[1]

---

[1] Some critics retain this distinction between document and work, which G.
Thomas Tanselle concisely summarized in "Literary Editing," *Literary & Historical
Editing*, ed. George L. Vogt and John Bush Jones (Lawrence: Univ. of Kansas
Libraries, 1981), 35–56. In his *Rationale of Textual Criticism* (Philadelphia: Univ. of
Pennsylvania Press, 1989), Tanselle reaffirms that editors "can choose either to present
the texts of documents, making no alterations in them, or else, by combining

Post-structuralist theory has radically undercut that distinction between document and literary work—witness Margreta de Grazia's and
Arthur Marotti's essays in this volume[2]—and emphasized that all texts
are "literary" in that they involve creation of personae and tones, and
that all texts are "historical" in that they are shaped by a culture as well
as by an author, thus collapsing arbitrary mid-century boundaries between history and literature.[3] Even the straightforward intended-for-pub-
lication criterion falls apart when we treat letters written at the Elizabethan and Jacobean courts, where manuscript letters often circulated far
beyond their named recipients, and women like Arbella Stuart had to
write with the consciousness that their court letters might be read aloud
in council and their familial letters be intercepted and read by unfriendly
factions. Nonetheless, when I speak with other textual editors about
letters, it is still the letter-as-document that is emphasized, both by traditional textual editors and by New Historicist and cultural materialist editors, the latter two of whom argue that a text does not exist without its
individual material embodiment: because the author's final intent cannot
be determined and would be irrelevant if we could discover it, they say,
our task is not to present a conflated, critical, definitive text, but to present the varied forms of a text as exactly as possible and examine their
cultural production in their various historical moments.[4]

When I talk to scholars in women's studies, however, the material
embodiment of the text is not the issue. Women's scholars want to bring
women from behind the arras of a male-determined canon and let them
share the stage. The emphasis is on the writer—the woman: her education, her varied roles within her culture, how she perceived herself in
relation to her society, how she constructed her everyday reality, how
she shaped herself in words, how her roles changed over time—and on
us as readers, on how we can interpret what she has to say. Scholars dis-

---

elements from different documents and admitting further alterations of their own, to
prepare reconstructions of the texts of works" (37–38). In treating authorial intent
with "works," Tanselle follows the theories of Fredson Bowers. Their positions have
been challenged by Jerome J. McGann, *A Critique of Modern Textual Criticism* (Chicago: Univ. of Chicago Press, 1983), and analyzed by D. C. Greetham, "Textual and
Literary Theory: Redrawing the Matrix," *Studies in Bibliography* 42 (1989): 1–24.

[2] Margreta de Grazia, "What is a Work? What is a Document?," and Arthur
Marotti, "Manuscript, Print, and the English Renaissance Lyric"; see above 199–221.

[3] Literary and historical editing were already merging by the early 1980s, as
evidenced by papers in Vogt and Jones.

[4] See Marotti, 214–15, *et passim*, above.

cuss women's entries into and retreats from the world of words, women as voices defending piety or challenging authority, whether or how women's voices are gendered, and whether or how our readings are gendered and thus affect what we hear.[5] Josephine Roberts entitled this session "Voices of Silence," reflecting the consensus of scholars at conferences like last month's Attending to Women in Early Modern England[6] that women, long silenced, must be enabled to speak. Those of us who edit women's letters, then, have to deal with the disjunction between an emphasis among editors on the text as a cultural and historical document and an emphasis among women's scholars on the writer and the reader. We must develop theoretical principles that incorporate recent work in these and related fields and adapt that work to our interdisciplinary, feminist editions. Those principles are what I intend to explore today, hoping to provoke further discussion by advocating a methodology, using the letters of Arbella Stuart as examples. I will argue that our guiding principle in editing women's letters should be to interfere as little as possible with the sound of their voices.

Anyone who has chosen to recommend an editorial system should explain her position. Unlike some New Historicists, I cannot discount the writer. Like most women's scholars, I feel a responsibility to a woman, in my case the Lady Arbella Stuart, who once existed in bodily form, walked on rush mats, laughed, and put her pen to paper. I want her to speak as directly as possible across the cultural and linguistic barriers that separate us. Surely many readers feel a kinship with Stephen Greenblatt when he says, "I began with a desire to speak with the dead." Many of us share his sense that the extant "textual traces" are filled with "lost life" and "uncannily full of the will to be heard."[7] That position

---

[5] See, for example, Anne M. Haselkorn and Betty S. Travitsky, eds., *The Renaissance Englishwoman in Print: Counterbalancing the Canon* (Amherst: Univ. of Massachusetts Press, 1990); Elaine V. Beilin, *Redeeming Eve: Women Writers of the English Renaissance* (Princeton: Princeton Univ. Press, 1987); Sheila Fisher and Janet E. Halley, eds., *Seeking the Woman in Late Medieval and Renaissance Writings: Essays in Feminist Contextual Criticism* (Knoxville: Univ. of Tennessee Press, 1989).

[6] An interdisciplinary symposium held November 8–10, 1990, sponsored by the Center for Renaissance and Baroque Studies at the University of Maryland, College Park.

[7] *Shakespearean Negotiations: The Circulation of Social Energy in Renaissance England* (Berkeley: Univ. of California Press, 1988), 1. Greenblatt goes on to argue the satisfactions of fictions, simulations "undertaken in full awareness of the absence of the life they contrive to represent." To some of us, women's letters are additionally meaningful because of the presence of life.

is especially appropriate to the Renaissance, when an oral culture was in the process of becoming a print culture, and spelling and punctuation were not yet fully fixed, but flexible, and thus especially reflective of the writer's internal voice. It is particularly appropriate to letters, which in early modern England often were dictated and thus sounded aloud as they were composed—and often as they were read, as well.

While reader response theory has convincingly argued that the voice we hear as we read is in part our own, it is ours *only* in part. Meaning is triggered by a specific text and resides between the text and the reader. Some traditional editors disagree—Fredson Bowers vigorously attacked Claire Badaracco for suggesting that the "text," by which she indicated meaning, could be separated from the document[8]—and some New Historicists and cultural materialists will find an emphasis on voice disturbingly author-centered. But our primary goal should be to treat early modern women fairly by retaining valuable textual signifiers of voice and eliminating aspects of the document that interfere with that voice for modern readers. Any edition is a translation.[9] Even a photographic reprint differs markedly from the experience of the original manuscript or book, as anyone who has ever worked with microfilms and photocopies is well aware. Thus, the editor should not try to duplicate the document in all its peculiarities, but edit it with consideration for the signifiers of value.

In general, original punctuation and spelling are important signifiers that should be maintained. In most cases, women's letters are extant in manuscripts either in the woman's own hand or in the hand of the scribe to whom she dictated her words.[10] Nothing offers a better sense of sound than the original punctuation and spelling, even if a few spellings

---

[8] Claire Badaracco, "The Editor and the Question of Value: Proposal," and Fredson Bowers, "The Editor and the Question of Value: Another View," *TEXT* 1 (1981): 41–43, 45–73. D. F. McKenzie discusses the two concepts of text, either as embedded in the physical document or as "independent of the documents which, at any particular moment, give it form," in *Bibliography and the Sociology of Texts*, The Panizzi Lectures, 1985 (London: The British Library, 1986), 50.

[9] Leon Edel's term, as cited in Robert Stephen Becker, "Challenges in Editing Modern Literary Correspondence: Transcription," *TEXT* 1 (1984, for 1981): 261, 265–66.

[10] Different texts pose different problems. In the discussion that follows on Renaissance women's letters, I assume that manuscripts are extant and that the editor is not working solely from Victorian printed texts many removes from the author.

need to be glossed. Modernization, especially of punctuation, strikingly distorts the woman's voice by inserting pauses, for example, that are not indicated in the manuscript. I may be biased because Stuart was so highly educated that her usage causes little confusion for a modern reader, but the majority of people who choose to read Renaissance texts are unlikely to be put off by original punctuation. The marks signal pace and tone and thus emotion, emotion wrenched from Renaissance women by nineteenth-century editors who desired to make them conform to a later code of literacy so as not to seem embarrassingly uneducated to a general audience.

When Emily Tennyson Bradley, a noted nineteenth-century historian (who like many early female scholars felt the need to disguise her gender by publishing under her initials as E. T. Bradley), based her biography of Arbella Stuart on contemporary letters, she radically altered the spelling, punctuation, and paragraphing to avoid lending, as she put it, "an illiterate appearance to letters written by the most highly educated people."[11] Most of the letters she cited were Stuart's, and Bradley apparently feared that Stuart, a learned woman comfortable in English, French, Italian, Latin, Greek, and Hebrew, would seem uneducated to a Victorian audience and thus reflect badly on women if her prose were not regularized and corrected. The result, in terms of altered emotional content, is sometimes startling. The following text is taken from a letter Stuart wrote to Sir Henry Brounker, Queen Elizabeth's representative, in March of 1603, on the anniversary of her friend Essex's execution and not long before Elizabeth's own death. Stuart was under strict house arrest in Derbyshire, denied access to friends, musicians, even her books, and she resented her treatment. In Bradley's book, Stuart's text appears like this:

> it is they who abuse her Majesty and wrong me, . . . who have made you present her Majesty with a misshapen, discoloured piece of stuff, fitting none, nor fit for her Majesty to look upon, which, if either I might be suffered, or not hindered, I will not say helped—but why should I not be helped, I pray you, in such a piece of work?—should have been presented to her Majesty in a form well beseeming her Majesty; whereas now it is so tossed up and down that it hath almost lost the gloss, and even by the best

---

[11] *Life of the Lady Arabella Stuart* (London: Richard Bentley and Son, 1889), 1:ix.

slubbered [*sic*] up in such haste, that many wrong stitches of unkind-
ness must be picked out, which need not have been so bestowed;
and many wrong-placed conceits ripped out, whereof some may be
cast away, but most being right placed will do very well. The more
you think to make, the more you mar; when all is done I must take
it [*in*] hand, and shape my own coat according to my cloth, but it
shall not be after your opinion of this world, God willing, but fit for
me, and every way becoming of that virtue in me, whether it be a
native property of that blood I come of, or an infective virtue of the
Earl of Essex; who could go neither friend nor foe knew whither,
till he arrived amongst his unwitting enemies, from whom he ever
returned with honour, and was received home with joy. Till. . . .[12]

By comparison, the text in original spelling and punctuation looks like this:

it is <they> who abuse hir Majesty and wrong me . . . <who> have
made you present hir Majesty with a mishapen discouloured peece
of stuffe fitting none nor fitt for hir Majesty to looke upon which if
either I might be suffered or not hindered I will not say helped but
why should I not be helpt I pray you in such a peece of worke?
should have binne presented to hir Majesty in a forme well beseem-
ing hir Majesty wheatas now it is so tossed up and downe that it
hath almost lost the glosse, and even by the best slubbred up in such
hast that many wrong stitches of unkindnesse must be picked out
which nedd not have binne so bestowed and many wrong placed
conceits ript out whearof somm may be cast away but most being
right placed will do very well, the more you thinck to make the
more you marre when all is donne I must take it hand, and shape
my owne cote according to my cloth, but it shall not be after the
fashion of this world god willing but fitt for me, and every way
becomming of that virtu in me whither it be a native property of
that bloud I comm of, or an infective virtu of the Earle of Essex
who could go neither frend nor foe knew whither till he arrived
amongst his unwitting enimies from whom he ever returned with
honour and was received home with joy till. . . .[13]

Aside from Bradley's errors in transcription (which are in general inter-

---

[12] 2:156–57.
[13] Cecil Papers, vol. 135, fols. 133v–34r, cited here with the kind permission of
the Most Hon. The Marquess of Salisbury.

esting and occasionally revealing), she did a good job of presenting Stuart's text in modernized form. What is lost, however, especially when the reader has the comparison of reading Stuart's usually highly pointed and carefully structured prose, is the emotional content indicated by the lack of punctuation and the run-on syntax, so completely unlike Stuart's other writing. What Bradley's editorial choice denied Stuart was her anger, the very fury at constraint that modern women were once told Renaissance women did not feel,[14] but which Stuart continues here for page after page after page. Nearly three centuries after Stuart's death, without intending to do so, Bradley, too, controlled Stuart, by "normalizing" her.

On the other hand, some aspects of the documents are not valuable as significations of sound and may actually interfere with the writer/ speaker's voice. There is every reason to regularize i/j and u/v, for example, and to expand some abbreviations silently, as A. R. Braunmuller did in his *Seventeenth-Century Letter-Book*.[15] To regularize in this way is not to distort the text except in the sense of the text-as-document, in which the editor tries to recreate that piece of paper. As the two letters i and j (as we consider them), like u and v, were regarded as two forms of a single letter well into the seventeenth century, not as separate sounds: m-a-i-e-s-t-y was pronounced "majesty" with a consonantal j between a and e, not a vowel; if the usage is not regularized, however, many modern readers may try to sound what they see, at least until they have worked long with Renaissance texts and no longer even hesitate over i-v-s-t as "just" (if that is ever fully accomplished). Similarly, abbreviations were largely a matter of saving space in an era when paper was hand-made, imported, and expensive,[16] and therefore were not reflective of emotion in the same way as was punctuation. Stuart does not use abbreviations only when she writes in haste, for example, and in this she seems representative of other Renaissance letter writers: she uses abbreviations even in formal presentation letters to other members of the court, and for words that she often writes out in full. If we

---

[14] In *Writing a Woman's Life* (New York: W. W. Norton, 1988), Carolyn G. Heilbrun comments on the degree to which women's anger has been seen as "unacceptable" and "unwomanly" until recent years (13–17).

[15] Subtitled *A Facsimile Edition of Folger MS. V.a. 321* (Newark: Univ. of Delaware Press, 1983).

[16] Giles E. Dawson and Laetitia Kennedy-Skipton, *Elizabethan Handwriting 1500–1650: A Manual* (New York: W. W. Norton, 1966), 6.

were to hear the text spoken, she—we—would say the word, not the abbreviation. The only abbreviations that Stuart never expands are those for Master, Mistress, and Saint, which I have left unexpanded in my edition according to her consistent usage. The words Stuart most often abbreviates—with, which, your, our, the, that—do not warrant the frequent, momentary pauses most modern readers make as they internally expand the abbreviations.

Additions and deletions to the text are signs that should be indicated, because they are the woman's voice pausing and then revising, saying the phrase over again. Revisions bring us closer to her mind. Unlike traditional literary editors, whose goal was not the process by which the text was produced but the author's "final intent," editors of women's letters must be interested in the process by which women chose their words and determined their rhetorical strategies. Most extant letters actually were sent, so the writer's corrections were available to the first reader/hearers, and few letters contain so many additions and deletions or additions and deletions within additions and deletions that they become unintelligible to the reader. Such sheets usually were destroyed, since few people then or now send or hold onto anything so scratched over as to be incoherent. Stuart's court letters are unusual, because her political importance as a claimant to the throne, niece to Mary Stuart, and cousin to King James, meant that some of her drafts were filed and became state papers or part of private collections. As a result, some letters exist in multiple drafts, and it is possible to see where and how Stuart reconsidered her wording and approach, not just in occasional phrases, but in the larger restructuring we mean by *re-vision*. These letters are psychologically and politically fascinating, but also unusual in the problems they pose for the editor, since Stuart's additions and deletions, transferred to print, may be too cumbersome to be deciphered. In my edition, the changes sometimes are discussed in the notes—as when Stuart changed all her "we"s and "our"s to "I"s and "my"s after deciding not to speak for her husband—and sometimes a letter is presented in more than one draft, with the substantial additions and deletions of each.

Explanatory notes and introductory materials pose difficult questions in terms of audience—how much and what kind of information the editor should include for the reader and where it should be placed. Letters are diverse, interdisciplinary texts, and—like all texts—embedded in the culture in which they were produced. As in autobiography, in a set of letters the central character in the narrative is the writer herself, which means that in order to listen with understanding when Stuart expresses relief in late 1603, the reader should know what Stuart did not have to say, that she had been exonerated of complicity in a plot to remove King James and place herself on the throne. Biographical background often is particularly difficult to locate for women, even women as prominent as Arbella Stuart, so the editor necessarily becomes archivist and biographer. Through the letters, the woman has fashioned herself in prose, which likely reflects unconscious conflicts and ambivalences as well. The editor becomes literary critic and psychologist. More than men's letters, women's often explore the private and domestic character of early modern life, hidden now *because* it was private and domestic. Even public activities—like serving as a godmother, sending gifts of sharp salad and red deer pie, handling loans and competing for monopolies, or offering one's grandmother the ends of one's hair clipped during the sixth day of the moon—occurred in contexts not fully clear four hundred years later. The editor becomes social and political historian, economist, and folklorist. Moreover, the letter was an elastic category in the Renaissance, including not only the personal and business letters we write, but what we would handle by telephone, the subtle political and social negotiations that we would conduct in person, and quasi-fictional preludes to the epistolary novel.

What we hear in Stuart's letters is not a single voice from which we can straightforwardly, magically, reconstruct the historical woman, but multiple voices, as Stuart enacts varied social and political roles—the imperious claimant, the deferential woman, the entertaining niece, the canny negotiator, the unjustly imprisoned citizen. To the extent that we can hear Arbella Stuart, we must hear her multiple voices in context. To hear her, we must go beyond her: there is no sound in a vacuum. Stuart's letters reflect a complex interplay of social and political forces; the letters are sometimes silent about what we would most like to know, because fundamental understandings need no articulation. As editors, insofar as we can, we should explore those contexts in light of rapidly changing interpretations of early modern England.

If we try to do so in detailed explanatory notes to each letter, however, either the Renaissance woman's voice will be continually interrupted as the reader switches between text and notes, and the reader's reading shaped by the editor's comments, or, in listening to the woman, the reader will overlook what could have helped make sense of what was said. In general, then, we should very lightly annotate the letters but provide lengthier and more complete introductions than have appeared with most collections of Renaissance letters, introductions in which we dare to cross disciplinary boundaries and treat the biographical, historical, social, political, psychological, economic, and rhetorical contexts in which the letters were produced, even when so doing means we enter disciplinary areas in which we feel uncertain. We need to accept the collapse of the distinction between document and literary work and embrace the opportunity to add the writer to what was once a historical artifact *and* to examine the cultural forces that fill the vacuum and enable voices again to be heard.

Much of what I say here can be applied to letters written by Renaissance men. But our responsibility right now is greater to the women who wrote, because so few women's texts are in print and because we are just beginning to develop a sense of women's writing within early modern culture. If the current publishing climate were so fertile that we could count on seeing many editions of various women's letters, then I would welcome fully modernized texts, excerpted texts, many and diverse forms of the texts. I welcome them anyway. But despite the encouraging signs of the Women Writers Project,[17] the current climate is not so warm and fertile. One of the best grant proposals I have ever read for an edition of a woman's writings was rejected recently because one evaluator, one of eight, said that anything worth reading by Renaissance women was already in print. Given the numbers of our colleagues who hold similar attitudes, multiple editions of many Renaissance women's letters may be a long way off. Even if we have no wish to claim ownership of an early modern woman's words in THE definitive edition, we may be providing what will be *de facto* THE edition for some time. And we should think carefully about the editorial choices that will best allow too-long-silenced women to step from behind the arras and speak of their human drama and, at the same time, be most responsive to the concerns of the audience that has come to hear them.

MONTANA STATE UNIVERSITY

---

[17] Sponsored by Brown University and the National Endowment for the Humanities. For additional information, contact the Project Manager, Elaine Brennan, Box 1841, Brown University, Providence, RI 02912.

Recreating the Letters of
Lady Anne Southwell

LA

JEAN KLENE, C. S. C.

HOULD THE TITLE OF THIS SESSION, "VOICES OF SILENCE,"
reach the Elysian fields, Lady Anne Southwell will undoubt-
edly shriek and then haunt us all, for a "silent voice," at least to
her own time, she was not. On the contrary, each of four prose
letters by her illustrates an insistent voice "play[ing] the Critik," as she
describes herself in one letter. She will accept nothing but agreement.
The letters argue, in brief, for the superiority of poetry over prose, with
Cecily Macwilliams; for a scorning of fortune's gifts and therefore some
consolation in humiliation, with the earl of Falkland; for Sir Richard
Edgecombe's rights to certain lands, with Sir Richard Boyle; and again,
for Edgecombe's rights, with Sir Thomas Browne. Surprisingly, not once
in any of the letters does she apologize for being a woman, even though
she often argues what is expected from a man—especially in the Renaissance. There is none of Shakespeare's Portia demurring, twice in one
speech, "I grant I am a woman, but withal...." (*Julius Caesar*, 2.1.292–
94).[1] In contrast to Portia, Lady Southwell often straightforwardly raises

---

[1] I wish to thank Laetitia Yeandle, Curator of Manuscripts at the Folger Shakespeare Library, who called my attention to Folger MS. V.b.198. All Shakespearean
quotations are taken from *The Riverside Shakespeare*, ed. G. B. Evans (Boston:
Houghton Mifflin Co., 1974).

what sounds, at least on occasion, like a feminist's voice.

Because most people have neither heard about nor read anything by this Renaissance woman, I will introduce the lady and her letters, two of which are part of the commonplace book, Folger MS. V.b.198, which I am editing. The emphasis in this short paper will not be on the letters-as-documents, although some physical aspects of the documents must necessarily be part of the discussion. I do not mean to slight their importance, but, within the limits of a brief paper, to introduce a Renaissance writer and discuss the editing of her letters. My aim is the re-creation of a voice that has rarely been heard for almost four hundred years.

One of the things that makes Lady Southwell worth listening to is her awareness of the female sex. She challenges the use of language by her society, for example, when she complains, "The man that for gods cause forbears to kill/ To sweare, lye, steale or droune his soll in wine/ and in a woord to bee the woorst of ill./ why hee is scornde and calde a femynine" (fol. 48r). Such use "abuse[s]" the Divine Maker himself, she points out. Often she praises the female who is clever and successful—in the Bible (like Rahab [fol. 3r], whose deviousness was far more beneficial to her and the chosen people than "Doegs truth" was), mythology (like Opis [fol. 19v], wife of Saturn, whose wily ways saved her children), and popular culture (like Pope Joan [fol. 46r], whose cleverness improved conditions in the Church—until she herself grew restless). Although Lady Southwell says that a wife "unwitty/ god sends to clogg a bad man to his grave" (fol. 48v), she still has no patience with the "wilfull herresye./ In thinkinge ffemales have so little witt/ as but to serve men they are only fitt" (fol. 26v).

A few biographical details may be useful in hearing Lady Southwell's voice; her commonplace book and public records offer many. She was born in 1573 to Elizabeth (Pomeroy) and Thomas Harris of Cornworthy, the second of their four children.[2] Because Mr. Harris was a Member of Parliament, the family occasionally lived in London. At the Church of St. Clement Danes Anne Harris married "Thomas Suthwell," country squire of Spixworth, Norfolk, on June 24, 1594. The couple may have lived in London or returned to one of Thomas's country estates, but they went to Ireland at some point, contributing to the "plantation of Munster." They lived at Poulnalong (meaning "ship-

[2] John Burke, *A History of the Commoners of Great Britain and Ireland* (London, 1836), 4:430–31.

pool") Castle, the ruins of which remain today, about seven miles up the Bandon River from Kinsale.[3]

Shortly after the death of Sir Thomas in 1626, Lady Anne married Captain Henry Sibthorpe, with whom she returned to Clerkenwell, on the outskirts of London. In 1631 they moved to Acton, where they lived in "Tennements" rented from Robert Johnson, believed to be the composer of the songs for Shakespeare's *Tempest*.[4] She died on October 2, 1636, according to Sibthorpe's testimonial on the last folio of Folger V.b.198, a testimonial also appearing on a plaque in St. Mary's Church at Acton, suggesting that she is buried there.[5]

The voice of Anne Southwell was also a strident one on occasion, as the records testify, albeit enigmatically. On May 15, 1603, Captain John Skinner, apparently assigned to send Mrs. Southwell from Berwick to London, writes to Cecil, insisting that he tried to get the lady started but failed. Mrs. Southwell, Skinner reports, "be took herself to her bed for two or three days and with vexing made herself ill indeed." She asserts that she will not go "except his Majesty send her allowance for her charge, . . . and men for attendance" lest she "be murthered." According to an expense account later submitted by Thomas Meade, "Mrs. Southwell's keeper," we know that, finally, she did make the journey, but little more about the problems surrounding it. Without more research, perhaps all we can conclude is that, in this case, she was neither silent nor obedient, at least to Captain Skinner.[6]

After the trip to London and the coronation of James I, her husband, now "Sir" Thomas, petitions Cecil to have the Southwell name cleared since, he insists, "It was the Queen's letters, that moved my wife's journey; if we had pretended without such a cause, there had been the less regard due to us."[7] Without further evidence, we cannot be sure

---

[3] I wish to thank Margaret J. Swarbrick, Chief Archivist of Westminster City Hall, for the data regarding the marriage at St. Clement Danes. See *The Peerage of Ireland* (Dublin, 1754), 4:223–28. Both of the letters for Sir Richard Edgecombe were sent from Poulnalong.

[4] *The New Grove Dictionary of Music and Musicians*, ed. Stanley Sadie (Washington, D.C., 1980), 9:681–82.

[5] *The Peerage of Ireland* (Dublin, 1779), pages on "Southwell, Viscount Southwell," sent by the present Viscount Southwell, 7.

[6] *Historical Manuscripts Commission Calendar of the Manuscripts of the Marquess of Salisbury Preserved at Hatfield House, Hertfordshire* (London, 1930), Part XV, 90–91, 124. I am grateful to Steven May for calling my attention to this.

[7] *H. M. C. Salisbury* (London, 1930), Part XV, 388.

about the details of this dramatic episode, but we can at least speculate that Mrs. Southwell was part of the group of ladies "of all degrees" sent from London to welcome Queen Anne in Berwick.[8] Judging from how aware Lady Southwell seems to be of prostitutes, pedlars, "Bawdes and Atturneyes," she could no doubt handle herself among many different kinds of people; and she could challenge a man's powers of stewardship. About the well-known dangers of travel, she was certainly correct.

During the years between Anne Southwell's death and today, however, her voice was indeed silent (at least to those of us who have not heard the female ghost, whom I am assuming for playful purposes is Lady Anne, said by the locals in Kinsale to stop passersby at the ruins of Poulnalong Castle—very late at night—with a question that no one has ever repeated).[9] Hence I grant whole-heartedly that this session is indeed appropriately named—especially in the sense Malraux was exploring in *Les Voix du Silence*, for in Lady Southwell's work "there survives for us the interior and invincible voice of a past civilization."[10]

As an editor at work on Folger MS. V.b.198, a bound volume of folios with watermarks dating before 1600, with the exception of the last two, which contain memorial verses and a testimonial by Lady Southwell's second husband, Captain Sibthorpe, I am still very much engaged in asking questions about the text, the paper on which the various selections are written, the many scribes and people addressed or mentioned. Even though all the answers could not be included in a literal edition for the Renaissance English Text Society because they may never be found, the search still helps in an understanding of the central voice of the folios. They also help in deciphering some of Lady Anne's own very

---

[8] Agnes Strickland, *Lives of the Queens of England* (New York, 1885), 3:648–49.

[9] I am grateful to journalist Molly Woulfe, who recently visited the ruins of Poulnalong Castle, listened to the tales of the locals in Kinsale and reported that a female ghost occasionally appears and asks a question—one which no one has repeated. She describes a desolation probably as true in 1626 as it is today: "The view was bleak. The Bandon River was dull, muddy and wide here, and there was a marshy area and a treeless field directly across. Strange, high bird cries came from the rushes and unseen cattle were lowing in the fields. The sun was bright but it was still a very lonely place. A week of rain would drive one to madness. Poor Lady Southwell! I'd have jumped ship" (in a letter of September 27, 1990).

[10] (Paris, 1958), 628, discussed in Jean Leymarie, "Malraux and the Creative Process," trans. by Robert Speaight, in *Life and Work*, ed. Martine de Courcel (New York: Harcourt, Brace, Jovanovich, 1976) 184–275. I am indebted to Renée Kingcaid for this reference.

difficult writing, angular and non-cursive as it is, which appears in the signature on fol. 2r, in notes for poetry on folios 44v–46r and 57r–58r, and in corrections on folios 13r, 22v, 32v, 33r and v, 49v, 50v, 51v, 52r, 53r, and 54v. Many of the folios contain compositions by Lady Southwell; others contain those which she probably collected—one by Sir Walter Ralegh and two by Henry King—inventories of her belongings, accounts of her payments for the rent in an Acton home, a mini-bestiary, scriptural and doctrinal commentary, and apothegms. As I ponder the collection, I am doing what D. F. McKenzie calls the carpentry necessary to construct a text:[11] searching the tomes of the Folger, questioning generous seventeenth-century scholars, writing to parish vicars and the offices of city records, and asking for information from librarians in Ireland, England, and the United States. As a result, I am relatively sure that very little of her work has been published, discussed, or even mentioned. Even her descendant, the present viscount Southwell, knew nothing about her, beyond what the Southwell pages of the *Complete Peerage of Ireland* report.

The story of what the world has heard from the lady begins with a publication during her own lifetime. Two brief prose pieces—a response to John Donne's "Newes from the very Countrey" and a response to Sir Thomas Overbury's "Newes from Court"—were published in *A wife now the widdow of Sir Thomas Overbvrye* . . . (London, 1614). A third contribution, "Certaine *Edicts* from a Parliament in *Eutopia*; written by the Lady Southwell" was added to the impression published in 1616 and renamed *Sir Thomas Ouerburie, his wife.* Two unpublished letters to be discussed in this paper, part of the Lismore papers, are now at Chatsworth in Derbyshire, England. She also wrote two lengthy meditations, now at the British Library, on commandments, titled Precept 3 and 4,[12] which are revisions of meditations first appearing in the commonplace book.

---

[11] *Bibliography and the Sociology of Texts*, The Panizzi Lectures, 1985 (London: The British Library, 1986), 5.

[12] I am indebted to Roberta Zonghi for xeroxes of Lady Anne's "Edicts" in the Overbury publication and for her comments on the book. Identification of John Donne's contribution is made in Geoffrey Keynes, *A Bibliography of Dr. John Donne*, 2nd ed. (Cambridge: The Univ. Press, 1932); it is discussed in Evelyn Simpson, "John Donne and Sir Thomas Overbury's 'Characters,' " *MLR* 18 (1923): 410–15. Her article is cited in John R. Roberts, *John Donne: An Annotated Bibliography of Modern Criticism 1912–1967* (Columbia: Univ. of Missouri Press, 1973). I am grateful to the British Library and its Curator of Manuscripts, Hilton Kelliher, for copies of Lansdowne 740, fols. 142–167b.

Although most of the world has never heard of Lady Southwell, her name and reputation have surfaced occasionally. In the eighteenth century, the writer George Ballard includes her name in a list of learned ladies in his *Memoirs of British Ladies*; Joseph Hunter, in "Chorus Vatum Anglicanorum," tells us that Anne, renowned for her learning and poetic skills, married Sir Thomas Southwell, and that Robert Herrick wrote an epithalamium for their wedding—highly doubtful, of course, since Herrick was but three years old in 1594 when they were married. For an anniversary, however, he may have done so. Editing Ralegh's poem, "The Lie," in 1929, Agnes Latham cites the twelve lines of the poem found only in Lady Southwell's commonplace book. Latham says very little about Lady Southwell, however, or the quality of her poetry. Finally, Jean Cavanaugh published the catalogue of books and Lady Southwell's letter to Lady Ridgeway.[13] Thus a surprising, albeit modest, amount by and about her does exist.

Research on the provenance of Folger MS. V.b.198 reveals that, having been bound with "Russia leather" in the nineteenth-century, it was purchased by Mr. Henry Folger from P. J. and A. E. Dobell in 1927, who had purchased it from Sir T. Phillipps in London in 1908. Although at least some of the sheets had begun life as an account book for John Sibthorpe, who signs ten of the fifteen accounts written in a clear sixteenth-century secretary hand, John's descendant Henry must have given it to his wife at their marriage in 1626. Exactly when some of the folios were added is impossible to tell. The watermarks of some inserted sheets, like the predominant Nicholas Lebe watermark of the 1580s (Briquet 8080) all date before 1600[14] and hence do not help us answer questions about when or why some folios were added. Sibthorpe may have decided, with Lady Anne, to include the letters, one to Lady Ridgeway and the other to the Lord Falkland, or, he may have inserted one or both after her death.

---

[13] Ballard (London, 1775), vii; Hunter, a transcript of British Library Add. MSS. 24487–24492, Vol. XI, under "Robert Southwell"; Latham, *The Poems of Sir Walter Ralegh* (London: Constable & Co., Ltd., 1929), "The Lie," 45–47, 152–59 and 256–58; Cavanaugh, *Studies in Bibliography* 20 (1967), 243–54; and "Lady Southwell's Defense of Poetry," *ELR* 14.3 (1984), between 284–85.

[14] I am grateful to Nati Krivatsy for showing me *Dobell's Catalogue of Poetical Manuscripts*, 2–5. I am grateful to Laetitia Yeandle, Curator of Manuscripts at the Folger, for helping in the identification of the watermarks, using C. M. Briquet, *Les Filigranes*, 4 vols., ed. Allen Stevenson (Amsterdam, 1970). I also used Edward Heawood, *Watermarks*, vol. 1 (Hilversum, Holland: The Paper Publications Soc., 1950).

Perhaps a brief digression on the shortest illustration of Lady Anne's wit will help us hear what resounds throughout the book as well as in the letters: wit and godliness. The speaker in the poem sounds like Shakespeare's Emilia, complaining about the double standard (*Othello*, 4.3.86–103):

> All maried men desire to have good wifes:
> but few give good example by thir lives
> They are owr head they wodd have us thir heles.
> this makes the good wife kick the good man reles
> [=reels].
> When god brought Eve to Adam for a bride
> the text sayes she was taene from out mans side
> A simbole of that side, whose sacred bloud.
> flowed for his spowse, the Churches savinge good.
> This is a misterie, perhaps too deepe.
> for blockish Adam that was falen a sleepe.   (fol. 16r)

Considering the challenging whimsy illustrated in this[15] and other poems, the silencing of her voice seems astonishing.

Not all of Lady Southwell's works, however, are equally inspiring, and it may be good news to hear that other authors did write a few of the poems. Checking in the first-line indices now available,[16] however, reveals that, in addition to the three poems by others mentioned above, only one other, Sonnet 1 on folio 1, appears in another book, Folger MS. V.a.339, dated 1630. Because Lady Southwell's is dated 1626, the other may have been copied from hers, or both could have been a copy of a popular poem. Even as some of Lady Anne's poems preach about our "clayey" weaknesses, however, other elements in the lines can fascinate a reader. When she is scolding those of us who "goosel" out the time, for example, her choice of a word like "goosel" can still amuse. Even the way she changes a biblical line into a more violent image, for

[handwritten note: 3 poems ("sonnetts") appear in E. Doughtie, Lyrics ... because they are in songbooks of the early 17th century]

---

[15] In the topos of Eve's superiority, Lady Anne may be echoing Agrippa, whose name and *De occulta* she mentions in Precept 3, stanza 82. Regarding the topos, see Linda Woodbridge, *Women and the English Renaissance: Literature and the Nature of Mankind 1540–1620* (Urbana & Chicago: Univ. of Illinois Press, 1984), 38–44.

[16] The Folger First-Line Index; Margaret C. Crum, ed., *First Line Index of English Poetry 1500–1800 in Manuscripts of the Bodleian Library Oxford* (Oxford: Clarendon Press, 1969). I am grateful to Hilton Kelliher, who has also checked the index—insofar as it has been completed—of the British Library. He has also said that he recognizes none of the first lines.

example, catches the imagination: the Christian paradox, "Unless the grain of wheat falling into the ground, die, itself remains alone," becomes "the grayne wee sow doth dy, rott, loose his shape,/ before it doth an other body take" (fol. 43v). Whatever the topic, she has no use for sentimentality.

The copies of two letters that she sent are also an important part of the commonplace book, contributing significantly to the sound of her voice. Although they are unique, as all letters are, in presenting themselves as writing,[17] editing them requires a study of the same knowable "facts" that the whole commonplace book requires, as A. R. Braunmuller, probably the reigning master-carpenter of Elizabethan letters, tells us. We look first at things like watermarks and handwriting and then at the letter's date and sender, its addressee, its place of origin, and its destination. Braunmuller also speaks of how an editor has to thread his way through the complexities of noble families, with all their titles and royal politicking.[18] Another possible metaphor for an editor's interdisciplinary *bricolage* work might be *bricolage*—or "puttering"—as a kind of academic jack-of-all-trades.[19] Whatever the metaphor, the work requires a great deal of time but offers amazing rewards.

Braunmuller's edition of *A Seventeenth-Century Letter-Book* superbly illustrates the method he advocates.[20] Among other things, his book also suggests that men wrote many more letters than women did. The numbers have increased, however, since the early sixteenth century. At that time, a collection of the 3,140 letters written to *from* Erasmus shows that only three of them came from women, one queen and two relatives of humanist government officials. The illiteracy among women and minimal attention given to writing for both sexes, as explained by David Cressy and Arthur J. Slavin and others,[21] also needs consideration in an examination of one woman's voice.

but see newer Early Modern Women's Letter Writing 1450-1700 James Daybell.

[17] Claudio Guillen, "Notes toward the Study of the Renaissance Letter," in *Renaissance Genres: Essays on Theory, History, and Interpretation*, ed. Barbara Kiefer Lewalski (Cambridge, Mass.: Harvard Univ. Press, 1986), 80.

[18] "Editing Elizabethan Letters," *TEXT* 1 (1984, for 1981): 185–99.

[19] I am indebted to Jeanne Rodes, for suggesting this and for reading this paper.

[20] *A Seventeenth-Century Letter-Book: A Facsimile Edition of Folger MS. V.a.321 with Transcript, Annotation, and Commentary* (Newark: Univ. of Delaware Press, 1983).

[21] Anne M. O'Donnell, S. N. D., "Sixth Annual Bainton Lecture: Contemporary Women in the Letters of Erasmus," *Erasmus of Rotterdam Yearbook Nine* (1989), 34–72. David Cressy, *Literacy and the Social Order: Reading and Writing in Tudor and Stuart England* (Cambridge: The Univ. Press, 1980), whose careful work shows how few women—outside of London and aristocratic homes throughout the country—learned

The first letter under discussion today, one of the two at Chatsworth, is not in the commonplace book, nor have I examined the originals, but I include them because they are prose documents contributing to our understanding of Lady Southwell and her voice. The first, written in 1623 in a clear italic hand, is addressed to Sir Richard Boyle, Earl of Cork, asking him "for the recoverie of certaine writings of Bodrugans landes detained by one Powre of Kilmeden" in behalf of Sir Richard Edgecombe, the "constant friend" of her "deceased father." So far, the letter sounds like the male discourse of property disputes. Then Lady Anne speaks as any citizen of County Cork might, recognizing the Earl's largesse and her own dependency on him. Finally, however, while demanding that the Earl of Cork comply with her request, Lady Anne speaks as only a woman would, illustrating, perhaps, what Elaine Showalter has called a "double-voiced discourse," i.e., "one that simultaneously acknowledges its dependence on the male and implies its own unique positive value."[22] Lady Anne says, "But if you will neither doe mee good in this respecte, nor tell mee why; I must bee forc'd to put up a petticion against you to the Countesse, who by this tyme (I hope) is stronge enough to putt you ten thousand pound in debt by the birth of another sonne or daughter." To a man whose wife had already delivered twelve children,[23] this was no idle threat. (Lady Boyle, incidentally, was to give birth to three more, the last being Robert, the famous scientist.) Few petitioners of either sex would tease an earl in this manner, but the threat of another child could only come, I suspect, from a female speaker.

---

to write (see especially 112, 115, 128, and 145); and *Education in Tudor and Stuart England* (London: Edward Arnold, 1975), quoting Richard Mulcaster on schooling for girls, in 1581. See also Arthur J. Slavin, *The Tudor Age and Beyond: England from the Black Death to the End of the Age of Elizabeth* (Malabar, Florida: Robert R. Krieger Pub. Co., 1987), who contrasts the limited amount of instruction in writing, for both sexes, to the larger amounts in reading, 196; and Foster Watson, *The English Grammar Schools to 1660: Their Curriculum and Practice* (Cambridge: The Univ. Press, 1908), chap. 11, 186–204, which explains that "written work had not ordinarily played any considerable part in school practice" (186). Writing, "in the earlier part of the 17th century, in the Grammar Schools, . . . if taught at all, seems to have been regarded as an extra and paid for by a special fee" (192).

[22] "Feminist Criticism in the Wilderness," *Critical Inquiry* 8.2 (1981): 179–205. The definition of Showalter's phrase comes from Barbara J. Bono, "Mixed Gender, Mixed Genre in *As You Like It*," *Renaissance Genres*, ed. Lewalski, 194.

[23] Nicholas Canny, *The Upstart Earl: A Study of the Social and Mental World of Richard Boyle First Earl of Cork 1566–1643* (Cambridge: The Univ. Press, 1982); see the list of the children and their dates of birth, 88.

One month after Lady Southwell's letter to the Earl of Cork, in November of 1623, she makes the same request to Sir Thomas Browne, a cousin to Sir Richard Boyle (not the well-known English writer). This letter, also at Chatsworth, is only nine lines long; she is writing "once more" to remind Browne "of Bodugans writings in Powres hands of Kilmeden, belonginge to Sir Richard Edgecombe." Searching the State Papers and histories of Ireland has not provided much information on this Sir Thomas Browne beyond things like the date of his being knighted in 1607 and his relationship (i.e., a cousin) to the famous Earl of Cork. Occasionally Browne signs a document as one of several, but there is no indication of how he functioned in the project at hand. One enigmatic letter from the Earl of Thormond to Boyle in 1613 sends greetings to Sir Thomas Browne and warns, "I hope he will have care, of sending away my hawkes." In a postscript, Thormond adds, "I have provided him [Sir T. B.] a brave hatt and feather to weare for his hauke this yeare."[24] Intriguing gifts notwithstanding, adequate editorial commentary on Sir Thomas Browne requires more research. What Southwell's letter to Browne does show clearly, however, is a determined writer pursuing a cause relentlessly for the friend of her deceased father.

A letter of more substantive importance in the search for Lady Anne's voice should be considered next in the chronological order of the four prose documents. She sent it to her close friend, Cecily Macwilliams, Lady Ridgeway of Londonderry, and a copy of it was written on folio 3 of the commonplace book. This letter argues for the superiority of poetry over prose, for which her friend, apparently, has stated a preference. Lady Anne emphasizes the power of art to organize and keep experiences and ideas. She also stresses some of the same ideas that Sidney does in his "Defense of Poesy." Like him, she praises David for his powerful poetry; like him and others, she too is concerned about harmony in the microcosm and the macrocosm. Poetry has by its very nature, she argues, the power to give a sense of balance to life. When Lady Anne denigrates popular epyllions, warning her friend against letting a "wanton Venus and Adonis," or "Hero and Leander," i.e., a "busy nothing," be a means to "skandalize this art" of poetry (fol. 3r), I am not sure whom she sees herself as echoing: male preachers, pious women engaged in "re-

---

[24] William A. Shaw, *The Knights of England* (London, 1906), 2:143. *The Lismore Papers . . . of Sir Richard Boyle, . . . Earl of Cork*, ed. A. B. Grosart, 2nd ser. (London, 1886–88), 1:148.

deeming Eve,"[25] or perhaps both. Whatever the case may be, the warning illustrates the cultural importance of poetry in general and Ovidian poems in particular, for both ladies know them well.

Occasionally, however, the voice in the letter differs radically from male voices. Her analogy for poetry, for example, describes it as the "silke thredd that stringes your chayne of pearle; which being broken, your jewells fall into the rushes; and the more you seeke for it, the more it falles into the dust of oblivion." Poetry, she argues, provides the unity of discourse that keeps the precious pearls together, i.e., in a context. Another statement, about her preference for orbicular forms (which also shows up in her poetry), sounds like another avenue needing investigation: the connection between women and the "iconography of centralized focus, [and] curved lines" recently explored by Lucy Lippard and Judy Chicago.[26]

Looking into the editorial "facts" about the letter shows that the copy in the commonplace book is written on paper tipped onto a blank sheet, with the watermark of a pot and a crescent moon above (similar to Briquet 12804 of 1588, or 12806 of 1600). The scribe's hand resembles that of Samuel Rowson, who signs as a witness to payments of the rent six times (fols. 71r and v and 72v); the hand is predominantly italic, clear and easily legible. It is possible that the folio was added after Lady Southwell's death, yet doubtful, for Samuel Rowson's signature does not appear in the two accounts after March, 1635. Another hand adds a note under the letter, affirming that it is a "vera copia." Although the date and other words are illegible, the original letter must have been written during or before 1627 when Lady Ridgeway died. An editor's task of explaining the friendship of the two women is alleviated by the two elegies for Lady Ridgeway which follow the letter: the first is a pretended one—a dramatic and witty chiding of the friend who has not written, and the second a sincere one, expressing shock and grief at the friend's actual death. What unfolds in the three works, even though no response from Lady Ridgeway appears, is a strong relationship between the two women. The pretended elegy by Lady Anne shows, as no other poem in the book does, how she could enjoy teasing her friend and mocking her-

---

[25] As explained by Elaine V. Beilin, *Redeeming Eve: Women Writers of the English Renaissance* (Princeton: Princeton Univ. Press, 1987).

[26] Showalter, "Feminist Criticism," 188 n. 21, citing Rich, *Of Woman Born: Motherhood as Experience and Institution* (New York, 1977), 62; and Lucy Lippard, *From the Center: Feminist Essays on Women's Art* (New York, 1976).

self simultaneously.[27] The very short sincere elegy following the pretended one forces a reader to recognize the profound grief of the writer. One indication, for example, comes in the fact that the pretended elegy extends for 124 lines of iambic pentameter, but the sincere one, for only eighteen lines of iambic tetrameter. As the first line of the sincere elegy says, Lady Anne's pen is now "choakt with gall."

The second letter in the commonplace book, addressed to Sir Henry Cary, the Lord Deputy Earl of Falkland, was written to console him in the humiliation of being demoted. History books record that, after strenuous efforts to govern in a rebellious land, Falkland was recalled to England. Examining the *Calendar of State Papers Ireland* lets us see that Lady Southwell is humanely returning a favor, for the Lord Deputy had written to King Charles I on October 4, 1627, seeking justice for Captain Sibthorpe, Lady Anne's second husband. Falkland insisted that Sibthorpe had served the king well in the 1625 Cadiz expedition, and that, in spite of his courageous service, he had still been overlooked while others less deserving were promoted. In addition, Falkland requested that Sibthorpe "be allowed the command of one of the substitute companies sent over" to Ireland.[28] The Deputy's kindness was not forgotten by Lady Southwell.

Paleographic study shows that the scribe's hand resembles that of Captain Sibthorpe, who writes and signs folio·74. The letters seem carefully formed, and the lines, with double dashes as fillers to justify the right margin, form a neat rectangle on the page—perhaps to give the letter a very business-like appearance. Although folio 4, like folio 3, is only a copy of the original, the scribe still seems to underscore the formality of the relationship between writer and recipient. The formality is reinforced by the two Latin phrases within only eighteen lines and the highly Latinate vocabulary of the whole letter. The other three letters contain no foreign phrases whatever. Examining these points makes me wonder

---

27   Poets, and Popeleings, are æquippollent
            Both makers are, of Gods, of like descent.
            Poets makes blinde Gods, whoe with willowes beates them,
            Popelings makes Hoasts of Gods, and ever eates them.
            But let them both, Poets and popelings, passe.
            Whoe deales too much with eyther, is an Asse   (fol. 20r, 81–86)
Lady Cecily or her ancestors may have been Roman Catholics, given her name, and Lady Anne, of course, was a poet.
28 *Calendar of State Papers Ireland* (1625–32), 273. For a discussion of Falkland's problems, see *A New History of Ireland*, eds. T.W. Moody, F.X. Martin, F.J. Byrne, vol. 3, Early Modern Ireland 1534–1691 (Oxford: Clarendon Press, 1976), 238–42.

whether this letter was copied and added to the book by a husband concerned to build up the image of his beloved wife. If the *topos* in epistolary theory holds true, that is, that the letter is "a halved dialogue, or part of a conversation with an absent friend,"[29] then Lady Southwell's stature increases with the importance of her friends.

In contrast to the letter's formal appearance, however, an unusual union of rhetorical strategy and paleography adds vivid color to at least one sentence. The last word in the line, "Nature, chance and death do dance the *Matechyne*," ends in a flourish, emphasizing the bravado of the dancers stomping out the Matechyne, an Arabian dance in which men swing swords rhythmically. (The line here has more power, incidentally, than the way she had written it earlier: "life, death, and time, do with short cudgels dance the Matachine" [*Ouerburie*, O6r].) Accenting four words in the text, as the scribe does—probably at Lady Anne's command—suggests a similar energy in the writer's attempt to persuade; she will accept nothing but Falkland's being consoled.

The same strong voice begins the letter, as Lady Anne asks permission to "play the Critick" about Falkland's language. She acknowledges his important position and his kindness, but then she needles him for indulging in despair by her focusing on the word that he must have used, either to her or others: "all." He has insisted, apparently, that he has lost *all*. She responds that he has lost but *one* of the gifts of "fleeteinge" fortune and therefore cannot despair. No voice calls a *serio ludere* in this letter; on the contrary, the writer remains reserved and respectful.

Editorial problems abound here. First, the watermark is undecipherable, for the paper, once folded in small squares of approximately 1 1/2", is now pasted flat on the folio. One also has to wonder why the copy of such a letter would have been folded into small squares. Did Captain Sibthorpe take it (out of his bottom drawer?) sometime during the last years of their life together and decide with her to include it? Or did he add it after his wife's death? And did he include it to impress readers with her importance? Another enigma lies in the misleading date. Although the note below the letter, in a different hand, gives the date "1628," it must be an error, for Falkland was recalled on April 1, 1629.[30] Does the error indicate that the letter was added to the book

---

[29] Discussed in Guillen, 77–78.
[30] *Complete Peerage* (London, 1926), 5:239; *New History*, 3:241; *DNB*, s.v., Cary, Sir Henry, first Viscount Falkland (1921–22, 3:1150).

long after the event? Another problem lies in describing the hand. Is it, in fact, that of Captain Sibthorpe, or did many scribes share the characteristics that suggest the versatile hand of the Captain? I am still speculating.

Questions about the addressees and their responses tease continually, for nothing on the folios indicates that the letters were actually sent to the recipients named in the title. Nor do we have a record of a response from these, or any of Lady Southwell's letters. They do have an urgency that convinces me they were indeed sent, but, without further evidence, I cannot be sure.

Judging from the people to, for, and about whom Lady Southwell writes, both in England and Ireland, she moved in (or at least wanted to move in) aristocratic circles. Beginning at the top of the human hierarchy, she prefaces the Precepts mentioned above with a one-page "Poetical Dedication to the King." Other people about or to whom she wrote, besides those addressed in letters, include Doctor Bernard Adams, bishop of Limerick; Sir George Touchet, Lord Audeley, first earl of Castlehaven; the duchess of Lennox; Queen Anne of Bohemia; Elizabeth Stuart, wife of the Palatinate; King Gustavus Adolphus of Sweden; the countess of Somerset; and Robert Johnson, respected court lutenist and composer. Lady Anne's world was not a narrow one. Ours will be made less narrow when we can clearly hear her voice.

SAINT MARY'S COLLEGE
NOTRE DAME

Some Problems in Editing
Margaret Cavendish

JAMES FITZMAURICE

I T IIAS BEEN UNDERSTOOD FOR A LONG TIME THAT MARGARET
Cavendish holds an important place in literary history as the first
woman in England to publish a great deal, and it is gradually
becoming apparent that Cavendish is an author of importance in
her own right. As the label "Mad Madge of Newcastle" ceases to be
taken to be a literal description and as Cavendish gains respect for her
autobiography, her plays, her letters, and even her science, we may expect to see a number of scholarly editions initiated. For prospective editors, there are substantial difficulties to be faced, but there are also some
daunting tasks that need not be performed.

First the tasks that require no work. There are no variant readings to
be gleaned from manuscripts, because there are no extant manuscripts for
what went to press. There are, of course, the manuscript letters that
passed from Cavendish to her husband,[1] but they are on the topic of
their impending marriage and do not bear directly on any of her pub-

---

[1] The letters may be found in *The Phanseys of William Cavendish*, ed. Douglas
Grant (London: Nonesuch Press, 1956), and in *Letters Written by Charles Lamb's
"Princely Woman"* (London: John Murray, 1909). The originals are in the Portland
Loan Collection at the British Library.

lished writing. Furthermore, with the exception of one possibility with
the poems, very few literary manuscripts are likely to turn up, for Cavendish herself tells us that she destroyed handwritten copies once the
printed texts appeared.[2] Many of the books that she wrote exist only in
the one edition that appeared in her life, so there is often only a single
authority on which to base a text. Thus, in many cases it will be unnecessary to compare various editions. Finally, there are almost no passages
offering difficulties in syntax or otherwise providing problems with literal
meaning. Cavendish often complains about errors produced by her
printers, but her lamentations are probably *pro forma*, for such errors are
few and easy to correct.

The poetry, of course, will make for a difficult project, and, from the
point of view of reception history, the poetry is extremely important.
Selections from it have been constantly in print since the middle of the
eighteenth century, but the reputation of Cavendish as a gentle eccentric
was a crucial factor in determining what was chosen for publication and
what was left unprinted. Early editors especially liked her poems on
Queen Mab and the fairy folk. Obviously, any edition produced in the
1990s will need to reconsider this placement of emphasis, but there are
more elusive problems.

Three editions of the poems appeared during the lifetime of Cavendish and a number of the poems were rewritten. Some poems were
dropped in the later editions and others added.[3] In addition, there are a
few marginalia to be found in a copy in the British Library. The marginalia are in a hand very like that used by Cavendish, and they may be her
revisions. Finally, Horace Walpole[4] and Mary Hays[5] both refer to the

---

[2] Margaret Cavendish, *CCXI Sociable Letters* (London: William Wilson, 1664), no. 143.

[3] A detailed and accurate bibliography of works by Cavendish printed in her
lifetime is to be found in Douglas Grant's *Margaret the First* (London: Rupert Hart-
Davis, 1957), 240–42.

[4] Walpole says in his text, "Three volumes more in folio, of her poems, are preserved in manuscript." He continues in a note, "Cibber, or Shiels, reports these to
have been possessed by Mr. Thomas Richardson and bishop Willis. Lives of the
Poets, vol. ii, p. 167. Mr. Nichols, in the notes to his Miscellany poems, says he was
informed that the MSS. of the Duchess had been given to St. John's College,
Cambridge, where they are now to be found in good order. Vol. iv. p. 353." *A
Catalogue of the Royal and Noble Authors of England, Scotland, and Ireland* (London,
1806), 3:148.

[5] Mary Hays writes: "In the library of the late Mr. Thomas Richardson, were the
duchess of Newcastle's poems, two volumes, folio, MS. Vid. Richardson's Cat. p. 50.

existence of manuscript poems. They seem to be referring to the same manuscript, which Walpole locates at St. John's College, Cambridge. Were these hand-made copies of what was already printed, or were they poems that had never seen the light in any form? Unfortunately, St. John's has no record of them. They may show up or may not, but there seems to be little an editor can do in an effort to try to locate them.

The editor of the poems probably has as his or her most important task in coming to grips with Cavendish as a poet. That is, he or she must decide what the later editions represent in the poetic development of Cavendish. Cavendish wrote a great deal about herself as writer, but much of that appears to have been involved with the creation of a public image, an image that was intended to protect her from the unpleasant fates of earlier woman writers like Elizabeth Cary and Lady Mary Wroth.[6]

The second most important book by Cavendish from the point of view of reception history is the life of her husband. We know it was respected by her near contemporaries, for it is the one book that was brought out in a second edition shortly after her death. It appears to have been used as a source by an important seventeenth-century historian, John Rushworth, and it provided a model for Mary Hutchinson's life of her own husband.[7] The life of her husband by Cavendish appears to have gathered dust during the eighteenth and first half of the nineteenth centuries, but that may be only an appearance. An editor will want to trace its influence with Civil War historians, an influence that may well be covert. Cavendish as Mad Madge could not be quoted by historians even though they might use her detailed accounting of facts. Although she claims quite the contrary, she had a fondness for giving exact locations, numbers of troops, dates, and names of officers. A heavily annotated copy in the British Library may provide clues to the use of the life by historians in the eighteenth and nineteenth centuries.

At the end of the nineteenth century and in the first fifty years of the twentieth, the life was frequently reprinted. Two editors, Firth and

---

In that of the late bishop Willis, is another MS. of her poems in folio. Vid. Cat. p. 55." *Female Biography or Memoirs of Illustrious and Celebrated Women of all Ages and Countries* (London: Richard Phillips, 1803), 1:523.

[6] See my "Fancy and the Family: Self-characterizations of Margaret Cavendish," *Huntington Library Quarterly* (Summer, 1990): 199–209.

[7] Sara Heller Mendelson, *The Mental World of Stuart Women* (Amherst: Univ. of Massachusetts Press, 1987), 61.

Lower, helped to bring the life as well as the autobiography to the general public,[8] which seems to have had an appetite for information about seventeenth-century aristocrats. It was during this time, too, that the first biographies of Cavendish and her husband were written.[9] The life of the husband and the autobiography, however, were not linked in print during the lifetime of Cavendish. She wrote and published her autobiography a full ten years before she completed the life of her husband and, perhaps significantly, included the autobiography with a group of short stories and poems titled *Natures Pictures*. The numerous reprints in one volume of the autobiography and life of the husband have no doubt suggested a false picture of early printing history. This distortion is especially striking, since the life of the husband is always placed at the beginning of the volume and the autobiography added as something of an appendix.

As a candidate for an edition itself, *Natures Pictures* involves the hidden dangers of source and influence. *Natures Pictures* along with another book, *The Worlds Olio*, may seem to be without the usual written sources, for Cavendish often claimed to have read virtually nothing. She frequently said that she depended solely on her fancy to spin original creations out of her mind, a little as a spider spins a web out of its body.[10] The more one reads Cavendish, however, the more one is surprised by her dependence on books. Who would have thought, for instance, that Cavendish read Philemon Holland's 1606 translation of Suetonius? Verbal echoes appear in *Sociable Letters* (Letter 162). Still, it will probably not be high-brow reading that mostly underlies *Natures Pictures*. It and *The Worlds Olio* are more likely to be indebted to books of plays, jest books, and romances.

While there is good reason to connect the publication of the autobi-

---

[8] Margaret Cavendish, *The Life of William Cavendish Duke of Newcastle to which is Added the True Relation of my Birth Breeding and Life by Margaret Duchess of Newcastle*, ed. C. H. Firth (London: George Routledge, [n.d.]), and *The Lives of William Cavendish, Duke of Newcastle, and of His Wife, Margaret Duchess of Newcastle*, ed. Mark Antony Lower (London: John Russell Smith, 1872).

[9] Richard William Goulding, *Margaret (Lucas) Duchess of Newcastle* (Lincoln: Lincolnshire Chronicle Ltd., 1925); [Thomas Longueville], *The First Duke and Duchess of Newcastle-upon-Tyne* (London: Longmans, Green, and Co., 1910); Henry Ten Eyck Perry, *The First Duchess of Newcastle & her Husband as Figures in Literary History* (Boston: Ginn and Co., 1918); A. S. Turberville, *A History of Welbeck Abbey and its Owners*, Vol. 1 (London: Faber & Faber, 1938).

[10] Sylvia Bowerbank, "The Spider's Delight: Margaret Cavendish and the 'Female Imagination'" *English Literary Renaissance* 14 (1984): 392–408.

ography of Cavendish with *Natures Pictures*, it will not always be easy to determine what item should be published with what. *The Blazing World* has attracted a good deal of attention lately, but it is not entirely clear whether or to what extent it is a part of *Observations upon Experimental Philosophy*.[11] It was published with *Observations* in 1666 and again in 1668, but it also appeared separately in 1668. There is yet another twist. A fragment titled "A Piece of a Play" was printed with *Plays* (1668),[12] and a note suggests that the fragment was intended for *The Blazing World*. The interrelationships among all of these items may turn out to be complicated.

The plays, especially those printed in the 1668 volume, are interesting from the point of view of reception history. In the first seventy-five years after her death, Cavendish was most often seen as a dramatist. In the later eighteenth century and throughout the nineteenth century, her plays were taken to be racy and were often passed over with little comment. Adolphus Ward said in 1899 that she "loses herself in unrefined fun, and at times falls into a license of coarse dialogue, resembling, [he] regret[s] to say, that in which the comedies of her contemporary, Mrs. Aphra Behn, abound."[13] Ironically, the comparison with Behn is liable to work to her advantage rather than against it these days. Although they have often been labeled "unactable," some of the shorter plays are tightly written and might be performed before appreciative audiences. There are no special editorial problems with the drama other than those that apply generally to editing Cavendish, problems I will shortly address.

As with the poems, a difficult area will be the scientific writing. Most people do not look to the science for literary merit, so it may be the last part of Cavendish to be edited. Nevertheless, there are a great many scholars interested in the history of scientific writing, and some of them already have been able to show that Cavendish was closer to the center of scientific orthodoxy than was earlier imagined.[14] The real problem

---

[11] Margaret Cavendish, *Observations upon Experimental Philosophy: To which is added, The Description of a New Blazing World* (London: A. Maxwell, 1668); *Observations upon Experimental Philosophy. To which is added, The Description of a New Blazing World* (London: Printed by A. Maxwell, 1668).

[12] Margaret Cavendish, *Plays Never Before Printed* (London: A. Maxwell, 1668).

[13] Adolphus William Ward, *A History of the English Drama*, vol. 3 (1899, repr. 1970).

[14] Lisa T. Sarasohn, "A Science Turned Upside Down: Feminism and the Natural Philosophy of Margaret Cavendish," *Huntington Library Quarterly* 47 (1984): 289–307.

is to determine the nature of the development of the thinking of Cavendish. It is sometimes suggested that the situation is not so much a matter of development as of accretion. That is, Cavendish added new thinking without removing the old or concerning herself much with consistency. There seems to be a great deal of repetition, say, on the theory of vacuum or the theory of atoms, and it could turn out that what seems to be an entirely new book on science is actually an enlarged version of something already published. On the other hand, the science is clearly stronger and subtler than hitherto was thought to be the case.

As for *CCXI Sociable Letters*, which I am in the final stages of editing, nearly all are literary constructions rather than transcriptions of what had been written to actual people. Many take the form of small essays that cover a variety of topics. As Margaret Ezell has pointed out, women often used letters as vehicles for formal writing.[15] Cavendish was unusual only in having her epistolary essays printed. Other letters in the volume are more dramatic in structure, involving descriptions of the interactions of men and women who function like characters in a play. In a preface, Cavendish suggests the likeness of *Sociable Letters* to a group of theatrical scenes (C2v), and it is clear that she liked to consider the same problem from various viewpoints using characters to articulate each position. This practice can be puzzling, for sometimes she sounds like a twentieth-century feminist, and sometimes she seems to revel in pointing out female inferiority. A comparison of selected passages in *Sociable Letters* with corresponding sections of, say, *The Worlds Olio,* will show that she is more a supporter of women's rights than an attacker of them. It is, however, not an easy job to pin her down.

In any event, the text of *Sociable Letters* is very straightforward, and it is the commentaries on individual letters that pose problems for an editor. There are the usual considerations of biography, historical backgrounds, and connections with other writing by the author, but these parts of the commentaries are easy enough to weave together. The problem comes with identifications of actual people who are represented by initials (with or without false titles) or by anagrams. Although many of the people she writes about are fictional characters, others are definitely not. B. J. is pretty obviously Ben Jonson (Letter 173) and Sir W. D. seems to be Sir William Davenant (Letter 127), but some initials are

---

[15] Margaret J. M. Ezell, *The Patriarch's Wife: Literary Evidence and the History of the Family* (Chapel Hill: Univ. of North Carolina Press, 1988), 64–83.

trickier. For instance, a man who admires Ben Jonson and who writes plays himself is called Mr. W. N. Given the context, that person must be the husband of Margaret Cavendish, William Newcastle, but the false title, Mr., makes this attribution less than straightforward.

Cavendish, as it turns out, is very playful in bringing actual persons into *Sociable Letters*, and she delights in self-parody. In letter fifteen, the Lord N. W. praises the Lady T. M. "up into the third heaven" and feels the lady is "fit to be the Empress of the whole world." Cavendish as letter writer feels the Lord N. W. is very silly, indeed, and she cannot "chuse but to smile." If the commentary on this letter is properly written, the reader should be smiling, too, for Cavendish is offering a parody of her husband and herself under the guise of anagrams. N. W. is a reversal of the initials of William Newcastle and T. M. is a reversal of the first and last letters of Margaret. In an introduction to *Sociable Letters* and elsewhere, Cavendish liked to speculate on what good she would do if she were empress of the world, and her speculations have often been used as evidence of her mild or not so mild megalomania. Her self-parody puts her into a whole new light.

Other letters bring about stickier problems with actual people, Cavendish included. In one (Letter 153), it appears that her husband has been keeping a mistress, while in another she seems to be saying that she, herself, is "light heeled" (Letter 113). The tone is playful in each case, but the image she creates for herself is a far cry from Charles Lamb's praise: "Thrice noble, chaste, and virtuous."[16] Also gone is the image of the humorless and pompous Margaret Cavendish invoked by Mary Evelyn.[17] The greatest puzzles, however, involve family members and persons associated with the Cavendishes during the interregnum. For instance, William Newcastle, husband to Cavendish, was asked by Hyde to stop a duel between the earl of Oxford and Colonel Slinger.[18] Letter sixty-eight tells the story of a duel and gives one of the participants the name V. A. Those initials work well as an anagram for Oxford, who was Aubrey de Vere. Unfortunately, Slinger and C. A. from the letter do not match up quite so well, and the story itself does not correspond exactly. For someone writing commentaries on *Sociable Letters*, the point is simply

---

[16] Charles Lamb, *The Essays of Elia* (London: J. M. Dent, 1925–28).

[17] Mary Evelyn, Letter to Dr. Ralph Bohn, in *Diary and Correspondence of John Evelyn*, ed. William Bray (London: Henry Coburn & Co., 1857).

[18] *HMC* Portland, 2:140.

that Margaret Cavendish liked to mix actual people with dramatized situations. Where anagrams in *Sociable Letters* are concerned, very little is simple or easy to understand.

Such are the individual problems with individual books by Cavendish. A host of problems for the editor of her writing derives from her penchant for interceding with copies of her books once they had been printed. There is no indication, as is the case with Ben Jonson,[19] that she made revisions based on proof sheets, but she did attempt to alter what already had been printed. In one case, the biography of her husband, she changed very nearly every copy produced. Of the forty-three copies I have seen, only one, that at the public library in the city of Nottingham, escaped the process of alteration. In other cases, as with *Sociable Letters*, she was in a position to change all copies but did not. She only changed those copies intended as gifts. Since her gift list was long and probably included all of the colleges at Oxford and Cambridge, it is not difficult to find an altered copy.

There are, however, problems in knowing when you have an unchanged copy and when there are changes that reflect the author's wishes. In the biography of her husband, for instance, Cavendish adds about a page to one of her prefaces. To a casual observer of either the original preface or the revision, there appears to be only one preface. Those skilled in bibliography might be able to detect signs of tampering, but others, myself included, would be likely to miss them. The lesson for anyone putting together an edition of any book by Cavendish is to personally compare a great many copies of the books in question with some standard, probably a photocopy.

This lesson is, of course, obvious to anyone constructing an edition, but there is always the touchy and often unexamined problem of practical limitations. At some point, the editor must determine that he or she has looked at enough copies and that further treks to libraries will have diminishing returns or even be a waste of time. After I had looked at twenty copies of *Sociable Letters*, people began to wonder if I weren't being a trifle silly to look at more. (I went on to look at a total of thirty-four). They were, I think, both right and wrong. I do not need to look at absolutely every copy I know to exist and, in fact, I don't have the financial resources to do so. Instead, I am trying to strike a compromise with myself, visiting some libraries and writing to others. I hope I phrase

---

[19] Percy Simpson, *Proof-reading in the Sixteenth, Seventeenth and Eighteenth Centuries* (London: Oxford Univ. Press, 1935).

my written questions in such a way that the libraries will be able to spot what is important to me.

Other interesting and probably important considerations remain when one has exhausted the obvious bibliographic tools used in locating copies in the United States and England. Margaret Cavendish and her husband lived in Antwerp, Rotterdam, and Paris for fifteen years. We know from thank-you notes printed after her death that she gave copies of her books to various individuals and institutions on the Continent.[20] It will behoove any editor to query libraries in Belgium, the Netherlands, and France. The National Trust no doubt has possession of a great many more copies, but it appears that such copies are not readily available to scholars undertaking editions. It would be a great help if there were some way to gain access to the Trust copies.

I hope that my recitation of this litany of problems does not discourage prospective editors of Cavendish. The study of Cavendish, like the reading of her plays, can be a great deal of "fun," sometimes "refined" and sometimes not. In any event, she provides an interesting topic. Samuel Pepys spent the whole of May Day in 1667 following her around. Pepys, it might be said, was fascinated by her, for elsewhere he writes that he sought, not just to observe her outward appearance, but to understand her character.[21]

She is, without doubt, an interesting person to study, a woman who put herself in the public eye when women generally did not. Whether she was isolated and as a result became the slightly daft "Mad Madge of Newcastle," as many people believe, or whether she carefully crafted a public image that worked to her own ends, as I take to be the case, it is clear that she looms ever larger in the landscape of seventeenth-century English literature.

NORTHERN ARIZONA UNIVERSITY

---

[20] The thank-you notes appear with either of two title pages: *A Collection of Letters and Poems* (printed for Langly Curtis in the Goat-Yard on Ludgate-Hill, 1678) and *Letters and Poems in Honour of the Incomparable Princess, Margaret, Dutchess of Newcastle* ([London:] Thomas Newcomb, 1675). It is not clear which title page is the cancel.

[21] In March of 1667, Pepys went to see *The Humourous Lovers*. Although it was written by her husband, Pepys thought the play to be the work of Cavendish. He had no use for the drama but was intent on deciphering the woman: "[I] did go by coach to see the silly play of my Lady Newcastle's called *The Humorous Lovers*, the most silly thing that ever came upon a stage; I was sick to see it, but yet would not but have seen it that I might better understand her" (Samuel Pepys, *The Diary of Samuel Pepys,* ed. Robert Latham and William Mathews [Berkeley: Univ. of California Press, 1970–83]).

Giving Voices to the Silent:
Editing the Private Writings of Women

JOHN W. VELZ

WHEN JOSEPHINE ROBERTS ASKED ME TO RESPOND AT the 1990 RETS meeting to three papers on editing women writers, I accepted because, despite my lack of experience in the special field, there are three peripheral backgrounds I can offer. First, at that time I was working on anonymity and authorship in medieval and Renaissance drama scripts, a study I have since completed. Then second, I once co-edited the private letters of a nineteenth-century Shakespeare scholar, who though male was more than a bit of a feminist, and, reclusive as he was, was himself a voice of silence, almost entirely unknown until 1975 when his manuscript letters turned up in the Folger Shakespeare Library. And third, I've been reflecting for several years on the gender question in editing, especially of letters and diaries.

About that first peripheral credential for this task, I'll say only that there were many male voices in the Middle Ages and the Renaissance that spoke out of the silence of anonymity, especially among playwrights where the art form was oral and the artifact took its authority from some agency other than an "author." I like to think, accordingly, that the feminist interest in women's private writing—a valid field in itself—is ultimately part of a larger phenomenon of broad cultural significance which has not yet been seen as a whole.

About the second credential, my own editorial co-labors on a set of letters, there will be reason to speak later in the response to today's three papers.

About the gender question in editing—this is the really interesting one: it now seems that everyone else is conscious of the relevance of gender as much as we in RETS are; everywhere one turns there are editors and transcribers eager to bring women's voices out of the past to the interested ears of modern listeners. *The New York Times* Book Review section for 9 December 1990 had accounts of Philip L. Gerber's edition of *The Homesteading Letters of Elizabeth Corey (1909–1919)*, who signed herself "Bachelor Bess" (7), and of Charles A. Le Guin's edition of *The Diaries of Magnolia Wynn Le Guin, 1901–1913*; he calls her "A Home-Concealed Woman" (24). These are only two of a dozen or more encounters I have had recently with editions of women's private writing. Part of Anaïs Nin's diary, published by Harcourt Brace Jovanovich as *Henry and June*, which *inter alia* transcribes many letters between herself and Henry Miller, is only the most sensational of them.

If it is permissible to digress briefly before properly confronting one's proper subject, I would note that there seems to be a preference among publishers and editors for the lives and letters of American farm women on the frontier, witness the two recent editions just mentioned. To them can be added Linda M. Hasselstrom's *Windbreak: A Woman Rancher on the Northern Plains* (Barn Owl Books, 1987) and Joanna L. Stratton's *Pioneer Women: Voices from the Kansas Frontier* (Simon and Schuster, 1981). Arthur M. Schlesinger, Jr., wrote a brief introduction to Stratton's book, articulating the truth that "History is lived in the main by the unknown and forgotten," though historians talk mainly about those few who leave public records behind (11). The interest in agrarian women is a contemporary cultural phenomenon I invite you to reflect on, though populist farm voices are far, very far, from the aristocratic voices of silence that have attracted the interesting labors of Jean Klene, Sara Jayne Steen, and James Fitzmaurice. Agrarian voices are being recovered today more often than voices from proletarian coldwater flats in big cities or voices from drawing rooms in the Gilded Age. So far as this is true, one is tempted to conjecture that in part it is traceable to a powerful cultural phenomenon, the enormous popularity for half a century now of the autobiographical, realistic-but-idealistic children's fiction of Laura Ingalls Wilder about her childhood in the wilderness of Wisconsin and on the Midwestern prairies. Two generations of Americans have subliminally been prepared for the voices of nineteenth-century American farm women by the Wilder books. Laura Ingalls Wilder herself is a role-model for women; she made money with her pen as Virginia Woolf thought a woman should be free to do, and she broke the silence that had been the lot of her mother Caroline Ingalls and all her foremothers. It is certainly true that the voices of farm women have been voices of silence. My wife Sarah once told me that an excellent book on the traditional rural art of quiltmaking was titled *Anonymous Was a Woman*, a variation on Virginia Woolf's well-known sentence in Lecture III of *A Room of One's Own*. Knowing what goes into a quilt in talent and womanhours and labor, from having watched Sarah spend months on some, even years on one, I was sobered and saddened by that book title, but I lightened up after I asked Sarah who had written that book, and she could not remember. Score up another "anonymous."

There are, of course, two great gaps between the voices of silence I have been commenting on here so far and the three voices of silence that we have heard scholarly papers about today. One is a huge gap in time—all of the women's voices I have been describing date from the nineteenth and twentieth centuries. And that is not incidental. The second gap is no less huge, one of social class: aristocrats in today's three scholarly papers and commoners in the examples I have gathered together. The two gaps of time and class are related to each other in that a commoner's silence in the Renaissance was quite likely to be total, un-voiced as it were, because what Retha M. Warnicke in *Women of the English Renaissance and Reformation* (Greenwood Press, 1983) calls "stark illiteracy" was so widespread among women of the lower class, even more than among men of that class. Only when—in the nineteenth century for all practical purposes—writing literacy among women of the middle and lower classes became common, can one find everywoman's letters, diaries, commonplace books, and sheafs of poems to edit, as such artifacts are now being edited. An Emily Dickinson, a glorious voice of silence in a bourgeois home, is next to unthinkable in the sixteenth or seventeenth century; we have to look to a lady—Jane Lumley for instance, or Margaret Cavendish, or Arbella Stuart or Anne Southwell—for any kind of analogue. Written in 1928, Virginia Woolf's words still seem cogent:

> By no possible means could middle-class [Renaissance] women with nothing but brains and character at their command have taken part in any one of the great movements which, brought together, constitute the historian's view of the past. Nor shall we

find [a middle-class woman] in any collection of anecdotes. Aubrey hardly mentions her. She never writes her own life and scarcely keeps a diary; there are only a handful of her letters in existence.[1]

There is a touch of irony in the publication, just at this writing, of Woolf's *A Passionate Apprentice: The Early Journals, 1897–1909;*[2] would Woolf smile if she knew that we, nearly a century after the fact, take an interest in her voice of silence? We do not have to accept Woolf's melodramatic fantasy of Shakespeare's "sister," Judith, to find poignancy in the portrait of middle-class women of the Renaissance quoted above. And the poignancy is made more bitter by the contrast between literature and life:

> [Woman] pervades poetry from cover to cover; she is all but absent from history. She dominates the lives of kings and conquerors in fiction; in fact she was the slave of any boy whose parents forced a ring upon her finger. Some of the most inspired words, some of the most profound thoughts in literature fall from her lips; in real life she could hardly read, could scarcely spell, and was the property of her husband.[3]

Virginia Woolf's dark scenario for the typical woman in the Renaissance, especially the matter of reading and writing, shows an awareness shrewdly beyond that of her contemporaries. Since Woolf's time, evidence has come to light that gives a bit of substance to her intuitive sketch, and the question of female literacy has taken center stage in New Historicist and feminist studies in the Renaissance. Editors must concern themselves with the question also, as Sara Jayne Steen and Jean Klene have both foreseen. I would like to follow Klene's lead in emphasizing a distinction between reading literacy and writing literacy, a distinction that until recent years had not been properly made by those concerned with the intellectual lives of women in the Renaissance. We need more information than we have available, but the information pool is not altogether valueless.

Contributions to the pool have been sociological studies of literacy as a phenomenon, especially the research of David Cressy that resulted in

---

[1] *A Room of One's Own* (Hogarth Press, 1928), 67–68.
[2] Ed. Mitchell A. Leaska (Harcourt Brace Jovanovich, 1990).
[3] Woolf, *A Room of One's Own*, 66.

his highly statistical *Literacy and the Social Order: Reading and Writing in Tudor and Stuart England*.[4] Of the approximately 3400 female deponents Cressy sampled in diocesan records for Norwich, Exeter, Durham, Essex, Hertfordshire, and London (City and Middlesex) from the last half of the sixteenth and the seventeenth centuries, percentages ranging from 76–98 signed with a mark. It is important to notice about Cressy's research that it tests for people's writing literacy, not at all for their reading literacy; the likelihood—for reasons given below—is that many more women could read than could write. By the last decade of the seventeenth century, women in London had attained a 48% literacy rate by Cressy's measurements, but as late as the 1720s women in Suffolk and Norfolk still had a 74% illiteracy rate (129; 144).

The statistical difference between London and the provinces surely has something to do with the urbanization of village and country people who had literacy among their survival skills and with the availability of schooling for women in London in the Tudor and Stuart periods (149). Mary Cathcart Borer offers a vivid account of Christ's Hospital founded in 1552 for the care and education of poor boys and girls (where boys seem to have outnumbered girls by as much as 6 to 1), and she emphasizes that petty schools that prepared boys under seven for grammar school by teaching them to read and write English and do sums also admitted girls.[5] Cressy shrewdly distinguishes between a woman's capacity to read and her lack of need to write: "Even among those social and economic groups where the men had regular dealings with paper and ink, the women were usually illiterate." He recounts a strange instance of the split between reading and writing literacy in early-eighteenth-century Sweden where the Lutheran Church systematically taught adult men and women to read "for confessional and liturgical purposes" and attained nearly 100% reading literacy in some fifty years; still, very low levels of writing literacy persisted (128; 178–79). In another book, Cressy quotes from *An Account of Charity Schools Lately Erected* (1706): The boys learn to write as soon as they can read "competently well"; the girls learn to read, sew, and knit—"several learn to write...."[6] Cressy's research methodology has been challenged in some quarters, but his con-

---

[4] (Cambridge Univ. Press, 1980), Tables, 119–21.

[5] *Willingly to School: A History of Women's Education* (Lutterworth Press, 1975–76), 56–65.

[6] *Education in Tudor and Stuart England*, Documents of Modern History, no. 139 (Edward Arnold, 1975), 114.

clusions are suggestive, however approximate: women unquestionably suffered seriously from illiteracy in Tudor and Stuart times, but many more could read than could write. Louis B. Wright has offered substantial evidence in *Middle-Class Culture in Elizabethan England*[7] that women in the sixteenth century were a reading audience recognized by enterprising authors and publishers. Yet silence is doubly oppressive when one can learn from the printed word but cannot express one's resulting thoughts in written language.

In response to the three papers, I would like to suggest one means by which the lost voices of some Renaissance women might be retrieved and to comment on aspects of the editorial process that impinge on gender, both in ways the three speakers today have underscored and in another way as well.

If we want to find out about the world of Renaissance women, narrow to the point of being stultifying yet of the utmost interest to cultural historians and New Historicists, we might not so much look for the letters of ordinary women—letters we are not very likely to find in any numbers—as to search in the familiar letters of men to their friends, letters in which wives, daughters, fiancées, and mothers may be mentioned, often unexpectedly, sometimes revealingly. Fifteen years ago, when Frances Teague and I read through the late-nineteenth-century letters of middle-aged Joseph Crosby to young Joseph Parker Norris expecting to find only scholarly discussion of the text of Shakespeare, we also found some wonderful accounts of Crosby's thirtysomething fiancée, Agnes Fillmore, who wooed him toward courtship and marriage by inducing him to help her found a Shakespeare Reading Club in Zanesville, Ohio. Norris saved the letters in question only because they were part of a corpus primarily about scholarly matters; he certainly did not save them to throw light on Agnes or on Joseph's love for her—on the contrary, he actively resented her because he feared that Joseph's marriage to Agnes would put a stop to his intimate epistolary conversations with Joseph about Shakespearian matters. Indeed, the only letter of Agnes known to survive is an excruciatingly polite and diffident note to Norris assuring him that the breach he feared was not about to occur. The Agnes that emerges from a series of Joseph's letters stretching over nearly a year of courtship and the first weeks of marriage is a far cry

---

[7] (Cornell Univ. Press for the Folger Shakespeare Library, 1935), 103–18.

from the prim Victorian speaker-in-formalities we meet once and once only in this sole surviving letter. Beneath a veil of propriety and reticence, Agnes emerges through Crosby's letters as witty, imaginative, ebullient, and independent-minded (Crosby cheerfully praises her for this independence, contrasting Desdemona, who would have been better off if she had some of Agnes's backbone). It is all supreme fun to find this cameo portrait of a middle-class woman, a hardware dealer's daughter, among those learned lexical notes on the text of *Cymbeline*, and *Lear*, and *Love's Labour's Lost*, and for Fran Teague and me it was serendipity. So I recommend combing *epistolae ad familiares*, if one can find a correspondent who has Cicero's interest in men and manners and an interest in the companionship of women besides.

My hypothetical analogue, Joseph Crosby, is two centuries and more behind the right date, and I have, moreover, not to this time joined in digging for Tudor and Stuart letters. But I am inclined to think that such letters as I have in mind may well turn up, beyond what Lawrence Stone found when he was working toward *The Family, Sex, and Marriage in England: 1500–1800*,[8] and even though A. R. Braunmuller makes only one passing reference to women as subjects of letters in his learned introduction to editing Elizabethan letters in *TEXT* 1. What is wanted, no doubt, is searching through many a *liber familicus*, many a household account, many a letterbook, a search in the manner of the REED combers of archives. I say without facetiousness that I would like to envision a *Records of Early English Women*. If such *Forschung* were to turn up women of the caliber of Agnes Fillmore, then a second desideratum would be met—a close look at unknown women worth knowing; one might anticipate the sort of emotional attachment we editors of letters regularly feel for the subjects of our labors.

Sara Jayne Steen's assessment of the role of the author in her letters insists on a real voice behind the cultural meaning we may find in what she is, what is written about her, and that an editor dealing with women's letters may need to serve two disciplines simultaneously: cultural history and biography. Cultural history will stand alone only if the woman in question is a dullard without idiosyncrasy. But if she is various and vibrant, as Agnes Fillmore was and as all three of this year's women writers were, we editors become biographers as well as cultural historians. As Sara Jane Steen advises: the cultural context is all-important

---

[8] (Harper and Row, 1977). See sections 2, 3, 4, and 5 of the Bibliography.

if we wish to hear the voice clearly. "There is no sound in a vacuum."

How much to annotate that cultural context is a perennial problem that must be solved by a policy decision made in light of the likely audience. In editing the letters of Joseph Crosby, Fran Teague and I established firmly at the outset that our audience was "the Shakespearean general reader," a woman or man who does not need to be told about the chronology of the Shakespeare canon or what works of Shakespeare were left out of the First Folio. Yet we aimed at providing plenty of informative notes where they were needed. We found the joys of running down allusions and writing about them succinctly to be superlative. Now an editor of a Renaissance woman's letters has a difficult choice to make, having two clienteles. One is sophisticated scholars, specialists in Renaissance textual questions and cultural historians (New Historicists included). The other is feminists interested in the history of women's writing, who may well be neophytes in Renaissance study—shall we say those brilliant young undergraduates at Girton and Newnham Colleges, Cambridge, whom Virginia Woolf addresses in *A Room of One's Own*? On the ground that well-schooled readers can slide without annoyance past notes they think nugatory, I recommend rather full annotation of cultural allusions when editing the letters of women—but also that you discuss your policy in the front matter to put the experts on notice.

One more comment on Steen's excellent approach to technical desiderata in editing letters: by all means include additions and deletions— and (if your publisher will agree) *in the text* for the sake of immediacy. Our method was to line out what was deleted in such a way as to make it still legible (~~this way~~); we used arrow-up (↑) and arrow-down (↓) before and after interlinear insertions. Editorial intervention in the form of ellipsis for economy's or continuity's sake ought to be avoided or minimized where possible; we capture the voice fully only when we hear *all* it says, not just its *bons mots*.

I want to spend a moment or two on "the Mad Madge syndrome." James Fitzmaurice proposes two interpretations: either isolation from the world made Margaret Cavendish a little daffy, or this clever woman "carefully crafted a public image" of daffiness for purposes unspecified. It might be that a third interpretation is appropriate to her interesting life. A woman who had opinions about everything, and unorthodox ones in a sufficient number of cases, and who published more in a lifetime than any Englishwoman before her and more indeed than many an English man of letters—it might well be that such a woman would be dismissed as "Mad Madge of Newcastle" by men who were threatened by this unabashed display of female assertiveness and by women who were secretly or even unconsciously envious of such an intellectual free spirit. In support of this explanation I offer the view of Lady Margaret offered by her contemporary, Dorothy Osborne, Lady Temple (as Virginia Woolf quotes her): "Sure the poore woman is a little distracted, shee could never bee soe rediculous else as to venture at writing book's and in verse too. . . ." Because Aphra Behn, another contemporary, allowed her stage women to engage in suggestive banter and bawdy wordplay with her stage men, because she dared write plays at all, and because she befriended Nell Gwynn, she too was by some labeled mad, crazed by lust. The shrewd defense of a male power-structure against a woman who oversteps the limits of female assertiveness is to label her "mad" with patronizing dismissal. Of Walter Pater's view of "manliness in art," Mary Ellmann writes: "The feminine is the not fully conscious, not fully assembled, the intemperate, incoherent, hysterical, extravagant and capricious."[9] We do a little better than society did in the late seventeenth century or the late nineteenth at accepting eccentricity and assertiveness in women—though I have seen the "Mad Madge syndrome" used in a whispering campaign against a female political candidate who dared to challenge the good-old-boy politicians in what they thought was their bailiwick. The phenomenon is as old as Socrates, whose wit and challenge to the Athenian establishment led to retaliation in the form of charges of atheism and corruption of youth. The irony of "the Mad Madge syndrome" in the seventeenth century is that a woman was not thought interesting enough to attract attention unless she was both outspoken and eccentric. But outspokenness and eccentricity exceeded the bounds of acceptable female assertiveness; it was a double bind for the likes of Margaret Cavendish.

One might wish that Fitzmaurice had offered more technical detail about the process of alteration in the already printed sheets of the Cavendish biography of her husband. The evidence about the stage-worthiness of Aphra Behn has actually been supplied in a fine Royal Shakespeare Company production of *The Rover* at the Swan Theatre in Stratford-upon-Avon in 1986.

Jean Klene has ferreted out a very strong voice from nearly complete silence. What she gives us of Lady Anne Southwell's wit and energy and intellectual and social daring, her insistence on having her own way

---

[9] *Thinking About Women* (Harcourt, Brace, and World, 1968), 44.

about the important things—all these make the prospect of a major edition of Lady Anne very appealing. But, for all that, the editorial process is a difficult one. We get a compelling sense in her paper of the encumbrances that lie in the way of the editors of Renaissance letters: the use of amanuenses, various styles in a single person's handwriting, the peculiarities of paper that obscure watermarks, reasons not to take some things (dates, for instance) at face value, the problem of whether a bit of verse or a translation is a copy in the letter under consideration or whether it originates with the author. These are the sorts of uncertainties that A. R. Braunmuller pointed to in his introductory essay on editing Renaissance letters, and here we see the problems reified *in situ*.

As I read about Lady Anne's advice to Cecily Macwilliams to steer clear of the erotic epyllion, I thought of Gabriel Harvey, who wrote in a copy of Speght's Chaucer about 1600, that "The younger sort take much delight in Shakespeares Venus and Adonis; but his Lucrece, and his tragedy of Hamlet, Prince of Denmarke, haue it in them, to please the wiser sort."

What I appreciate especially in Klene's paper is the brief but informative remarks about literacy for women in the Tudor and Stuart periods, especially the distinction between the ability to write and the ability to read and the references to David Cressy and to Arthur Slavin in her note 21. It seems to me that this is an area for research in time to come. Louis B. Wright's briefly stated evidence that middle-class women read more than a little—sometimes in genres that their puritanical male counterparts could not approve of—should be played off the statistical evidence David Cressy has piled up that women in England in the Tudor and Stuart periods lived under the constraining silence of writing illiteracy.

UNIVERSITY OF TEXAS

Manuscript Circulation at the Elizabethan Court

STEVEN W. MAY

T HE NEW HISTORICISM HAS THUS FAR MADE SCANT PROG-
ress in its efforts to discover an Elizabethan courtly aesthetic
or to define the relationship between poetry, patronage, and
power in late Tudor society. In the absence of any historical
methodology, scholars have investigated a canon far too indiscriminate to
shed light upon actual conditions at court. It is as if a modern critic
hoped to penetrate the inner workings of the White House or State
Department through the writings of Neil Simon or Kurt Vonnegut. This
is not to say that works by such authors as Edmund Spenser and George
Puttenham, George Gascoigne, Robert Greene, Thomas Nashe, and the
like were unknown at court. It is simply beyond demonstration that
these authors were widely read or highly regarded by those who controlled the nation's power and patronage. Even less likely is the notion
that such out-of-court writers knew enough about conditions at court to
give them authentic representation in their works.

Unlike modern Washington, creative writing was cultivated at the
highest levels of the Elizabethan power structure. The queen, her chief
minister, Lord Burghley, such privy councillors as Sir Thomas Heneage,
Thomas Wilson, Sir John Wolley, the second earl of Essex, and Sir
Robert Cecil, with many others were practicing poets. Scores of

Elizabethan courtiers wrote and collected verse and patronized poets. We can find out, at least to some degree, what poetry "did" at the apogee of Elizabethan society—but this will require a wholesale rewriting of the canon. We must begin to investigate a very different array of authors and works from those that have been studied to date; in addition, scholarly analysis of the transmitting media must shift from print to manuscripts.

A literary canon of the court can be assembled from two primary sources of evidence. First, catalogs of aristocratic libraries reveal the kinds of books that elite Elizabethans kept and, presumably, read. I cannot analyze this body of evidence in detail here beyond noting that most of the printed belles lettres in Elizabethan aristocratic libraries were written in Latin or the continental vernaculars. To the extent that courtiers wrote or read English literature, most of those works circulated in manuscript. Thus the currents of manuscript circulation provide the surest guide to the literary tastes of the court, and the study and editing of these manuscripts is vitally important to any accurate understanding of the role of literature at court.

The task is complicated, however, by the fact that very few Elizabethan poetic anthologies actually owned by courtiers have survived or thus far been identified as such. In this paper I shall analyze four collections which provide an authentic cross section of the kinds of creative writing that circulated at court in the late sixteenth century.

British Library MS. Additional 38823 is Sir Edward Hoby's personal collection of prose records plus twelve poems in English, French, and Latin verse, three of them by Hoby himself. Sir Edward, son of the translator of Castiglione's *Courtier*, was allied by marriage with the Carey family, lords Hunsdon. Through his mother, Lady Russell, he claimed kin as well to the Cecils. He was a regular at court from the mid-1580s to the end of the reign, during which time he followed in his father's footsteps by publishing three books in translation.

The *Arundel-Harington Manuscript*, so entitled and edited by Ruth Hughey,[1] is the personal anthology of two courtiers, John Harington of Stepney and his son, Sir John of Kelston. The Elizabethan contents of this anthology were primarily transcribed, I believe, under Sir John's supervision during the 1580s and 1590s. Harington attended court with some regularity from the late 1580s if not before. His translation of

---

[1] *The Arundel-Harington Manuscript of Tudor Poetry*, ed. Ruth Hughey, 2 vols. (Columbus: Ohio State Univ. Press, 1960).

Ariosto, his epigrams, devotional verse, and other writings make him the most prolific of the Elizabethan courtier poets. He had also been a friend of Hoby's since their school days together at Eton College.

No other literary anthologies owned by Elizabethan courtiers have been identified, to the best of my knowledge, but two manuscripts have survived which were compiled in court-connected households. Their contents derive from varied sources including identifiable printed books, yet both manuscripts show signs of tapping into courtly veins of circulation as well.

British Library Egerton MS. 2642 is an unedited collection of verse and prose to a length of 418 folios. Its scribe was Robert Commander, chaplain to Sir Henry Sidney.[2] Commander served in Ireland with Sir Henry in 1566–67 and later became chaplain to the Council of Wales while Sidney was its lord president. Commander assembled his anthology, which includes nearly 200 English poems, during the last quarter of the sixteenth century. A smattering of elite texts, including verses by the queen and a copy of her oration at Oxford University in 1592 (fol. 413), reveal this manuscript's ties to the court.

A similarly well-connected scribe was Henry Stanford, chaplain to George Carey, 2nd Lord Hunsdon and lord chamberlain of the royal household in the last seven years of Elizabeth's reign. My edition of Stanford's anthology, Cambridge University Library MS. Dd.5.75, was published by Garland Press in 1988.[3] Stanford resided in one of the great patronage-dispensing households of the Elizabethan age. Compiled from about 1580 through 1610, his manuscript includes substantive texts by some of the most prestigious courtier poets and was clearly derived in part from the most elite levels of circulation at court.

The contents of these four manuscripts reveal a taste and emphasis very different from the printed canon and from the styles and genres studied thus far by the New Historicism. Love poetry makes up a significant but not dominant part of the Hoby, Harington, and Stanford anthologies, but it is totally lacking in Commander's manuscript. All four manuscripts pay significant attention to political and religious verse satire

---

[2] Commander matriculated at King's College, Cambridge, at age sixteen in 1548. He left in 1550 without taking a degree and, regrettably, was charged with destroying " 'many good books in the College library' " (Venn and Venn, *Alumni Cantabrigienses* 1 [Cambridge, 1922], 377).

[3] *Henry Stanford's Anthology, An Edition of Cambridge University Library Manuscript Dd.5.75* (New York, 1988).

as well as personal libels. Devotional and philosophical verse form a second genre well-represented in these collections, along with elegiac verse.

To what extent do these four manuscripts suggest that their owners drew upon a common and homogeneous body of courtly literature? The overlap of the Egerton, Cambridge, and Arundel-Harington anthologies with Hoby's, which contains only a dozen poems, reveals their joint access to a common pool of texts. Hoby's manuscript preserves two political-religious satires that appear in one or more of the remaining anthologies. His copy of "The Scottishe Coqalane" (cockalane, fol. 69v), a satire of Scottish affairs in the mid-1580s, also appears in Commander's manuscript (fol. 325). Hoby transcribed the French original of a political satire beginning "The state of France as now it stands," which occurs in both the Egerton and Cambridge collections.[4] Hoby's anthology also shares with the Egerton manuscript a philosophical quatrain beginning, "He that spareth to speak hath hardly his intent." The verses occur in at least three other Tudor collections and may have been written by the elder Harington.[5] Of Hoby's three love lyrics, "Like hermit poor" also occurs in the Arundel-Harington manuscript; the poem survives without attribution in two more Elizabethan anthologies and two prints but was incorrectly ascribed to Sir Walter Ralegh in a print of 1644. Thus, of the nine poems in the Additional manuscript not written by Hoby himself, four occur as well in one or more of the other three anthologies.

Hoby's collection is instructive beyond this evidence that all four manuscripts drew upon common currents of circulation. Despite its limited sample, Hoby's manuscript provides a representative cross section of the kinds of poetry that courtiers copied into their anthologies. Satires, devotional and moral poetry, and elegies vie with love lyrics as major genres of courtier interest and taste.

Satiric verse forms a significant component of the manuscript anthologies—one that has gone almost wholly unstudied as either literature or social history. Four of Hoby's texts are political-religious topical

---

[4] For a critical text with analysis of the poem's popularity see my " 'The French Primero': A Study in Renaissance Textual Transmission and Taste," *English Language Notes* 9 (1971): 102–8.

[5] In *John Harington of Stepney* (Columbus: Ohio State Univ. Press, 1975), Ruth Hughey edits the poem as Harington's by virtue of its attribution to "I H" in Trinity College, Dublin, MS. D.27. Other texts occur in British Library Harl. MSS. 7392, fol. 59v, and 2296, fol. 138.

satires, three of them in French verse. In addition to the Scottish and French satires, Commander added to the Egerton MS a satire of French affairs in English verse beginning "The lords do crave all." He included as well a dozen anti-Catholic works and Queen Elizabeth's verses against Mary, Queen of Scots, and the Northern Rebellion of 1569–70 (fols. 236, 237v). Harington copied the companion poems by Sir Henry Goodyer and Thomas Norton which deal with the Duke of Norfolk's involvement with Mary after her imprisonment in England. (Hughey 147–8). The shift from topical to personal satire is represented by Stanford's text of an attack on the Queen of Scots in Latin verse beginning "O Maria scota meretrix" (214). The Cambridge and Arundel-Harington manuscripts preserve the elaborate slander of Edward Bashe, the queen's victualler of the navy, known as the "Bashe Libel" (Harington 182–83; May 212–13). In addition, Harington copied the libels of Oxford and Cambridge Universities (180–81), poems which chronicle at length and in salacious detail the illicit sexual escapades of named members of both academic communities. Rounding out the list of personal invectives in these manuscripts are entries in the Cambridge collection against the traitor William Parry and a satiric elegy on Robert, earl of Leicester (110, 181).

Non-satiric elegiac verse also forms a prominent part of these anthologies. Hoby copied not only the widely circulated "death verse" of Chidiock Tichborne ("My prime of youth"), but his own Latin epitaph for his stepfather, John, Lord Russell. Stanford preserved elegies for the composer Thomas Tallis and Lady Anne Lee, wife of Sir Henry Lee (18, 28). Arundel-Harington includes verse epitaphs for the first earl of Southampton, Sir Philip Sidney, and Queen Elizabeth's tutor, William Grindal, in addition to one for an unidentified lady (295, 225, 285, 257). Commander's anthology preserves verse epitaphs for Elizabeth, daughter of Mary and Sir Henry Sidney (d. 1567), for Catherine, countess of Huntingdon (d. 1576), plus Latin epitaphs for Bishop John Jewel, Edward VI, Chaucer, and a number of the Marian martyrs (fols. 213–19v, 226–6v).

Although Hoby did not copy explicitly religious verse into his anthology, devotional works form a significant part of the other three collections. In addition to the earl of Surrey's translation of Ecclesiastes and the texts of Wyatt's Psalms, Arundel-Harington contains translations of penitential Psalms by John Dudley and his brother Robert, later earl of Leicester (289–90). Verse prayers and Thomas Smith's text of the Ten Commandments in English verse round out the devotional component

in Harington's collection (264, 283, 288, 323–24). Stanford copied
hymns and Christmas carols into the Cambridge manuscript (281–83),
and Commander included biblical paraphrase and prayers in Latin and
English in the Egerton collection.

A similar and related emphasis on verse proverbs and wisdom literature occurs in all four manuscripts. Commander devoted five folios of his
anthology to proverbs (fols. 221–22v, 246v–48), with dozens more
scattered throughout the volume. Harington copied thirty-nine such
poems under the title "dyvers sentences" (24–63) and included another
half dozen aphorisms elsewhere in the manuscript (92, 252, 254–55,
315–16). Stanford transcribed substantial moral verses on the world's
vanity (114, 215) and the value of a settled, loyal mind (225), along with
shorter aphorisms on a variety of subjects (140–46).

These genres form a canon profoundly unlike what has thus far been
proposed as the basis for an Elizabethan courtly aesthetic. The devotional
works and aphorisms, for example, are conservative and orthodox rather
than subversive. The elegies are sincere, lending further testimony to the
fact that courtiers considered poetry an entirely acceptable medium for
public expression of serious feelings and beliefs. The satires, especially the
personal invectives, are "subversive" insofar as they attack their subjects,
as all satires must. Manuscripts preserve the bulk of Elizabethan subversive literature in prose and verse. Yet in general, the tone and manner of
these satires are blunt and direct. The author of the Bashe libel, for
example, wonders whether his victim's "turkey coloured snowt/ Be
bigger then his mouthe about?" "Loe thus they deale with the lowt," he
continues, "But I doe know & dare avow, that he is wasted like a cowe/
Made like a bull of brest & brow & somwhat snowted like a sow"
(212.169–75). This falls somewhat short of that artful dissimulation, that
deft and subtle handling of a subject which we have come to associate
with the courtly manner.

Finally, what of the amorous verse which, except for Commander's
collection, makes up a quarter to one half of the contents of these manuscripts? These proportions alone indicate that love poetry was only one
among several genres of verse which appealed to courtier taste, although
it is usually considered as almost the only one. The three anthologies in
question here preserve some of the finest Elizabethan love lyrics, but the
commercial poets are notably missing from their pages. In fact, the better
out-of-court poets—Drayton, Daniel, Lodge, Campion, and the like—
saw little or no manuscript circulation in or out of court circles. To this
list we might add Spenser, Puttenham, George Peele, and George

Gascoigne. Nor do the printed works of these authors commonly appear in the catalogs of aristocratic libraries. Instead, the Harington and Stanford anthologies contain amorous verse by such poets as Sir Edward Dyer, Fulke Greville, Queen Elizabeth, Sir Arthur Gorges, and Ferdinando, fifth earl of Derby, as well as such better known courtier poets as Ralegh and Sidney. Moreover, all three of the love lyrics in Hoby's collection are anonymous, along with scores of the better poems in the other two anthologies. Thus the canon of the court must expand to consider not only a much wider range of authors than has yet been dreamt of in New Historicist methodology, but a range of anonymous texts including religious, elegiac, and satiric verse as well as love poetry.

This canon must be formulated from the extant manuscripts, and many other anthologies have survived with indications that they tapped into veins of court circulation, even if at some remove from the court itself. Professor Doughtie's edition of Bodleian MS. Rawl. poet. 148 and Professor Sullivan's edition of the Dalhousie manuscripts are two such collections.[6] Important Elizabethan anthologies which are either unedited or unpublished include British Library Harl. MSS. 6910 and 7392, Bodleian MS. Rawl. poet. 85, Marsh's Library, Dublin, MS. 183, Folger MS. V.a.89, Dyce MS. 44 in the Victoria and Albert Museum, and Rosenbach MS. 1083/15.

What will these anthologies tell us about the taste of the court? No definitive answer is possible until these manuscripts have been edited and fully analyzed, yet I will risk a few preliminary conclusions. First, no single genre of creative writing is likely to emerge as an overwhelming favorite of courtier taste. Even if love lyrics dominate the anthologies, they will share in popularity not only with the genres I have singled out in these four manuscripts, but with riddles, short narratives, epigrams, and verse letters among other popular forms. Second, no single aesthetic of the court is likely to be discernible either in courtier works edited from these manuscripts or in the corpus of anonymous writings they preserve. The generic diversity of these collections is matched by a diversity in style, tone, and approach to the subject that confounds any single formulation. True, many of the works of Sidney, Greville, and Ralegh are ambiguous, multi-faceted, and subject to varied interpreta-

---

[6] Edward Doughtie, *Liber Lilliati* (Newark: Univ. of Delaware Press, 1985); *The First and Second Dalhousie Manuscripts*, ed. Ernest W. Sullivan, II (Columbia: Univ. of Missouri Press, 1988).

tions. But many other works by Queen Elizabeth, the earl of Essex, Lord Burghley, and Dyer for example, are direct and transparent expressions. Instead of a single courtly aesthetic, the manuscripts will reveal the kinds of literature that appealed to the courtier elite, and these parameters of quality, style, and genre necessarily govern the patronage extended or denied to out-of-court, professional writers. We may someday be able to explain why Spenser, Gascoigne, and Nashe found it nearly impossible to secure royal or courtier favor, while such authors as Thomas Watson, Thomas Churchyard, and Anthony Munday were relatively successful in their quest for patronage.

GEORGETOWN COLLEGE

John Ramsey's Manuscript
as a Personal and Family Document

EDWARD DOUGHTIE

O N READING ARTHUR MAROTTI'S ARTICLE ON "MANU-
script, Print, and the English Renaissance Lyric," I was
pleasantly surprised to discover that what I had thought of
as my old-fashioned edition of an old manuscript was on
the cutting edge of—something.[1] Although I had had a glimpse of the
new interest in sociocentric textual study in Ted-Larry Pebworth's *SEL*
article on coterie texts as performances,[2] I had been distracted lately by
other matters and am grateful to Marotti for catching me up on all that's
been going on with McKenzie, McGann, Shillingsburg, et al.[3] The
New Editorialism's emphasis on the social conditions that produced different forms of texts can be applied to manuscript versions, which are
not necessarily to be regarded as simply corrupt copies of the author's
original. Clearly, some works need an authorcentric treatment. Ben Jon-

---

[1] Arthur F Marotti, "Manuscript, Print, and the English Renaissance Lyric" (see
above, 209–21); he refers to my edition of Bodleian MS. Rawlinson Poetry 148, *Liber
Lilliati: Elizabethan Verse and Song* (Newark: Univ. of Delaware Press, 1985).

[2] Ted-Larry Pebworth, "John Donne, Coterie Poetry, and the Text as Performance," *Studies in English Literature* 29 (1989): 61–75.

[3] For a review of many of these studies, see G. Thomas Tanselle, "Textual
Criticism and Literary Sociology," *Studies in Bibliography* 44 (1991): 83–143.

son cared about his texts and his role as author. And we should not abandon the useful if imperfect tools of textual analysis that can sometimes get us closer to what an author wrote. But within certain coteries or groups, there can be a communal attitude toward a work, and a given text may be best perceived as a performance suited for a particular occasion and audience. Moreover, there may be a greater range of kinds of coteries and attitudes towards the text than may at first appear.

At one extreme is the oral work, such as the folk ballad. These ballads were probably not recreated at each performance from a store of formulas like Homeric or Slavic epics, but neither was the idea of a fixed text or an individual author as strong as in the literary tradition.[4] Even before Child, editors of ballads had abandoned the notion of an author-centric text, and the common way of presenting a ballad—the "work"— is via a number of versions or "texts" that record specific performances. Even within the literary tradition, orally-transmitted texts may be more numerous than one might think. Just as the joke is still a vital oral form (now enhanced by faxes and electronic mail), joke-like verses clearly had an oral life among the undergraduates and templars of the sixteenth and seventeenth centuries. Of the epitaph on the bellows-maker who died because he "could not make breath," John Davies said that it was "in every mans *mouth*" (my emphasis), and the many copies vary as one would expect.[5] The same is true of a popular anagram on the letters of the word *wife* and of the epitaph on Christ College's privy member, Mr. Prick.[6] Outside oral tradition, but still treated as communal property, are popular poems and songs to which various hands contributed, resulting in varying texts. For example, a poem beginning "Now what is love" appears in three poetical miscellanies and was set to music by Robert Jones. The formula it uses to define love is easily expanded, and several manuscript copies add a number of extra stanzas, most of which are obscene.[7] Manuscript collections of verse may reflect the interests of a

---

[4] For a recent account of the dispute over the application of oral-formulaic theory to ballads, see William B. McCarthy, *The Ballad Matrix* (Bloomington: Indiana Univ. Press, 1990), 1–13.

[5] British Library MS. Cotton Faustina E.v., fol. 171v. For a collation of other versions, see *Liber Lilliati*, 148–49.

[6] *Liber Lilliati*, 152–53; on Prick, see, e.g., Bodleian MS. Malone 19, fol. 55, Folger MS. V.a.103, fol. 23, or Huntington MS. HM 116, p. 47.

[7] British Library MS. Add. 22601, fols. 104–6, and Rosenbach MS. 1083/15, 98–100; see my *Lyrics from English Airs* (Cambridge, Mass.: Harvard Univ. Press, 1970), 504–10.

particular coterie, and may not contain anything that cannot be found in a number of similar manuscripts. But they may be highly individualistic. A given manuscript may contain some items found elsewhere, but much of its contents may reflect the special interests of its compiler, a coterie of one.

My current topic is the manuscript of John Ramsey, known as Bodleian Douce 280.[8] This manuscript provides an extraordinary amount of material concerning the cultural and social interests of its maker. It reeks of historical particularity. First, it contains an autobiography of Ramsey from which I was fascinated to learn several things. Ramsey, born in 1578, was the oldest surviving son of William Ramsey of Mount Surrey. He was educated first at boarding schools and came to Peterhouse, Cambridge, in 1601. He left Cambridge in 1603 at the age of twenty-five because his kinsman, Sir John Ramsey, persuaded him to try being a courtier to the new king. Sir John was later viscount Haddington and earl of Holderness and was probably, according to Professor Sullivan, the source of the material for the Dalhousie manuscripts.[9] Our John Ramsey did not like the court, so he retired to the country, where he discovered that he had better learn something about the law. He came to the Middle Temple, but soon fell victim to a six-year illness. Recovering in time to accompany the prince Palatine and his bride home in 1613, Ramsey stayed on the continent on an extended grand tour. After returning to England, he lost the use of his right hand in a duel in 1618, making it easy for the reader to recognize which entries were made after that date. He married in 1620 and fathered eight children. Then, in 1633, at age fifty-five and with one good hand, he wrote that "because my life beinge all waies active & not having employment to my desire" he had determined to set out on a "noble voyage" to Guiana in South America (fols. 5–8v). That's the last we hear of John Ramsey.

Aside from this intriguing life story, the manuscript contains many other curious items, such as prescriptions, descriptions of dance steps, "A Rule to find the goulden or prime nomber," and an essay on "Hypo-

---

[8] MS. Douce 280 has been rebound and a number of its leaves rearranged. Therefore in the following references I cite the more recent, continuous foliation, not Ramsey's.

[9] *The First and Second Dalhousie Manuscripts*, ed. Ernest W. Sullivan, II (Columbia: Univ. of Missouri Press, 1988), 5.

chondriacke Melancholye" (fols. 1, 61, 62v–64, 65–66bv). Ramsey's reasons for including any item must range from the practical to the whimsical. But one reason may underlie many of the entries, and that is concern for his own status and that of his family. This concern, as I hope to show, will have some bearing on the literary contents of the manuscript.

Many entries testify directly to this concern with the family. The autobiography itself could be presumed to be of interest mainly to Ramsey's family, and it expresses values that are conventionally appropriate for enhancing the family. For example, references to his father express filial piety, and mention of a family quarrel by which Ramsey seems to have lost some of his patrimony represses much; although he expresses pain at the "wicked enterprises attempted by some of mine own house," he wishes the episode to be "evermore buried in the obscure pitt of oblivion" (fol. 6v). He gives an elaborate genealogy of four branches of the family from the Norman Conquest to 1620, with spaces for additions (fols. 72–76). He sketches and describes his coat of arms (fol. 111v). He frequently identifies himself as being of the Ramseys of Mount Surrey, even though his own estate is in Whitsgreen, Surrey; he also relates the activities of his kin in the Scottish branches, as well as the relative who was lord mayor of London. He carefully records his marriage, the name of his father-in-law (but not his wife's given name), and the names and birthdays of his children (fols. 8, 180). A draft of his will in English made during his sickness in 1606 is supplemented by a Latin will apparently made before 1618 but heavily revised in 1627 (fols. 94, 89–90). His manuscript shows expectation of and preparation for a family of his own years before he began one. Although Ramsey did not marry until 1620, in 1607 he wrote—or copied—a set of instructions to his as yet unborn son (fols. 92–93v). Within these rather predictable instructions he inserts cross-references to parts of his manuscript in which he gives advice for travel and lists persons whose conversation he esteems. In an adjacent part of the manuscript, also written before 1618, he gives directions to his spouse as to how his son should be raised if he himself should die before the son came of age (fols. 90v–91). This part is also conventional, and may have been copied from some other source, but it has been adapted to reflect Ramsey's own wishes—such as that his son should go to Cambridge, as he did. Other miscellaneous information in the manuscript could be seen as further supplements to the education of his children or the functioning of his family. Ramsey not only gives reading lists for his son, he catalogs his own books (fols. 117–21v). He lists tradesmen, their specialties and addresses (fols. 115v–116). He lists nobles, state officers, bishops, and kings from the Conquest through Charles I (fols. 96–110v). He includes patriotic historical essays on the "Ancient English nation," with special attention to the Ramseys, and on the history of the conflict with the Spanish in the Low Countries (fols. 10–12, 71). An essay on the benefits of country life (fol. 70v) may be seen as an encouragement to his descendants to stay on the land and look after it—though there is evidence that Ramsey himself spent considerable time in London.

The nature and use of the literary contents of the manuscript are affected by the approximate date of entry and the context in the manuscript. The earliest entries appear to be copies of poems, notably works printed in the 1590s. Three of these are from Spenser's 1591 *Complaints*.[10] A spot check reveals some variants, but not of the number or sort to suggest independent origin; Spenser is credited with authorship in each case. He also copies selected verses from *Pasquil's Mad-Cap* (1600; STC 3675), usually attributed to Nicholas Breton; Ramsey gives no author (fol. 122r–v). There is also a copy of *The Fissher-mans Tale* and of its sequel *Floras Fortune*, both printed in 1595 as the works of Francis Sabie, who subsequently published two more books. But Ramsey puts his own name at the end of these poems, and even copies much of the title page of the second, substituting his initials for Sabie's. He dates the latter copy 1596 (fols. 128–44, 161v–80). Ramsey also appears to take credit for "The nativitie of Christ" (fol. 180v), which is from Robert Southwell's *Saint Peters Complaint* (1595), and for "Troyes lamentation for the death of Hector" (fols. 162–68v), which had been printed in 1594 by one "I. O." (possibly Sir John Ogle).[11] Ramsey tells us that between the ages of fourteen and eighteen his mother had kept him at home, "to my noe small detriment in the exsecuting of my studdyes," and that around 1596 he was again sent to a tutor (fol. 5). There are various indications that Ramsey began his book around this time, so these poems may have been copied as exercises in penmanship or in some other connection with his studies. The manuscript also contains translations of parts of Caesar's *Gallic Wars* (dated 1599) and Virgil's

---

[10] He includes "Prosopopoeia or Mother Hubberds Tale," fols. 22–34v; "The Teares of the Muses," fols. 36–43; and "The Visions of Petrarch," fols. 44–45.

[11] I. O., *The Lamentation of Troy for the Death of Hector*, ed. Elkin Calhoun Wilson (Chicago: Institute of Elizabethan Studies, 1959), xix–xxii.

Aeneid (dated 1596), which look like academic exercises and which have Ramsey's name at the end of each (fols. 46–60v, 144v–61v). Perhaps he put his name on all these items as modern students do their assignments, or as testimony to his labor as a copyist, or out of some self-centered late-adolescent sense of possession. At any rate, his practice must cast doubt on the attribution of other items entered at this time in the manuscript, especially ones he claims for himself. A poem on "Arion of Lesbos," dated 1597 and subscribed "Jo: Ramsey" (fol. 181), is not known to me in any other source, but I would not assign it to Ramsey on the basis of this subscription.

Another group of poems presents similar problems to the author-centric. These poems were entered later than the first group, but before the 1618 duel, are ascribed to "Montanus," and all seem to relate to love affairs. The first is headed "To the Fayrest. A Sonnett. In laudem dominae suae. A: B: E. E: D." In the margin is this note: "Montanus to Flora"; it is subscribed "By him that must loue or not liue. Poore J R." (fol. 35). Although Montanus is the name of a character in Lodge's *Rosalind* and appears in other pastoral contexts, Ramsey may have adopted it in reference to his ancestral estate, Mount Surrey. I have tried some Malvolian crushing of the initials in the heading, but cannot easily make them fit anyone else named in the manuscript, or his wife, the daughter of Sir Edmund Bell of Beauprey in Norfolk; moreover, these verses were entered several years before his marriage. They are almost entirely stolen from Spenser's *Amoretti* 64. On the same page is another poem subscribed "Sheephearde Montanus" and addressed "To Alexis." This second poem is an imitation of the second stanza of a poem by Anthony Munday, "Beauty sat bathing by a spring," which was printed in his *Primaleon of Greece* (1596? 2nd ed. 1619), reprinted in *Englands Helicon* (1600) and set to music by Robert Jones, Francis Pilkington, and William Corkine.[12] Another poem by "Montanus" is also an imitation—or plagiarism—of a poem by Munday from his play *Fedele and Fortunio* (1584) and also printed in *Englands Helicon*, where it is headed "Montana the Sheepheard, his loue to Aminta," and begins "I serue Aminta, whiter then the snowe."[13] Ramsey's version, probably based on *Englands Helicon*, is headed "Montanus the Sheephearde his loue to Flora" and

---

[12] *England's Helicon*, ed. Hyder Edward Rollins, 2 vols. (Cambridge, Mass.: Harvard Univ. Press, 1935), 1:28–29; *Lyrics from English Airs*, 527–28.

[13] *England's Helicon*, 1:107–8.

begins "I serue sweete Flora brighter then Cinthiaes light" (fol. 45v). Ramsey includes two more poems by "Montanus" (fols. 35v, 43v) for which I have not found models; but at this point one cannot be confident about their originality. Ironically, Ramsey quotes the couplet of a sonnet in which Michael Drayton wittily steals from Sidney: "Divine Sir Philip I avouch thy writt / I ame noe pickepurse of anothers witt."[14] At least he subscribes Drayton's initials.

Another group of poems Ramsey includes in his manuscript would seem to be straightforward copies of the texts of madrigals and airs he liked or wished to select for the education of his children (fols. 67–70). He credits his sources, naming "Mr Jno. Dowland. first booke" or "Mr Rob: Jones. 2. booke." Ramsey had specified that his son should be taught to "playe on the Lute, & singe to it with the Dyttye." A marginal note by this instruction says, "See Dowlands bookes"; Dowland was also listed among the "Personages to converse with" (fols. 90v, 91v). Most texts are simple copies; but Ramsey substitutes a stanza of his own for the second stanza of Robert Jones's "Fie what a coile is here" and gives a different first stanza and highly varied subsequent stanzas for another Jones song.[15] Ramsey does not seem to hesitate to adapt the works of others to his own uses.

Two other poems demand some attention. One is an apparently unique text of a song called "E. Essex Downe," beginning "Say, what is loue? a foolishe toye I can well proue" (fol. 67). Steven May has accepted this poem as part of the small canon of verse by Robert Devereux, earl of Essex.[16] This may indeed be a text by Essex, who was known to have his verses sung to the queen. But it may be words to fit a tune named in his honor, like Dowland's Essex galliard, or like the dance Ramsey describes on a nearby leaf called "The Earle of Essex measures" (fol. 65v). Ramsey also has a copy of a poem that is ascribed to Essex in many manuscripts. This is "The Bee," beginning, "It was a tyme when

---

[14] Fol. 124v; Michael Drayton, *Idea's Mirror* (1594), dedicatory sonnet to Anthony Cooke. See Drayton's *Works*, ed. J. W. Hebel (Oxford: Shakespeare Head Press, 1931–41), 1:96; in the manuscript this couplet follows a heavily annotated copy of Drayton's sonnet beginning, "The World's faire rose, & Henries frostye fire," which was first printed as an addendum to *Englands Heroical Epistles* (1599 ed.), sig. P2; see Hebel's edition, 2:308.

[15] *Lyrics from English Airs*, 503–4 and 487–88.

[16] *The Poems of Edward de Vere, Seventeenth Earl of Oxford and of Robert Devereux, Second Earl of Essex*, ed. Steven W. May, in *Studies in Philology* 77.5 (1980): 46, 92.

silye bees could speake"; Ramsey heads it "E. Essex" (fols. 123–24v). Since some good manuscripts ascribe the poem to Essex's secretary, Henry Cuffe, Steven May puts this poem among the *dubia*; moreover, Ramsey's text is from a group of versions that lacks a stanza, and it seems to be rather far down the chain of transmission.[17] Yet since these attributions do not conflict with Ramsey's personal agenda, and since he may have felt some cachet in having poems by such a famous and tragic historical personage in his collection, they may be as good as any such attribution. Ramsey wrote elsewhere of Essex that he was "the very Hercules, Achilles, or Julius Caesar of his tyme but most vnfortunate" (fol. 108).

What generalizations can be drawn from this examination of Ramsey's manuscript? Although there needs no ghost come from the grave to tell us, Ramsey's manuscript does suggest that editors find out as much as they can about the individual manuscripts they consult. I could list a number of suggestive corollaries to this warning, but Mary Hobbs has already done so, based on many more seventeenth-century sources, in her article in *English Manuscript Studies*.[18] Ramsey's manuscript provides reinforcement from a slightly earlier period, and an extreme example of the power of a reader to assume control of the texts he encounters.

RICE UNIVERSITY

---

[17] *Essex*, ed. May, 109–13.

[18] Mary Hobbs, "Early Seventeenth-Century Verse Miscellanies and Their Value for Textual Editors," *English Manuscript Studies 1100–1700*, ed. Peter Beal and Jeremy Griffiths (Oxford and New York: Blackwell, 1989), 1:182–210.

The Renaissance Manuscript Verse Miscellany: Private Party, Private Text

ERNEST W. SULLIVAN, II

NYONE WHO HAS SEEN A RENAISSANCE MANUSCRIPT VERSE miscellany knows why they are called miscellanies. Even so, I was surprised by the apparent chaos of the First and Second Dalhousie Manuscripts (henceforth TT1 and TT2), probably because I, like most people who work with manuscripts, harbor a residual assumption that a manuscript is an artifact copied by one person from one source in sequence over a relatively short and continuous period.[1] Donne scholars are particularly prone to this textually monolithic conception because Grierson and subsequent Oxford Donne editors chiseled it in their stemmata and descriptions of Donne manuscripts. Yet while TT1 and TT2 are not bibliographical monoliths, they are "monoscripts" in a larger sense—they had their genesis in a single, personal, vision. And TT1 and TT2 (as well as some other texts I will discuss briefly) suggest that textual bibliographers will not fully understand our own texts until we see such artifacts (whether manuscript or print) not as "miscellanies,"

---

[1] For a detailed physical description of the First and Second Dalhousie manuscripts, see my *The First and Second Dalhousie Manuscripts: Poems and Prose by John Donne and Others* (Columbia: Univ. of Missouri Press, 1988), 1–3.

but as monoscripts—each having its specific, private, experiences informed by a single vision.

Even though Peter Beal classifies TT1 and TT2 as Group II manuscripts,[2] neither is monolithic. Five distinct hands, not always in contiguous segments, appear in TT1; four, not contiguous, in TT2. Neither manuscript derives from a single source. The contents, their sequence, headings, attributions, and texts of the poems in TT1 and TT2 establish that much of TT1 probably shares an ancestor with British Library MS. Lansdowne 740 (Sullivan, 7–10) and that much of TT2 derives from TT1. Yet even in shared poems in the main copyist sequence, the texts of TT2 do not always derive from TT1: lines 14–16 of Donne's "The Curse" in TT1 (fol. 17) have the text of the Group II Donne manuscript tradition ("Or maye he, for her vertue reuerence/ Her y^t hates him, only for impotence/ And equall traytors be she; and his senc,"), but TT2 (fol. 11) has the text of the Group I tradition ("in earely scarcenesse, and longe may he rott/ for land, wch had been his, if he had not/ himselfe incestuouslie an heire begott.") Thus, even though copyist D of TT2 got the texts of the rest of the Donne poems in the fols. 5–21 sequence from TT1, he got the text of "The Curse" (on fol. 11) not just from another manuscript, but from a manuscript textually unrelated to TT1. Further, different hands and dates of the materials prove that various segments of the manuscripts were copied at different times rather than during a relatively short and continuous period.[3] Only the uniform watermark in each manuscript hints that the Dalhousies might be monoscripts of some sort.

Only when I took off my bibliographer's uniform and donned the raiment of the New Historicist was I invited to the Dalhousie party to meet the monoscript ancestor of the Dalhousies, as well as Lansdowne 740, Trinity College, Dublin, MS. 877 (I), and the entire Group II Donne manuscript transmission tradition. The fact that the Dalhousies represent a private party provides insight into the circulation and

---

[2] *Index of English Literary Manuscripts* (London: Mansell, 1980): 1.1:251. According to Helen Gardner, the Group II manuscripts derive from a single manuscript Γ that was completed around 1625 and that grew by accretion from a smaller collection preserved in British Library MS. Lansdowne 740 (*John Donne: The Elegies and the Songs and Sonnets* [Oxford: Clarendon Press, 1965], lxvii–lxviii).

[3] The transcription of the main sequence (fols. 1–62) in TT1 must postdate 12 May 1613 and predate August 1617, with the materials in various segments from fols. 62v to 69v having been transcribed from August 1617 to shortly after 30 July 1624; the materials in TT2 were transcribed between 28 September 1622 and shortly after 23 August 1628 (Sullivan, 4).

function of manuscript verse in the Renaissance and has implications for our study of the texts of that verse.

Both Dalhousies contain evidence in every gathering and in the work of every copyist that they derive immediately from documents preserved by one or more members of the Essex family. Some of the poems may have been collected from the papers of Robert Devereux, second earl of Essex, statesman, soldier, poet, literary patron, and husband of Frances Walsingham, the widow of Sir Philip Sidney.[4] Another "private party" collecting the poems would have been Penelope Devereux, sister to the second earl, the Stella of Sir Philip Sidney's *Astrophel and Stella*, and literary patroness. The "private party" after the 1601 and 1607 deaths of the second earl and Penelope would have been the third earl[5] (a copy of the testimony for his divorce trial involving Lady Frances Howard begins TT1) or Lady Lettice Carey and Mrs. Essex Rich, daughters of Penelope Devereux, to whom Donne wrote "A Letter to the Lady Carey, and Mrs. Essex Riche, From Amyens" in 1611, about the time the collection reached that state preserved by the Dalhousies.

The most likely copyist or conduit from the Essexes to the Dalhousie family would have been Sir John Ramsay, viscount Haddington and earl of Holderness (1580–1626). Sir John Ramsay would have had an interest in the particular poetry in the collection as well as access to the poetry in circulation through his membership in the Inner Temple (where several of the poets represented in the Dalhousie collection studied law) and as a favored member of the court of James I. Sir John also had a likely connection to the Dalhousies—the *DNB* (16:701) identifies him as the second son of James Ramsay of Dalhousie and brother of George Ramsay, first lord of Dalhousie. Interest in preserving materials associated with the Essex family would have been strong for the Dalhousies: William Ramsay, second baron and first earl of Dalhousie (d. 1674), eldest son of George Ramsay, signed the letter of covenanting lords of 19 April

---

[4] Donne's literary connection to the Sidney family lasted at least until his poem "Upon the translation of the Psalmes by Sir Philip Sidney, and the Countesse of Pembroke his Sister," written after the death of the countess on 25 September 1621.

[5] Robert Coddrington testifies to the third earl's status as a patron: "And if ever any unseverer houres of leisure offered themselves in his study, hee would imploy that time in the perusall of some labourd Poeme, and having great judgment especially in the English Verse, it was his custome to applaud the professors of that Art, as high as their deserts and to reward them above it" (*The Life and Death, of the Illvstrivs Robert Earle of Essex* [London, 1646], 11), Wing C 4877.

1639 to the third earl of Essex and served with him in the Civil War against Charles I.

The Essex/Dalhousie manuscripts party had a very restricted guest list.[6] A few poets were members or friends of the family: William

---

[6] The relationships among the authors and the Essex family are as follows: Sir Henry Wotton was secretary to the second earl from 1595 to 1601 and accompanied him on the ill-fated expedition to Ireland in 1599 (see Donne's verse letter "*H. W. in Hiber. belligeranti*"). John Donne served with the second earl in the expedition to Cadiz in 1596–97 and also worked for Sir Thomas Egerton the elder, who, as Arthur Marotti points out, was "one of the Earl of Essex's most important clients" (*John Donne, Coterie Poet* [Madison: Univ. of Wisconsin Press, 1986], 116). Alexander B. Grosart prints two letters by the second earl recommending Josuah Sylvester (1563–1618) for secretarial positions in 1597 (*The Complete Works of Joshuah Sylvester* [London: Printed for private circulation, 1880], 1:xiv). Sir John Harington (1560–1612) served the second earl as commander of the horse in Ireland and was knighted by him on 30 July 1599. Edward de Vere, seventeenth earl of Oxford, as lord great chamberlain oversaw the elevation of Walter Devereux to the earldom of Essex on 4 May 1572. Sir John Davies (1569–1626) became solicitor general for Ireland on 18 September 1603 and would have known Essex either through Essex's service as lord lieutenant of Ireland from 9 March 1599 to June 1600 or through their mutual Inns of Court acquaintances Sir John Harington, John Hoskyns, and Richard Corbett—all poets represented in the Dalhousie collection. Sir Thomas Overbury (1581–1613), a close friend of the third earl, was murdered by Lady Frances Howard and her second husband, Robert Carr, earl of Somerset, for his opposition to their marriage. Interestingly, the selection of Overburian characters in TT1 might have had particular relevance for the third earl: W. J. Paylor argues that these three characters are by Overbury and that "A Very Very Woman" and "Her Next Part" are not only the antitheses of "A Good Woman" but also are a specific attack on Lady Frances (*The Overburian Characters* [Oxford: Basil Blackwell, 1936], 109–11). Sir John Roe (1581–1608) served with the second earl in Ireland in 1599 and may have been knighted by him. Sir Walter Ralegh served with the second earl at Cadiz and the Azores. Thomas Campion was a volunteer in the 1591 Essex expedition to Dieppe. Francis Beaumont's poem, "To the Countesse of Rutland" (TT1, fols. 52v–53), has topical links to the second earl: her husband, Roger Manners, fifth earl of Rutland (1576–1612) accompanied Essex on the 1599 Irish Expedition, was knighted by Essex, and participated in the Essex "plot" of 1601 against Queen Elizabeth. John Hoskyns, a member of Donne's coterie (Marotti, 34), knew enough of the second earl to use "And the speciale for the perticular, as the Earle is gone into Ireland for E: E" as an example of synedoche in his "Direccions For Speech and Style" (Louise Brown Osborn, *The Life, Letters, and Writings of John Hoskyns, 1566–1638* [New Haven: Yale Univ. Press, 1937], 124). Richard Corbett's "An *Elegie* on the late *Lord William Haward* Baron of Effingham, dead *the tenth of December*. 1615" eulogizes one of the four squadron leaders in the second earl's expedition to Cadiz and his companion in the Azores expedition. Francis Bacon (1561–1626) was a longtime friend of the second earl, but later prosecuted him in the 1601 trial for treason against Elizabeth. William Herbert's "When my Carliles Chamber was on fire" (TT2, fol. 32v) may be

Herbert, third earl of Pembroke; Edward de Vere, seventeenth earl of Oxford; Sir John Davies; Sir Thomas Overbury; Francis Bacon; George Morley; and John Hoskyns. Sir Henry Wotton and Josuah Sylvester served the Essex family in a civil capacity. The largest number of contributors representing by far the greatest number of poems comes, not unexpectedly, from the main interest of the Essex family—those who served with the earls in their various military campaigns: John Donne, Sir John Roe, Sir Walter Ralegh, Thomas Campion. Poets writing about those who served the earls in a military capacity include Francis Beaumont, Richard Corbett, and the anonymous author of "An Epitaph vpon the Duke of Buckinghame." In fact, the only identifiable Dalhousie poets not connected to the Essex family are the Scottish poet Sir Robert Aytoun and Jonathan Richards (one poem each). Evidently, men who had served the earls in civil or military capacities sent their poetry to them in hopes of patronage and preferment, and the poems were then collected by the Essex family.

The private nature of the Dalhousie poems and poets has literary and textual significance. The most problematical poems in the Dalhousies for the Donne canon are "Elegie: The Expostulation" and "Faustus." Even though "Elegie: The Expostulation" was first published in Donne's 1633 *Poems*, its subsequent publication in the posthumous second volume of Ben Jonson's *Workes* (London, 1640) sparked a continuing debate:[7] Gardner's 1965 edition of the elegies lists "Elegie: The Expostulation" as dubious (94–96). The presence of "Elegie: The Expostulation" in long sequences of poems by Donne in TT1 and TT2, manuscripts containing chiefly poems (including the majority of elegies) by Donne and none by

---

linked to the Essex family by both subject and author: "Carlile" may be Lucy Hay, countess of Carlisle (1599–1660), subject of many poems during the period and granddaughter of the first earl of Essex. Herbert was also the nephew of Sir Philip Sidney, whose widow, Frances Walsingham, had married the second earl in 1601. George Morley's "On the Death of King James" is related to the third earl by topic (the third earl was prominent in the court and military of James I) and author (Morley edited the third earl's *Pious advice to his son the late Earl of Essex* [London, 1683], Wing C 469). The anonymous, unique "An Epitaph vpon the Duke off Buckinghame" would have several links to the third earl who served under Buckingham in the Palatinate and in the 1625 naval assault at Cadiz: Buckingham befriended Archbishop Abbot, opposed the earl of Somerset, and married Katherine Manners, daughter of the earl of Rutland.

[7] For a review of the arguments, see D. Heywood Brock's "Jonson and Donne: Structural Fingerprinting and the Attribution of Elegies XXXVIII–XLI," *Papers of the Bibliographical Society of America* 72 (1978): 519–27.

Jonson, persuasively augments the evidence of the manuscript traditions utilized by Evelyn Simpson to assign authorship to Donne.[8]

In 1967, John T. Shawcross first published "Faustus" and, on the basis of its presence amid other Donne poems and its attribution to "J D" in National Library of Scotland MS. 2067 (Hawthornden MS. XV), assigned its authorship to Donne.[9] "Faustus" also occurs amid other Donne poems and is attributed to "J D" in National Library of Scotland MS. 6504 (Wedderburn MS.). The evidence provided by the Dalhousies for Donne's authorship of "Faustus" is not as strong as it was for "Elegie: The Expostulation": "Faustus" is not positioned in a sequence of Donne poems; no other Donne epigrams occur; and three poems by Sir John Harington, Donne's chief competitor for authorship, are nearby ("Of the commodities that men haue by their Marriage," fol. 56v; "Of a Precise Tayler," fol. 57; and "Of Women learned in the tongues," fol. 57). Nonetheless, the appearance of "Faustus" even without attribution in a main Donne textual tradition adds considerably to the evidence for Donne's authorship.

The discovery that the Dalhousies were private party monoscripts has enormous significance for the bibliographical study of Donne's texts; and the existence of other private party "monoscript" manuscript and print artifacts for other Renaissance authors suggests that bibliographers and critics are going to have to rethink the very nature of Renaissance literary works.

Let me illustrate how a private party monoscript like TT1 is indispensable in establishing the text of a Donne poem whose text and context so presently confused that it does not even have a name. The poem, headed *Another Eligie vpon the death of M^{ris} Boulstred* in TT1, begins, "Language thou art to narrow and too weake." Simply headed "*Elegie.*" in Donne's 1633 *Poems* (296–98) and "ELEG. XI. *Death*" in the 1635, 1639, 1649, 1650, and 1654 editions and "ELEGIE XI." in

---

[8] TT1 has twenty-six Donne poems, from "The Legacie" on fol. 44 to "Womans constancy" on fol. 56, broken only by Hoskyns's "A Poem upon Absence" on fol. 45 and Beaumont's "To the Countesse of Rutland" on fol. 52v; and TT2 has fifteen Donne poems from "The Legacie" on fol. 22v to Womans constancy" on fol. 29v, broken only by Beaumont's "To the Countesse of Rutland" on fol. 26. See Evelyn Simpson, "Jonson and Donne: A Problem in Authorship," *Review of English Studies* 15 (1939): 274–82.

[9] "John Donne and Drummond's Manuscripts," *American Notes & Queries* 5 (March 1967): 104–5.

the 1669 edition, the poem has been variously headed by its editors with some variant of "Elegie: Death," "ELEGY," and "DEATH"—with only Grosart (1872–73), Smith (1971), and Milgate (1978) adopting a version of the manuscript heading "Elegie upon the Death of Mistress Boulstred."[10]

The poem occurs in twenty-six manuscripts and all seven seventeenth-century collected editions/issues of Donne's *Poems*. The manuscripts form two closely related families of textual transmission (essentially the traditional Group II and Group III). TT1 and the 1633 collected edition belong to the Group II tradition, though the later six seventeenth-century collected editions emend the 1633 text with readings from a Group III manuscript. The net result: a confusing mass of relatively nondistinctive variants. How to choose a copy-text? The poems in the TT1 family had been invited to the Essex party, a party which would have had every reason to expect a very authoritative representative from Donne. Internal comparison showed that of all the manuscripts in the TT1 family, the Trinity College, Dublin, MS. 877 (I) probably had the text that best preserved the original, and it became the copy-text for the forthcoming Donne Variorum. Of the twenty-two manuscripts in either family which have a heading, only South African Public Library MS. Grey 7 a 29 and National Library of Scotland MS. 6504 fail to identify the poem with the death of Cecilia Bulstrode, daughter of Edward Bulstrode, on 4 August 1609 at Twickenham Park, the residence of her relative and Donne's patron, Lucy, countess of Bedford. Even so, the fact that the family of manuscripts related to Essex had headings establishing a connection to Cecilia Bulstrode helped Claude Summers prove that Donne's first elegy on the death of Cecilia Bulstrode, "Death I recant," Lucy, Countess of Bedford's, "Death be not proud, thy hand gave not this blow," and this second Donne elegy on the death of Cecilia Bulstrode form a sequence caused by Lucy's lukewarm reaction to Donne's first elegy.[11]

As Ted-Larry Pebworth and I have been arguing for some time (he

---

[10] "Elegie: Death" (by Tonson [1719], Bell [1779], Anderson [1793], Chalmers [1810], Lowell [1855], Grierson [1912], Hayward [1929], and Shawcross [1967]); "ELEGY" (Alford [1839], Lowell [1895], and Patrides [1985]), "Elegie upon the Death of Mistress Boulstred" (Grosart [1872–73], Smith [1971] and Milgate [1978]); and "DEATH" (Chambers [1896] and Bennett [1942]).

[11] "Donne's 1609 Sequence of Grief and Comfort," *Studies in Philology* 89 (Spring 1992): 211–31.

longer than I),[12] Renaissance manuscript miscellanies (and printed texts) contain alternative, authoritative versions of some poems—a fact that challenges the implicit assumption that literary texts are inevitably singular. The forces behind these multiple authoritative versions would seem to include the circumstances of the composition, thus the creation of "private" text versions—texts created in a specific set of circumstances for a specific set of readers or even a single reader. As Marlowe and Shakespeare created different texts of *Doctor Faustus* and *King Lear* for different performances, so did other Renaissance authors create private texts for private readings (or "performances") of their texts.

Ben Jonson offers an example where manuscripts preserve the private text of a public poem. As C. H. Herford and Percy and Evelyn Simpson argue,

> First drafts of the 'Epistle to the Countess of Rutland' (xii) survive in Harley MS. 4064 and Rawlinson poetry MS. 31; they are valuable for giving the concluding lines 93–100, which were not printed in the Folio text. The Folio version breaks off at line 93, with a note '*the rest is lost.*' It was not lost, but tactfully cancelled. The poem was written in the first year of the marriage, 1599, and ended with the hope that, before the year was out, the Countess would bear a son. The earl was impotent, if not at the time of the marriage, at any rate shortly after it. The impotence was current gossip long before the Folio appeared, and the original conclusion would have excited derision in Court circles, apart from the pain it would have given the Countess.[13]

Henry Wotton's "A shorte Hymne by Sr Hen: Wotton In a nyght of his present sicknes," probably written in 1638 (Pebworth and Sullivan, 49), exemplifies the deliberate creation of two manuscript versions of a poem for different audiences. In manuscripts dating from the late 1630s, the poem is preserved in two versions: one jibes at Roman Catholicism's veneration

---

[12] See Ted-Larry Pebworth, "Sir Henry Wotton's 'O Faithless World': The Transmission of a Coterie Poem and a Critical Old-Spelling Edition," *Analytical & Enumerative Bibliography* 5 (1981): 205–31, and "The Editor, the Critic, and the Multiple Texts of Donne's 'A Hymne to God the Father,' " *South Central Review: The Journal of the South Central Modern Language Association* 4 (1987): 16–34, as well as our "Rational Presentation of Multiple Textual Traditions," *Papers of the Bibliographical Society of America* 83 (1989): 43–60.

[13] *Ben Jonson* (Oxford: Clarendon Press, 1947), 8:10.

of relics, as the speaker, in line 8, professes to need "Noe raggs of saintes; noe purging fier"; the other avoids the unflattering reference to Roman devotional practice by reading line 8 "No new borne drams of purging fire." Even though a staunch Protestant, Wotton had close friends among the English Roman Catholic community (notably Sir Kenelm Digby); and in preparing copies of his hymn for Catholic friends, Jonson likely altered line 8 in deference to their religious sensibilities.

Such deliberate sensitivity to religious differences also appears in the two versions of the 1661 edition of Owen Felltham's *Resolves*. As Ted-Larry Pebworth has shown, three copies of the 1661 edition contain as a cancel Felltham's "Form of Prayer," an "amended" version of the "Anglican morning and evening prayer services designed to circumvent the letter of the 1645 act of Parliament proscribing the use of the *Book of Common Prayer* in private family devotion."[14] Pebworth proves that "What is now clear is that the 1661 folio was set into type with the 'Form of Prayer' included; that the printer pulled at least a few copies of the book in that state; and that before the printing of copies for general sale, the liturgy itself and the sentence referring to it in 'To the Reader' were excised" (209–10). The cancelled version with the "Form of Prayer" is a deliberate private text—by printing the "Form of Prayer" in a discrete gathering "Fff" at the end of its run of signatures and the sentence in the preface on discrete lines (except for one word) for removal with no effect on the rest of the paragraph, Felltham could preserve the "private," Anglican version of the work undetected.

Thus the Renaissance manuscript (or even printed) verse miscellany as "monoscript" private text for a private party has important implications for the textual and literary study of Renaissance verse and culture. Textual scholars need to ponder why as well as how a text and its versions were created; literary critics need to recognize the bibliographical and artifactual evidence for multiple, authoritative versions of texts. And we all need to think about the intensely private interchange between the original writer and reader when we simultaneously reenact and reinterpret their performance, or we will lose both text and meaning.

TEXAS TECH UNIVERSITY

---

[14] "An Anglican Family Worship Service of the Interregnum: A Canceled Early Text and a New Edition of Owen Felltham's 'A Form of Prayer,'" *English Literary Renaissance* 16 (1986): 206.

Index

318

International Advisory Council

The Renaissance English Text Society was founded to publish scarce literary texts, chiefly nondramatic, of the period 1475–1660. Subscriptions at $25.00 per year should be sent to Mario A. Di Cesare, Department of English, SUNY, Binghamton, NY 13902–6000, USA. Institutional members are requested to provide, at the time of enrollment, any purchase order numbers or other information required for their billing records; the Society cannot provide multiple invoices or other complex forms.

Copies of volumes X–XII may be purchased direct from Associated University Presses, 440 Forsgate Drive, Cranbury, NJ 08512, USA. Copies of earlier volumes still in print or of volumes XIII on may be ordered from MRTS— LNG–99, SUNY, Binghamton, NY 13902–6000.

FIRST SERIES

Vol. I. *Merie Tales of the Mad Men of Gotam* by A. B., edited by Stanley J. Kahrl, and *The History of Tom Thumbe*, by R. I., edited by Curt F. Buhler, 1965. (o.p.)

Vol. II. Thomas Watson's Latin *Amyntas*, edited by Walter F. Staton, Jr., and Abraham Fraunce's translation *The Lamentations of Amyntas*, edited by Franklin M. Dickey, 1967.

SECOND SERIES

Vol. III. *The dyaloge called Funus*, A Translation of Erasmus's Colloquy (1534), and *A very pleasaunt & fruitful Diologe called The Epicure*, Gerrard's Translation of Erasmus's Colloquy (1545), edited by Robert R. Allen, 1969.

Vol. IV. *Leicester's Ghost* by Thomas Rogers, edited by Franklin B. Williams, Jr., 1972.

THIRD SERIES

Vols. V–VI. *A Collection of Emblemes, Ancient and Moderne,* by George Wither, with an introduction by Rosemary Freeman and bibliographical notes by Charles S. Hensley, 1975. (o.p.)

FOURTH SERIES

Vols. VII–VIII *Tom a' Lincolne* by R. I., edited by Richard S. M. Hirsch, 1978.

FIFTH SERIES

Vol. IX. *Metrical Visions* by George Cavendish, edited by A. S. G. Edwards, 1980.

SIXTH SERIES

Vol. X. *Two Early Renaissance Bird Poems,* edited by Malcolm Andrew, 1984.
Vol. XI. *Argalus and Parthenia* by Francis Quarles, edited by David Freeman, 1986.
Vol. XII. Cicero's *De Officiis,* trans. Nicholas Grimald, edited by Gerald O'Gorman, 1987.
Vol. XIII. *The Silkewormes and their Flies* by Thomas Moffet (1599), edited with introduction and commentary by Victor Houliston, 1988.

SEVENTH SERIES

Vol. XIV. John Bale, *The Vocacyon of Johan Bale,* edited by Peter Happé and John N. King, 1989.
Vol. XV. *The Nondramatic Works of John Ford,* edited by L. E. Stock, Gilles D. Monsarrat, Judith M. Kennedy, and Dennis Danielson, with the assistance of Marta Straznicky, 1990.

Special Publication. *New Ways of Looking at Old Texts: Papers of the Renaissance English Text Society, 1985–1991,* edited by W. Speed Hill, 1993.

New Ways of Looking at Old Texts consists of twenty-three papers about ways of editing Renaissance manuscripts and texts, from panels sponsored by the Renaissance English Text Society at annual MLA conferences. Topics addressed include the theory and practice of transcription, editing women writers of the Renaissance, New Historicism and the editing of Renaissance texts, editing the letters of Renaissance women, and editing manuscript poetical miscellanies, and the contributors include A. R. Braunmuller, Richard Proudfoot, Elizabeth McCutcheon, Josephine Roberts, Arthur F. Marotti, and Margreta de Grazia.

◆

W. Speed Hill, Professor of English at Lehman College, City University of New York, is general editor of the Folger Library Edition of *The Works of Richard Hooker* (in six volumes, 1977–1993). He has published widely on Renaissance subjects, particularly on Richard Hooker and on editing questions and theory. He has served as President of the Renaissance English Text Society and as chair of the Committee on Scholarly Editions of MLA. He has been a senior research fellow of the National Endowment for the Humanities, and has held fellowships from American Council of Learned Societies and the Folger Library-British Academy.

ⲘRTS

ⲘEⲆIEVAL & RENAISSANCE TEXTS & STUⲆIES
is the publishing program of the
Center for Medieval and Early Renaissance Studies
at the State University of New York at Binghamton.

ⲘRTS emphasizes books that are needed —
texts, translations, and major research tools.

ⲘRTS aims to publish the highest quality scholarship
in attractive and durable format at modest cost.

104 Philips
p 167
172 - Ralegh

127, Roberts on Ov & Wroth